The Pilgrim and the Book

American University Studies

Series IV
English Language and Literature

Vol. 42

PETER LANG
New York · Berne · Frankfurt am Main

Julia Bolton Holloway

The Pilgrim and the Book

A Study of Dante, Langland and Chaucer

PETER LANG
New York · Berne · Frankfurt am Main

Library of Congress Cataloging-in-Publication Data

Holloway, Julia Bolton.
   The pilgrim and the book.

   (American university studies. Series IV, English
languages and literature; vol. 42)
   1. Pilgrims and pilgrimages in literature.
2. Poetry, Medieval—History and criticism.   3. Dante
Alighieri, 1265–1321. Divina commedia.   4. Langland,
William, 1330?–1400? Piers the Plowman.   5. Chaucer,
Geoffrey, d. 1400. Canterbury tales.   I. Title.   II. Series.
PN682.P5H64   1987   821'.1'09355   86-20180
ISBN 0-8204-0345-8
ISSN 0741-0700

CIP-Kurztitelaufnahme der Deutschen Bibliothek

Holloway, Julia B.:
The pilgrim and the book: a study of Dante,
Langland and Chaucer / Julia B. Holloway.-New
York ; Berne ; Frankfurt am Main ; Lang, 1987
   (American university studies ; Ser. 1,
   English language and literature ; Vol. 42)

ISBN 0-8204-0345-8
NE: American university studies / 04

Printed by Weihert-Druck GmbH, Darmstadt (West Germany)

DEDICATED TO

THREE PILGRIMS

TABLE OF CONTENTS

The Ellesmere <u>Canterbury Tales</u>' Pardoner
in scarlet garb with "vernicle," scrip.
The Henry E. Huntington Library and
Art Gallery

ILLUSTRATIONS

The Ellesmere Canterbury Tales Pardoner
The Huntington Library and Museum

PLATES

PROLOGUE

> How should I your true love know
> From another one?
> By his cockle hat and staff
> And his sandal shoon.
>
> <u>Hamlet</u>

Chaucer opened his <u>Canterbury Tales</u> with a General
Prologue in which he presented the characters of his poem,
twenty-nine pilgrims in all, himself among them, gathered at
the Tabard Inn in London to ride towards Canterbury's shrine
of St. Thomas Becket on the following day. This is however,
a <u>caveat lector</u>, a warning to the reader. His true-seeming
Prologue is, actually, a "Canterbury tale," a lie. Pilgrim's
tales, "Canterbury tales," were considered to be lying
fictions; therefore pilgrimage poems ought themselves to be
suspect. Chaucer's famous portraits shape our perceptions of
the medieval pilgrim. We are no longer aware of Chaucer's
satire in presenting them as he does on horseback, many in
bright clothing, and including in their company members of
the cloistered clergy. The satire can, however, be
understood by contrasting these carnal figures from a comic
work with depictions in art of medieval pilgrims, one from
Italy, one from England. In these, paradoxically, we shall
find reality to be stranger than poetry, fact more extreme
than fiction.

In the Spanish Chapel of Florence's Santa Maria Novella
a mural was frescoed in the late 1360s of an allegorical
pilgrimage, the funds for this being given by Buonamico di
Lapo Guidalotti under the impact of the Black Death. It
includes the figure of an aged and real pilgrim, garbed in a
goat or camelskin sclavin, with a shell, a vernicle, and one
other badge upon his hat, who kneels and leans upon his
staff, and whose white beard is worn parted in two (Plate I
a). At this period, in the twelfth through fourteenth
centuries, pilgrim hats were conical and brimless.

A manuscript of <u>Piers Plowman</u> (Bodleian MS Douce 104, fol. 3; Plate Ib) gives a sanguine drawing of a palmer in the poem's margin. The pilgrim figure is dressed in a fleece sclavin hung about with shells, has a brimmed hat, typical of the fifteenth century, and holds a staff which has a Jericho palm bound to it. His pilgrim hat is adorned with a hundred lead ampulles, catherine wheels (from St. Catherine's Monastery at the foot of Mount Sinai), and shells. His cloak bears the Jerusalem cross and the keys of Rome; and he wears, too, the Veronica veil of the Roman pilgrimage. Langland, in his portrayal of this much-traveled palmer, exaggerates and caricatures the medieval figure of the literal pilgrim, his satire the opposite of that of Chaucer. Yet these and almost all other representations of pilgrims show them as soberly clad, and not in brilliant colors, and as pedestrian, rather than equestrian.

During the fourteenth century in which Dante Alighieri's <u>Commedia</u>, William Langland's <u>Piers Plowman</u> and Geoffrey Chaucer's <u>Canterbury Tales</u> were written, pilgrims in truth traveled throughout Christendom and told their lying tales while dressed in this absurdly distinctive manner. Their figures, with "cockle hat and staff," are mirrored, though "through a glass darkly," in these poems. Dante writes his <u>Commedia</u>, turning the tragedy of exile into the comedy of pilgrimage; Langland and Chaucer write <u>Piers Plowman</u> and the <u>Canterbury Tales</u> under the shadow of the Black Death and in the belief that pilgrimage could avert pestilence. Each of their poems is as a <u>speculum peregrinorum</u>, a mirror for pilgrims, presenting true and false images, juxtaposing folly and wisdom, that their readers may choose how best themselves to be as pilgrims. Each pilgrimage poem is self-consciously, self-referentially, self reflectively, about poets and poetry. Each makes use of the figure of the poet, in his own image, within his poem and as a pilgrim.

We thus, in reading these texts, find ourselves in a medieval version of Douglas Hofstadter's <u>Gödel, Escher, Bach</u>, in a looking-glass world where we are mirrored in the poet, the poet in us, through the medium of the text--which thus also mirrors the medieval/modern world we share. We have, therefore, to step beyond New Criticism, into the newer criticism, which itself is locked in a "looking-glass war" between Deconstructionism and Marxism, between theory and <u>praxis</u>. We will actually find that critics, ancient, medieval and modern, are talking the same language, playing the same games and seeking the same goals. What is important with medieval pilgrimage poems is to remember that we are

dealing with texts that intertextually emmesh themselves
with the Bible and that they are playfully about theology
as much as they are about poetry. These texts require that
we work within their terms of reference, suspending for a
while our disbelief.

Each pilgrimage poem uses the figural typology of the
Exodus and Emmaus stories, granting to these a "local
habitation and a name," setting those ancient stories in
fourteenth-century Italy and England and using them to
justify poetry, minstrelsy and fabling. The premise of a
work of fiction is that it is not flesh and blood reality,
that it is fable and not fact. However, pilgrimage poetry is
both fiction and fact, both allegory and reality, both lie
and truth, both fable and sermon. It transgresses beyond the
bounds of fiction and incorporates reality within its poetry
as flesh and blood people metamorphosed into words,
combining fiction and fact, mirror-reversing God's word made
flesh. Dante based his Commedia upon the allegory to be
found in Psalm 113, "In exitu Israel de Aegypto," which
retells the historical Exodus in an allegorical way. The
double use of Egyptian gold, for fashioning first the
profane Calf and then for adorning the sacred Ark, has been
argued by Augustine to justify the use of pagan poetry's
lies in Christian sermons. Each pilgrimage poem uses the
Emmaus story, of the disguised Christ and the two disciples
who "sermon" and "fable" on the road to the inn. Both
stories, of Exodus and Emmaus, are of conversions and
paradoxes. Thus we have here an intertextuality of fact and
fiction, truth and lies, the past and the present.

The Puritan heritage of modern readers has us read
texts as either piously serious or impiously comic, as
either sacred or profane. Yet pilgrimage poetry, as Dante's
poem title suggests and as Bakhtin has shown to be true of
the Two Worlds of medieval culture, can be piously comic,
profanely sacred, and fabulously true. Therefore these poems
include perverse, "up-so-doun," echoes of the Emmaus tale
from romances such as Tristan and Isolde and from beast
fables such as the Roman de Renart. Poems using the Exodus
and Emmaus themes have double structures that permit rich
paradoxes in which the "Two Worlds" of body and soul, nature
and culture, fables and sermons, and Carnival and Lent are
conjoined. They are "Janus" poems, capable of dual readings,
one, with folly, the other, with wisdom, which both
contradict and reconcile each other. Charles Singleton
discussed this quality to medieval texts in his Essay on the
Vita Nuova. His insights deserve to be expanded to these
larger fourteenth-century works. Nor should we forget here
the playfulness of Barthes on the pleasures of texts.
A prime example, of course, of such a text is the Roman de

la _Rose_. The serious pilgrimage texts, such as the _Commedia_, jokingly model themselves upon this profane one.

New Criticism believed in working with the text alone, working with the literal level of the text: "The text, the whole text and nothing but the text." But to do that can result in a lost dimension; in only looking at the art, we lose sight of the life that it mirrors and opposes, we lose its truth and only see its lies, naively taking these for eternal verities rather than _ambages pulcerrime_. Medieval modes of reading texts were different. The allegorical reading of a text then depended largely on the literal context as a means for decoding its "irony," a common medieval definition of allegory. Thus one text could then have two equal and opposite ways of being read, a Janus or _boustrophedon_-like quality, classical writing having originally been written like the ploughing of oxen in a field, forward and backwards as well (modern computers having returned to this method). This has confused many modern readers and New Critics of these texts. Yet to restore this doubleness is to achieve a richer and truer version of the poets' pilgrimages.

In working this medieval vein of textual interpretation one should be cognizant not only of the text, but also of the reader and the interaction with the author. Methods applied here derive in part from Stanley Fish's _Surprised by Sin: The Reader on Paradise Lost_ and from his essay "Affective Stylistics" (he appears to have independently arrived at "reader response," "reception aesthetic" and "deconstruction" from Jauss, Isser and Derrida, the latter being also his _Self-Consuming Artifacts_). An example of the restoration of a medieval way of reading a text could well be Terry Jones' controversial book, _Chaucer's Knight_, in which he discusses the General Prologue's satire of the Knight, presenting it as irony, as allegory, against the literal backdrop of the sordid nature of mercenary war in fourteenth-century Christendom, a contextual backdrop his audience well knew. Terry Jones achieves--or re- achieves--that doubleness through his analogy, his typology, of fourteenth-century _condottiere_ and the Vietnam War's similarly perceived loss of a chivalric, martial code. Sir John Hawkwood, "Gianni Acuto," and the scenes of rape, arson and pillage he wrought upon the Italian landscape, depicted in the Sienese _Mal Governo_ fresco, and the modern film, _Apocalypse Now_, are parallel. In them, life and art, its commentary, are context and text, code and cypher, signified and sign. To forbid that _boustrophedon_ doubleness of meaning is to censor the text (whose _ironia_ already presents it with a hermenutics of censorship), to destroy what Foucault has spoken of as its _parrhesia_, its

obligation to speak the truth at personal risk for the
common good. Empson's work on ambiguity, pastoral and double
plot at the beginning of his career, became, at its ending,
a study of censorship. These texts, the pilgrimage poems,
make use of Aristotle's _Ethics_ and intensely believe
that art is a handmaid to ethics and politics. It is a
poetic that uses _parrhesia_, in a direct continuum of that
classic tradition and obligation. Perhaps it is possible to
use literary criticism in a likewise parrhesiastic way, to
investigate what is dangerous and true, rather than what
would be safe and prestigious to do so. The Pilgrim and the
Fool are related figures; perhaps the scholar studying them
likewise needs to don their garments of sanctuary and
immunity. "'Tis a naughty night to swim in," Gerhart Ladner
remarks in his seminal   essay on medieval and Renaissance
pilgrimage literature.

        Each poem has pilgrimage be as an allegory and
apology for fabling poetry, while conjoining to it
theological truths. There are two basic sorts of allegory.
One, of pagan origin and which still prevails today, is
personification allegory representing abstract virtues and
vices. In Greek, "allegory" means that which is alien to the
agora, the market place, to reality. Dante is to call this
the "allegory of the poets," in which philosophical morality
is taught by the truth being concealed "beneath a beautiful
lie," fact veiled by fiction. Interestingly, the "pilgrim"
also means one who is "alien." The other sort of allegory is
Christian and is concerned with flesh and blood reality,
because of the Incarnation, of the word made flesh. Dante
called this the "allegory of the theologians," seeing it as
historically true and requiring a carnal basis. The two
sorts of allegory are combined in medieval pilgrimage
poetry. Erich Auerbach in his essays, "St. Francis of Assisi
in Dante's _Commedia_" and "_Figura_," described this with Cato
in _Purgatorio_ I-II and Amyclas in _Paradiso_ XI. In Greek
philosophy body and soul were to be dichotomized; in
medieval theology body and soul were to be in harmony.
Pilgrimage and its poetry are as a "carnal allegory" that
mirrors the four-fold scriptural senses, being polysemously
literal, allegorical, tropological and anagogical; being at
once carnal, figural, moral and concerned with salvation.
(Angus Fletcher, in a footnote, brilliantly analogized the
medieval four-fold allegoresis to the Aristotelian material,
formal, efficient and final causes.)

        Each poem is written in the vernacular--in the same
century that Wyclif translated the Bible. We recall that
this is a revolutionary period in England, a proto-Marxist
time, in response to the social breakdown brought on by the
Black Death. The people's languages are being used in

these texts to make them available to all. These texts are
responses to traumata, crises; exile in Dante's case, plague
in Langland and Chaucer's. In them exilic or revolutionary
breakdown is replaced by artistry, chaos by order. But such
figures as St. Francis and Amyclas are the stuff of revolutionary "worlds-upside-down," anti-heros of another ilk,
Everyman figures, common people, not Kings or Popes. A text
related to pilgrimage material is Thomas More's egalitarian
Utopia. Yet, Victor Turner reminds us, to permit such a
"world-upside-down" in life, ritual, art and--one could add
--scholarship, is the best way of averting real bloodshed.
For, along with the vernacular, each pilgrim text also
borrows from the Latin heritage, Europe's church and state
textual community, thereby empowering the people; prior to
this time, scribal literature had been a community for the
elite, the educated few alone. Leslie Fiedler has noted how
important the figure of the stranger really is--the distant
mirror of ourselves. These texts enfranchise us.

That textual community had wedded, to cite Matthew
Arnold, Hellenic and Hebraic traditions, resulting, as
Fredric Jameson has shown in "Metacommentary," in the four-
fold scriptural senses. Each poem uses the liturgical
material associated with pilgrimage, and especially the
Officium Peregrinorum, the liturgical drama of the Pilgrims
at Emmaus, enacted each Easter Monday in Benedictine
monastaries and which were likewise accompanied by the
chanting of Psalm 113. These poems also use, to varying
degrees, the "Chartrian," pedagogic, encyclopedic vision
poetry of the twelfth century, shaped by Cicero's and
Boethius' neo-Platonist and Stoic Somnium Scipionis and
Consolatio Philosophiae. Chaucer's Troilus and Criseyde is
stated by Chaucer himself to be a "philosophical poem."
These pilgrim poems in question are "theological" poems.

What is found in these three poems applies also to
other works, notably to Deguileville's trilogy of the
Pèlerinage de la vie humaine, the Pèlerinage de l'âme, and
the Pèlerinage Jhesucrist, likewise written in the
fourteenth century, and to the early Christian Pastor of
Hermas and to Bunyan's Pilgrim's Progress, of the
seventeenth century. The triadic form is also present in
Dante's Inferno, Purgatorio, and Paradiso, in Langland's
Vita de Dowel, Dobet and Dobest and even in Chaucer's
Prologue, Fables and Sermon. Dante knew the thirteenth
century mock pilgrimage poem, the Roman de la Rose,
which in turn was modeled upon the Latin encyclopedic poetry
of the twelfth century. Deguileville also knew the Roman de
la Rose and states that his poem was modeled upon it.
Chaucer was familiar with all of these, the "Chartrian"

poetry, the Roman de la Rose, the Commedia and the
Pèlerinages. Langland perhaps knew none of them save for the
Latin poetry, yet paradoxically he mirrors their structures
the most closely while Chaucer does so the least of all this
group of pilgrim poets. Peculiar to its form is its
mirroring of the scriptures in its own moment in time and in
its own region, and its inclusion within the poem's text of
its poet as a pilgrim. Also inherent to its genre is that
the paradigms are not so much static archetypes as they are
progressing entelechies. The reader in this way
participates in the persona's education, in the pilgrim's
progress, thus envisioning himself in the speculum
peregrinorum, the book as mirror held up to pilgrims.

     The scholarship on Dante, Langland and Chaucer is
massive. I do not pretend to have read it all. In the main
it fails to address the issue of pilgrimage as it is used in
these poems. Instead, I have attempted to explain the cruxes
in the texts concerning pilgrimage by examining records of
pilgrimage's manifestations in history, geography, theology,
liturgy, music, art and literature. While I have been
influenced by structuralists first, then by critical
theorists, I have tried to avoid their terminology. Between
the Scylla and Charybdis of Saussurian and Lévi-Straussian
dyads of binary polarities and Derridan deconstructions of
texts, pilgrimage best charts a course that can be
understood in Victor Turner's mediating paradigms of the
harmonies of opposites, of triads which are paradoxically
unities. I would argue that theology is the critical theory
of medieval pilgrimage poetry. I have applied iconography
and musicology to the study of literary texts. I have also,
as well as using anthropologists', musicologists' and art
historians' findings, made use of Paul Piehler's
psychoanalytic interpretation of Dante, The Visionary
Landscape, and Julian Jaynes' The Origin of Consciousness
in the Breakdown of the Bicameral Mind, the latter work
giving a rationale for pilgrim incubation rites and dream
visions.

     Pilgrimage poems are as "twice-told tales."
Therefore, I analyze each poem twice over, boustrophedon,
once in the light of the Emmaus paradigm, then again in
the light of the Exodus pattern of Psalm 113. Medieval modes
of thought--and consequent art--were not linear but
cyclical, chiastic and symmetrical. I have copied this mode
of thought, inherited by the Middle Ages from the Classical
period, in my writing about its paradigms. As Chaucer said,
"The word moot nede accorde with the dede" (IX.208). Caveat
lector, reader beware! This text needs a medieval, rather
than a modern reading. I have also tried to reconstruct for

the allegorical poetry its conscious palimpsest of carnal
reality, of Dante's Italy and Langland's and Chaucer's
England of the fourteenth century, upon which are reenacted
ancient pilgrimages of Exodus and Emmaus.

Jonathan Sumption has claimed that pilgrimage is an
image of medieval religion. Ralph Baldwin has spoken of it
as the _sovrasenso_ of the _Canterbury Tales_. Victor Turner has
suggested it is even more than that. One can use medieval
pilgrimage, as Clifford Geertz has used the Balinese cock
fight, to understand the symbolic structures of medieval
culture. Yet, as Turner has shown, it is an anti-structure,
in opposition to the society's structures. In opposition
to medieval society's rigid hierarchies, pilgrimage
presented a world in which all were equal, women with men,
beggars with kings. Thus, to understand medieval society,
we must do paradigm shifts backwards through time
and investigate not only its structures, but also its
opposing anti-structures, which serve to define its
culture. Chaucer noted, in _Troilus and Criseyde_, that
things are declared by their contraries. Blake, likewise,
deeply respected that Gothic principle. Foucault defined our
modern culture through the prism of the prison. And here I
should like to thank Ronald Herzman for his invitation to
lecture on Dante in Attica State Prison, for which I made
use of Foucault's _Surveiller et punir_, an experience that
taught me more than any classroom or study could about
Dante's _Inferno_. Pilgrimage, part of medieval culture's
penal system, can enable us to investigate these major
literary texts and the society which produced them. I also
wish to thank Fathers Gerard Farrell and Mark Thamert,
O.S.B., the first the Chant Master, the second, the Christus,
for performances of Fleury liturgical plays produced in
connection with this book.

I use Dante Alighieri, _La Commedia secondo l'antica
vulgata_, ed. Giorgio Petrocchi, Verona, 1967, 4 vols.;
William Langland, _Piers Plowman: The B Version_, ed. George
Kane, E. Talbot Donaldson, London, 1975, restoring, however,
the median dot; Geoffrey Chaucer, _The Canterbury Tales_, in
The Works of Geoffrey Chaucer, Boston, 1957; Guillaume de
Deguileville, _Le Pèlerinage de la vie humaine_, in the
translation by John Lydgate, _The Pilgrimage of the Life of
Man_, ed. F.J. Furnivall, London, 1888-1904, New York, 1975,
Early English Text Society, Extra Series 77, 83, 92, the
untranslated _Le Pèlerinage de l'âme_ and _Le Pèlerinage
Jhesucrist_, ed. J.J. Stürzinger, Roxburgh Club, London,
1895, 1897. My reason for restoring the median dot to the
Langland text is that the manuscripts, and Thomas Wright's
(London, 1832, 1856) and W.W. Skeat's (Oxford, 1886)

editions, took pains to show the caesura. The verse in this form presents the Old English quality of the alliterative line with its typical caesura and also the Judaeo-Christian quality of the antiphonal psalm chanting which was, probably, Langland's livelihood. See J.B. Trend, "The First English Songs," Music and Letters, 9 (1928), 127-128, for a discussion of this. Abbreviations used are EETS for Early English Text Society publications, London; DACL for the Dictionnaire d'archéologie chrétienne et de liturgie, ed. Fernand Cabrol, Henri Leclercq, Paris, 1939; TDNT for the Theological Dictionary of the New Testament, ed. Gerhard Friedrich, Grand Rapids, 1967; journals according to PMLA. Scriptural texts, the Vulgate and, where translated, the King James Bible; other translations, generally my own.

Studies on pilgrimage, the metaphor of the book and these poems are: Gerhart B. Ladner, "Homo Viator: Medieval Ideas on Alienation and Order," Speculum, 42 (1967), 223-259; John V. Fleming, The Roman de la Rose: Allegory and Iconography, Princeton, 1969; Ernst Robert Curtius, "The Book as Symbol," European Literature and the Latin Middle Ages, trans. Willard R. Trask, New York, 1953, pp. 302-347; Charles S. Singleton, An Essay on the Vita Nuova, Cambridge, Mass., 1958; Georg Röppen and Richard Sommer, Strangers and Pilgrims: An Essay on the Metaphor of Journey, Oslo, 1964; John C. Demaray, The Invention of Dante's Commedia, New Haven, 1974; Barbara Nolan, The Gothic Visionary Perspective, Princeton, 1977; Ralph Baldwin, "The Unity of the Canterbury Tales," Anglistica, 5, Copenhagen, 1955; Frank Cook Gardiner, Jr., The Pilgrimage of Desire: A Study of Theme and Genre in Medieval Literature, Leiden, 1966; Gabriel Josipovici, The World and the Book: A Study in Modern Fiction, London, 1971, pp. 52-99; Christian K. Zacher, Curiosity and Pilgrimage: The Literature of Discovery in Fourteenth-Century England, Baltimore, 1976; Donald R. Howard, The Idea of the Canterbury Tales, Berkeley, 1976, and his more recent short study of pilgrimage accounts. Background studies on pilgrimage are: J.J. Jusserand, English Wayfaring Life in the Middle Ages, trans. Lucy Toulmin Smith, London, 1889, 1961; Daniel Rock, The Church of our Fathers, London, 1903, vol. III; G. Hartwell Jones, Celtic Britain and the Pilgrim Movement, London, 1912; Edward L. Cutts, Scenes and Characters of the Middle Ages, London, 1922; Pellegrinaggi e culto dei santi in Europa fino alla I^a Crociata, Todi, 1963; Jonathan Sumption, Pilgrimage: An Image of Medieval Religion, Totowa, 1976. Books that are similar to this one were published after I had completed its writing: William Anderson, Dante the Maker, London, 1980; Peter Armour, The Door of Purgatory: A Study of Multiple Symbolism in Dante's Purgatorio, Oxford, 1983.

Professors Judson Boyce Allen, Lorrayne Y. Baird-Lange, Theodore Bogdanos, Kenneth Burke, Franco Cardini, Jonathan Culler, Phillip Damon, Horton Davies, John Demaray, William Empson, Leslie Fiedler, John V. Fleming, Patrick Geary, Gail McMurray Gibson, Laila Gross, Renata and James Fernandez, William S. Hecksher, Robert Hollander, Julian Jaynes, Spiro Kostoff, Murray Krieger, William LaFleur, Lawrence Lipking, Anthony Luttrell, Anne Middleton, Millard Meiss, Edward P. Nolan, Brendan O Hehir (who taught me to see poetry as having a historical geography), Norman Rabkin, Barbara Reynolds, Thomas P. Roche, Jr., Richard J. Schoeck, Raymond St. Jacques, Victor Turner, Dunstan Tucker, O.S.B., Rev. David Green, and others were hosts, guides and foresters to this pilgrim.

Pilgrims are given charity. I wish to thank the National Endowment for the Humanities for a Summer Seminar with Professor John V. Fleming at Princeton, 1973; the Surdna Foundation for a summer grant, 1976; Princeton University's Committee on Research in the Humanities and Social Sciences for a grant, 1977, and to that Committee and the Department of English for photography, typing costs and travel funds to pilgrimage to Compostela and Santo Domingo de Silos, 1979; the University of Colorado's Committee on University Scholarly Publications for enabling this publication; the libraries of the University of California at Berkeley, the Marquand Library, the Index of Christian Art (with special thanks to Rosalie Green, Elizabeth Home Beatson and Adelaide Bennett), the Firestone Library and the Robert H. Taylor Collection, Princeton University, the Rosenbach Collection, Philadelphia, the Bibliothèque Nationale, Paris, and the Vatican Biblioteca Apostolica in which I worked, and the libraries and museums which sent me photographs and answered queries, the British Library, the Bodleian, the Prado, Heidelberg University, the New York Metropolitan Museum, the Huntington Library and Museum, and many others. I also wish to thank Rev. Rex M. Ware of Winchelsea Rectory, Rev. John Bowers of Ashby-de-la-Zouche Vicarage, Rev. D. Conrad Evans of Llanfihangel Abercywyn Vicarage and Rev. K.J. Gillingham of Llandyfodwg Vicarage for photographs and information concerning the crusader and pilgrim effigies in their churches. Part of Chapter VIII appeared, in a condensed version, in <u>Studies in Medieval Culture</u>, 12 (1978). Some of the book's material was published in an article in the <u>American Benedictine Review</u>, 32 (1981). A shorter version of the argument of this book will appear as an essay in <u>Allegoresis</u>, New York, 1986.

My three sons have shared in the labors of this book and in many of the pilgrimages it prompted, to Malvern and Canterbury, to Florence and Rome, among others. They and Signor Amato Morrone of Rome greatly helped with the book's photography. My brother, Richard Rothwell Bolton, and his wife, Maria Antonia, encouraged the pilgrimage to Spain, and it was with them that I saw the cloister sculptures of the Emmaus Pilgrims and the Doubting of Thomas at Santo Domingo de Silos. _Gratias ago_

Easter Monday, 1986
University of Colorado
Boulder

CHAPTER ONE: PILGRIMS AND EXILES

   The figure of the pilgrim, with his "cockle hat and
staff, and his sandal shoon," whether medieval or
Renaissance, stood at a joining of roads: on the one hand
lay a Hellenic past, on the other a Hebraic one. These two
traditions, though opposed to each other, were reconciled in
the concept of the "Exile," the "Pilgrim," which yoked their
contrary modes into one being.[1] In flesh and blood, the
figure of Everyman as pilgrim acted out the words of books,
of the Odyssey and the Bible.

   Odysseus, the wily teller of lying tales, was a
traveler and therefore under the protection of Zeus. The
texts of Homer show that such a pilgrim in the ancient world
was honored. He was to be greeted, fed, clothed and housed,
and then asked his name and provenance. If such a stranger
or exile, ΞΕΝΟΣ or ΜΕΤΟΙΚΟΣ , were even to have been a
murderer fleeing revenge, or some foul beggar, ΠΤΩΧΟΣ, he
would still be under Zeus' protection.[2] Telemachus, Homer
shows us, is perturbed at the suitors' neglect of the
stranger at the gates who is really the goddess Athena
"disguised as a foreigner" [ΕΙΔΟΜΕΝΗ ΞΕΙΝΩ] (I.105),
and Eumaeos, once a king's son, now a slave, declares to
the disguised Odysseus, the king as beggar:

   "Stranger [ΞΕΙΝ'], it would not be right for me to
   dishonor a stranger, not if one worse than you came. In
   Zeus' care are all strangers and beggars [ΠΡΟΣ ΓΑΡ ΔΙΟΣ
   ΕΙΣΙΝ ΑΠΑΝΤΕΣ ΞΕΙΝΟΙ ΤΕ ΠΤΩΧΟΙ ΤΕ] (XIV.56-58)

When Odysseus has Eumaeos accompany him to the palace
he asks him for a staff and a scrip (XVII.195-199). He then
appears with intense dramatic irony amidst the suitors in

his own palace and begs bread and meat from them with which to fill his scrip. (St. Francis, many centuries later, will repeat this scene.) Antinoos alone denies him and, provoked by Odysseus, hurls his footstool at him, whereupon another suitor chides Antinoos:

> " . . . you did not do well to hit a hapless stranger. You are cursed, if he perhaps is some heavenly god. Yes, the gods in the semblance of alien strangers appears in all guises and go among the cities looking upon the pride and moderation of men." (XVII.483-487)

Penelope will address Odysseus, her own husband, as stranger [ξείνε] until the anagnorisis or recognition. The pilgrim is both the stranger and ourselves, both "Noman" and "Everyman." Thus Homer shapes the paradoxical and dramatic theme of gods-going-a-begging in the world.

The Greek traveler typically carried a staff, cut from the olive and wreathed with wool, and wore the petasos, a hat suitable for journeys, and sandal shoon, his guide being the psychopomp Hermes, whose staff was the caduceus, whose sandals were winged, and who likewise wore the petasos. The distinctive garb, with associations with the kingdom of the dead, despite differences in time and space, signified that the right of sanctuary belonged to the individual wearing it.[3] Worn next by Byzantine pilgrims, it was to become medieval pilgrim garb, the sanctuary right still intact (Plate I a,b, Figure 1). Similarly, though Homer's text was lost to the Middle Ages, was the pilgrim Odysseus to be reencountered as Ulysses in Dante's Commedia; while Pietro Alighieri says that Virgil in Dante's Commedia is Mercury, Hermes.[4] Virgil is thus Dante's psychopomp, his soul guide.

The Odyssey provided a word, and with it a legal and theological context concerning exile, with which to translate "stranger" in the Hebrew scriptures: גֵּר: ger, became ξένοι : xenoi, "strangers." The later city states made use of πάροικοι : paroikoi, for "resident aliens," which translated תּוֹשָׁב: toshab, "pilgrim." Greeks, besides, made use of pilgrimage and incubation for purposes of healing, journeying especially to the shrine of Aesculapius at Epidauros, much as the medieval world will journey to the shrines of thaumaturgical, miracle-working Christian saints, such as that of St. Thomas Becket at Canterbury, and there seek epiphanies of hero or saint in visions. The classic Roman world brought Aesculapius' caduceus from Epidauros to the ship island in the middle of the Tiber in time of plague and today that island is still a center of healing, Italians journeying to its now Christian hospitals.

Pagan elements contaminated Judaeo-Christian pilgrimage, among them perhaps the use of the labyrinth. Labyrinths, used formerly at Epidauros, are found on medieval cathedrals' floors and these are thought, probably erroneously, to have functioned as miniature penitential pilgrimages. In pagan initiation rites, in which success spells life, failure, death, labyrinths were frequently traced by the initiand bearing a staff, which could be sacrificed at need in place of its bearer. In these rites the labyrinth represented the female, the staff, the male.[6]

This Hellenic background to pilgrimage explains much. However, the Hebraic background consciously shaped medieval theology and pilgrimage. The appearance of the medieval pilgrim is partly to be explained by Hellenic texts, partly by Judaeo-Christian scriptures, especially the books of Genesis, Exodus, Luke, Hebrews and Apocalypse. In Genesis Adam and Eve sin and are expelled from Eden. The text has God garb the parents of mankind as were medieval pilgrims to be: "Fecit quoque Dominus Deus et uxori eius tunicas pelliceas et induit eos" [Unto Adam also and to his wife did the Lord God make coats of skin, and clothed them] (3.21). A mosaic at Monreale shows Adam and Eve so clothed while the Fra Angelico Annunciation in the Prado presents them in the haircloth of medieval penitents (Plates II a,b).

The word for "pilgrim" in Hebrew texts, implied with Adam and Cain, occurs first, however, in Abraham's phrase, "strangers and pilgrims" (Gen. 23.4), in which it refers to the Hebrews' nomadic status. David was to theologize the legal phrase as meaning man's alienation from God after the Fall (Psalm 39.12; I Chron. 29.15). Jerome translated the scriptural "strangers and pilgrims" " גר :ger, and " תושב: toshab, of Hebrew and the "πάροικοι : paroikoi" and "ξένοι : xenoi" of Greek into the "peregrini et advenae" of Latin. Moreover, the typical pilgrim garb of skins imposed an additional meaning upon peregrinus: "stranger." Cassian called the monastic fleece garb a "pera," though elsewhere that word meant "leather scrip," the pilgrim's skin tunic or cloak more often being called a "sclavin." "Peregrinus" in the vernacular languages became "pellegrinus, pèlerin, pilgrim," both in accordance with linguistic rules and also because of its association with "pelle" or skin. In the Middle Ages these words meant not only "homo viator," "traveler," "stranger" or "exile," but also "one who goes about clad in skins" or naked.[7] It is even unclear in the Blessing of the Pilgrims, the Benedictio peregrinorum or Benedictio pere et baculi, or in the Officium Peregrinorum, whether "pera" meant scrip, fleece tunic or cloak of skin.

Sclavins of fleeceskin are found in medieval art garbing the first parents, prophets, desert fathers and pilgrims. Such was the early monastic dress of the Egyptian desert of the Thebaid and also in Celtic lauras in Ireland and Britain. Palladius gave Pachomius' Rule: "Let them each have a goatskin cloak," besides which they were to wear leather belts and white cowls with Tau crosses worked on them in deep red. Cassian in the early fifth century said that the dress of the cenobitic "milites Christi" [knights of Christ], signifying their dying to the world, imitated Elijah and John the Baptist who clad themselves in hair and camelskin (such as we see in the Wilton Diptych of Richard II and his patron saints), and the "strangers and pilgrims' who "wandered about in sheepskins and goatskins . . . in deserts, and in mountains, and in dens and caves of the earth" of Hebrews 11. 37-38.[8] The garb of these scriptural wilderness dwellers was clearly patterned upon the skins with which God clothed the exiled Adam and Eve. With Christianity, first it was the garb of patristic hermit monks, then it was assumed by medieval lay pilgrims.

Dante Alighieri in _Paradiso_ XXV.7 speaks of his garb as a "vello" [fleeceskin] and of returning in it from exile to his "bello ovile" [fair sheepfold] of St. John's in Florence. Will Langland, in the A and B texts of _Piers Plowman_, is clad in a sheepskin, like a sheep: "I shoop me into a shroud . as I a shepe weere."[9] Northern pilgrims adopted the sheepskin rather than the camel or goatskin for their garb, a practice reinforced by the imagery of Revelation whose heavenly Jerusalem is as a sheepfold, and by the Blessing of the Pilgrims which speaks of the travelers as sheep questing their shepherd (Appendix I). The _Roman de la Rose_, which is a mock pilgrimage poem mirrored seriously by the _Commedia_, counters the earthly and idolatrous garden of delights of Amant and his rose with the heavenly park where the apocalyptic lamb is the shepherd of the saved flock (20191-20272). The Cistercian monk Guillaume de Deguileville is obliged to wear monastic garb and tonsure but to these he adds pilgrim accoutrements in his _Pèlerinage de la vie humaine_, while in his _Pèlerinage de l'âme_ his figure is startlingly naked save for his scrip and staff.[10] Medieval frescoes and illuminations often have pilgrims garbed in skins (Plates I, II, III, Figure 12).

The medieval pilgrim dramatized the state of Everyman in God's world. Expiatory penitential pilgrimage consciously mirrored the exile from Eden of Adam and Eve. This is stated in the Ash Wednesday Expulsion of Penitents and echoed in the liturgical action of the Pilgrim Blessing. Pilgrimage

also reflected the wanderings of Cain who was outlawed by
God for murdering his brother Abel. When Cain protested that
" . . . everyone that findeth me shall slay me," God marked
Cain to protect him from such revenge. The Tau mark in
Exodus, Ezekiel and Revelation granted a similar protection
to its bearers.[11]   Consequently the Egyptian Desert Fathers
and St. Francis adopted the Tau cross for their sign. The
signs and phials medieval pilgrims wore similarly protected
them under Christendom's laws. Andrea da Firenze's pilgrim
wears three such signs on his hat, a Roman vernicle, a
Galician cockle shell and one other, and Langland tells of
many more worn by his Palmer (Plates Ia,b). The Musée de
Cluny preserves many pilgrim badges and London museums
possess a good number dredged from the Thames' mud.
Sometimes these signs were branded upon the pilgrim or cut
with a sword point upon the shoulder or forehead. Dante in
Purgatorio IX receives seven such sword-inscribed cuts upon
his brow, each in turn to be expiated and then removed upon
the terraces of the penitential mountain.[12]

Cain, in Genesis 4.16, is said to have built a city,
ceasing to plough the blood-stained land, and in Hebrews
11.4 and 13 the shepherd Abel is named as one of the
"strangers and pilgrims" who sought not worldliness but the
heavenly city. Augustine yoked together the statements of
Genesis and Hebrews: "it is recorded of Cain that he built a
city, but Abel was a pilgrim and built none," and from this
opposition he created his City of God.[13]   Samuel Purchas was
to rephrase this concept in his seventeenth-century travel
book, Purchas his Pilgrimes: "And thus is Mans whole life a
Pilgrimage either from God as Cains, or from himselfe as
Abels."[14]   Cain had lamented to God: "from thy face shall I
be hid: and I shall be a fugitive and a vagabond in the
earth" (Gen. 4.14). Man created in God's image could
recreate that image within by pilgrimage or deny it by
remaining exiled and alienated from God. It is therefore
significant that the Roman badge of pilgrimage was the
vernicle which bore the face of God.

The word peregrinus embraced the oppositions of exile
and pilgrimage, of the profane and the sacred. Medieval
pilgrims enacted this doubleness. There were those who vowed
a religious pilgrimage and performed it for the love of God,
being thereby as an Abel. There were those who had committed
a crime, had been tried in ecclesiastical or secular courts
and been sentenced to penitential exile, being thereby as a
Cain. A Cain-like murderer could become a pilgrim, rather
than be hanged, but were he in turn murdered his murderer
would be instantly slain, no expiation being tolerated for
such a crime. Such a pilgrim exile in Carolingian times

could be stripped naked and laden with chains into which
were forged the weapons of his crime, or who was branded or
cut with a cross or other mark, to expiate his sin. Dante's
nude sinners in the Inferno and the Purgatorio are similarly
appropriately punished. Yet the religious pilgrim and the
penitent criminal were garbed alike, the service of the
Pilgrim Blessing said over them was the same; they were
similarly treated in the communities through which they
passed, and given bread, water and lodging for twenty-four
hours. Like Cain, they were under the protection of God.[15]

Dante, soon himself to be exiled, in the Vita Nuova
prophetically defined the pilgrim as an exile: "I have said
'pilgrim' according to the broad sense of the word: for
'pilgrim' can be understood in two ways, one broad, the
other strict. In the broad sense, a 'pilgrim' is one who is
a stranger, and exile; in the strict sense 'pilgrim' is not
meant unless he travels toward the shrine of St. James or
elsewhere." Cesare Ripa in his Renaissance emblem book, the
Nova Iconologia, concurred, giving the figure of the Exile,
Esilio, as the figure of a pilgrim (Figure 1). The emblem
shows a pilgrim who has journeyed to Compostela, signified
by the cockle or scallop shell he wears, and who intends a
voyage to Jerusalem, that vow indicated by his sign of the
cross, and who therefore exemplifies the extremes of either
piety or criminality, the gravest offenses requiring the
farthest pilgrimages as expiation.[16]   Dante defines these
types of pilgrims:

> E dissi 'peregrini' secondo la larga significazione del
> vocabulo; ché peregrini si possono intendere in due
> modi, in uno largo e in uno stretto: in largo, in
> quanto è peregrino chiunque è fuori de la sua patria;
> in modo stretto non s'intende peregrino se non chi va
> verso la casa di sa' Iacopo o riede. E però è da sapere
> che in tre modi si chiamano propriamente le genti che
> vanno al servigio de l'Altissimo: chiamansi palmieri
> in quanto vanno oltremare, là onde molte volte recano
> la palma; chiamansi peregrini in quanto vanno a la casa
> de Galizia, però che la sepultura di sa' Iacopo fue più
> lontana de la sua patria che d'alcuno altro apostolo;
> chiamansi romei in quanto vanno a Roma, là ove questi
> ch'io chiamo peregrini andavano.

> [And "pilgrims" is said according to the broader
> significance of the word; that pilgrims can be
> understood in two ways, in a broad and in a narrow; in
> the broad in that a pilgrim is whoever is outside of
> his country, in the narrow, a pilgrim is only one who
> goes to the shrine of Saint James or elsewhere. And
> there are three kinds who are properly called the

HVOMO in habito di Pellegrino, che con
la deftra mano tiene vn bordone, & con
la finiftra vn falcone in pugno.

Due Efilij fono, vn publico, e l'altro priua
to. il publico è quando l'huomo, ò per colpa,
ò per fofpetto è bandito dal Prencipe, ò dalla
Republica, & condannato à viuere fuor di patria perpetuo, ò à tempo.

Il priuato è quando l'huomo volontaria-
mente, e per qualche accidente fi elegge di ui-
uere, e morire fuor di patria, fenza efferne cac-
ciato, che ciò fignifica l'habito del pellegrino,
& il bordone.

Et per il publico lo dinota il Falcone con i
getti alli piedi.

Figure 1   Emblem of Esilio
            Cesare Ripa, Iconologia

people who go in the service of the most high: they are
called "Palmers" when they go overseas from whence many
times they bring back the palm; they are called
"Pilgrims" when they go toward the shrine of Galicia,
because the sepulchre of St. James is the farthest from
his homeland of any of the Apostles; they are called
"Romei" when they go toward Rome, where these whom I
call "pilgrims" were going.] (XL)

For over a thousand years, the figure of the pilgrim
was both holy and a criminal, both the pilgrim and an exile,
as he journeyed to Jerusalem, Rome, Compostela, Canterbury
or elsewhere.

The pilgrim was to lay aside his weapons and journey
great distances barefoot; he was not to sleep twice in one
place, he had to fast and pray, and he could not set iron on
hair or nail.[17]   From this last custom came the distinctive
beard of the male pilgrim, typically worn parted in two. The
pilgrims in the Via Veritatis fresco and in the engraving of
Esilio have such untrimmed beards (Plate Ia; Figure 1).
However, Chaucer's Pardoner is unable to grow one. Many of
Chaucer's pilgrims are armed, likewise in defiance of canon
law. The pilgrim, above all, was to be chaste: "Dearly
beloved, I beseech you as strangers and pilgrims, abstain
from fleshly lusts, which war against the soul" (I Peter
2.11). What then are we to make of the lustful Wife on
pilgrimage from Bath? Or of the golden brooches, in lieu of
pilgrim badges of lead, adorned with a "loveknotte" and the
motto: "Amor vincit omnia" that the Monk and Prioress wear
(I. 160-162, 195-197)?

Chaucer's Canterbury Tales in our day is thought to
describe medieval pilgrims with some verisimilitude. In its
own day, however, the General Prologue would have been read
as ludicrous satire. "Commune penaunce," Chaucer's Parson
says, "is that preestes enjoynen men communly in certeyn
caas, for to goon peradventure naked in pilgrimage or
barfot" (X.104). He preaches these words at the beginning of
his penitential sermon to the worldly, gaily clad, armed,
lustful and, above all, equestrian pilgrims of Chaucer's
mocking fiction. To ride a horse for the whole journey
invalidated the pilgrimage. Kings, even Henry VIII, and
knights, including the Sire de Joinville, walked barefoot on
pilgrimage. An ass was permitted for those too infirm to
journey otherwise, in imitation of Christ; staves were
jokingly called pilgrims' mules.[18]   The satire deepens with
the figure of the beardless Pardoner who wears a pilgrim hat
to which is fastened a vernicle of the bearded Christ--whom
he ought to imitate but will not and, being a eunuch,
cannot.[19]   His scrip, moreover, is hung about his horse's

neck in the Ellesmere illumination to the Pardoner's Tale in
a manner that outrageously defies pilgrimage iconography
(Frontispiece).

Whether the pilgrim chose out of piety to undertake the
pilgrimage, or whether he was an exile abjured from the
realm, before he set out he had to make his Will and
Testament as if he were dying. Piers Plowman, Guillaume de
Deguileville, Margery, Sir Richard Guylforde and many more
do so. Family affairs were to be settled, debts paid, and
the bishop's license obtained without which the pilgrim
would be liable to arrest. Chaucer's merchants set forth on
pilgrimage without paying their debts (I.279-280;
VII.233-234), which would not have been allowed. The pilgrim
was then exempt from taxes and tolls, except those exacted
by Byzantine and Saracen authorities, and from other
financial and even feudal obligations which were now owed
only to God and his saints, not the world and its lords.[20]
The pilgrim in law was as if dead in the temporal world in
his quest for eternal life.

Adam and Eve, Cain and Abel, Abraham and Jacob are
pilgrim figures. The Pilgrim Blessing, the Benedictio
Peregrinorum, quoted the words Abraham said over his servant
Eliezir sent to what would be Jacob's Well to find a bride
for Isaac: "The Lord God of heaven, which took me from my
father's house, and from the land of my kindred . . . ."
Earlier texts cited God's more direct words to Abraham: "Exi
de terra tua et de domo patris tua, et vade in terram quam
tibi monstravero" [Get thee out of thy country, and from thy
kindred, and from thy father's house, unto a land that I
will show thee] (12.1), a command that Abraham obeyed,
pilgrimaging from Chaldea to Canaan. In the Dark Ages
fleece-clad Irish monks, like those of the Egyptian Thebaid,
revered this concept of peregrinatio, which they called
"ailithre" [other land], and their saint's lives echoed
God's command to Abraham in both word and deed. Irish
pilgrims based their lives upon Adam, Abraham, Moses,
Elijah and John the Baptist, after the manner of the Thebaid
monks. While Celtic Christians adapted Thebaid monasticism
to their ocean-girt islands, similarly building lauras or
communities with separate eremitic cells, their pilgrimages
often took the form also of a sea voyage without rudder, oar
or sail, followed by a land wandering. Four Irish monks came
in this manner to Anglo-Saxon King Alfred. Irish monks
preceded the Icelandic settlers. Both forms of pilgrimage,
on land and sea, expressed the paradox of dying to the world
to attain eternal life.[21]

Monasticism, eremeticism and peregrination in their

origin were one. With time they diverged. The earlier form,
of the Thebaid and Ireland, exemplified by St. Anthony,
stressed the solitary hermit who departed from the city for
the wilderness in _peregrinatio_, on _ailithre_. The later, of
the Roman Church's centralized monasticism, stressed
communal life, St. Benedict's Rule condemning the earlier
monastic pilgrimage.[22]   The cloistered life was now as an
interior pilgrimage, but not a physical one; it stressed
community, not individuality; its cloistered garden was as
an Eden, the world outside it as a wilderness of exile.

Eastern Christianity still retains the earlier
practices, for instance in Mount Athos' lauras of bearded,
leather-belted eremitic monks, though Ireland no longer does
so. After the Council of Whitby in A.D. 664 chose Roman
Benedictinism over Celtic monasticism, physical
peregrinatio was carried out by the laity rather than by the
clergy. Chaucer's Monk and Prioress in the fourteenth
century were definitely forbidden to be on the Canterbury
road of pilgrimage though they could have traveled so in the
fourth century. Chaucer, well aware of the Benedictine
Rule's prohibition against external pilgrimages being
performed by cloistered clergy (I.179-181), wrote of that
monastic pair with great irony.

In the thirteenth century the fraternal mendicant
preaching orders resurrected external _peregrinatio_ among the
clergy. St. Francis' disciple Bernard was converted by the
same text that had prompted St. Anthony, Matthew 19.21,
"sell that thou hast, and give to the poor," and St. Francis
himself spoke often of the Friars Minor as "strangers and
pilgrims."[23]   In the interim the lay populace
enthusiastically took up the concept of pilgrimage abandoned
by the monastic clergy. Lay pilgrims of the fourteenth
century were to be found dressed as were the Egyptian and
Irish monks of the fourth through eighth centuries. Secular
pilgrims preferred group travel, not only to the Holy Places
about Jerusalem but also to European shrines housing
precious relics of miracle-working saints. Rome, Compostela,
Canterbury and many other places were as if substitute
Jerusalems.[24]   Pilgrimage had become an expression of lay
piety; therefore, pilgrimage poetry became the form most
chosen by lay poets. Such poetry satirized monks, friars and
pilgrims because it sought the reform of clergy and laity.

Genesis' tale of Adam and Eve expulsed from Eden and of
Abraham's monastic wanderings from Chaldea to Canaan were
tales of exile become pilgrimage. Moses' and Aaron's Exodus
from Egypt and their pilgrimage in the Sinai Wilderness
toward Israel added to medieval pilgrimage its relics housed

in shrines of gold, silver and jewels and its associations
with plague. Also it gave the medieval pilgrim his
distinctive staff and sandal shoon—which Christ forbade. At
the beginning of the Exodus pilgrimage a Paschal Lamb was
slain and eaten, its blood marking the doorposts with a Tau
cross to protect the Israelites from the tenth plague, the
death of the first born, meted out to the Egyptians. God
commanded the Israelites: "thus shall ye eat it; with your
loins girded, your shoes on your feet, and your staff in
your hand: and ye shall eat it in haste; it is the Lord's
Passover" (Exod.12.11). Christ, however, told his followers
to go forth with "nor scrip for your journey, neither two
coats, neither shoes, nor yet staves" (Matt.10.10: Luke
10.4). The Pilgrim Blessing contained these Gospel words,
together with the version of God's Commandment to Abraham:
nonetheless it blessed the Exodus' scrips and staves the
Gospels' words condemned.

The pilgrims of the Middle Ages kept their staves and
leather belts with scrips and sandal shoes, though Christ
forbade them. Thus Genesis garbed pilgrims with skins of
animals and Exodus added to that garb, scrips, staves and
shoes. The pilgrim first fulfilled Abraham's Covenant and
Moses' Law, then upon his pilgrimage's completion laid aside
his scrip, staff, and sclavin upon the altar in his
reconciliation to Christ. This pattern of a pilgrim's
progress is important also in literature. Deguileville's
Pèlerinage de l'âme has the saved souls in this manner lay
aside their scrips of faith and their staves of hope when
they have attained the realm of charity.[25]

John of Climacus in the Ladder of Divine Ascent, a work
written at St. Catherine's Monastery at Sinai, Joachim of
Fiore in the Liber Figurarum, St. Bonaventure in the Itinerarium mentis in Deum, Dante in the Purgatorio, and many
more, all make use of the Exodus pattern.[26] Real pilgrims
in the Middle Ages were conscious of themselves as mirroring
the Exodus' Israelites wandering in the Wilderness of Sinai
and of likewise carnally lusting after the "fleshpots of
Egypt." Depictions of pilgrims through the thirteenth
century show them with the pointed hats Jews were required
to wear in Christendom (Plate Ia).[27] Then, in the
fourteenth century, the petasos, the broad-brimmed Greek
traveler's hat, became the fashion (Plate Ib), in the
fifteenth century its brim being turned up in front and if
the pilgrim came from Compostela fastened with a shell
(Figure 3). Such a garb, whether Hebraic or Hellenic, to the
medieval mind, signified sinfulness pilgrimaging to truth.

Pilgrims were also aware of their scrips' and staves'

priapic connotations as in the <u>Roman de la Rose</u>'s consummation (Plate IVb,c), though pilgrimage and lust, Christ and Venus, were opposed: "Dearly beloved, I beseech you as strangers and pilgrims, abstain from fleshly lusts, which war against the soul" (I Peter 2.11). However, though these staves and scrips countered Christ, they are nevertheless shown on pilgrim tombs (Figure 2); on Doomsday portals pointed hats and scrips are worn by the joyous elect at God's right hand (Plate XIV); and Christ himself, contradicting his own words, wears all these as an Emmaus pilgrim in medieval illuminated manuscripts, frescoes and sculptures (Figure 4, Plates IIIa,b, VIa,b).[28] In Deguileville's <u>Pèlerinage de Jhesucrist</u> Jesus does so to demonstrate his incarnation as word become flesh, God imaged forth as Adam. Elsewhere, as in the liturgical drama, the <u>Officium Peregrinorum</u>, and in Dante's <u>Vita Nuova</u>, he is spoken of as "Amor" when in this garb. Such paradoxes abound in pilgrimage material.

The sclavin, signs, scrip, staff and sandals have been explained. The pilgrim palm and shell now await their turn. After the Exodus the Israelites were commanded by God to commemorate that event with thrice-yearly pilgrimages to Jerusalem, at Passover, Pentecost and Tabernacles. At the feast of the Tabernacles the Hebrew pilgrims were to dwell in booths and to bring palms to lay on the horns of the Temple's altar while singing the Hallel, a group of psalms which included Psalm 113. Dante was to base his <u>Commedia</u> upon Psalm 113 as it had become, likewise, the psalm Christian pilgrims sang at Jerusalem and elsewhere.[29] John in writing Revelation 7.9 used these aspects of Hebrew Temple pilgrimage and liturgy in his vision of the heavenly Jerusalem and placed the martyred souls about the Passover Lamb as garbed in white and holding such palms in their hands. Early Roman martyr tombs were therefore marked with such a palm and were visited by Christian pilgrims, themselves clad in white.[30]

Jerusalem and Rome were obvious goals. But the third pilgrimage shrine Dante listed in the <u>Vita Nuova</u> was that of Compostela's supposed tomb of St. James in Spain's western province of Galicia. Dante notes that it was the shrine farthest from the Apostle's homeland, thereby being the most peregrinate. The figure of the legendary pilgrim saint deeply impressed itself upon medieval culture. Pilgrims who completed their pilgrimage to him crossing the limen or threshold of his shrine, were in his image with his scallop shell fastened on their hat and scrip and were shown so in art throughout Latin Christendom, and were remembered even in the poetry written by Protestant Shakespeare: "How should

I your true love know From another one? By his cockle hat
and staff And his sandal shoon." The scallop or cockle
shell, usually associated with Venus, has no scriptural
significance and its Compostela meaning is a mystery. In
Latin St. James' name is Jacobus, mirroring the Jacob of the
Old Testament, likewise a pilgrim figure in medieval
commentary, whom God named "Israel," as one "face to face
with God."[31]

The Autun tympanum shows besides a Jerusalem pilgrim a
Compostela one with a shell upon his scrip (Plate XIV). A
naive and startling effigy, at Llandyfodwg, Wales, is of a
pilgrim with staff, scrip, two sets of keys of the Roman
pilgrimage, two Jerusalem crosses and a shell of the
Galician pilgrimage (Figure 2).[32] The aged pilgrim of the
Florentine Spanish Chapel fresco (Plate Ia) has reached the
distant shrine and wears the Galician shell in his hat
beside a Roman vernicle. His garb is that of Adam's coat of
skins, his staff is from Exodus.

Such a pilgrim would have journeyed through the
Alyscamps and Roncesvalles (Inferno IX.112; XXXI.16), regions
famous for their associations not only with the Santiago
pilgrimage but also with the landscapes of Charlemagne's
crusading Paladins. In the pilgrim churches along the way,
built to house the crowds of pilgrims who slept in them on
the eves of saints' feastdays in order to experience visions
and miracles, relics were shown not only of saints but also
of these knights, such as the Oliphant of Roland, and
legends were ably fostered by Cluniac monks in which the
Emperor Charlemagne is himself anachronistically a pilgrim
crusader to St. James, led to his shrine by a galaxy of
stars.[33]   All Europe knew of tales of miracles of the
Santiago pilgrimage road. A famous one is of a wicked
innkeeper who places silver cups in the scrip of a boy on
pilgrimage with his parents. The boy is hanged for the
supposed theft but St. James holds him up until his parents
return from Compostela. Another is of a band of pilgrims of
whom twenty-eight do not aid a dying companion, while the
twenty-ninth does so and is rewarded by St. James. Chaucer's
Canterbury pilgrims number "wel nyne and twenty in a
compaignye" (I.24). The Compostela road was therefore
associated with the telling of pilgrim sermons, legends and
fables.[34]   Many of these deliberately encouraged a Christian
pilgrimage into a largely Saracen-held land in order to
counter and counterfeit the Mohammedan haj to Mecca and
Cordoba.

In Spain, in the eighth century, at the same time that
mention was first made of St. James' tomb as being there,

Figure 2   Effigy of a Pilgrim
Llandyfodwg, Wales

fine illuminated manuscripts of Beatus' Commentary on the
Apocalypse began to be copied. The Apocalypse text stresses
the opposition between Babylon and Jerusalem and speaks of
Babylon as Egypt (11.8). Interestingly, in the Middle Ages,
Cairo in Egypt was known as "Babylon" whose Saracen Soldan
ruled Spain's Moslem population. St. James, in legends,
became not only the pilgrim but also the crusader saint, the
Matamoros, or "Moor Slayer," who rode into battle upon an
apocalyptic horse to free Spain from the Infidel.[35]   Thus
the Beatus Apocalypse had much to do with shaping a
crusading division between the Moors and Christians. The
eleventh-century Chanson de Roland continues this division
in juxtaposing the Christian forces as those of Jerusalem,
mirrored in Charlemagne's capital, Aix-la-Chapelle, and the
Saracen forces of the Soldan's Babylon in Egypt.

The twelfth-century Compostela Codex Calixtinus states
that Charlemagne and Archbishop Turpin of Reims conceded a
plenary indulgence to those who fought against the infidel
in Spain and that this concept was taken up by Pope Urban at
Clermont in 1095, granting a similar plenary indulgence to
those who fought against the infidel in the Holy Land with
the sign of the Jerusalem cross on their shoulder.[36]
Crusading pilgrimage was considered "satisfaction." For the
remission of sins "confession" and "contrition" were still
also required, despite lying claims such as those made by
Chaucer's and Langland's false pardoners.

Contemporary historians described the Reconquest and
the Crusades in the light of the Apocalypse. Richard Coeur
de Lion visited apocalyptic Joachim of Fiore before voyaging
to the Holy Land. Spain's and Jerusalem's crusaders took the
allegorical and apocalyptic concept of monastic hermits and
pilgrims as "milites Christi" [knights of Christ]
(Rev.19.11-14) literally. Though the clergy were not to bear
arms, nor likewise were pilgrims, armed monastic orders such
as the Hospitallers and the Templars were formed to wage war
against the Saracen and to protect the Christian pilgrim.
These orders combined monasticism and militarism, the knight
with the pilgrim. Thus Christendom sought to regain
Jerusalem, whose name means "vision of peace," by means of
war.[37]

On the road these contrary pilgrims clustered together;
the warrior knight with the peaceable civilian; the pilgrim
who out of piety had vowed a pilgrimage; the pilgrim whose
journey was penitential punishment; the chaste pilgrim and
the lustful one. Chaucer's Canterbury Tales gives us villain
and saint, the worst and the best, riding side by side.
Similarly does the Duchess of Burgogne's fifteenth-century

Book of Hours' illuminations for the months of April and
September in which pilgrims are seen who journey to and from
St. James of Compostela beneath Taurus and Libra. Very few
of these pilgrims ride. Most walk barefoot in the true
pilgrim manner. Some of the criminals fight, other pilgrims
step in to break up quarrels. The pilgrims returning from
Santiago have scallop shells upon their hats and festooning
the scrips' straps.

In the fourteenth and fifteenth centuries guilds and
confraternities were established to organize group
pilgrimages, such as we see with Chaucer's gildsmen and
their wives. Ludlow had a Palmers' Guild, commemorating
Edward the Confessor's gift of a ring to a poor pilgrim who
was St. John the Baptist in disguise, who then, in turn,
gave the ring to two Ludlow pilgrims to return to the
saintly king.[38]

The Church gained great revenue from the sales of
indulgences, pardons and jubilees. There are lists in
Rymer's <u>Foedora</u> of pilgrim ships and of their gold-carrying
passengers setting sail for Compostela and Jerusalem and of
pilgrim licenes granted by bishops and by kings. There are
also guidebooks and diaries written by pilgrims noting their
great expenses. Important fairs, such as the Lendit of St.
Denis, grew up around pilgrimage shrines' feast days. There
was at the same time considerable criticism of the
mercantilism present in pilgrimage, though papal decretals
similarly protected merchants and pilgrims.[39]   Shakespeare
was to write aptly: "there are pilgrims going to Canterbury
with rich offerings, and traders riding to London with fat
purses" (<u>I Henry IV</u>.I.iii.139).

Despite the growing mercantilism of medieval pilgrimage
its ideals continued to be upheld. In the midst of the
world's hierarchies, pilgrimage presented the opposition of
a theocracy in which all are equally in the image of God. In
accord with the Greek tradition of the disguised pilgrim who
was no stranger; with Abraham's hosting of three strangers
who were God (Gen.18.1-33); with God's command that
Israelites honor strangers since they were themselves
strangers in Egypt (Exod.22.21); with Christ's request that
Christians shelter pilgrims as if they were himself
(Matt.25.35-36); with the Pilgrims at Emmaus; monastic
rules, whether Thebaid, Irish or Benedictine, required that
the stranger be greeted as if he were Christ in disguise.
The <u>xenodochia</u> or guest house was built to house such
strangers in the earliest monasteries. Travel-stained and
hungry guests first thanked God for their safety, then had
their feet washed by the Abbot or by one of his monks, in

Of ryches vnprofytable.

Yet fynde I folys of another sorte
Whiche gather and kepe excessyfe ryches
With it denyeng their neyghboures to conforte
Whiche for nede lyueth in payne and wretchydnes
Suche one by fortune may fall into distres
And in lyke wyse after come to mysery
And begge of other, whiche shall to hym deny.

Fig. 3 Dives and Lazarus
Barclay's Ship of Fools

imitation of Christ's washing of the disciples' feet on
Maundy Thursday, and they were fed well and sheltered for
the night.[40] At San Marco in Florence, Christ is shown as a
fleeceskin-clad pilgrim greeted by two Dominicans as if at
Emmaus; at Pistoia, reversing Maundy Thursday, he has his
feet washed by hospitallers (Plates IIIa,b). The modern
hospital derives from those built out of charity to house
pilgrims, including those who were sick and dying.

The Wilton Diptych shows Richard II, Chaucer's king,
resplendent in cloth of gold, yet humbly kneeling before the
figures of ascetic John the Baptist holding a lamb in his
arms, King Edward the Confessor, the ring of the pilgrim
legend held in his fingers, and Edmund the Martyr King with
his arrow. The painting sternly contrasts Richard's opulence
to the Baptist's poverty at the same moment that it links
English kings to pilgrimage. The Ship of Fools shows foolish
Dives counting out his money while at the gate sits poor
Lazarus in the garb of a Compostela pilgrim with dogs who
lick his sores (Figure 3). Pilgrims achieved a fleeting
theocracy, a law unto their own, or rather of Christ, all
being created equally in that Emmaus image which shadowed
that of Exodus.[41] The two modes coexisted, the one of
medieval hierarchy, the other of Christian equality.
Chaucer's Parson, Lollard writers and others spoke openly of
"evene-Cristenes" (X.394). Fourteenth-century pilgrimage
poems stressed pilgrimage's apocalyptic theocracy. Dante's
"Ma noi siam peregrin come voi siete" [But we are pilgrims,
like yourselves] (Purg.XI.234); Langland's "for pilgrimes
are we alle" (B.XI.234); Chaucer's "And pilgrimes were they
alle" (I.26), echo in turn this universal concept of
Christian justice and mercy. Medieval Christendom and its
poetry considered men and women to be as sinful exiles who
could, if they chose, become godly pilgrims. About the
figure of the medieval pilgrim was an air of modern freedom
and equality--though perhaps this also is for us a dream
vision.

CHAPTER TWO: EMMAUS INN

In the cloister of Santo Domingo de Silos in Spain a
scene is sculpted in stone of the Emmaus Pilgrims' Play
acted on Easter Mondays in Benedictine Abbeys. It shows Luke
carrying the book of his Gospel, Cleophas noting that the
sun is setting, and Christ, the unrecognized third, with the
cockle shell of the pilgrimage to St. James upon his scrip
(Plate Va). It dates from the eleventh century. On the
fourteenth-century ceiling above are painted scenes, in rich
reds and blues, from beast fables and romances of lust.[1]
The Roman de Renart, the learned and literary expansion of
such popular beast fables, even includes a parody of the
action of the Pilgrims at Emmaus in having the Jungian
trickster-saviour fox Renart be as Christ, and Belin and
Benart, the sheep and the donkey, be as Luke and Cleophas
in one of its episodes (Plate Vd). The Roman de Tristan
likewise parodies the Pilgrims at Emmaus, having Tristan be
as a Christ in meeting two pilgrims at Tintagel (Figure 5).
In medieval culture this juxtaposition of Gospel sermoning
profanely commented upon by beast fable and by romance did
not result in a negation of either fable or sermon but in an
intensification of both. The two worlds, of Lent and
Carnival, existed side by side, each defining the other.[2]
"By his contrarie is every thyng declared," Chaucer observed
in Troilus and Criseyde, and "of two contraries is o lore"
(I.637,645).

Luke 24's tale of pilgrims telling tales, which shapes
pilgrimage poetry, has the stark simplicity of a Greek
drama's recognition. Three days after the Crucifixion, two
sorrowing disciples journey from Jerusalem. "And behold, two
of them went that same day to a village called Emmaus, which
was from Jerusalem about three-score furlongs. And they
talked together of all these things which had happened. And
it came to pass, that, while they communed (fabularentur)

together and reasoned, Jesus himself drew near, and went
with them. But their eyes were holden that they should not
know him. And he said unto them, what manner of
communications (<u>sermones</u>) are these that ye have with one to
another, as ye walk, and are sad? and one of them, whose
name was Cleopas, answering said unto him, Art thou only a
stranger (<u>peregrinus</u>) in Jerusalem, and hast not known the
things which are come to pass there in these days?" (13-18)."
Though "fabularentur" and "sermones" in classical Latin
referred merely to the act of conversation, for the medieval
audience the text appeared to yoke pilgrim "fabling" with
"sermoning," the one a reprehensible activity, the other a
worthy one.[3]   The remainder of the journey from Jerusalem
was spent by the three pilgrims in narrating of Jesus and
his prophetic types, beginning with Moses of the Exodus.
Though the one pilgrim spoke the truth, the other two
believed he fabled. Similarly, when the Holy Women told the
Apostles that Christ was risen: "their words seemed to them
as idle tales, and they believed them not" (Luke 24.11).

The pilgrim story continues. "And they drew nigh unto
the village (<u>castellum</u>), whither they went: and he made as
though he would have gone further. But they constrained him,
saying, Abide with us: for it is toward evening, and the day
is far spent. And he went in to tarry with them. And it came
to pass, as he sat at meat with them, he took bread, and
blessed it, and brake and gave to them. And their eyes were
opened, and they knew him: and he vanished out of their
sight. And they said to one another, Did not our heart burn
within us, while he talked with us by the way, and while he
opened to us the scriptures?" (28-32). Thus the recognition
by the fabling two of the sermoning third in their midst
occurs not in the sacred Temple of Jerusalem but in a
profane inn at Emmaus. These paradoxes, of sermon and fable,
of Temple and Inn, shaped the tale's ambiguities.

The Emmaus tale was linked to pilgrimage because Luke's
Gospel text had Cleophas term Christ "peregrinus,"
"stranger," or, as it was understood in the Middle Ages,
"pilgrim." The story appealed to all Christendom. An Irish
poem in the margin of a Sedulius manuscript evokes it:

Techt do Ròim,
   mòr saitho, becc torbai;
In Rì con-daigi i foss,
   manim bera latt nì fhogbai

Who pilgrims to Rome,
   labors much, yet little gains.
Your King is there only
   if he traveled with you.[4]

Antiphons were sung from the Gospel of Luke 24, becoming in turn the liturgical drama, the Officium Peregrinorum,
or Office of the Pilgrims, which was usually performed on
its commemorative day, Easter Monday, in Benedictine abbeys.
However, the Orléans manuscript Officium Peregrinorum whose
final scene is of the Doubting of Thomas was acted on Easter
Tuesday when the Doubting of Thomas story was the Gospel of
the day. Because the setting of the tale is eventide, the
Officium Peregrinorum was sung and acted at Vespers, having
the Gospel's words become as a fabling sermon of flesh and
blood. At Emmaus itself the Franciscan guide and the
pilgrims, as if Christ, Luke and Cleophas, recited its
story.[5]   Medieval sculpture, stained glass and illuminated
manuscripts further mirrored forth the monastic dramas'
enactment of the pilgrimage to Emmaus (Figure 4; Plates
Va,b).[6]

The liturgical dramas performed in monasteries and
their reflection in art and poetry were much influenced by
Christ's chiding of his disciples for their foolish dullness
of understanding: "O stulti et tardi corde ad credendum" [O
fools and slow of heart to believe]. In the iconography and
in the vernacular Emmaus Pilgrims' Plays one of the foolish
disciples was generally held to be Luke, the wise writer of
the Gospel in which the pilgrim tale appears: the other,
Cleophas, is named in the Gospel. The Officium Peregrinorum
is typically in three parts: the first showing the folly of
the two disciples, Luke and Cleophas, in not recognizing
Christ; the second, their account of the Emmaus recognition
to their fellow disciples in Jerusalem; and the third, the
Doubting of Thomas who was not present before and who now
insists upon thrusting his hands into Christ's wounds. The
theme of the play is the dispelling of theological folly and
doubt in its actors and audience.[7]   The Officium
Peregrinorum participants were not truly Luke, Cleophas,
Thomas, or the disguised, resurrected Christ. They merely,
in a playful manner, pretended to be so. Their play yoked a
recognition to a resurrection, a comedy to a tragedy, and in
doing so attained the magic of the theatre where actors can
lie that they do not know each other's disguises--though the
audience does--and likewise can lie that they die and return
to life. Above all, it must be remembered that these
participants were Benedictine monks forbidden by their Rule
to be pilgrims though the manuscripts of the plays have them
be playfully garbed in pilgrim dress, borrowed, of course,
from their abbey's guests.[8]   (One suspects, too, that the
part of the Christus as Pilgrim was enacted by their Abbot.)

The Officium Peregrinorum is unusual among the

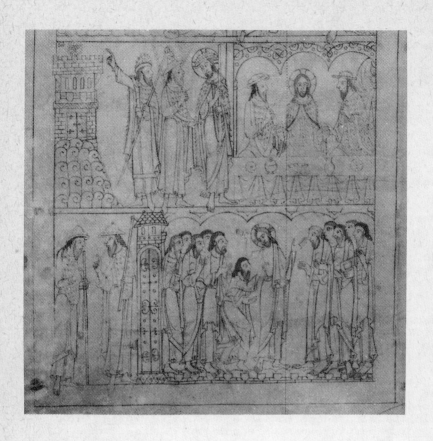

Figure 4   Emmaus Pilgrims
           Corpus Christi College, Oxford, MS 201

liturgical dramas of the Latin West in that its text is
mostly derived from actual dialogue in the Vulgate Gospels
of Luke and John, with some interpolations from Isaiah (Luke
24.13-53; John 20.23-29; Isaiah 63.1,3), and that many of
these scriptural passages were already incorporated, with
the music they would continue to have in the drama, in the
Gregorian antiphons of the Easter service. The Codex
Hartker, St. Gall, of the tenth century and the thirteenth
century Salisbury antiphonal give the music. The liturgical
drama is best shown by Bibliothèque Municipale d'Orléans, MS
201, a manuscript which probably contains the liturgical
dramas as they were performed at the Abbaye St. Benoit-sur-
Loire, anciently called Fleury, in the eleventh through
thirteenth centuries. The text that follows is from Edmond
de Coussemaker, <u>Drames liturgiques du Moyen Age</u>.[9]

Ad faciendum similitudinem dominice apparitionis in
specie peregrini que fit in tertia Feria Pasche ad
vesperas, procedant Duo a competenti loco, vestiti
tunicis solummodo et cappis, capuciis absconsis ad
modum chlamidis, pileos in capitibus habentes et
baculos in manibus ferentes, et cantent modica voce:

Jesu nostra redem-pti-o, a-mor et de-si-de-rium.

Et ceteros versus.

[For making the likeness of the Lord appear in pilgrim garb
which is done in Feria III in Eastertide at Vespers, let two
process from a convenient place, dressed only in tunics and
copes, their cloaks being hoodless, having hats on their
heads and carrying staves in their hands, and singing in a
moderate voice:

Jesus, our redemption, love and desire.
And the other verses. [10]]

Hoc his cantantibus, accedat Quidam alius in
similitudine Domine, peram eam longa palma gestans, bene
ad modum peregrini paratus, pileum in capite habens,
hacla vestitus et tunica, nudus pedes, latenterque eos
retro sequatur, finitisque versibus, veniat eis:

Qui sunt hi sermones quos offertis ad invicem ambulan-

les, et estis tristes? Al-le- luia!

Alter autem ex duobus, converso vultu, ad eum dicat:

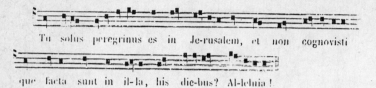

Tu solus peregrinus es in Je-rusalem, et non cognovisti

que facta sunt in il-la, his die-bus? Al-leluia!

[Having sung this, another approaches in the likeness of the Lord, with a scrip and carrying a long palm, dressed well in the manner of pilgrims, having a hat on his head, dressed in a hacla and tunic, with bare feet, following them from behind and to the side; these verses finished, he comes to them:

What are these things you speak of together as you walk and are sad. Alleluia!

The other of the two, turning his face, says to him:

You surely must be a stranger in Jerusalem not to know what has been done there in these days? Alleluia!]

Cui Peregrinus:

Que?

Ambo Discipuli:

De Jesu Na-zareno, qui fuit vir propheta, potens in o-

pere et sermone coram Deo et o-mni po-pu-lo. Quomodo

tradide-runt e-um summi sacerdotes et principes nostri in

damnati- o-nem mortis et cru-ci-fi- xerunt e-um, et super o-

mnia, terti- a dies est quod hec facta sunt. Al-lelu-ia!

[To whom the Pilgrim:
      What?
Both Disciples:
      Of Jesus of Nazareth, who was a prophet, powerful in
      deed and word in the heart of God and all the people.
      Who was betrayed by our high priest and princes to the
      damnation of death and they crucified him, and more-
      over it is now the third day since these things were
      done. Alleluia!]

His dictis, Peregrinus gravi voce, quasi eos increpando,
cantare incipiat:

O stu-lti et tardi corde ad credendum in o-mnibus

que lo-cu-ti sunt Prophete! Al-le-lu-ia! Nonne sic opportuit

pa-ti Christum et intrare in gloriam su-am? Al-le- luia!

Quo facto, fingat se velle discedere; ipsi autem
retineant eum et dicant:

Sol occasum ex-pe-tit, jam hospita-ri ex-pedit. Sane no-

li de-serere nos jam instante ve- spere. Sed ma-ne nobis-

[This having been said, the Pilgrim in a stern tone, as if
to scold them, begins to sing:
      O fools and slow of heart to believe all that the
      prophets have said: Alleluia! Is it not right that
      Christ should suffer and enter into his glory?
      Alleluia!

26

This done, he moves as if he wishes to leave; they draw him
to them and say:
    The sun is setting, let us seek lodging. It would be
    wise not to leave us now that vespers is imminent. But
    remain with us.]

cum, Domine, quo sa-ti-e-mur ple-nissime, quo dele-cte-mur

maxime tu-i sermonis· dul-ce-di-ne. Mane nobiscum quo-

niam advesperascit et in-clinata est jam di-es. Al-le- luia!

Sol vergens ad oc-casum su-a-det ut nostrum ve-lis hospi-

cium; placet e-nim no-bis sermo-nes tu-os, quos confers de

resurre-cti-one magi-stri nostri. Al-le- lu-ia!

[Lord, who so deeply satisfy us, with the delight of
your most sweet words. Remain with us while evening
and the day ends. Alleluia! The sun is about to set and
we would seek an inn. Your words have so pleased us,
who speak of the resurrection of our master. Alleluia!]

His dictis, eant sessum in sedibus ad hoc preparatis et
afferatur eis aqua ad lavandum manus suas. Deinde
mensa bene parata, super quam sit positus panis
inscissus, et tres nebule, et calix cum vino. Accipiens
autem panem (Peregrinus), elevatum in altum dextra
benedicat, frangatque, singulis partibus, cantando:

Pacem relinquo vobis. Pacem meam do vobis.

Deinde det uni eorum calicem, et dicat:

I-sti sunt ser-mones quos dice-bam vo-bis cum es-sem.

Al-le-lu-ia! Alle- lu-ia! Sicut dile-xit me Pater et ego di-

le-xi vos. Manete in di-le-cti-o- ne mea.

[This said, they are seated on benches prepared for this and are offered water for washing their hands. Then a table is well prepared on which is placed uncut bread, and wafers, and a chalice with wine. Then taking the bread (the Pilgrim) blesses it with his raised right hand, and breaks it into single parts, singing:
Peace I leave to you. My peace I give to you.
Then he gives to each of them the chalice and says:
These are the words which I said to you when I was with you. Alleluia! Alleluia! As my father loves me, so do I love you. Remain in my love.]

His dictis, illis mandacantibus de nebulis, ipse latenter discedat, quasi illis nescientibus. Intervallo autem parvo facto, aspicientes ad invicem, et illo non invento inter se, quasi tristes, surgant, et eum, relicta mensa querere incipiant, et, suaviter incedentes, hos versus alta voce dicant:

Nonne cor nostrum ardens e-rat in nobis de Jesu, dum

loqueretur nobis in vi-a et a-pe-ri-ret nobis scriptu-ras?

Heu! miseri! u-bi e- rat sensus noster quando in-tel-

le-ctus a-bi-e- rat? Alle-luia!

[This having been said, as they are eating the wafers, he
leaves from the side, as it were without their knowing.
After a short interval, they both look about and not seeing
him in their midst, as if sad, rise, and leaving the table,
they begin to seek him and softly say these verses in a high
voice:
    Was not our heart burning within us of Jesus, when he
    spoke with us on the road, and opened to us the
    scriptures? Alas! Where were our senses when we should
    have understood? Alleluia!]

Venientibus in choro, Chorus dicat:

Surre-xit Dominus et appa-ru-it Pe-tro. Al-le- luia !

Interim veniat Dominus, colobio candido vestitus, cappa
rubra superindutus, ob signum passionis crucem auream
in manu gestans, infulatus candida infula cum
aurifrisia; stansque in medio eorum, dicat:

Pax vo-bis! e-go sum, noli- te ti- me-re.

Et Chorus dicat:

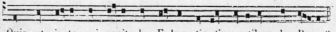

Quis est i-ste qui venit de E-dom, tin-ctis vestibus de Bosra?

Tunc Dominus

Pax vobis !

[They come into the choir, the choir singing:
    The Lord has risen and appeared unto Peter. Alleluia!
Then the Lord enters, dressed in a white alb, a red cope
over it, with the sign of his passion as a cross of gold
held in his hand, wearing a white fillet with gold
ornamentation; he stands in the middle of the choir, saying:
    Peace to you! It is I, do not be afraid.
And the Chorus says:
    Who is this who comes from Edom, in vestments dyed of
    Bosra?
Then the Lord:
    Peace to you!]

Et Chorus

I-ste for-mosus in stola su-a, gradiens in multi-tu-dine

forti-tu-di-nis sue.

Et tercio Dominus:

Pax vo-bis!

Et Chorus:

Surre- xit Do- mi-nus de se-pulchro, qui pro no-bis pe-

pendit in li- gno. Al-le-lu-ia! Al- le-luia! Al-le- luia!

Et Dominus:

Quid tur-bati e- stis et cogita-ci- o- nes ascendunt in cor-

da vestra? Solus cal-ca-vi torcu-lar, et de gentibus non est

vir mecum.

[And the Choir:
    He is beautiful in his garb, increasing in the vastness
    of his strength.
And the third time, the Lord:
    Peace to you!
And the Choir:

The Lord is risen from the sepulchre, who hung upon the
cross for us. Alleluia! Alleluia! Alleluia!
And the Lord:
Why are you troubled and why do these thoughts arise in
your hearts? I only am the trampler in the winepress,
and of all the peoples there is no man with me.]

Et monstret manus ejus et pedes minio rubicatos:

Videte manus meas et pe-des me-os, quia e- go i-

pse sum. Al-leluia! Al- le-lu-ia!

Et adjicit:

Palpa- te et vi-dete, quia spiri-tus carnem et os-sa non

habet, si-cut vi-detis me habe-re. Jam credite.

Quae dum cantaverit, accedant discipuli, palpent ejus
manus et pedes. Hoc peracto, dicat Dominus extenta manu
super illos:

Acci- pi- te Spiritum sanctum; quorum remise-ri-tis

pec-cata remittentur e- is. Allelu-ia!

[And he shows them his hands and feet rubricated with red:
See my hands and my feet, that it is really I,
Alleluia! Alleluia!
And then:
Feel and see, for a spirit does not have flesh and
bones as you see me to have. Now believe.
Having sung this, he goes up to the disciples, they feeling
his hands and feet. This carried out, the Lord extends his
hands over them, saying:
Accept the holy spirit; those who repent of their sins
are forgiven them. Alleluia!]

Quo percantato, Dominus exiens per ostium ex adverso chori. Discipuli autem appropinquant, pedetentim incedentes, alternando hos versus:

Adam no-vus ve-terem duxit ad astra; crea-to-rem re-colit jam crea-tura. Sancta Ma-ri-a Jaco-bi cum Magdale-na et Ma-ri-a Salo-me ferant unguenta. Quid dixit An-ge-lus in veste al-ba; resurrexit Dominus, morte calca-ta. Fracta linquens tartara et spoli-a-ta, refert secum spoli-a victor ad a-stra. Se demonstrat poste-a forma preclara dilectis di-scipulis, in Gali-

[While this is being sung, the Lord exits through the door of the opposite choir. The disciples then draw near, walking slowly, alternating with these verses:
The new Adam leads the old to the stars, the creator renews now the created. Holy Mary Jacobi with Magdalen and Mary Salome brought ointment. The angel in white garb said this: "The Lord is risen, death is overcome." The broken and spoiled Tartar is left, the victor bears the spoils to the stars. This he has already clearly shown to his beloved disciples in Galilee.]

le-a. Comes factus increpat latens in vi- a. Scriptu-re reserat

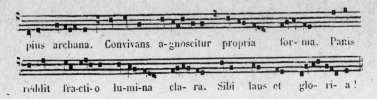

pius archana. Convivans a-gnoscitur propria for- ma. Panis

reddit fra-cti-o lu-mi-na cla- ra. Sibi laus et glo- ri- a!

[He made a meal openly in the way. He unlocked the
old and holy scriptures. He ate with them without
their recognizing his true face. He broke bread in
broad daylight. To him be praise and glory.]

Interea veniat quidam in similitudinem Thome, vestitus
tunica et chlamide serico, baculum in manu habent et
pileum aptum in capite, cui discipili:

Tho-ma, vi- dimus Do-minum.

Thomas:

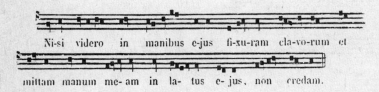

Ni-si videro in manibus e-jus fi-xu-ram cla-vo-rum et

mittam manum me- am in la- tus e- jus, non credam.

[Then comes one in the likeness of Thomas, dressed in a
tunic and Jericho cloak, having a staff in his hand and a
pilgrim hat on his head, to whom the Disciples:
        Thomas, we have seen God.
Thomas:
        I will not believe until I have seen and placed my
        hands where the nails pierced his hands and his side.]

Interim veniat Dominus, colobio candido et cappa rubra
vestitus, coronam gestans in capite ex amicto et
phylacteris compositum, crucem auream eum vexillo in
dextra, textum Evangeli habens in sinistra; qui, dum
chorum intraverit, dicat:

Pax vobis !

Chorus:

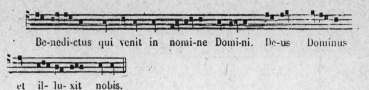

Be-nedi-ctus qui venit in nomi-ne Domi-ni. De-us Dominus

et il- lu- xit nobis.

[Then the Lord comes, dressed in a white alb and red cope,
wearing a crown on his head made of a covering and
phylacteries, with a gold cross and banner in his right
hand, the Gospel book in his left, who, in the midst of the
Choir, says:
    Peace to you!
Chorus:
    Blessed is he who comes in the name of the Lord. The
    Lord God has revealed himself to us.]

Dominus:

Pax vobis !

Et Chorus:

A Domino factum est et est mirabile i-stud in o-cu-

lis meis.

[The Lord:
    Peace to you!
And Chorus:
    This deed of the Lord is marvelous in my eyes.]

Dominus:

Pax vobis! Ego sum; noli- te ti-mere vos.

Et Chorus:

Hec est di-es quam fe- cit Dominus; e-xulte-mus et le-te-

mur in e- a.

Deinde Dominus dicat ad Thomas:

Tho-ma, fer digitum tuum huc, et vi-de ma-nus meas.

Et monstret vulnera, dicens:

Mit-te manum tuam et cogno-sce loca clavorum. Al-le-

luia! Et noli esse incredulus, sed fi-de-lis. Al-le-lu-ia!

[The Lord:
  Peace to you! It is I; do not be afraid.
And Choir:
  This is the day which the Lord made, let us rejoice and
  exult in it.
Then the Lord says to Thomas:
  Thomas, place your finger here, and see my hands.
And shows his wounds, saying:
  Put your hands and know the places of the nails.
  Alleluia! And do not doubt, but believe. Alleluia!]

Palpatis autem a Thoma cicatricibus Domini, procedat ad
pedes ejus, dicens:

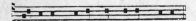

Do-minus meus et Deus meus!

Tunc Dominus:

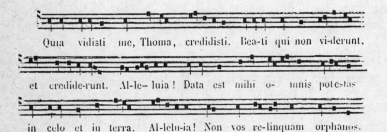

Quia vidisti me, Thoma, credidisti. Bea-ti qui non vi-derunt,

et credide-runt. Al-le- luia! Data est mihi o- mnis potestas

in celo et in terra. Al-lelu-ia! Non vos re-linquam orphanos.

Al-le-luia! Vado et veni-o ad vos. Al-le-luia! Et gaudebit cor vestrum. Al-le-lu-ia! Euntes in mundum u-niversum et pre-dica-te e-vangeli-um o-mni crea-tu-re. Al-le-lu-ia! Qui credi-derit et ba-pti-zatus fu-erit, salvus e- rit. Al-le-luia!

[Then Thomas feels the wounds of the Lord; he proceeds to his feet, saying:
     My Lord and my God!
Then the Lord:
     Because you have seen me, Thomas, you have believed.
     Blessed are those who do not see and believe.
     Alleluia! Given to me is all power in heaven and
     earth. Alleluia! I will not leave you orphans.
     Alleluia! I go and am returning to you. Alleluia!
     And rejoice in your heart. Alleluia! Go into all the
     world and preach the Gospel to all creatures.
     Alleluia! Who believes and is baptized, will be saved.
     Alleluia!]

Tuncque Discipuli accedentes, ducant eum per chorum ut videatur a populo, cantantes:

Salve, fe-sta dies.

     Sic finitur.

[And then the disciples process, leading him through the choir that the people might see him, singing:
     Salve, festa dies.
So it ends.]

While the Orléans manuscript gives the best account of the entire play and its accompanying music from which it had evolved, a Rouen manuscript also ably discusses the staging and costuming of the Officium Peregrinorum for that cathedral. It tells of two priests dressed with fake beards (pilgrims were bearded, priests were clean-shaven) and wearing pilgrim hats, scrips and staves which Christ forbade, who are to enter the church singing. They are to be met by a third priest who has the cross of the Jerusalem pilgrimage upon his right shoulder and who is barefoot in contrast to their sandal shoon. At the center of the church they are to beseech him to stay with them pointing out to him the castellum (village or castle) of Emmaus with their staves. The Rouen text tells us: "Et ita canentes ducant eum usque ad Tabernaculum medio navis Ecclesiae in similitudinem castelli Emaux praeperatum." [And then they lead him singing to the tabernacle in the middle of the church nave which is fashioned like the village of Emmaus.][11]

Often in the plays and depictions of the Emmaus Pilgrims, but not always, Christ is barefoot, obeying his own dictate: "Nor scrip for your journey, neither two coats, neither shoes, nor yet staves," though he may wear the insignia of the Compostela pilgrimage or the Jerusalem one, the shell or the cross (Plates Va,b). Frequently he carries the palm of martyrdom and pilgrimage. Depictions of Luke and Cleophas often demonstrate their folly by their being dressed as if Exodus pilgrims with shoes, wallets and staves. Sometimes one is shown as old, the other young, one as a pilgrim, but not so the other. The Orléans Officium Peregrinorum likewise has the part of Cleophas be sung by a man, that of Luke by a boy chorister. This contrasting of the two, of aged Cleophas and youthful Luke, may be intended to show that one will remain in his folly, while the other will convert to wisdom. Thomas of Celano noted that Francis first dressed himself as a hermit with a leather belt and carried a pilgrim staff, but that he laid aside that garb when he heard the Gospel of Luke 10.4 preached where Christ forbade scrip and staff. Francis thus recognized the one as of the old, the other of the new pilgrimage, the one of Exodus, the other of Luke. [12] The Pilgrims' Plays' audiences would similarly have recognized this iconographical language as opposing the Israelites and Christian pilgrimages as folly and wisdom at the same time that it paralleled and celebrated them both.

On the Compostela pilgrimage route are fine sculptures of Officium Peregrinorum scenes. On one side of a cloister column at Santo Domingo de Silos Christ is shown as a pilgrim with the shell of St. James upon his scrip, wearing

a pilgrim hat and holding a staff, at his side Cleophas
speaks to him, beyond walks Luke, his Gospel book carried
beneath his arm, and all three pilgrims are barefoot (Plate
Va); the next side of the column, at right angles, gives
the scene of all the disciples assembled at Jerusalem and
Doubting Thomas thrusting his hand in Christ's wound. The
sculpture has translated these figures, as likewise had the
liturgy and its drama, from Israel to Spain, from Emmaus/
Jerusalem to Silos. Another Spanish work, an ivory diptych
leaf now in the New York Metropolitan Museum, also clusters
together two scenes from the Officium Peregrinorum in some
versions; this time of the three bearded pilgrims, Christ
with the Jerusalem cross upon his scrip and a bottle on his
staff, Christ and Cleophas with staves, Luke again carrying
the book of his Gospel, with the scene of Christ and Mary
Magdalen in the garden (Plate Vb). All these scenes are of
recognitions, anagnorises and epiphanies, by Cleophas, Luke,
Thomas and Mary Magdalen, of Christ. Both sculptures in
having Luke carry the Gospel book in which the pilgrim fable
is told, stress the authorial, self-referential
participation in the narrated tale's conjoined folly and
wisdom.

Long before the liturgical drama came to fruition the
paradox of the pilgrimage of folly had been woven into
sermons by Augustine, Gregory and many more. Gregory
preached on Luke 24, stating that the eyes of the body
(oculis corporis) knew him not, while the eyes of the heart
(oculis cordis) recognized him.[13]   Other favorite texts in
sermons were II Corinthians 5.6-7: "Audientes, igitur
semper, scientes dum quoniam sumus in corpore, peregrinamur
a domino (per fidem enim ambulamus, et non per speciem)" [".
. . therefore you know that while we are in the body, we
pilgrimage from God (for we walk by faith, not by sight)"]
and I Corinthians 13.12: "For now we see through a glass
darkly; but then face to face: now I know in part; but then
shall I know even as also I am known." Galatians 3,
likewise, discussed the paradox of folly as wisdom. Such
material disparaged physical world wandering while it
praised a spiritual pilgrim's journey to God, yet saw the
two as yoked to each other. Fourteenth-century pilgrimage
poetry was to inherit these arguments along with a knowledge
not only of the Gospel text of Luke but also of the Officium
Peregrinorum's music and staging. The Renaissance likewise
remembered the paradigm of Emmaus folly. Erasmus' Praise of
Folly is based upon its paradox and More's Utopia upon the
convention of travelers' lying tales. The Twelfth Night joke
of a painting of two fools, titled "We Three," is but a
further development of this Emmaus matter as speculum
stultorum, as a mirror for fools that teaches wisdom.

Gregory in the _Moralia_, drawing upon classical philosophy, spoke of the inn as that which opposes pilgrimage in tempting the pilgrim away from the goal of the heavenly city by means of the lusts of the flesh which war against the soul.[14] The classical world had dichotomized body and soul; Christian theology, because of the doctrine of the Incarnation, sought to harmonize them. In Christian thought, therefore, was to be found that doubleness between the inn as the flesh opposed to the soul, its inheritance from classical thought, and the inn also as twice the site of epiphanies, at Bethlehem and Emmaus, of God showing himself forth as of flesh and blood. In the Rouen Pilgrims' Play the profane inn is even set up within the sacred cathedral. A Renaissance painting, deeply aware of this Emmaus paradox, shows a priapic and Chaucerian ale stake and garland at the door, Christ at the table.[15] Chaucer, in the _Canterbury Tales_, will play with the juxtaposition of the tavern's profane cakes and ale and the church's sacred bread and wine and with the Tabard Inn of London and the cathedral of Canterbury. Dante quotes a proverb: "ma ne la chiesa coi santi, e in taverna coi ghiottoni" ["in the church with the saints, in the tavern with the gluttons"] (_Inf_. XXII.14-15). The monks themselves, putting on their play, would have been aware of such playful contradictions. Their Rule not only forbade them to be pilgrims; it also forbade them to stay at inns or to eat any meal while away on a day's journey. And though their scriptorium at St.Benoit-sur-Loire had copied and illuminated Terence's _Comedies_ it would also have had a Boethius and an Augustine whose _Consolation of Philosophy_ and _Confessions_ speak out sternly against the lusts of the theatre.[16] The Emmaus pilgrim tale and the _Officium Peregrinorum_ based upon it both playfully negate and affirm their being. Chaucer stated of such ambiguities: "Of two contraries is o lore."

Medieval pilgrims had the unsavory reputation of being great liars though they sought, as Langland said, St. Truth. Shakespeare was to note, in _Rape of Lucrece_, "As palmers' chat makes short their pilgrimage" 9791). Chaucer in the _House of Fame_ spoke of pilgrims' "scrippes bret-ful of lesinges"["scrips full of lies"] (2123); Langland, of pilgrims and palmers who to "seken Seint Iame . and Seintes at Rome; Wenten forþ in hire wey . wiþ many wise tales, And hadden leue to lyen . al hire lif after" (B. Prol. 47-9), while his doctor of divinity pontificates: "for pilgrymes konne wel lye" (XIII.178); tall stories went by the epithet even of "Canterbury tales."[17] The Lollard William Thorpe at his trial said: "If they be a month out in the pilgrimages, many of them shall be an half year after great janglers, tale-tellers and liars." Thorpe disapproved also

of the playing of lusty bagpipes to solace the barefoot
pilgrim who has stubbed his toe on the Canterbury
pilgrimage, thereby reminding us that pilgrims traveled in
this manner in reality even if they did not do so in
Chaucer's lying poetry. Chaucer, after all, is writing a
"Canterbury Tale."[18] This reputation of medieval pilgrims
as liars clearly contaminated the Emmaus Pilgrims' Plays
whose protagonist was the "via et vita et veritas" ["the
way, the truth and the life"], with interesting
consequences. The Emmaus episode came to be used to justify
pilgrim poetry which could progress through folly to wisdom,
through lies to truth, through fables to a sermon.

The pilgrim scrip, such as that which Christ wears at
Silos with a Santiago shell upon it, carried both bread for
the journey and written documents. Pilgrims had to carry a
license from their bishop permitting them to perform the
pilgrimage; otherwise they were arrested. They were,
moreover, the letter carriers of the Middle Ages.[19] In one
Emmaus Pilgrims' Play, that of Padua, Christ carried the
bread for the supper with him in his scrip, wine in his
bottle.[20] In the Orléans Officium Peregrinorum he blessed
this bread and wine, stating that they were the prophetic
words, the sermons, the parables he had preached. The
Shrewsbury Officium Peregrinorum, partly in Latin, partly in
English, has Cleophas say concerning this supper: "Hark
brother! help to hold him here, Ful nobel talis wil he vs
telle!"[21] The vernacular Corpus Christi plays also used
the analogy. The Towneley Pilgrims' Play's disciples beseech
the unknown third pilgrim to remain with them, again on
account of his skill as a teller of tales.[22] Pilgrims'
Plays thus yoked not only sermoning and fabling, but also
bread and wine with words. Chaucer in the Canterbury Tales
speaks of the unbuckling of "males" or scrips from which
fable and sermon will emerge (I.694;I.3115;X.26). He uses
the term of the Pardoner in a profane context, of the Parson
in a sacred one. In the case of the Pardoner Chaucer's
reference is to the bawdy medieval analogy of scrip and
staff as the male genitalia (Plates IVb,c)--which the
Pardoner lacks. In the case of the Parson it is to the
"fructuous" words of truth he sows by means of his sermon.

The text of Luke 24.32, "Nonne cor nostrum ardens erat
in nobis?" ["Did not our heart burn within us?"], and the
liturgical drama's use of the hymn, "Iesus, Amor et
Desiderium," preceding the performance of the Officium
Peregrinorum, permitted a doubleness to the Emmaus story in
which Amor could be perceived foolishly and cupidinously or
wisely and charitably, as either Cupid or Christ. "Dearly
beloved, I beseech you as strangers and pilgrims, abstain

from fleshly lusts, which war against the soul" (I Peter
2.11). The pilgrimage of lust, largely a literary
convention, may have been further shaped by the knowledge
that pilgrims journeyed to Jerusalem where Hadrian had built
a Temple to Venus above the Holy Sepulchre which the Empress
Helena had then pulled down to find in its ruins the True
Cross.[23]   This was upon May the third, a date Chaucer was
to use over and over again to symbolize the Janus aspects of
Venus and Christ in his poetry.

The theme of the pilgrimage of lust obstinately
prevailed in medieval literature. The Roman de la Rose uses
it, its consummation effected by Amant's priapic scrip and
staff (Plate IVa,b,c).[24]   Dante, in the Vita Nuova, plays
with the theme, encountering Amor in pilgrim guise. Indeed
his Vita Nuova and Commedia's pilgrimage has all the
doubleness of the Emmaus material: he "seems" to think his
pilgrimage is to Tintagel and to Carthage rather than to
Jerusalem for he shadows his love for Beatrice with that of
Tristan for Isolde, that of Aeneas for Dido. In the
Heidelberg Manesse codex the Minnesinger Johannes von
Hadlaub is shown in pilgrim disguise, with three Compostela
shells upon his hat, presenting a poem to the lady for whom
he lusts, as she enters church, her lapdog in her arms.[25]
In Ophelia's song the pilgrim with "cockle hat and staff and
his sandal shoon" is either a mortal lover--or Christ at
Emmaus.

The romance of Tristan is a splendid example of the use
of the Emmaus pilgrimage theme. Tristram, set on shore at
Tintagel by Norwegian seamen, meets two Venetian pilgrims
who have come to visit Cornwall's St. Michael's Mount. The
three journey on together but Tristram soon shows his true
colors and becomes involved in a hart hunt, that old pun of
"venerie" and is then brought to the King's court, the two
pilgrims still accompanying him. A thirteenth-century red
and white clay tile at Chertsey Abbey shows the scene with
the two pilgrims in their pointed hats and scrips, one
bearded, one too young to be so, behind the young Tristram
(Figure 5). The monk who had that picture made was clearly
familiar with the iconography of the two pilgrim disciples,
one as old, one as young, of the Officium Peregrinorum, as
they meet with a third. A further tile depicts the scene
where Tristram disguised as a pilgrim carries Ysolt from the
barge so that she may fable truthfully to King Mark that she
has lain in no man's arms save his and those of the pilgrim
who aided her.[26]   Upon these tiles monks, vowed to chastity
and forbidden to be pilgrims, walked with downcast eyes,
themselves thus consciously mirroring the folly of the
Emmaus pilgrim disciples who had held their eyes upon the

Figure 5   Tristan with Two Pilgrims
            Chertsey Abbey Tile

ground so that they did not know him. In 1270, at the same
time that these tiles were made, Prince Edward, Henry III's
son, as a pilgrim crusader took with him to the Kingdom of
Jerusalem the romance of Tristram and there, before the Fall
of Acre, plays were performed about the Fall of Camelot
through the lusts of Lancelot and Tristram.[27]   The literary
pilgrimage of folly through lust was quite deliberately
didactic. Its seeming profane fable was also as a moral
sermon, Dante in De Vulgari Eloquentia, called Arthurian
fables "pulcerrime ambages," the "most beautiful
ambiguities."

A different kind of pilgrimage was that of trickery, or
"renarderie." Because pilgrims had the right of sanctuary
about their person those who were unscrupulous could take
advantage of it. Troilus thinks of "Hymselven lik a pilgrym
to desgise" in order to visit Criseyde (V.1577).[28]   The
Roman de Renart shows its hero as frequently employing this
device. Those episodes will be discussed at greater length
in connection with the Canterbury Tales. What is of interest
here is that at one point in Renart's life he almost
sincerely repents his many sins and sets off to Rome to seek
absolution from the Pope for his many crimes. On his way he
meets with Belin and Benart, the sheep and the ass, and they
join with him, in an unholy parody of the Emmaus Pilgrims
(Plate Vd). Their pilgrimage, too, ends at an inn--but
falls apart entirely in a drunken brawl.

These up-so-doun parodies of the Emmaus tale of
pilgrims telling tales became in turn the tales pilgrims
told upon their journeys. They were the joking fables that
heightened, rather than negated, a serious sermon central to
Christian pilgrimage, a sermon whose text was drawn from
Luke 24. That text yoked folly and wisdom, doubt and faith,
the old and the new, and, above all, death and life. Mirk's
Festial, for St. James' day, gives a whole sermon fabricated
out of pilgrims' fables.[29]   Pilgrims carried with them
romances of Arthur, legends of Roland, fables of Aesop and
miracles of St. James, both as written books and as spoken
tales with which to wile away the tedium of journeys and
voyages. Aesop's fables, sculpted and painted in church and
cloister, and ornamenting Psalter and Bible margins,
satirized pilgrims, showing Renart so disguised, sometimes
with his pilgrim companions, Belin and Benart, sometimes, as
a pilgrim or friar or priest or bishop, preaching to
gullible barnyard fowl whom he would devour at his sermon's
conclusion. Renart was as a false priest who guided pilgrims
wrongfully into danger, death and, even worse, damnation.
Yet Renart was also a "trickster-saviour" who served to
teach truth through treachery.[30]   Similarly did pilgrim

poets make use of both lying fables and the Emmaus Gospel of truth; they both betray and save their readers. They could do so because that Gospel account, Luke 24, contained within it--seemingly--both pilgrim fables and pilgrim sermons, lies and truth, being thereby as if a defense of pilgrim poetry.

CHAPTER THREE: "COME NE SCRIVE LUCA"

    In a Purgatorio simile Dante describes the meeting of
himself and Virgil with a third poet, Statius, as like that
meeting of the disciples Cleophas and authorial Luke with
Christ on the road to Emmaus.

        Ed ecco, sì come ne scrive Luca
    che Cristo apparve a' due ch'erano in via,
    giù surto fuor de la sepulcral buca,
        ci apparve un'ombra, e dietro a noi venìa,
    dal piè guardando la turba che giace;
    né ci addemmo di lei, sè parlò pria,
        dicendo: "O frati miei, Dio vi dea pace."

    [and here, even as Luke writes of it that Christ
    appeared to the two who were on the way, when new
    risen from the sepulchral cave, a shade appeared to us,
    coming from behind us, while we were watching the crowd
    that lay at our feet, nor did we notice him until he
    spoke, saying, "O my brothers, God give you peace."]
                                            (XXI.7-13)

    Dante's Commedia gives us Dante himself as both a pagan
and a Christian pilgrim who journeys through its landscapes
and seascapes of pilgrimage. He is both as a pilgrim Ulysses
and as the Gospeler Luke. Upon his pilgrimage he is
accompanied by another, first by pagan Virgil of the Aeneid,
then by Christian Beatrice of the Vita Nuova, who guide him.
These pilgrims encounter others. Each encounter is shadowily
that of two disciples meeting a third, a stranger on the
road--who is no stranger and no shadow--the pattern of
Emmaus. The liturgical drama and the iconography generally
give one disciple as ancient, as if of the Old Testament,
the other as young, as if of the New, one as Cleophas, the
other as Luke, the author of that tale and who carries the

book in which that tale is told. So here do manuscript illuminations show Virgil as venerable and bearded, Dante as a beardless youth, carrying the book in which the tales of Aeneas first, then of Luke, appear (Plate Vc).

Dante in the Inferno had declared he was neither Aeneas nor Paul: "Io non Enëa, io non Paolo sono" (II.32). That statement is neither true nor false. The poet Virgil is present to shadow forth his hero Aeneas' wanderings, and the poet Dante becomes as if a Luke, the writer of the Gospel telling of the pilgrims at Emmaus and of the Acts of the Apostles concerning Paul's voyage and shipwreck, events of which Luke, by tradition, was eyewitness. Aeneas recounted the Fall of Troy: "quorum magna pars fui" (Aeneid II.6) and Paul stated: "Only Luke is with me" (II Timothy 4.11). The text and the illuminations (Plate Vc) imply that Dante was reading Aeneid VI and had fallen asleep while doing so, for when he encounters that poet and shade he says: "vagliami 'l lungo studio e'l grande amore che m'ha fatto cercar lo tuo volume" [may the long study and the great love avail me that made me search your volume] (I.83-84). Dante, instead of reading the Gospels' truth, has been reading Virgil's pagan fable. Like Chaucer's Physician, his study seemingly has been "but little on the Bible" (CT.I.438). Virgil, Dante has him say truthfully, lived during the time of the "dèi falsi e bugiardi" [false and lying gods] (I.72), of columned idols of deities, emperors and beasts requiring lustrations of sacrificial blood.[1] He is associated with Roman law, implying also the Mosaic Law (I.124-126). Augustine in the Confessions stated that Virgil fabled for historically Aeneas and Dido had not lived in the same century. The book that Dante carries through Hell is both the sybilline and aenigmatic Aeneid of laws and lies, and Luke's Gospel of the via et vita et veritas; like his own Commedia, it is of both lies and truth. Such had been the quality of the discourse on the road to Emmaus, Cleophas and Luke clinging to the lie, in their folly, doubt and despair, of the death of God, the stranger seeming to lie in speaking, in faith, hope and charity, of the prophesied resurrection.

Virgil's name had become so spelled, instead of the classical form, "Vergilius," because of that poet's patristic and medieval associations with education and magic, with the staff or virga of the pedagogus and the necromancer.[2] The Pilgrims' Blessing declared to pilgrims Christ's injunction: "Nolite possidere . . . virgam" [Provide neither . . . staves for the journey] (Matt. 10.9-10). Virgil, at the obscure beginning of the pilgrim's progress, of its initial vision "per speculum in aenigmate" [through a glass darkly] (I Cor. 13.12), is as Dante's

Passover staff, the _virga_ required of Exodus pilgrims in the
Old Testament, yet condemned by Christ in the New. So had
Cleophas in Emmaus iconography frequently carried a staff
while Luke carried the book of the Gospel he did not yet
comprehend (Plate Va,b,c).

A major work shadowing Dante's poem is the _Roman de la_
Rose whose poet hero consummates his lust by means of a
pilgrim yet priapic scrip and staff. His idol is a red rose,
spoken of as his shrine housing relics, towards which he
perversely pilgrimages (Plate IVb,c).[3] The act of touching
relics with a staff is typical of the pilgrims' desire to be
as close to the shrine's contents as could be permitted,
many shrines for this purpose having niches into which
pilgrims could insert their staves, their hands or their
heads.[4] But where Dante comes to Beatrice, Virgil as
staff and book is laid aside (_Purg_. XXX.43-57). Similarly
did Shakespeare's Prospero renounce his staff and book of
magic at the _Tempest_'s conclusion. Virgil functions as
Dante's pilgrim staff, his "Falstaff," even upon this
labyrinthine pilgrimage. Thus he represents poetry's lies
pilgrimaging to truth. The Emmaus paradigm and the paradigm
of Boethius' _Consolation_ of folly and despair juxtaposed to
wisdom and love, demands his presence within the poem.

Dante's _Vita Nuova_, precursor to the _Commedia_, several
times weaves into its text the paradigm of the tale of the
Emmaus pilgrims from Luke 24. In the ninth part of the work,
Dante speaks of how he has to leave the city of Florence and
ride through the countryside:

> E tutto ch'io fosse a la compagnia di molti, quanto a
> la vista, l'andare mi dispiacea sì, che quasi li
> sospiri non poteano disfogare l'angoscia che lo cuore
> sentia, però ch'io mi dilungava de la mia beatudine. E
> però lo dolcissimo segnore, lo quale mi segnoreggiava
> per la vertù de la gentilissima donna, ne la mia
> immaginazione apparve come peregrino leggeremente
> vestito e di vili drappi. Elli mi parea disbigottito,
> e guardava la terra, salvo che talora li suoi occhi mi
> parea che si volgessero ad uno fiume bello e corrente
> e chiarissimo, lo quale sen gia lungo questo cammino là
> ov'io era.

> [And though I was in the company of many, it seemed,
> the going so displeased me that my sighs could not lift
> the anguish that my heart felt because I was apart from
> my beatitude. And then the sweetest lord, he who rules
> me through the virtue of that most gentle lady,
> appeared in my imagination to me as like a pilgrim,
> lightly dressed and in sordid clothing. He seemed lost,

and he cast his eyes to the ground except that
sometimes it appeared to me that his eyes turned to a
beautiful river, swift and most clear, which ran beside
the road where I was.]

Dante follows this with the sonnet, "Cavalcando l'altr'ier
per un cammino," in which we learn that the lover is
improperly riding on horseback while Amore walks beside the
stream on foot in the proper pilgrim manner, and with eyes
downcast, "per non veder la gente a capo chino." In the
razio that follows Dante notes that in the first section he
sees Amore and in the second part Amore speaks to him. But
he only gives a part of what Amore had said to him, letting
the rest remain secret from the reader. In the third part
Dante speaks of Amore's sudden disappearance from him.

Dante, true to the Emmaus Officium Peregrinorum whose
initial hymn spoke of Christ as Amor, has here shown his
Amore in pilgrim garb, shadowily echoing Luke 24. To this
scene Dante juxtaposes another, more obvious one, for he has
partially progressed from folly to wisdom. In section forty
of the Vita Nuova Beatrice has died and all Florence, like a
widowed Jerusalem, mourns:

Dopo questo tribulazione avvenne, in quello tempo che
molte gente va per vedere quella imagine benedetta la
quale Jesu Cristo lasciò a noi per esemplo de la sua
bellissima figura, la quale vede la mia donna glorio-
samente, che alquanti peregrini passavano per una via
la quale è quasi mezzo de la cittade, ove nacque,
vivette e morio la gentilissima donna. Li quali
peregrini andavano, secondo che mi parve, molto pensosi; ond'io pensando a loro, dissi fra me medesimo:
"Questi peregrini mi paiono di lontana parte, e non
credo che anche udissero parlare di questa donna, e non
ne sanno neente; anzi i loro penseri sono d'altre'cose
che di queste qui, ché forse pensano di li loro amici
lontani, li quali noi non conoscemo." Poi dicea fra me
medesimo: "Io so che s'elli fossero di propinque paese,
in alcuna vista parrebero turbati, passando per lo
mezzo de la dolorosa cittade."

[After this tribulation it happened at the time when
many go to see the blessed image which Jesus Christ
left for us as a pattern of his fair face which my lady
sees most gloriously, that some pilgrims were passing
along a road that lay through the midst of that city in
which the gentlest lady was born, lived and died, and
as they went, it seemed to me, that they were very sad.
When I thought of them I said to myself, "These
pilgrims seem to be from afar and I do not believe

they have heard my lady spoken of, and that they know nothing of this, and this thoughtfulness is of another thing; perhaps they think of their distant friends, whom I do not know." Then I said to myself, "I know that if they were from nearby they would in some way appear disturbed as they passed through the midst of our dolorous city."]

Dante's sonnet then begins: "Deh peregrini che pensosi andate."

His narration contains deliberate echoes of the Emmaus Pilgrims, a careful intertextuality with that tale. Cleophas had asked Christ: "Tu solus peregrinus es in Jerusalem et non cognovisti quae facta sunt in illa his diebus?" [Art thou only a stranger in Jerusalem, and hast not known the things which are come to pass there in these days?] Dante's Janus pilgrimage is no longer to the living wife of another man, in which case his goal was the same adultery that had destroyed Troy and Camelot, but to the memory of the dead Beatrice—who dwells with God in a heavenly Jerusalem and, perhaps, even a heavenly Rome, "of which Christ is Roman" (Purg. XXXII.102).

In both the Vita Nuova and the Commedia, Dante deliberately makes Rome function as if it were Christendom's New Jerusalem. Indeed, Latin Christendom itself sought to substitute the one city for the other because Acre, the last Crusader stronghold of Outremer, had fallen to the Saracen in 1291, and it was now obvious that Jerusalem was lost. Both Dante's Vita Nuova with its handling of the Emmaus theme set in an Italian landscape and his Commedia with its dating of the Roman Jubilee year of 1300, reflect this sub- stitution of the one city and country for the other. Tales of the appearance of Christ's face as still present in the mosaic apse at the Lateran and the showing forth of the Veronica veil at Easter at the Vatican encouraged pilgrims to think of the Roman pilgrimage as not so much a pilgrimage to St. Peter, signified by his crossed keys, as rather one to the Volto Santo, the Holy Face of Christ, signified by the vernicle, the miniature Veronica veil so proudly worn by many a medieval pilgrim (Plate Ia; Frontispiece).[5]

In Dante's mind, as he wrote the Commedia year after year, was the memory of the Lateran's use as medieval Rome's liturgical center. However, Dante wrote the Commedia after the Lateran had burned in 1308, and after the Papal Curia had moved to Avignon in 1305 (the "Babylonian Captivity"), and after his own exile from Florence in 1302, an exile he had not known of when he had defined pilgrims as exiles in the Vita Nuova,[6] yet he pretended that he experienced

his prophetic vision in 1300, the year in which Boniface
VIII proclaimed the Roman Jubilee from the Lateran Basilica.
Boniface's bull, <u>Antiquorum Relatio</u>, granted indulgences to
pilgrims who visited the Holy City in that year. For this
purpose the Pope yoked the Hebrew Jubilee festival at which,
every fifty years, the Temple's Jubilee trumpets sounded,
all slaves were freed, all debts forgiven, the land lying
fallow (Leviticus 25.8-7), with that of the annual Feast of
the Tabernacles at which Hebrew pilgrims came and laid palms
on the horns of the Temple's altar to commemorate the
pilgrimage of the Exodus. Boniface's intent was to make the
Roman Lateran Basilica serve a similar function as had the
Jerusalem Temple. The Temple's Jubilee trumpets were brought
from Jerusalem to Rome by the Emperor Titus.[7]   They were
also remembered in the Apocalypse and in Doomsday programs
as at Autun (Plate XIV). Giotto frescoed the 1300 Jubilee
showing Boniface making his pilgrim proclamation at the
Lateran. A manuscript commentary of Dante's <u>Commedia</u> at
Chantilly shows Roman Jubilee pilgrims, one clad in a fleece
sclavin, clustered about the feet of Boniface at the
Lateran.

St. John Lateran was the goal of pilgrims at other
times than in the Jubilee year. Excommunicated persons were
reconciled to the Church by the Pope. Pilgrims, dressed in
wool or hair sackcloth or in sclavins of fleece, would have
first been led out from their own churches after having lain
on the floor in the shape of a cross as in the Ash Wednesday
expulsion of penitents. These penitents and pilgrims were
denied the sacraments and their pilgrimages were made most
often in Lent. At the reconciliation, which would take place
at St. John Lateran for severe offenses, in their own
diocesan cathedral for lesser ones, such pilgrims could for
the first time in their pilgrimage cut their hair, wash and
be dressed in white linen. They then waited outside the
ecclesiastical edifice by the west Doomsday portal within
which sat their bishop or the Pope. The seven penitential
psalms (which Dante translated into Italian) were chanted,
and from time to time messages of comfort were sent out to
them. At length, the bishop, or Pope, would lead the
penitents, each holding the other's hand as in a carol,
across the edifice's threshold, its Janus-like <u>limen</u> (Figure
6). Outside the structure the carol would be of profane
lust, as it is in the <u>Roman de la Rose</u> and the <u>Via Veritatis</u>
(Plate XIII); within, it is its opposite and sacred.[8]
Dante echoes the expulsion and reconciliation liturgy in
<u>Purgatorio</u> IX.70-145 and elsewhere.[9]

The liturgy here is a memory of Genesis, of Exodus, of
the Gospels and of the Apocalypse. The Apocalypse in turn is

Figure 6   Reconciliation of Penitents
           Pontifical of 1520
           Herbert Thurston

a memory of Jerusalem Temple liturgy with its white-clad,
palm-bearing pilgrims and its Jubilee trump. These Christian
penitent and reconciled pilgrims in their white garb--even
if they had been criminals, even if they had been
murderers--paradoxically were now become as the saved souls
of Revelation 7.9, the "great multitude who stood . . .
before the Lamb, clothed in white robes, and palms in their
hands." A similar ritual in the early Church was the Easter
baptism. During Lent the neophytes were prepared by
ecclesiasts and finally were robed in white (candida) as
baptismal candidates. Dante echoes it in Purgatorio I.
94-96, 123-129. At Rome St. John Lateran was the basilica at
which these two Eastertide rituals, of pilgrimage and of
baptism, took place with the greatest frequency.[10] Thus
the Lateran was as if Rome's Jerusalem Temple and because of
this Dante speaks of St. John Lateran as the "tempio"
[Temple] of a pilgrim's vow (Par. XXXI.43-5).

     Dante describes such an exile's and excommunicate's
reconciliation to his own "bello ovile" [fair sheepfold]
(Par. XXV.5), of St. John's Baptistery in Florence which
mirrors that in Rome. Poignantly, Dante, along with other
White Guelfs, had been not only exiled by the Blacks from
Florence; his party had at the same time been excommunicated
by the Pope in Rome.[11] His fictive poem is his political
and theological reconciliation to Florence and to Rome; it
displaces, by means of poetry, a bitter and lifelong
reality. And perhaps what aids in that conversion is the
Emmaus theme which speaks out against the need for the
centrality of the Jerusalem Temple and instead shows that
Christ may be found upon a pilgrimage anywhere. The Emmaus
tale, likewise, allows for the mixture of lies with truth.
The Commedia, shaped by the Emmaus theme, metamorphoses the
poet's exile into his poem's pilgrimage.

     The Commedia, though not giving a physical pilgrimage,
nevertheless constantly compares and contrasts, using epic
similes to do so, the two travelers as fictive pilgrims
within the vision poem to pilgrims of flesh and blood upon
the pilgrimage roads of the then known world.[12] Dante had
discussed pilgrimage in the Vita Nuova (XL), defining
peregrini there as those who journey to Jerusalem, Rome or
Compostela. He borrowed this definition from Alfonso el
Sabio's writings, which he perhaps knew through Brunetto
Latini who had journeyed there along the pilgrim road from
Italy to Spain to go on embassy to that king. Dante gave
Latini a copy of the Vita Nuova fittingly speaking of it in
an accompanying sonnet as a "Janus" work.[13] In the
Commedia Dante describes true pilgrims and pilgrimages being
performed in the Jubilee year, A.D. 1300, in both space and
time. These erupt into the fictive, lying poetry.

The journey to St. James of Compostela for Italian
pilgrims lay through Arles and the famed Alyscamps. Where
Dante and Virgil enter the city of Dis it is not a city of
the living but of the dead, Dante comparing it to the
pilgrim road at Arles which was bordered with Roman and
Christian tombs, a necropolis, and he compares it to the
necropolis likewise at Pola;

> Sì come ad Arli, ove Rodano stagna,
> sì com'a Pola, presso del Carnaro
> ch'Italia chiude e suoi termini bagna,
>   fanno i sepulcri tutt'il loco varo,
> così facevan quivi d'ogne parte,
> salvo che'l modo v'era più amaro:

[As at Arles, where the Rhone stagnates, and as at
Pola, near the Quarnaro gulf which shuts up Italy and
bathes its borders, the sepulchres make all the place
uneven; so they did here on every side, only the
manner here was more bitter.]   (*Inf*. IX.112-117)

At Autun the great tympanum had shown the souls of the
saved rising from their sepulchres, among them a Compostela
pilgrim and a Jerusalem one (Plate XIV). For the non-pilgrim
souls within these infernal and poetic sepulchres there can
be no such hope. Arles' Alyscamps or Elysian Fields,
reminiscent of *Aeneid* VI, were believed to entomb
Charlemagne's Paladins, the heroes of the *Chanson de Roland*,
crusaders who were assured of salvation at Doomsday. So
sacred became this necropolis at Arles that many arranged to
be buried there, convinced that their proximity to the
blessed Paladins would also save them. The pagan tombs were
recycled by the monks for Christian burials and are placed
in disorder beside the church--exactly as Dante described
them and exactly as they are shown in illuminations to the
Commedia. Elsewhere in the *Inferno* is heard the *Chanson de
Roland*'s horn winding in doomed despair (XXXI.16-18). It was
a relic shown to pilgrims at Roncesvalles as they passed
through on their way to Compostela. The Alyscamps simile
describes not so much pilgrims as the mortal landscapes of
pilgrimages, though relieved by tales. The classic world had
stressed the metaphor of life as a journey, death its
ending, by bordering the roads beyond city walls with tombs.
Christian pilgrimage inherited the concept. Pilgrims, in
law, were as if dead, and indeed many died on these
journeys. Such pilgrims were assured of salvation.[14]   Not
so, Dante's infernal exiles here.

We next hear of pilgrims, though again in the infernal

pages they cannot be named as such, in Canto XVIII. Dante
described how naked pandars and seducers run in file
opposite each other, scourged by demons:

> come i roman per l'essercito molto,
> l'anno del giubileo, su per lo ponte
> hanno a passar la gente modo colto,
> che da l'un lato tutti hanno la fronte
> verso'l castello e vanno a Santo Pietro,
> da l'altra sponda vanno verso 'l monte.

[thus the Romans, because of the great throng, in the
year of the Jubilee, upon the bridge have taken means
to pass the people over, so that, on one side, all have
their faces toward the Castle and go to St. Peter's, at
the other ledge, they go towards the Mount.] (28-33)

At the moment that Dante and Virgil in Dante's fantasy
view pandars and seducers being scourged around the eighth
circle in opposite directions, crowds of Jubilee pilgrims in
the real world above traverse the bridge of the Castel Sant'
Angelo on their way to and from St. Peter's, above them
looming the figure of the Archangel Michael, with drawn
sword, upon the Castle's top (a medieval statue in lieu of
today's Renaissance one), before the pilgrims the Porta
Sancti Petri, the literal gate of St. Peter's, leading into
the Vatican's confines. Such pilgrims traversed Rome from
the Lateran and its Volto Santo and the Vatican and its
Veronica along the Via Sacra. Singleton included photographs
of both the Alyscamps and the Ponte Sant'Angelo in his
Inferno commentary. [15] Illuminations can image forth the
Inferno landscapes, but, except where they are fashioned out
of actual pilgrim landscapes, photographs cannot be taken of
them. Pilgrim landscapes are physical reality; the _Inferno_'s
are mental constructs that borrow from that reality.

In Canto XXI, Dante encounters the Barrators in a
bolgia of infernal pitch. The scene is compared to the
Venetian Arsenal, a sight familiar to pilgrims who embarked
for Jerusalem from Venice on ships whose sails bore
Jerusalem pilgrim crosses (Plate VIb).

> Quale ne l'arzanà de' Viniziani
> bolle l'inverno la tenace pece
> a rimpalmare i legni lor non sani,
> ché navicar non ponno--in quella vece
> chi fa suo legno novo e chi ristoppa
> le coste a quel che più viaggi fece;
> chi ribatte da proda e chi da poppa;
> altri fa remi e altri volge sarte;
> chi terzeruolo e artimon rintoppa--:

[As in the Arsenal of the Venetians, in winter boils
the clammy pitch for caulking their damaged ships, they
cannot navigate; and instead, one builds his ship anew,
one plugs the ribs of that which has made many voyages,
one hammers at the prow and another at the stern,
another makes oars, another twists ropes, one mends the
jib and mainsail.]   (7-15)

When Sir Richard Guylforde passed that way on his pilgrimage
to Jerusalem where he was to die, he and his secretary
chaplain, because it was nearer Easter, observed the lesser
activity of rope-making, the Jerusalem ships being already
caulked and afloat, awaiting their pilgrim cargo.[16]

The three _Inferno_ similes do not paint pilgrimage
attractively. The first sees the road of a deadly pilgrimage
to the west lined with tombs.[17]   The second has pilgrims be
like sinners and subjects them to a perilous crossing, above
them the Archangel Michael upon the Castle brandishing his
sword as if in a scene from a Doomsday tympanum. The third
dwells on the wintry boiling of pitch for mending and
caulking ships in the Venetian Arsenal during the months of
storm. To sail to Jerusalem in winter was to invite
shipwreck and a watery death (Plate VIa). Though in each
simile the word "peregrin" [pilgrim] is absent, each, in
turn, describes aspects of the Galician, Roman and Jerusalem
pilgrimages which Dante had listed in the _Vita Nuova_. Each
simile pegs down the _fantasia_ (_Par_. XXXIII.142) of the poem
to reality.

The _Purgatorio_ is different. Its similes are borrowed
from the Jerusalem voyage and the Emmaus tale, while the
landscapes about them within the poem are largely taken from
the Exodus' pilgrimage between Egypt and Israel. The word
"peregrin" [pilgrim] is uttered for the first time in the
Commedia, in the _Purgatorio_ by Virgil who (for he is a
stranger there, being instead a citizen of Dis, of the
Inferno and _Aeneid_ of exile) tells a group of pilgrims that
he does not know where they are. He thereby echoes the
Emmaus tale's Cleophas' use of the word "peregrinus" as
"stranger."

                    "Voi credete
          forse che siamo esperti d'esto loco;
          ma noi siam peregrin come voi siete."

     ["You think perhaps we have knowledge of this place;
     but we are strangers, like yourselves."] (II.61-63)

The Emmaus tale with its use of "peregrinus" [stranger]

belongs to the geography of Jerusalem. Pilgrims journeying
from the pilgrim port of Jaffa passed through Emmaus on
their way to the Holy City. Here the encounter, however,
takes place in the geography of Exodus, at the foot of a
mountain which Carol Kaske and John Demaray have shown to be
Sinai.[18]   The two landscapes are merged in the poem just as
were the two pilgrimages in practice.

    In Canto VIII, Dante compares the evening mood to that
of voyages and pilgrims:

        Era già l'ora che volge il disio
    ai navicanti e'ntenerisce il core
    lo dì c'han detto ai dolci amici addio;
        e che lo novo peregrin d'amore
    punge, se ode squilla di lontano.

    [It was now the hour that turns back the longing of
    voyagers and melts their hearts the day they have said
    farewell to dear friends, and that pierces the new
    pilgrim with love if from afar he hears the chime that
    seems to mourn the day that dies.]   (1-6)

The double simile recalls Joinville's sorrow at leaving his
castle and his two children as he walked barefoot away to
sail with his king on crusade.[19]   It echoes, too, Dante in
Vita Nuova XL. Earlier, and again in a simile, Dante had
compared his passage as like "gente che pensa a suo cammin,
che va col cuore e col corpo dimora" [folk who ponder on the
road, who go in heart and in body stay] (II.11-12).
Gregory's Moralia had allegorically so divided the pilgrim
soul from the carnal body, the soul desiring to journey
onward, the body to remain at the inn.[20]   That division, of
soul from body, was more pagan and philosophical than
Christian. Illuminations to the Commedia show Dante in his
study writing his poem, or in his bed dreaming his poem,
"col corpo" [in body], while his dream self essays to find
the mountain or is lost in the dark wood, "col cuore" [in
soul] (Plate VIIa). One especially fine illumination to the
Purgatorio shows Dante as writing that canticle on
shipboard, imaging forth his metaphor of his poem as pilgrim
ship in which his reader sails with him to Jerusalem (Purg.
I.1-6; Par. II.1-18), while, within the initial P, Dante,
the real Dante this time, can be seen in his study, carnal,
earthbound, yet writing the identical words (Plate VIIb).
Dante's double simile here compares himself to a pilgrim and
to voyagers, journeying towards the goal in body, yet
lingering in heart. Gregory's metaphor of body and soul to
inn and pilgrim were in accord with the earlier single
simile, not the later double one. Dante is shaping
conflicting emotions within the Purgatorio pilgrimage that

contrast with the inexorable and eternal exile of <u>Inferno</u>.
Here voyages are begun and not yet completed; here journeys
are yet in progress.

In Canto XXI, after the earthquake, Dante and Virgil
meet another, the soul of Statius, the poet who lived in the
time of the Emperor Titus, and whom Dante claims to have
been a Christian. Three poets--as three pilgrims--meet; the
first of pagan Augustan Rome, born <u>sub Iulio</u>, and an
idolator (<u>Inf</u>. I.70-71), the second, of Titus and the coming
of the Jerusalem Temple's spoils to Rome's Temple of Peace
(<u>Purg</u>. XXI.82-87), and secretly a Christian, the third, of
the Christian Florentine Republic, though soon to be an
exile. Time is collapsed while the three poets, from
different eras, reenact the Emmaus drama.

> Ed ecco, sì come ne scrive Luca
> che Cristo apparve a' due ch'erano in via,
> giù surto fuor de la sepulcral buca,
> ci apparve un'ombra, e dietro a noi venìa,
> dal piè guardando la turba che giace;
> né ci addemmo di lei, sì parlò pria,
> dicendo: "O frate miei, Dio vi dea pace."

[and lo, even as Luke writes of it that Christ appeared
to the two who were on the way, when new-risen from the
sepulchral cave, a shade appeared to us, coming from
behind us, while we were watching the crowd that lay at
our feet, nor did we perceive him till he first spoke,
saying, "O my brothers, God give you peace."] (7-13)

As in Luke's account where Cleophas and the other
disciple held their eyes so that they did not recognize
Christ so here Virgil and Dante cast their eyes downwards.
The iconography of the Emmaus Pilgrims stressed one as old,
the other as young (Plate Va,b). The music did so likewise,
Cleophas' voice being a man's, Luke's a boy's. Here Virgil,
of oldness, and Dante, of newness and carrying the book--of
the <u>Aeneid</u>, of the Gospel?--encounter the "Christian" poet
Statius, the patterning being analogous to Emmaus', yet of
poetry's realm; the encounter of Statius by Virgil and Dante
being shadowily that of Christ in the Gospel by Cleophas and
Luke, yet culled from lying Greek and Roman poetry (Odyssey
XI.206-8; <u>Aeneid</u> VI.700-702) and enacted by fabling poets.
The scene borrowed from the Gospel is also enhanced by the
liturgical drama's <u>Officium Peregrinorum</u> in which, after the
blessing and breaking of the bread, Christ sings to the two
disciples: "Pacem meam do vobis" [I give you my peace].
Statius' association with Titus' Temple of Peace links
Christ as "Prince of Peace" together with Jerusalem as
"Vision of Peace" and with Rome of the "Pax Romana."[21]

The Emmaus image of the two pilgrims joined by a third
is suggested again by a further pilgrim simile in Canto
XXIII:

> Sì come i peregrin pensosi fanno,
> giugnendo per cammin gente non nota,
> che si volgono ad essa e non restanno.
>
> [Even as pilgrims lost in thought, who overtaking
> strangers on the road, turn round to them and do not
> stop.]   (16-21)

All encounters in the Commedia by two of a third
shadowily, intertextually, reflect that fabling on the road;
though, until Purgatorio XXI, the reader, himself an Emmaus
pilgrim, in a mirroring of Dante pilgrim as the foolish
viator of Emmaus, Luke, does not realize this.

Yoked with the Emmaus image of Purgatorio XXI is
another, of the Samaritan woman at the well who recognizes
the Messiah, again in an epiphany involving a traveler,
where Dante likens his thirst to that which is never
quenched: "se non con l'acqua onde la feminetta samaritana
domandò la grazia" [save with the (baptismal) water where
the poor Samaritan woman asked for grace] (2-3). Emmaus,
Jacob's Well at which Christ spoke with the Samaritan woman
and the Holy Sepulchre were Holy Places visited by Jerusalem
pilgrims. The oblique references to these sites in these
pilgrimage similes set them apart from the very specific
Inferno similes concerning Arles, Venice and Rome's Castel
Sant' Angelo. The Inferno similes are associated with
Italy's geography; the Purgatorio's with Israel. The
Purgatorio similes, while they mention the word "peregrin,"
refuse to be carnal and tend to emphasize the allegorical
meaning of "peregrinus," the Gregorian yearning of the soul
for God in tension with the body's physical desires. These
pilgrims do not quest the shrines of "corsaints," but only
mention an empty sepulchre, a well that cannot satisfy the
travelers' thirst and a shadowy Emmaus road, while
pilgrimaging to Beatrice and God.[22]   Their settings, of the
Holy Places, are of a geography lost to 1300's Christendom.

The Paradiso similes cluster in Canto XXXI and are once
again carnal and in time and space. Moreover, they are of
Rome, not Jerusalem. First we are told of wandering
Barbarians who gaze upon the large grandeur of the Lateran,
in Dante's day, the Papal Basilica:

> Se i barbari, venendo da tal plaga
> che ciascun giorno d'Elice si cuopra,

rotante col suo figlio ond'ella è vaga,
  veggendo Roma e l'ardüa sua opra,
stupefaciensi, quando Laterano
e le cose mortali andò di sopra;

[If the Barbarians, coming from such a shore which day
is spanned by Helice, wheeling with her son for whom
she yearns, on seeing Rome and her arduous works--what
time the Lateran surpassed mortal things--were
stupefied.]   (31-36)

Dante compares his wonderment at the sight of the City
of God to these Barbarians at the gates of the city of Rome
marveling at its size. As Dante writes these lines he
himself could remember the Lateran's glory. He writes in the
past tense. Though the Basilica was spared in the fifth
century by the Barbarian Goths, Huns and Vandals, by Alaric,
Attila and Genseric, in 1308 it had burned. Dante recalls
now its past Jubilee splendor of 1300, its present desolate
ruin after 1308. The bitter irony of Dante's lines on the
Lateran would have seared themselves upon early fourteenth-
century Italian readers, recalling, perhaps, Leviticus 26.
3-33, where God told Israel: "If ye walk in my statutes
. . . I will set my tabernacle among you . . . . And if ye
walk contrary to me and will not hearken unto me . . . I
will make your cities waste, and bring your sanctuaries unto
desolation." [23]

Dante pens another simile, a few lines later, this time
of a pilgrim, not a barbarian (though both are strangers),
to show how his wonder augments:

    E quasi peregrin che si ricrea
nel tempio del suo voto riguardando,
e spera già ridir com'ello stea.

[And as the pilgrim who is renewed within the temple of
his vow as he looks around, and already hopes to retell
how it was.]   (43-45)

Such a tale-bearing pilgrim in St. John Lateran would have
entered the doors and stood within the massive Sergian
Basilica (which had replaced the original Constantinian
Basilica Aurea destroyed in A.D. 896 by earthquake), his
eyes passing from pillar to pillar to come to rest on the
famed face of Christ in the apse mosaic. This Basilica
contained the Ark and its treasures, including Aaron's
virga, brought from Jerusalem to Rome by Statius' Emperor
Titus; the camelskin of St. John the Baptist, the white
robes of St. John the Divine; and the heads of Saints Peter

and Paul. It was as Rome's Jerusalem Temple; its Sancta
Sanctorum as that Temple's Holy of Holies. Though this
"tempio" [Temple] in <u>Paradiso</u> XXXI.44 engendered pilgrim
memories, when Dante was writing, the temple of that
pilgrim's memory was truly only a memory. Though rebuilt
much later in the century it never again dominated over
Rome; the Vatican, after the return from the Babylonian
Captivity, replaced it as the seat of Popes. Rome, as well
as Jerusalem, Dante bitterly repeats, lost her Temple of
Peace for having bought and sold Christ (<u>Par</u>.IX.127-142).

Considerably later in Canto XXXI occurs a further
pilgrim simile, this time situated in St. Peter's and viewing
the Veronica:

> Qual e colui che forse di Croazia
> viene a veder la Veronica nostra,
> che per l'antica fama non sen sazia,
>   ma dice nel pensier, fin che si mostra:
> "Segnor mio Iesù Cristo, Dio verace,
> or fu sì fatta la sembianza vostra?"

> [As is he who comes perhaps from Croatia to look on our
> Veronica, and who because of its ancient fame is not
> satisfied, but says in thought so long as it is shown,
> "My Lord Jesus Christ, true God, was this the fashion
> of your semblance?"]   (103-108)

The Jubilee pilgrim has come "facie ad faciem" [face to
face] but merely with an impression of that face left in the
world as a relic, not with the living reality in heaven Dante
says he sees (XXXIII.130-132). Dante's text here puns upon
"fama" [fame], the reading of all the manuscripts, and
"fame" [famine], as Petrocchi's emendation gives it, the
phrase "non sen sazia" [is not satisfied] requiring this.[24]
Thus, ambiguously, the relic in Dante's language is both
famous and inadequate; Dante's pilgrim's response to it,
that of Doubting Thomas in the <u>Officium Peregrinorum</u>. The
Lateran and Vatican depictions of Christ were reputed to be
"not made with hands, which are the figures of the true; but
unto heaven itself . . . ." These simile pilgrims, or is it
only one who has now traversed the city's Via Sacra, the
pilgrim route, from Lateran to Vatican, passing under Titus'
Arch sculpted with the Jerusalem Temple's treasures and over
the Ponte Sant'Angelo, guarded by the Archangel Michael,
quest the face of God, carnally, in this world, while
Dante does so in "alta fantasia" [high fantasy], in an
<u>itinerarium mentis in deum</u>, a mental journey to God, within
his poem. The Virgilian similes of Christian pilgrims are
deliberately literal, deliberately unsatisfying. They make

the flesh and blood pilgrims be of poetry's lies; the lying
poet the true pilgrim.

Dante's Commedia is termed a poem, Dante himself its
poet, the unpopular Greek words for both being used by
Dante. The pagan and lying fables of poets were held in
disrepute by Christian theologians--much as they had been in
Plato's Republic--though Augustine stated they might be used
like Egyptian gold to adorn God's Ark and Luke, in Acts, had
noted that Paul quoted fabling and pagan poetry in his
Christian and truthful sermon at the Areopagus (17.28).
Dante so used pagan poetry in the Commedia. Scarcely a page
goes by without a reference to a classical myth, or without
the borrowing of a convention from pagan poetry, now yoked
to Christian ends. One such convention is that of the
metaphor of the poem as if a ship upon which the reader and
the poet embark. The magisterial Ernst Curtius traced the
convention from classical pagan to patristic and medieval
Christian writings in European Literature and the Latin
Middle Ages, with reference to Dante's use of the convention
in the Commedia.[25] It is true here that Dante is borrowing
both the introduction metaphor and the idea of such poem
voyages as the Odyssey, the Argonautica and the Aeneid, but
all of these are as foils to the pilgrim ship voyage to
Jerusalem.

Pilgrimage to Jerusalem required sea voyages. The
Crusaders even called their Jerusalem kingdom "Outremer."
The port of Venice was well equipped for the Jerusalem
pilgrim trade. Sir Richard Guylforde's secretary chaplain
on pilgrimage with his employer described the bustle of
the Arsenal or shipyard, and Dante's similar account, his
simile of the Venetian Arsenal, is part of the landscape
and seascape of medieval jerusalem pilgrimages (Inf.XXI.
7-15).[26] In winter, pilgrim ships were repaired there and
caulked with pitch, to set forth after Ascension Day, their
sails, marked with Jerusalem Crosses, billowing forth in
the wind and their cargoes of pilgrims joyfully singing,
"Veni, Creator Spiritus."[27] Sermons would be preached on
shipboard concerning the allegory of the Ship as the Church,
the Sea as the World. These voyages were often dangerous.
Saewulf wrote down a fine description, filled with echoes
from the Bible and Virgil, of multiple shipwrecks in a storm
he saw at Jaffa after he had disembarked in his zeal to
reach the Holy Places. Joinville also movingly recounts such
an event.[28]

That Jerusalem pilgrim ship voyage in turn in Dante's
poem is likewise a metaphor; Dante's Jerusalem of the Holy
Places having become Italian Rome, to pilgrimage to which

required no ship voyage. Luke had written of Paul's voyage
to Rome, including its shipwreck (Acts 27). Not only the
text of the Commedia but also the illuminations play with
the metaphor. The ship's sails are shown marked with
Jerusalem crosses (Plate VIb).[29] One manuscript takes pains
to show Dante as writing the Purgatorio's opening line, "Per
correr miglior acqua alza le vele" [To course over better
waters raise the sails], on shipboard, while within the
initial P Dante is shown on land and in his study writing
the self-same words; the two depictions of Dante in each
other's image, the one, the poetry, the other, the truth
(Plate VIIb). The Paradiso threatens the careless reader
with shipwreck (II.1-6). The Inferno had begun with a dual
image which, read one way, has the reader experience the
shipwreck of Aeneas and his shipmates upon Carthaginian
shores (Augustine in the Confessions told how the love
affair of Aeneas and Dido was but a fable), while another
reading is of historical Israelites gazing upon the
drowning Egyptian soldiery in the Red Sea waves:

> E come quei che con lena affannata,
> uscito fuor del pelago a la riva,
> si volge a l'acqua perigliosa e guata.

> [And as he, who with laboring breath has escaped from
> the deep sea to the shore, turns to the dangerous
> waters and gazes.]   (I.22-24)

One reading is of Ulysses' lying words, of the Aeneid's
lying poetry, the other of Exodus and Luke's truthful
scriptures; in one the voyage is associated with Troy and
with Carthage, in the other the journey is to Jerusalem and
to Rome; one is of the "allegory of the poets," the other of
the "allegory of the theologians."

In Inferno XXVI, Virgil and Dante encounter Ulysses
and are told of his voyage beyond the Pillars of Hercules,
in a lying tale culled from pagan poetry and, by Dante,
fabricated anew, a further fictional pilgrim's progress, or
rather, its reverse. The medieval world knew that Eden, the
"hortus deliciarum" [garden of delights], lay across
Oceanos and that it could be reached westward by sea,
eastward by land, though God forbade that pilgrimage to
fallen mankind.[30] In Canto XXVI Ulysses describes how he and
his crew, before Columbus, and with ship sails unmarked by
crosses, crossed the Ocean and sighted a huge mountain in
the New World:

> quando n'apparve una montagna, bruna
> per la distanza, e parvemi alta tanto
> quanto veduta non avéa alcuna.

    Noi ci allegrammo, e tosto tornò in pianto;
ché de la nova terra un turbo nacque
e percosse del legno il primo canto.
    Tre volte il fé girar con tutte l'acque;
a la quarta levar la poppa in suso
e la prora ire in giu, com'altrui piacque,
    infin che'l mar fu sovra noi richiuso."

["when there appeared to us a mountain dim with
distance, and to me it seemed the highest I had ever
seen. We rejoiced, but soon our joy was turned to
grief, for a tempest rose from the new land and struck
the forepart of our ship. Three times it made her whirl
round with all the waters, at the fourth lifted the
stern aloft and plunged the prow below, as pleased
another, till the sea closed over us."] (133-142)

    Here, unlike Aeneas, or scriptural Paul--and Luke with
him (Acts 27), or the Israelites crossing the Red Sea of
Exodus 14, or Dante in il primo canto, the first canto, of
the Commedia, tale-telling Ulysses does not survive. The
waves similarly close over him as, in Exodus, they did over
Pharoah's pursuing cavalry. Ulysses has reached antipodal
Mount Purgatorio with its hortus deliciarum, but drowns at
its harbor for his Adam-like disobedience to God.[31]
Aquinas, Paradiso XIII.136-139, describes that shipwreck:

    e legno vidi già dritto e veloce
correr lo mar per tutto suo cammino,
perire al fine a l'intrar de la foce.

[and I saw a ship sail straight and swiftly on its
course over the sea, to perish at its goal at the
harbor mouth.]

    An illumination of Canto XXVI could well have derived
from Aeneid II's depiction of the Trojans' shipwreck, which,
but for Neptune, would have similarly wrought their deaths
(Plate VIa). The Alpha of the Commedia had been of allusions
to shipwreck (Inf. I.22-27), its Omega will be a nude
Neptune marveling at the Argo's maiden voyage (Par. XXXIII.
94-96; Plate VIc), which Jean de Meun called the first
pilgrim voyage in this simile Dante intertextually stole
from him:

    "N'estoit lors nul pelerinage,
N'issoit nus hors de son rivage
Por cerchier estrange contree;
N'onques n'avoit la mer passee
Jason, qui prime la passa,

64

Quant les navies compassa
Por la toison d'or aler querre
Bien cuida estre pris de guerre
Neptunus, quant le vit nagier
. . . enragier."

[There was then no pilgrimage, no man went forth from
his own shore to seek foreign lands. Jason had not yet
passed over the sea, and he was the first to do so when
he organized the ships for the journey to seek the
Golden Fleece. Neptune, when he saw the ships sailing
along, well knowing this to be their prize of war . . .
raged.]   (9471-9486)[32]

Why does the Paradiso conclude with the pagan god,
Neptune, against whom Augustine spoke in De Doctrina
Christiana, III.vii, declaring that figure to be an idol;
and why the pagan hero Jason, Ulysses' counterpart, punished
with him in Inferno? Villani's History of Florence links
Florence and Troy, Troy being founded by Fiesolan Dardanus.
Hercules and Jason destroyed Dardanus' citadel, Jason first
sailing to Colchis to obtain the Golden Fleece. Dante has
repeated the theft of the Golden Fleece associated with a
war upon Troy and used it for his white and gold rose, his
"pacifica orifiamma" [peaceable oriflamme] of Jerusalem; and
from the idolatrous Aeneid and the Roman de la Rose he has
stolen the marveling pagan idol, Neptune, to adorn his
Christian poem, both defying and obeying Augustine,[33]   as
had Ulysses stolen the Palladium. He has borrowed Greek
gold. In Virgil's text, Neptune does not rage, but instead
peaceably calms the ocean (Aeneid I.124-127). These are
Janus images whose doubleness--as "ambages pulcerrime"--can
be exploited by poets (De Vulgaria Eloquentia I.10).

In Inferno V, Dante shows the evil wrought by fabling.
Paolo and Francesca, through their pornographic, Barthesian
reading of the tale of Lancelot and Guinevere, a "Miroer aus
Amoreus," similarly commit adultery. The murdered lovers
tell the pilgrim Dante: "Galeotto fu'l libro e chi lo
scrisse" [the book, and he who wrote it, was a Gallehault]
(137). Gallehault was the go-between in the affair, a
pandar. What is not generally known is that "galeotto" in
Italian is "oarsman." Even here, therefore, Dante's nautical
metaphor is at work and he refers not only to the writer of
the Arthurian romance in French but to the writer of the
contemporary murder story (one could call it "The Ring and
the Book") in Italian, Dante himself. In Inferno V Dante is
a pornographic poet and the result is nearly--in the lying
poetry--fatal. For Dante, our galeotto, himself falls at our
feet "come corpo morto cade" [as a dead body falls] (142).

But at this stage of our pilgrimage we are almost too moved by pity--as was Augustine over the death of Dido--to perceive the lesson of this Fall. It is "una verità ascosa sotto bella menzogna" [a truth concealed beneath a beautiful lie]. We are in _Inferno_ yet, whose Emperor is the Father of Lies, and the mirror is most murky, even tinged with blood. Yet the tale is an inversion of Augustine's _Confessions_, a conversion to lust; it parodies its very words.[34]   Both Augustine and Francesca state that that day they read no further; but the one turned to the Emperor of Heaven, the other to his parody, the Emperor of Hell.

The Boethian pattern of consolation, of folly become wisdom, permeates the _Commedia_ and mediates between lying pagan poetry and scriptural truth. As had Luke in the Emmaus account, Boethius' strategy was to show himself a fool at the beginning of the _Consolation_, acquiring wisdom by its ending. Dante established similar, yet opposing states in Canto XIII of the _Inferno_ and in Canto VI of the _Paradiso_ of folly and wisdom. In the latter Dante and Beatrice encounter a Romeo within a pearl because on earth he wandered in humility: "Persona umile e peregrina" [in poverty and a pilgrim] (135). This pilgrim tale of Romeo, because of his name, associated him with the Roman pilgrimage,[35]   the legend telling how he came to Raymond of Berengar's court in Provence on his way from St. James of Compostela, and stayed on as a trusty advisor, marrying Raymond's daughters to the king of France, the saintly Louis of the Crusades, and the King of England. But Romeo was to be unjustly accused of embezzlement, as also was Dante, through envy, and therefore he requested to be allowed to depart with only his mule, scrip and staff as recompense for all his service.

Romeo's pilgrimage contrasts with the despair and suicide of the similar figure, likewise unjustly accused of a crime he did not commit, Pier delle Vigne. There Dante in the _Inferno_ had been tested by Virgil as to his memory of the Virgilian text and found sadly wanting (XIII.28-48). Had Dante, the student of Virgil, truly read the _Aeneid_, rather than falling asleep over the text, he would have known that to pluck the tree branch was wrong. This is no Sybilline Golden Bough, but one of blood and words and error. Had Dante, the pilgrim of folly, truly read the _Consolation_ he would have known Romeo's pilgrimage to have been the moral response to injustice, and not Pier's exilic suicide.[36] Instead, he reels back in terror--and with him so does the reader, though both would have known the _Aeneid_ text from which this scene is borrowed. These are "up-so-doun" parallels to Luke being uncomprehending of Christ, the word become flesh, at whose side he walks, whose life he writes,

whose book he carries. The reader, with Dante, draws back in
horror, at words and blood comingling incarnately. The
fiction, here, of this fiction, is that it is not fiction.
Thus does Dante, by his lying pilgrim fabling, jolt his
reader awake to the truth. But it is also a parody of the
Mass and Crucifixion, a Black Crucifixion, fitting for these
infernal pages. Dante, like Milton, has surprised his reader
with sin.

Virgil, in the poem, is as Dante's pedagogue, Dante's
schoolmaster. Dante had had another, Ser Brunetto Latini, to
whom he had once given a copy of the Vita Nuova, speaking of
it as a Janus work, like Boethius' Consolation of
Philosophy. The Commedia is modeled both upon Virgil's
pilgrim Aeneid and upon Latini's pilgrim Tesoretto. The
Tesoretto is a dream vision that transpires where Latini,
returning from an embassy in Spain, learns in the pilgrim
pass of Roncesvalles from a Bolognese student that he has
been exiled from Florence in his absence. He describes
himself, troubled in thought, becoming lost:

> Pensando a capo chino   Perdei il gran cammino
> E tenni a la traversa   D'una selva diversa,
>
> [Deep in thought I lost the high road and took the
> crossroad into a wilderness.]   (187-190) [37]

at which point, in his mind, the vision and its allegorical
landscape lie before him. Later in the work, he returns to
that visionary landscape with the words: "Mi ritrovai. . . "
[I found myself again . . .](2896). These are lines which
Dante will borrow for the commencement of the Commedia,
shadowily making of that valley of shadows a pilgrim pass of
Roncesvalles; using a poetic form of double entry book-
keeping:

> Nel mezzo del cammin di nostra vita
> mi ritrovai per una selva oscura,
> ché la diritta via era smarrita,
>
> [In the middle of the journey of our life I found
> myself again in a dark wood where the straight way was
> lost.]   (I.13)

and for his dialogue in the Inferno with the soul of Ser
Brunetto Latini; where two meet with a shadowy third:

> "Là sù di sopra, in la vita serena,"
> rispuosio lui, "mi smarri' in una valle,
> avanti che l'età mia fosse piena."

[There above, up in the clear life," I answered him, "I
lost myself in a valley, before my age was full."]
(XV.49-51)

He tells Latini how Virgil appeared to him and guided him
downward on this path to Hell. Latini's shade tells Dante of
Florence and of the exile from her they are to share. Dante
then watches his former maestro, who in running seems to be
one who wins, not loses, the "drappo verde a Verona" [the
green cloth at Verona]. "Ver" puns upon spring, green and
truth amidst this landscape of winter, darkness and lies. It
shadows Dante's own pilgrimage, from Florence to Verona.
Both Pier delle Vigne and Brunetto Latini are poets. Both
Latini's Tesoretto and Dante's Commedia are pilgrimage
poems. They are both written by Florentine exiles.

Brunetto Latini gives a simile in the Tesoretto of the
player at dice in a tavern:

E un altro per impiezza   A la zara s'avezza
E giuoca con inganno   E per far l'altrui danno
Sovente pigna 'l dado,   E non vi guarda guado;
E ben presta un unzino   E mette mal fiorino;
E se perdesse un poco   Ben udiresti loco
Biastemiare Dio e' santi   E que' che son davanti.

[Another impiously played zara with skill and made the
others lose as often as he threw the die without
caring; then all at once he played with a bad florin
and started to lose a little, and then you should have
heard in that place how he cursed God and the saints
and those who came before.]   (2775-2786)

Dante intertextually metamorphoses the simile into:

   Quando si parte il gioco de la zara,
colui che perde si riman dolente,
repetendo le volte, e tristo impara;
   con l'altro se ne va tutta la gente;
qual va dinanzi, e qual di dietro il prende,
e qual dallato li se reca a mente;
   el non s'arresta, e questo e quello intende;
a cui porge la man, più non fa pressa;
e così de la calca si difende.

[When the game of zara breaks up, he who loses is left
sorrowing, repeating the throws, and sadly learns. With
the other all the people go along; one goes in front,
one plucks him from behind, and one at his side recalls
him to mind. He does not stop and listens to this one

and to that one; those to whom he stretches out his
hand press on him no more, and so he saves himself from
the throng.]   (<u>Purg</u>. VI.1-9)

The first simile described the dice player who loses,
despairs and blasphemes; the second gives both winner and
loser, the loser not blaspheming but sadly learning from his
error, his loss becoming thereby more profitable than the
winner's gains. The simile is, in reality, to Dante, who has
lost at Fortuna's game of zara, and hence, like Boethius,
learned Philosophia's wisdom. From others' literary
pilgrimages, mapped by Virgil, Boethius and Latini, and
wrought from their despair, Dante learns his own of hope.
That progress from folly, doubt and despair is the pattern
of the Emmaus pilgrimage. Dante, like Luke, has used
Ulyssean lies and God's truth, sea voyages and land
journeys, as Janus tales, to tell of Emmaus encounters by
two pilgrims with many another.

In _Paradiso_ XXXIII, Dante's will is revolved equally
with love, Dante at its conclusion saying they turn as upon
a wheel:

Ma già volgeva il mio disio e'l velle,
sì come rota ch'igualmente è mossa,
   l'amor che move il sole e l'altre stelle.

[But now my desire and my will were as if turned like a
wheel moved by the love which moves the sun and the
other stars.]   (143-145)

The reader then returns to reread the Janus poem, this
time knowing of its ending and therefore no longer affected
by the tragic, willful, despairing folly of the _Inferno_'s
Boethius-like _persona_, Dante as exiled Adam. Though in that
canticle the word "peregrin" cannot be uttered, the entire
Commedia's pilgrimage is now present in the mind during a
second reading, in lieu of a first reading's bitter and
exilic ignorance. The text is as a twice-told tale, the
first of exile, the second of pilgrimage; it progresses as
in the Emmaus paradigm from lies to truth. In the
ingathering of these opposites in memory, the pilgrim--both
poet and reader--can comprehend the center.

Thus Dante's _Commedia_ pilgrimage is circular, rather
than linear. So also is _Piers Plowman_'s pilgrimage. In both
poems the ends are revolved to become again the beginning in
which the poet, and the reader mirrored in him, refind
themselves ("mi ritrovai") in that initial, Adamic
landscape. A carnal outward pilgrimage transpires in time
and space, in Fortuna's realm; the "journey of the mind in

God," the _itinerarium mentis in deum_, seeks instead the
center of all time and space. Boethius, using the figure of
the circle and the center, tells us of this shape of time
and eternity, bondage and freedom, man and God. In _Vita
Nuova_ XII, Love tells Dante: "Ego tamquam centrum circuli,
cui simili modo se habent circumferentie partes: tu autem
non sic." [I am at the center of the circle, equidistant
from all parts of the circumference; but you are not.] Yet
the reader who has completed the _Vita Nuova_ or the _Commedia_
or _Piers Plowman_ is, in memory, also as if at the center of
these works, equidistant from all parts, knowing their
beginning and ending, _alpha_ and _omega_.[1]

    In the Prologue to _Piers Plowman_ the reader encounters
the poet's _persona_, English Will, as a wanderer and a roamer
in a wilderness landscape, just as in _Inferno_ I the reader
had encountered Italian Dante as a lost and despairing
traveler, full of sleep, in a "selva oscura e selvaggia" [a
dark and wild wood]. Each work reflects the other, not
because either borrowed from the other, but because they
share in Christendom's culture and mirror its Bible in their
books.[2] Langland gives us an Adam in England:

> I was wery forwandred . and wente me to reste
> Vnder a brood bank . by a bourne syde,
> And as I lay and lenede . and loked on þe watres
> I slombred into a slepyng . it sweyed so murye,
> Than gan I meten . a merueillous sweuene,
> That I was in a wildernesse . wiste I neuere where.
>   (7-12)

At the poem's ending Will's sickness and approaching
death, like Boethius', prompts not authorial Will but
Conscience, the human will reformed in Christ's image, to
reform that pilgrimage to regain Love, the leech of Life:

> 'By crist!' quod Conscience þo . 'I wole bicome a
>   pilgrym,
> And wenden as wide . as þe world renneþ
> To seken Piers þe Plowman'.   (XX.380-382)

Conscience, as in the _Commedia_, joins the end to the
beginning, the inside to the outside, Love with Will, as in
a Möbius strip, a Gödelian loop, reconciling their
contradictions. The reader thus likewise retraces the
passus, the steps of the poem, to regain the _vita Christi_
embedded in the English text of _Piers Plowman_, just as the
Jerusalem pilgrim, the _viator_, must trace the steps of
Christ, the _via et vita et veritas_. Medieval art showed
depictions of Adam and Christ on opposing pages which, when
the book was closed, became one. Similarly the Book God held

gave on one page <u>alpha</u>, on the other <u>omega</u>, and had
originally been a scroll written <u>intus et foris</u>, on the
inside and the out, which though opposed to each other are
yet united at the closing and rolling up of God's Book. In
the fiction of the poem, if the reader would follow Will as
Adam following Piers as Christ he has but to turn from the
last page, the Doomsday <u>omega</u>, to the first, the <u>alpha</u> of
creation, making <u>Piers Plowman</u>, like the <u>Commedia</u>, a comedy.
Even if he ignores the book, closing it ("that day we read
no further"), its opposites still become a unity. Though
Dante had his reader complete his reading on comedy's
upswing, "Regno" [I reign], Langland does so on what
compares to tragedy's downswing, "Regnavi" [I reigned], of
Fortuna's Wheel; nevertheless, at the center of both poems
is the refinding of, in Dante's case, Beatrice as Christ,
in Will's, of Piers as Christ. Each comes "face to face"
with the one whom he had sought in his exile and upon his
pilgrimage. Thus neither poem is to be read as a tragedy.

Readers of <u>Piers Plowman</u> become as bewildered as does
Will himself concerning the structuring of the poem's
pilgrimage. It pretends to be triadic, with the Vitae of
Dowel, Dobet and Dobest, when really it is one Vita. Within
one pilgrimage, undertaken by two pilgrims, by Piers and by
Will, Will quests Piers--and follows behind him in his
<u>passus</u>, his footsteps, yet falls far short of the ideals he
should follow. "The spirit is willing but the flesh is
weak." Essentially there are two groups of threes, one
overlapping upon the other, some sections of which are
negative, some of which are positive. Piers is seen as a
progression, being in turn Dowel, Dobet and Dobest; Faith,
Hope and Charity; Ploughman, Monk and Knight; Abraham, Moses
and Christ; and then a fourth state which falls short of all
his former states--could one call it "Do ill"?--as Pope and
as Peter. Will can be seen first as a "Ne'er-do-well," and
then, sarcastically, as "Dowel," "Dobet" and "Dobest." He is
really "Ne'er-do-well" throughout. Yet both Will and Piers
are aspects of the poem's poet, much as both Boethius and
Philosophia are aspects of the <u>Consolation</u>'s author, who can
thereby present us with both his folly and his wisdom.

It is possible to give the triadic, cyclical structure
of the work, mapping its pilgrim's progress as a diagram.[3]
In this pilgrim's "progress," it can be seen that the part
of the poem having the most positive value corresponds to
the Gospels' account of the Incarnation, of the <u>vita
Christi</u>, XVII-XVIII. Elsewhere, the terms "Dowel, Dobet and
Dobest" frequently become a sarcastic commentary on
Christendom's failure to imitate Christ. The figure of Will
mirrors that of Adam not only within the author but also
within ourselves; the figure of Piers, that of Christ, whom,

Mede

	Visio Prol-VII	Vitae VIII-XVI	XVII-XVIII	XIX-XX	
					Apocalypse
				Folly	
				Body	
				Adam-	
	Will	"Dowel"	"Dobet"	"Dobest"	
	Ne'er-do-well	Student	Minor orders	Aged and dying	
	Hermit	Lent	Easter	Pentecost	
Haukyn	May −	−	+	−	Decretals
					Book/Gospels
	Piers	Elijah/John	Christ	Peter	
	Abraham/Moses	Dobet/Hope	Dobest/Charity	"Do ill"	
	Dowel/Faith	Monk	& Knight	"Unity"	Wisdom
	Ploughman +	+	Abraham Moses +	Pope −	Soul
					Christ+

Genesis · Exodus · Pardon/Covenant · Prophets · Charter/Law · Gospels · Book/Gospels · Decretals · Apocalypse

Ecclesia

as pilgrims, we ought to quest. The structures should be
thought of as a circle, Adam's on the outside, Christ's
within, the diagram, as it were, folded along the center and
the ends joined together, or its terms engraved upon a ring
inside and out, or best yet, upon a Möbius strip, to
represent the poem's yoking of opposites, body and soul,
Mede and Holichirche, minstrelsy and truth, doubt and faith,
despair and hope, anger and charity, folly and wisdom, and a
multitude more. Even the triads of faith, hope and charity,
doubt, despair and anger in the poem are actually unities,
the third term uniting the opposing first two despite Will's
initial failure to perceive this concept. <u>Piers Plowman</u>
presents a negative epistemology, only to have it be
simultaneously a positive epistemology.

We first meet the sheepskin-garbed Will resting from
his wandering by a "bourn-syde" in Pentecostal May.[4] The
word "pilgrim" of Will is left unsaid (as indeed Dante does
not mention that word during the infernal journeying), yet
Langland shows by allusion that Will's dress and wandering
are part of the practice of pilgrimage. He does this by
garbing his <u>persona</u> in a sheepskin: "I shoop me into a
shroud . as I a sheep weere" (2). Palladius and Cassian had
noted this to be the correct garb of Thebaid hermits in
obedience to Hebrews 11.37-38, whose strangers and pilgrims
"wandered about in sheepskins and goatskins . . . in
deserts, and in mountains, and in dens and caves,"[5] and this
became, after Benedict's Rule forbade clerical pilgrimage,
the dress of the medieval lay pilgrim traveling through the
wilderness of this world. The Emmaus Pilgrims' Plays dress
their three travelers in this manner (Plate IIIa,b; Figure
4). Dante, Langland and Bunyan are all sensitive to the
correct landscape of a pilgrimage and accordingly place
their <u>personae</u> amidst mountains, wildernesses, dens,
Langland curiously localizing his scene upon English
"Maluerne hilles," yet maintaining it is also as an Egyptian
wilderness. Will is presented to us as an English Adam and
as an English Israelite.

Langland has Will see upon the "fair feeld ful of folk"
mirror images of himself, tale-telling pilgrims and lazy
louts of hermits:

Pilgrymes and Palmeres . pli3ten hem togidere
For to seken Seint Iame . and Seintes at Rome;
Wenten forþ in hire wey . wiþ many wise tales,
And hadden leue to lyen . al hire lif after.
I sei3 somme þat seiden . þei hadde ysou3t Seintes;
To ech a tale þat þei tolde . hire tong was tempred to
    lye
Moore þan to seye sooþ . it semed bi hire speche.

Heremytes on an heep . with hoked staues
Wenten to walsyngham . and hire wenches after;
Grete lobies and longe . þat loþe were to swynke
Cloþed hem in copes . to ben knowen from oþere;
Shopen hem heremytes . hire ese to haue. (46-57)

These he lists with friars and with pardoners as evil-doers
who exploit others. This satire upon pilgrims and hermits,
coming so soon after Langland's description of himself as
one of their number,

I shoop me into a shroud . as I a sheep weere;
In habite as an heremite . vnholy of werkes,
Wente wide in þis world . wondres to here, (2-4)

acts as a commentary upon that self-portrait, explaining the
garb, the ambivalent intent of the journeying, the
characteristic trait of pilgrims, as of poets, of telling
tales more false than true. The commentary casts doubt,
even, upon Will's tale of his Vision of Piers the Plowman,
as it does upon the Emmaus tale of tale-telling pilgrims,
one of whom is Truth. Pilgrim tales deconstruct. Pilgrim
poets are unreliable narrators: "Trust not the teller, trust
[not even] the tale." Yet their very untrustworthiness
paradoxically becomes their means for telling truths.

Will's garb is described as a sheepskin.[6] Pilgrims in
their sclavins were likened in the Benedictio Peregrinorum
of the Sarum Rite to sheep questing their shepherd, Christ
(Appendix I). A familiar medieval image, derived from the
Greek Aesop and metamorphosed into clerical satire as the
Roman de Renart, is of Renart the fox garbed as a pilgrim in
a sheepskin preaching to gullible barnyard fowl whom he will
devour at the sermon's conclusion.[7] A further image is
present, which Robertson and Huppé mention in other contexts
to the poem, Matthew 7.15: "Beware of false prophets, which
come to you in sheep's clothing, but inwardly they are
ravening wolves."[8] Which is Will, innocent sheep, or
guileful fox or treacherous wolf? All these senses could be
present in Piers Plowman's Visio.

The ambiguity, reflected in the beginning and ending of
the poem, and in Will's sheepskin garb, reverberates, too,
throughout. Will asks the question Bunyan's Christian will
echo in Pilgrim's Progress, "How may I saue my soul?"
(I.84), a question asked by a rich young man of Christ who
in reply told him that if he would do well he should keep
the commandments, if he would do best he should sell all and
give to the poor, gaining treasure thereby in heaven (Matt.
19.16-22; Luke 18.18-30).[9] It was this text that wrought the

peregrinate conversion of Egyptian St. Anthony and Italian
St. Francis.[10] Holichirche in her simple garb confronts and
opposes opulent Mede. The pilgrim could renounce the things
of this world and attain God, or claim Mede and by
possessing her be an exile from God. Holichirche and Mede
dramatize for Will--and the reader's will--this choice
between God and the world, between "Dobest" and "Do ill."
Will--like ourselves--makes the wrong choice.

Mede appears, resplendent in scarlet, gold and gems:

```
. . . a womman . wonderliche ycloþed,
Purfiled wiþ Pelure . þe pureste on erþe,
Ycorouned in a coroune . þe kyng haþ noon bettre.
Fetisliche hire fyngres . were fretted with gold wyr
And þeron riche Rubies . as rede as any gleede,
And Diamaundes of derrest pris . and double manere
    Saphires,
Orientales and Ewages . enuenymes to destroye.
Hire Robe was ful riche . of reed scarlet engreyned,
Wiþ Ribanes of reed gold . and of riche stones.
Hire array me rauysshed . swich richesse sau3 I
    neuere.                                (II.8-17)
```

The poet only noticed Holichirche's beauty, not her
garb; in one line he stated "A louely lady of leere . in
lynnen ycloþed" (I.3), but with Mede he is absorbed for
many lines with a catalogue and inventory of the wealth of
her dress. He had asked Holichirche: "Kenne me by som craft
to knowe þe false" (II.4). Holichirche complies by intro-
ducing him to the seductiveness of "Fals," that he may
experience its dialectical opposition to her Truth.
Holichirche had come to Will from the East, Jerusalem's
direction; but Mede, the Babylonian Whore, "arrayed in
purple and scarlet colour, and decked with gold and precious
stones and pearls" (Rev. 17.4), advances from the left, the
bastard sinister of heraldry, and indeed (like Langland
himself) she proves to be of bastard birth. She is "Fals."
Many, including Skeat, have seen her as Edward III's
mistress, Dame Alice Perrers. We will find scarlet-clad Dame
Alice of Bath is her kin.[11] She approaches Will from the
Castle of Care where Wrong dwells, who had counseled Adam
and Eve to sin and Cain to slay Abel. She is the opposite
of pilgrimage.

Holichirche, clothed in the pilgrim simplicity of white
linen, had descended from the East, coming geographically
from Herefordshire Beacon, Langland's dream poem's sun-clad
Tower of Truth. Behind this beacon and the other, of
Worcestershire, nestle the towns of Great Malvern with the

Benedictine priory, the sister institution to Westminster
Abbey, and another at Little Malvern, where, perhaps,
Langland received his education.[12] It is a landscape that
echoes Dante's delectable mountain of _Inferno_ I.77, from
which lying Virgil guided him. Alan Bright tells of an old
castle dungeon diked about with a moat into which the walls
were crumbling (now Old Castle Farm) as being on Langland's
left if he were on the banks of Ledbury's Promeswelle or
Pewtress Spring, a mile from Longland's Farm (A.VIII.130-
131) and as representing Mede's and Wrong's Castle of Care.
On his right he would have seen the Norman keep atop
Herefordshire Beacon as the Tower of Truth, and before him
would have stretched the vision's Field Full of Folk. R.W.
Chambers agreed that it is the one spot in Malvern hills
that equals the poem's landscape description.[13] Langland has
localized the vision of St. John's Apocalypse in
fourteenth-century England. (The Van Eycks, in the
fifteenth century and in Flanders, were to do the same with
their Ghent Altarpiece.)

After the episode with Holichirche and Lady Mede, the
tension between the World and God is given a subtler twist.
The folk on the plain, in attempting to seek Truth, meet
first a palmer and then Piers. Their encounters are both
with a false pilgrim, then with one who is true. The palmer
is

> Apparailled as a paynym . in pilgrymes wise.
> He bar a burdoun ybounde . wiþ a brood liste,
> In a wiþwyndes wise . ywounden aboute.
> A bolle and a bagge . he bar by his syde.
> An hundred of Ampulles . on his hat seten,
> Signes of Synay . and shelles of Galice,
> And many a crouch on his cloke . and keyes of Rome,
> And þe vernycle bifore . for men sholde knowe
> And se bi hise signes . whom he sou3te hadde.
>
> (V.516-525)

The pilgrims ask where he has been:

> 'Fram Synay', he seide . 'and fram þe Sepulcre.
> At Bethlem, at Babiloyne . I haue ben in boþe,
> In Armonye, in Alisaundre . in many oþere places.
> Ye may se by my signes . þat sitten on my hatte
> That I haue walked wel wide . in weet and in drye
> And sou3t goode Seintes . for my soule hele.'
>
> (526-531)

They question him further:

> 'Knowestow au3t a corsaint', quod þei . 'þat men calle
>   truþe?
> Kanstow wissen vs þe wye . where þat wye dwelleþ?'

'Nay, so god glade me' . seide þe gome þanne.
'I ne sei3 neuere Palmere . wiþ pyk ne wiþ scrippe
Asken after hym . er now in þis place.' (532-536)

They speak of Truth as carnal, as a "corsaint," forgetting
that in the Holy Sepulchre of the risen Christ, who is
veritas, the Truth, there is no corpse. They shadow forth
the folly of the pilgrim disciples at Emmaus. But the palmer
they have met is himself a fool, and by no means the Christ,
the Truth, whom they seek. Piers Plowman suddenly burst on
the scene (he almost bursts through the parchment of the
page as he puts "forþ his hed" [537], intruding upon this
world of fiction and lies from that of fact and truth) and,
exclaiming "Peter!," tells the rest that he is acquainted
with Truth, and has promised to serve him forever now that
Conscience has shown him where he dwells. For Piers counters
the palmer's mendicant pilgrimage with honest ploughing.

Langland with this scene does two things. He describes
the attributes of the literal medieval pilgrim, such as we
have observed in Andrea da Firenze's mural detail and in the
Douce manuscript illumination (Plate Ia,b). And he
exaggerates the polarity between the carnal and the true
pilgrim in order to prove a point about pilgrimage. This
palmer is a caricature. His hundred ampulles were fashioned
of lead and pewter and jet. In such a quantity they would
have been heavy indeed to be borne in his hat. Such ampulles
were bought, for instance, by pilgrims at Canterbury where
they contained the healing water and blood of St. Thomas'
Well (Figure 8). The "signes of Synay" were St. Catherine
wheel emblems, for her monastery and shrine were points of
pilgrim interest at Sinai, as well as the mountain being the
historic site of God's presentation of the Law to Moses in
Exodus. The Galician shells were those gathered near the
shrine of St. James of Compostela in Spain or fashioned from
jet in the shape of such shells. The "many crouch on his
cloke" were the sign of intent to journey to the Holy
Sepulchre at Jerusalem. The crossed keys represented those
of St. Peter and the papacy at Rome, and the "vernycle
bifore" was a miniature of the revered Roman relic, St.
Veronica's napkin, upon which was printed the face of
Christ. This pilgrim has been, according to his signs, to
Canterbury, Sinai, Compostela, Jerusalem and Rome. To this
list he adds Bethlehem and Babylon (in fact, Cairo), Armenia
(where he could see Noah's Ark), and Alexandria (once the
Gospeller Mark's resting place until his theft by
Venetians).[14] Thus Langland's palmer presents the semiotics
of pilgrimage, the medieval audience being fully aware of
the code; though not, perhaps, the modern one.

The palmer has a pilgrim staff, his "burdoun," and around it is twined a broad "liste" which is compared in turn to a woodbind. The olive staff of the classical traveler had similarly had wool wreathed about it. The Ripa engraving of a pilgrim shows this riband on the pilgrim staff (Figure 1) and the illumination of Lydgate presenting his translation of Deguileville's _Pilgrim_ to Thomas, Earl of Salisbury, shows that book literally as a pilgrim with a wreathed staff among his other attributes (Figure 11). Langland's Palmer has besides, his begging bowl for food and alms and his scrip or bag. Owing to his foreign travels he is dressed in "paynym" clothes. Douce Manuscript 104 in the Bodleian Library gives a fine depiction of this palmer at folio 33 (Plate Ib). It shows the "liste" twined about the staff as if it were a caduceus, the pilgrim hat crowded with "benedictions," the fleece garb hung about with objects and a scrip at the left side, its strap crossing the right shoulder. The palmer has a white beard. That he is termed a "paynym" in garb would serve to signify, in medieval thought, that he was an infidel. There is evidence that medieval pilgrims consciously dressed as Jews, to represent their journeying as an Exodus recapitulation. However, the word "paynym" seems to imply that this palmer also partakes of the supposed Muslim worship of idols, of mawmets. It turns out that he is pagan, a "paynym," not knowing Truth, which alone could save his soul ("Ego sum via et vita et veritas") though he has visited many a shrine for his "soules hele." He is an Adamic pilgrim, not a Christian one. His signs signify the letter only, not the spirit. The signifier and the signified here become the same in a meaningless tautology. The palmer is thereby an idolator, his leaden pilgrim signs, paradoxically, his idols.

The readers who think, like Will, that the answer to the quest for Truth is to be found in carnal pilgrimage are brought up short with the realization of the failure of that method spelled out before their eyes by this "paynym" figure. Pilgrimage here deconstructs. The poet has played them false in much the same manner as had Dante with his pilgrim similes. The personification presents us with the folk's practice and corresponding belief in pilgrimage. It meets them as they embark upon their pilgrimage as if to mirror themselves. They do not come to St. James in their likeness at Compostela, nor to the parousial Veronica at Rome, nor to Christ who is Truth at an Emmaus inn. They meet only themselves, foolishly asking themselves, where is the "corsaint" Truth. It is a question Holichirche has already answered but neither Will nor the folk have heeded her words:

It is a kynde knwyng . þat kenneþ in þyn herte.

(I.143)

They must perform an <u>itinerarium mentis in deum</u>, a
pilgrimage within, to find there themselves in the image of
God. Instead, like Pilate, they foolishly ask, "What is
Truth?" (John 18.38), of Truth, that scene Dostoevsky will
so powerfully repeat with Christ before the Grand
Inquisitor.

In the poem, Will progresses from carnal pilgrimage to
the <u>via veritatis</u>. The ambiguity in pilgrimage is enhanced
to stress this point; pilgrimage cannot be "by feet alone,"
but is the alienation from the things of this world, even
such things as ampulles, catherine wheels, crosses, keys,
shells, vernicles, staffs, lists, scrips, bowls, pardons,
indulgences, bulls, though they are supposedly indicative of
pilgrimage and salvation; the quest is not to dispersed
shrines in outlandish places but for the mirroring within
one's soul of Christ who is Truth and Charity (V.605-607).
It is an internal pilgrimage that is sought. External,
physical pilgrimage is ridiculed. Pilgrimage poems thus
paradoxically disparage actual pilgrimages; they, in effect,
cancel themselves out; they are poems that deconstruct; they
are self-consuming artifacts.

After Piers puts forth his head and tells the pilgrims
he knows where Truth dwells they offer him payment for his
services as guide. They impose upon Piers the role of the
Saracen guide in the Holy Land who for a sum of money gives
pilgrims protection and escort. Christian Piers swears by
"Seint Thomas Shryne" he will accept no payment, not even a
farthing. The Thomas of the oath is the English St. Thomas
Becket, patron of Canterbury and Acre. In medieval thought,
Thomas epitomized the true churchman. As the crusaders'
patron he protected Jerusalem pilgrims; he died in order to
defend the spiritual realm against the demands of Mede; his
shrine was deeply revered by pilgrims at Canterbury.[15]

Piers' ploughing as pilgrimage has confused many
critics.[16] First Piers preaches upon pilgrimage, though the
pilgrimage he describes is one within an allegorical,
Bunyanesque landscape. Then he tells the pilgrims, repeating
Holichirche's teaching, that:

> . . . if grace graunte þee . to go in þis wise
> Thow shalt see in þiselve . truþe sitte in þyn herte
> In a cheyne of charite .   (V.605-607)

The assembled pilgrims respond variously to the sermon and
the directives Piers delivers to them. At times he seems to
say that the half-acre must be ploughed before the

pilgrimage proper can commence (VI.63); at times he declares
the ploughing is the pilgrimage (VI.57-62). Some assent to
Piers' directives, others back out. The knight humbly
pledges himself to Piers, "by seint Iame," invoking the
saint of pilgrims and crusaders (VI.5). His action echoes
that of those crusading knights and pilgrims who heard St.
Bernard preach the Crusade. Yet the task he will perform has
none of the glamour of a Crusade and it is odd indeed to
envision a medieval knight trespassing categories and
estates and humbly asking to be taught how to plough the
earth (VI.22-23).[17] The three estates of medieval society,
the ecclesiasts, the warriors, the laborers, were a triad.
Piers Plowman unites them.

Piers then dresses himself, he says, as a pilgrim:

'And I shal apparaille me', quod Perkyn . 'in pilgrymes
    wise
And wende wiþ yow þe wey . til we fynde truþe.'
He caste on his cloþes . yclouted and hole,
His cokeres and his coffes . for cold of hise nailes,
And heng his hoper at his hals . in stede of a Scryppe:
'A busshel of bredcorne . brynge me þerInne,
For I wol sowe it myself . and siþenes wol I wende
To pilgrymage as palmeres doon . pardon to haue."
                                            (VI.57-64)

The language is deliberately ambiguous. His intent to be a
pilgrim makes of him a mirror of Will and of the palmer; his
ploughing and his workman's garb, their antithesis.

Piers equates ploughing with pilgrimage. Yet he does
not go barefoot as a pilgrim ought, but gaitered with
ploughman's leggings and with wrappings on his wrist against
the cold, such as we see the ploughman in the Luttrell
Psalter and in the Duc de Berry's Très Riches Heures
illuminations to wear. He has but a patched coat, no staff
and his scrip is his hopper from which he sows the seed as
he walks. This apparent illogicality can be explained by the
Gospel words of Christ, who as veritas, Truth, would have
been heeded in this context, words which were in fact read
at the service of the Benedictio Peregrinorum (Appendix I).

Nolite possidere aurum neque pecuniam in zonis vestris
non peram in via neque duas tunicas neque calceamenta
neque virgam; dignus enim est operarius cibo suo.

[Provide neither gold, nor silver, nor brass in your
purses, nor scrip for your journey, neither two coats,
neither shoes nor yet staves: for the workman is worthy
of his meat.]   (Matt.10.9-10)

Medieval man was thus well aware of the contradiction
involved in pilgrimage. One form is Mosaic, the other
Christian. This dictate appears also in Luke 10 where it is
preceded by an analogy drawn between the disciples and their
ministry of the word to laborers and harvesting. It is
followed by the parable of the Good Samaritan, which
Langland will adapt to the structuring of Piers Plowman.
Langland's ideal Christian pilgrim is there Piers the honest
plowman, rather than the exilic "paynym," the mercenary
palmer; yet we are presented with both figures contrasted
to one another, as we had been earlier with Holichirche
and Mede.

Because medieval pilgrimage was a dying to the world,
the medieval pilgrim upon setting out wrote his Will and
Testament.[18] Piers is no exception. He dictates his bequest
(titled in the C Text the Testamentum Petri Plouhman) in
the name of God. He wills his soul to God, to defend from
the devil; his body to the church, for he has paid his
tithes; to his wife, his friends and his children, that
which he has earned truly; he owes no man money, having
always repaid before nightfall; and he concludes:

> And wiþ þe residue and þe remenaunt . by þe Rode of
> Lukes!
> I wol worshipe þerwiþ . truþ by my lyue,
> And ben his pilgrym atte plow . for pouere mennes sake.
> My plowpote shal be my pik . and putte at þe rotes,
> And helpe my cultour to kerue . and close þe furwes.'
> (VI.100-104)

The Rode of Lucca was a famed pilgrim relic, a portrait of
Christ said to have been painted by St. Luke, and mentioned
also by Dante (Inf.XXI.49).

Piers' pilgrim Testament echoes Luke 10 (whose symbol
is the ox of ploughing, XIX.263) and he is no longer
ambiguous about his pilgrimage as being ploughing, the
plough pike, his pilgrim staff. He vows by the Holy Face of
Lucca that this is his pilgrimage.[19] Like Cain the ploughman,
he quests God's face--in order to be as Abel the pilgrim. He
is the example that pilgrims should follow, not as an exilic
beggar with a bowl, but as an honest laborer worthy of his
hire. Piers Plowman is a poem whose central metaphor is of a
harvest, both carnal and spiritual, that harvesting being in
turn true pilgrimage and honest labor.

Both Will and Piers participate in the pattern of the
Pilgrims at Emmaus, a pattern that becomes central to Piers
Plowman. In the Visio we had met Will aimlessly wandering
about, clad in a sheepskin, garbed as an Adamic pilgrim. He

had then met, in his own image, the "paynym" palmer who knew
not where Truth dwelt. Following that, Will encountered
Piers who knew Truth. It is as if Will were Luke; the
Palmer, Cleophas; and Piers, Christ. At the beginning of the
Vita, Will is again a _peregrinus_, like a friar "yrobed in
russet," of rough grey cloth (VIII.1) and roaming about,
though this time he has a goal. He seeks Dowel. He meets two
friars on a Friday (a scene where two travelers are
overtaken by a third, in medieval thought generally
represented the Pilgrims at Emmaus, but that was on a
Monday) and he asks them where Dowel is. They preach at
length but do not enlighten him. This is another shadowy,
deconstructing Peregrini. The three on the road, each garbed
in coarse russet cloth, mirror each other.

After the encounter with the "paynym" palmer who knows
not Truth, Piers the Plowman explicates Truth as conjoined
with Charity (V.606-607), echoing in turn the words of
Holichirche: "That Treuþe is tresor . þe trieste on erþe"
(I.137) and "For truþe telleþ þat loue is triacle of heuene"
(I.148). She had already chided him, echoing Christ's
chiding of his Emmaus disciples: "O stulti, et tarde corde
ad credendum . . . ": "'Thow doted daffe!" quod she . 'dulle
are þi wittes . To litel latyn þow lernedest, leode, in þi
youþe'" (I.140-141). Now, in the Vita, after Will's futile
education at the university, Scripture skips to the pulpit
and preaches on salvation, taking as text the parable of the
feast to which many were summoned but few were chosen. Will
angrily proceeds to dispute this (XI.115-136) and pagan
Trajan suddenly comes to his aid. It is thus neither an
unlettered Christian ploughman nor a traveled "paynym"
palmer who unravels the enigma but, even more paradoxically,
it is a pagan emperor who rescues Will from his Malvern and
Oxonian mists of misunderstanding. Latin Trajan, called
"Troianus" by Langland (the Ricardian English believed they
were descended from the Trojans and called London "New
Troy"), proclaims most rudely, "Ye, baw for bokes!' (140)
and insists that without Charity all Latin learning is
worthless. The Douce manuscript (Plate XIIc) illuminates
Trajan in the margin as thumbing his nose at books, even at
the book of _Piers Plowman_ itself, as he says this, and shows
him as a grotesque with none of the classic dignity Dante's
poem gives him; yet for all that Langland's treatment of him
is the more powerful one. Dante and Langland similarly had
access to the tale of Trajan, the widow and Pope Gregory, as
they were the matter of Christendom.[20]

Trajan movingly tells Will that Christ roams the world
disguised as a poor man, a pilgrim (as he was at Emmaus),
and sees all. Because all, rich and especially poor, are

created in the image of their Creator, whoever helps them
does likewise to Christ. Trajan explains his plea for the
charitable treatment of the poor, with the statement that
all are pilgrims:

> Why I meue þis matere . is moost for þe pouere;
> For in hir liknesse oure lord . lome haþ ben yknowe.
> Witnesse in þe Pask wyke . whan he yede to Emaus;
> Cleophas ne knew hym no3t . þat he crist were
> For his pouere apparaill . and pilgrymes wedes
> Til he blessede and brak . þe breed þat þei eten.
> So bi hise werkes þei wisten . þat he was Iesus,
> Ac by cloþyng þei knew hym no3t . so caitifliche he
>   yede.
> And al was in ensample . sooþliche, to vs synfulle here
> That we sholde be lowe and loueliche . and lele ech man
>   to oþer,
> And pacient as pilgrymes . for pilgrymes are we alle.
>   (XI.232-242)

The paradox of the teller and the tale, of the pagan
teller of a Gospel tale, of the imperial narrator of
theocratic equality, heightens its power. The encounter,
first of the poor widow with the powerful Emperor in pagan
Rome, then of the Pope Gregory of Christian Rome with these
two figures from the past, told in the Golden Legend, is
shadowily an Emmaus triad, of newness meeting with oldness,
of love with law. The rest of the tale has Gregory weep for
Trajan, the Pope's tears thereby baptising the Emperor.

Langland, as a boy in a Benedictine priory, would have
taken part in the Officium Peregrinorum performed on Easter
Mondays. He could well have sung the part of Luke which
requires a boy's voice, rather than a man's. In the monastic
context, that tale clashes with its setting. Monks acting
the roles in the liturgical drama of the pilgrim disciples
of Luke's Gospel going to supper at an inn and telling
pilgrim tales--known traditionally to be lie-filled--were
playfully, paradoxically, disobeying the Benedictine
Rule--which forbade monks to be pilgrims, forbade them to
eat when on only a day's journey, forbade the telling of
idle tales and forbade them to put up at secular inns and
taverns.

The liturgical drama of the Officium Peregrinorum would
have been familiar to Malvern inhabitants. We have partial
proof of this in the splendid East Window of the Benedictine
Priory at Great Malvern which presents the scenes of "Pask
wyke" from Christ's entry into Jerusalem on Palm Sunday to
Pentecost, which echoes the liturgical time scheme of Piers
Plowman XVIII-XIX, and which includes, at its center, the

journey to Emmaus. L.A. Hammond describes it: "The scene is
laid in a landscape among green trees, with a battlemented
tower . . . Of the figure of Jesus, standing on the left,
the cross-nimb survives . . . He is dressed as a pilgrim,
brown pilgrim's hat with scallop shell hanging behind His
head, and holding in his right hand a pilgrim's staff, and a
finely patterned wallet at His side . . . a curved scroll
bearing the text . . . '(Qui sunt) hiji: sermones quos: co
(n)fertis: ad: I(n)vice(m): What manner of communications
are these that ye have one to another as ye walk, and are
sad?' (Luke 24.17). Of His companions, the two disciples,
the head of one remains . . . in pilgrim's hat with scallop
shell, and the head of his staff, with a few other
fragments."[21] The window for this glass was built in
Langland's day, the glass added in the century after the
writing of <u>Piers Plowman</u>. The C Text was much circulated in
the Malvern region. Though there is no reason for <u>Piers
Plowman</u> to have influenced either this scriptural depiction
in glass or the carved wood misericord there of the cat hung
by rats of popular beast fable (another such scene is to be
found upon the ceiling at Santo Domingo de Silos), these
artifacts are of iconographical significance to the poem;
they all share in a common culture.[22] Langland, indeed, could
certainly be influenced by such Benedictine drama and by
such Benedictine humor in his writing of Prologue 145-209
and XI.232-242.

Will's garb reflects that of the pilgrim progression of
the <u>Officium Peregrinorum</u>; it alters with the progression of
the poem. We met him first as a vagrant, clad in a sheepskin
cloak, considering himself to be a hermit as he wanders in
Pentecost's Maytide upon Malvern hills. In Passus VIII we met
him "yrobed in russet," like the friars he encounters. In
Passus XVI.172 it is mid-Lenten Sunday, the period of
penitence, and in Passus XVIII, he is therefore "wolleward"
(in <u>Love's Labours Lost</u>, V.ii.717, that phrase referred to
the penitent's garb) upon Palm Sunday, the feast which was
originally the Hebrew pilgrimage of the Tabernacles where
palms were brought to the Temple's altar. Langland's garb
reflects that not only of a pilgrim but of a penitent
expelled from the church on an Ash Wednesday not to return
until Maundy Thursday. Finally, Will, on Easter Sunday, is
in eastern London, not western Malvern, and dressed
"derely," attends Mass with his wife and his child, and sees
Piers there as if Christ.[23]

In Passus XIX, Will sees Piers as at the Resurrection
on Easter Sunday, in his vision, while at Easter Sunday
Mass:

                    sodeynly me mette

> That Piers þe Plowman . was peynted al blody
> And come in wiþ a cros . bifore þe comune people,
> And ri3t lik in alle lymes . to oure lord Iesu.(5-8)

As with Dante's view of God who "mi parve pinta de la nostra
effige" [seemed to me as if painted in our image] (Par.
XXXIII.131), so here does Langland use the word "peynted."
Dante's phraseology probably implies a painting or a mosaic
such as that at St. John Lateran, the image of which is said
to have floated into the Golden Basilica of Constantine at
the dedication and which was revered by pilgrims,[24] and that
of God as Pantocrator in the Baptistery of St. John in
Florence. Langland speaks not of an artifice on apse or dome
but of an actor, Piers as the priest in the role of Christ
in the Easter Officium Peregrinorum, who is dressed first as
a pilgrim and who walks up the nave with the priests acting
the parts of Cleophas and Luke who knew him not, who then
appears to the disciples at Jerusalem (acted by the
choristers within the church's choir) while holding a cross,
his hands, feet and side "peynted al blody," with sanguine
ink, and last, who comes to the actor who plays unbelieving,
Doubting Thomas, likewise often in pilgrim garb, Will's own
role. Will, through this Christian drama of the liturgy,
within his vision sees Piers as like Jesus, just as does the
priest in the Officium Peregrinorum appear before choir and
congregation like the risen Christ. Will, the congregation
and the reader thereby see the imago dei. Petrus id est
Christus, Piers is become as Christ; viator and via are face
to face.

We know from autobiographical remarks that Langland
lived on Cornhill (C.VI.1-101) and that he earned his
family's livelihood, for he was married and had a daughter,
by saying prayers for the dead in return for payment. His
illegitimacy and his marriage would have barred him from the
priesthood, making of him a cleric in minor orders only. As
such a chantry cleric he would have been attached to the
nearest church, which was actually St. Peter's, Cornhill.
Pilgrim texts and maps show that the titular saints were
thought to appear to incubating pilgrims with all their
attributes.[25] When Langland, with his wife and daughter,
attends Easter Mass "derely" dressed, having laid aside his
penitential, Adamic garb, he sees Piers as Christ. It is a
typical thaumaturgical pilgrim vision of the titular saint
of the Cornhill church in his apostolic role of "Petrus, id
est Christus," Peter as Christ, that Will, the pilgrim,
views. The apostles, and above all, Peter, "counterfeited"
Christ and were in his image. Langland has combined pilgrim
vision and pilgrim drama.

In Passus XIII, Conscience, Clergy and Reason dine with
Will. At the door of the palace they meet Pacience dressed
as a pilgrim and who begs them for alms:

> Ac Pacience in þe Paleis stood . in pilgrimes cloþes
> And preyde mete 'pur charite . for a pouere heremyte.'
>   (29-30)

This was the medieval practice. Pilgrims were entitled to
fresh bread, water, lodging and coarse, sober clothing. In
memory of the parable of Dives and Lazarus, Pacience,
therefore, stations himself by the palace gates (46-66). A
fifteenth-century Ship of Fools woodblock shows Lazarus as a
Compostela pilgrim, like Pacience, while Dives has the ass's
ears of a fool for ignoring him (Figure 3). Conscience,
however, appropriately calls him in

>   . and curteisliche seide
> 'Welcome wye, go and wassh . þow shalt sitte soone.'
>   (31-32)

The scene reminds us of the hosting of first Athena and then
Odysseus on Ithaka.

Pacience, at that banquet, speaks of Dowel, Dobet and
Dobest as "Disce, doce, dilige inimicos" (137), to learn, to
teach and to love one's enemies as his lemman, Love, had
once taught him. The learned doctor of the church, presiding
at the feast, promptly accuses Pacience of peregrinate lying
minstrelsy for saying this--though it comes from the
Gospels. Pacience says love can bring peace to Christendom.
The doctor scorns: "'It is but a dido,' quod þis doctour, 'a
disours tale . . . for pilgrimes konne wel lye'"
(XIII.172-178). Perhaps the doctor assumes that Pacience
speaks of love in romance terms, as lust, not charity.
Conscience rises to the challenge, telling the doctor, "'Me
were leuer, by oure lord, and I lyue sholde,/Haue pacience
parfitliche . þan half þi pak of bokes'" (200-201), echoing
Trajan's "'Ye, baw for bokes!!'" (XI.140). Neither minstrelsy
nor books, nor even Piers Plowman speaking of both, is of
use, unless they learn and teach love and truth.

Yet Ymaginatif had told Will that the dialectical
Clergy and Intelligence are as a mirror by which men can
amend their faults, and that they guide learned and
illiterate people. All, Ymaginatif tell Will, is learned
first from books, whether it be logic or law, and men
without them would be as though blinded. However, this
learning, this intertextuality, comes first from God:

> Alþou3 men made bokes . þe maister was god
> And seint Spirit þe Samplarie . & seide what men sholde
>   write.   (XII.101-102)

The Ark in the old law could only be kept by the Levites;
only the clergy could lay hands on that chest (113-114).
Book-despising Trajan, after all, is pagan. <u>Piers Plowman</u>
centers upon such dialectic, contradiction and paradox as
the means by which to present its pilgrim's progress from
folly to wisdom. It presents Janus arguments, <u>ambages</u>, a
double vision, a complementarity, in order to achieve Truth.

Conscience joins Pacience on his pilgrimage, and on
their way, as the two speak of Dowel (again reminiscent of
the disciples journeying to Emmaus speaking of the Passion),
they meet with Haukyn Activa Vita, the minstrel and teller
of lying pilgrim fables. The medieval versions in drama and
verse of the Emmaus tale emphasized the story-telling role
of Christ himself during that journey. Thus, behind the
lying figures of pilgrims telling of fables and minstrelsy
is that first pilgrim and exemplar for all the rest, who had
himself told tales upon the road, Christ who is Truth.

Activa Vita mirrors Will's own pilgrim's progress. Like
Will he is a poet. Unlike Will he is not lazy. He is not a
Malvern pilgrim but a London baker. He is a blend of that
first Piers the Plowman and the unholy hermit, Will; a human
medley of virtue and vice. He trusts in his pardon with its
seals of lead, stamped with "two polles amyddes" (XIII.246),
the heads of St. Peter and St. Paul, relics of the Lateran
Basilica, which he has bought from a priest hoping for
protection from the plague.[26] He fails to realize that such
pardons cannot be bought and sold. Later Langland has the
Samaritan tell Will that the man who is unkind to his fellow
Christian, his "euenecristene," though he does penance and
purchases pardons at Pamplona and Rome, will be damned
(XVII.254-260). The true pardon and the true pilgrimage is
that which Piers has already received from St. Truth in the
Visio, that which Moses has also just received (XVII.1-13)
and that which Book will narrate to Will and the reader
(XVIII.228-257), the life lived in the imitation of Christ,
with love for God and man.

Haukyn Activa Vita is a minstrel and a waferer, a baker
of communion wafers, among others. He speaks of his desire
that the Pope would heal the people from their physical
sickness and plague as had Christ. Then he could feed all
the people, poor as well as rich. He speaks of the Easter
famine of 1370.[27] But he himself has sinned so often, his
coat of Christendom is so spotted and soiled with lies and
tales told in taverns and town and false oaths and boasts,
that Conscience has him confess his misdeeds. Haukyn says of
his carnivalesque minstrelsy, "For tales þat I telle . no

man trusteþ to me" (XIII.332). This we have seen in
Langland's initial description of the pilgrims and palmers
of the Field Full of Folk, in the description of Liar, and
in the doctor's stock response, that pilgrims and minstrels
tell lying tales.

Langland at this point inveighs against sin, in the
form of minstrel tales, and offers his solution, that lords
should have their minstrels be clerics who will tell of
Christ, their jesters be poor blind men, and bedrid women be
their flatterers, for these same beggars "ben goddes
minstrales" (XIII.439). Will had seemed, at Piers Plowman's
beginning, to be a vagrant pilgrim telling lying tales. Now
he himself is revealed authorially, like Francis, as "goddes
minstrale" in his Lenten writing of Dowel, Dobet and Dobest.
To do this Langland makes use of a curious juxtaposition. It
is not normal to find a minstrel who is a cleric, yet he
portrays Will, himself, as such. Nor is it common to find a
Cornhill baker who is also a minstrel. Yet he has Haukyn be
such. The Gospels (Matt 4.3; Luke 4.3; John 6) linked bread
and flesh.[28] The manner in which the Emmaus Pilgrims theme is
handled in medieval drama and poetry show how people were
aware of the analogy of bread with words and the Word.
Langland's poetry ceases to deal with minstrelsy and instead
weaves into his words the preaching of the Word. Langland
becomes "goddes gleman" and "goddes minstrale," his poem,
Haukyn's wafers which feed the faithful as pilgrim manna in
the desert. William Langland is thereby a poet "dignus
operarius cibo suo" [a laborer worthy of his hire]. All of
this is part of the poem's harvest metaphor, from the
ploughing of the Malvern half-acre to London's wheaten
bread.

Langland self-consciously and self-defeatingly builds
up a case for poetry, for pilgrim's tales, for all
minstrelsy, as being turpiloquio. He deconstructs his text.
When he had first described the pilgrims and palmers on the
Field Full of Folk he had mentioned their trait of telling
lying tales (Prologue 46-52). Then at the routing of Mede at
the court of Westminster, he had told of Liar being forced
to flee and go into hiding. At first he is not welcomed "for
his manye tales" (II.220), but the pardoners then have pity
on him and pull him into their houses. They clean him up and
train him to preach in churches with pardons for sale. Next
the doctors seek him out to live with them and aid them in
their craft which they teach him. Then the minstrels get
him:

Ac Mynstrales and Messagers . mette with hym ones
And wiþhelden hym . an half yeer and elleuene dayes.
(II.230-231)

In Passus V Reason had preached to the king, holding in
his hand a cross in iconographic similitude to that later
vision Will will have of Piers as the resurrected Christ at
Mass on Easter Sunday. The sermon prompts the folk to
confess and the confessions of the Vices follow. Accidie or
Sloth is afraid because romances are more memorable to him
than are prayers:

> I kan no3t parfitly my Paternoster . as þe preest it
>   syngeþ
> But I kan rymes of Robyn hood . and Randolf Erl of
>   Chestre,
> Ac neiþer of oure lord ne of oure lady . þe leeste þat
>   euere was maked.   (V.394-6)

The same comment had been made by Deguileville of
Ydelnesse's preoccupation with romances. So also had Dante
had Paolo and Francesca's sin and murder be wrought by
idleness and the reading of romances, in an inversion of
Augustine's bookish conversion.[29] What we have here is a
self-referentiality within the text to reader response,
presenting a spectrum of such textual reception.

Sloth continues:

> I am occupied eche day . halyday and ooþer,
> With ydel tales at þe Ale . and ouþerwhile in chirches;
> Goddes peyne and his passion . pure selde þenke I on.
>   (402-406)

The argument concerning minstrelsy, as of turpiloquio
where it merely entertains its audience with lying tales, as
godly where it narrates of the Gospels, is to be found
throughout Piers Plowman. It reflects upon Will, who is
reflected in turn in the figure of Sloth, the manuscript
illuminations of the sleeping Will and the sleeping Sloth
equating the one figure with the other (Plate Xb). Sloth,
similarly, for his penance vows to go on pilgrimage, not to
Rome, but to Truth (V.460), though he had earlier described
himself as a lover of "ydel tales" (403). He will now
reform. That reform is an indictment of the idle
tale-telling pilgrimage to Rome which engenders more lies
than truth.

In Passus X, Langland speaks of the minstrels who
delight wealthy lords at their banquets. These lords reward
harlots for their harlotry, "Iaperis and Iogelours and
Iangleris of gestes," with gifts of worldly goods (30-31).
Langland bitterly adds:

> Ac he þat haþ holy writ , ay in his mouþe
> And kan tell of Tobye . and of þe twelue Apostles

> Or prechen of þe penaunce . þat Pilate wro3te
> To Iesu þe gentile . þat Iewes todrowe
> On cros vpon caluarye . as clerkes vs techeþ,
> Litel is he loued or lete by . þat swich a lesson
>   techeþ.   (32-37)

The banquets are nothing but "lecherie, losengerie and
losels tales; Glotonye and grete oþes" (50-51). Meanwhile
the hungry wait at the gate, like Pacience the pilgrim at
the palace door, like Lazarus at Dives' great mansion. The
tale that the pilgrim Christ told, the parable of Dives
and Lazarus, is reflected in the tale Langland tells of
Holichirche and Mede. The lying tales about greed teach
charity and truth. Thus had St. Thomas Aquinas in the Summa
contra Gentiles and the Summa Theologiae taught, by means of
lies, true doctrine, giving equal time to each in the
epistemology presented to the reader of the text and thus
permitting the reader to choose and choose aright, according
to the freedom, rather than bondage, of the will.

It is when speaking to Anima, the most inward part of
his being, and the closest to Truth, that Will comes to
understand that therein, as Holichirche and Piers had told
him, is the shrine of Truth and Charity that he seeks. He
had not found it where he went to school with diverse and
external teachers. Nor was it present amidst the minstrelsy
of the world. In the Visio, Holichirche had spoken of Truth
and Charity as residing within, in the soul. She had also
said:

> For who is trewe of his tonge . telleþ noon ooþer,
> Dooþ þe werkes þerwiþ . and wilneþ no man ille,
> He is a god by þe gospel . a grounde and o lofte,
> And ek ylik to oure lord . by Seint Lukes wordes
>   (I.88-91)

The other paths down which Will wanders are the false
directions he takes. "Heu michi quia sterilem duxi vitam
Iuuenilem" [Woe is me for the useless life I led as a youth]
(142). Dante had also observed this to be the trait of the
adolescent, the wandering in the wood of vices, unable at
first to find the true direction. This behavior is
symptomatic of the diseased Will, brought about by the Fall,
causing each man to recapitulate the Adamic wanderings in
the wood and in the desert of the wilderness's pilgrimage
and be exposed there to the temptation of the world, the
flesh and the devil.

We see that historical replication occur before our
eyes in the interior vision of the Tree of Charity. In
Passus XVI we have Anima tell Will of this tree. In the B
Text it is known as "Trinite"; in the C Text it is found in

the country "Corhominis" and is "highte Ymago-dei," its
fruit, "Caritas" (XIX.4-14). Piers is to guard it and at
that name, Will swoons into the inner vision where he meets
Piers who explains the allegory of the tree propped by three
poles, the power of the Father, the wisdom of the Son and
the will of the Spirit, against the world, the flesh and the
devil. But man, because his will is free, chooses to sin by
his will, and is left in the snares of the enemies. Will, in
a mirroring of that first event where Adam sinned, asks
Piers to cast him down an apple. Piers, as did God at the
Fall, assents. The devil gathers up the fallen fruit, souls
of the dead who were "strangers and pilgrims" on earth,
Adam, Abraham, Isaiah, Samson, Samuel and St. John the
Baptist, but Piers, "for pure tene," in an echoing of his
Mosaic tearing of the Pardon, here grasps the pole of the
Son and chases the devil to get back the stolen fruit.[30]

Both Dante and Langland cause their readers to
participate in sin by having their Everyman authorial
personae, in the one case, be asked by Virgil to pluck the
twigs of the vine/bramble tree that is punningly the
suicide Pier delle Vigne, in the other ask Piers to pull
down an apple from the tree that grows in the country the
B Text says "liberum arbitrium" [free will] has to farm.
Poets in both cases lead them astray. Both incidents fill
the authorial personae and the reader with horror and guilt
at the consequences of these thoughtless acts. This is
reader reponse and reception with a vengeance.

Piers Plowman is a speculum peregrinorum, a mirror for
pilgrims. Where the pilgrimage is inadequate, the pilgrim
readers comes upon an inadequate goal, meeting that face to
face, instead of the face of God. This occurs where Langland
has his pilgrims on the plain meet the "paynym" pilgrim who
has traveled everywhere and learned nothing. Where the
education is completed, the mirroring is true rather than
false, and Will no longer views his own and imperfect
double, in Thought, Wit and others, but Piers in the
likeness of Christ. The poem presents these images of Will
in a pilgrim progression, at first Adamic, unsatisfying and
inadequate, but then fulfilled. Will's life in its waking
state is vagrant and literal; in his dreams he quests Piers,
his pilgrim saint, and at last in "Pask wyke" finds him in
his soul in his own and Christ's image.[31]

At the same time there are two geographic landscapes:
the waking one is England's and of the fourteenth century;
the visionary one is Biblical and of all time. The one
commences at Malvern and concludes in London, the other
begins upon the Egyptian wilderness of Exodus progressing

toward Israel, and concludes with Jerusalem's Pentecost.
Thus Will within western England attains eastern and Easter
Jerusalem.[32]

At the poem's Pentecostal ending, which is close to an
Apocalypse, Will lies dying. Therefore Conscience resolves
to go on pilgrimage:

> 'By crist!' quod Conscience þo . 'I wole bicome a
>   pilgryme,
> And wenden as wide as . þe world renneþ
> To seken Piers þe Plowman.   (XX.380-382)

This resolution to be a Pascal pilgrim and Langland's waking
conclude the poem. The poem has been circular with beginning
and ending, alpha and omega, having pilgrimage as its motif,
though that first authorial pilgrim is, like Luke at Emmaus,
unaware of his pilgrimage, while the second has come to
understand his quest and know his goal. Piers Plowman, like
Dante's pilgrim Commedia, returns its reader, at its ending,
back to its beginning. Will is now metamorphosed as
Conscience, who can journey with wisdom, instead of with
folly.

CHAPTER FIVE: "UNBOKELED IS THE MALE"

The "Book of the Tales of Canterbury" begins under the
zodiacal sign of Aries or of Taurus. Chaucer elsewhere tells
us that in that season the world began and Adam was made by
God (VII.3187-3188). Dante called Aries the "dolce stagion"
[the sweet season], for at that time not only was Adam
created, though he fell, but Christ was crucified, then
resurrected, redeeming mankind.[1] The <u>Canterbury Tales</u> is
in three parts, Prologue, Fables and Sermon. It uses themes
of Emmaus, astrology and alchemy and knits these together by
means of the concept of the poet as "soules leche," as
physician to the soul. Both Chaucer and Luke write pilgrim
fables and sermons--and Luke, moreover, is a physician.

It opens with an Adamic vision, an English Genesis,
seen through the senses, with the Gregorian eyes of the
body:

    Whan that Aprill with his shoures soote
    The droghte of March hath perced to the roote,
    And bathed every veyne in swich licour
    Of which vertu engendred is the flour;
    Whan Zephirus eek with his sweete breeth
    Inspired hath in every holt and heeth
    The tendre croppes, and the yonge sonne
    Hath in the Ram his halve cours yronne,
    And smale foweles maken melodye,
    That slepen al the nyght with open ye.

The fallen reader shares in the unfallen vision from the
beginning of time. But then Chaucer's text pivots upon the
line, "So priketh hem nature in hir corages," and is changed
from a corporeal, priapic and prelapsarian vision to one of
the Gregorian eyes of the heart, to the insight of
redemption from the fall through pilgrimage to their
Christlike saint.[2]

> Thanne longen folk to goon on pilgrimages,
> And palmeres for to seken straunge strondes
> To ferne halwes, kowthe in sondry londes;
> And specially from every shires ende
> Of Engelond to Caunterbury they wende,
> The hooly blisful martir for to seke
> That hem hath holpen whan that they were seeke.(I.1-18)

Thus England's martyr and England's poet can restore English pilgrims and readers upon their progress to lost Eden.

Pilgrimage, essentially, was imitation, the imitation of the saint one sought, who in turn imitated Christ. The Codex Calixtinus states that pilgrims to Santiago imitate that saint since St. James, the first apostle to suffer martyrdom, was closest in imitation to Christ. That imitation is borne out in the iconography of Saint and Compostela pilgrim who mirror each other with their "cockle hat and staff and [their] sandal shoon." St. Andrew was famous for his adoration of Christ's cross, to be mirrored in his own crucifixion, and St. Jerome wrote, "nudum crucem nudus sequens" [naked, following the naked cross], Renaissance artists portraying him in penitential nudity before a crucifix.[3] England's imitation of Christ was Thomas Martyr who was born in worldly London and who died in holy Canterbury. Thus, in imitation of his vita, which imitates that of Christ, these pilgrims journey from London, the place of his birth, to Canterbury, the site of his martyrdom. Only where their imitation is a true one, can they gain salus, both salvation and healing.

Their pilgrimage begins, as did the vita Christi, at an inn:

> Bifil that in that seson on a day,
> In Southwerk at the Tabard as I lay
> Redy to wenden on my pilgrimage
> To Caunterbury with ful devout corage,
> At nyght was come into that hostelrye
> Wel nyne and twenty in a compaignye,
> Of sondry folk, by aventure yfalle
> In felaweshipe, and pilgrimes were they alle,
> That toward Caunterbury wolden ryde,
> The chaumbres and the stables weren wyde,
> And wel we weren esed atte best.   (19-20)

Christ was born in the stable of an inn. He traveled on a pilgrimage with his disciples to an inn supper at Emmaus. This pilgrimage begins at an inn and its stables are stressed. It is to end with an inn's "soper at oure aller cost" (I.799). Chaucer is thinking of both the vita Christi

and of Gregory's <u>Moralia</u>. Samuel Purchas phrases the first
in this manner:

> Christ indeed vouchsafed, even in literall sense, to
> honour peregrinations in his owne person, whose blessed
> Mother . . . is by Caesars Edict brought . . . that in
> an Inne at Bethlehem, this Pilgrime might in a
> Pilgrimage bee borne . . . . And there from a remote
> place by Pilgrimes of the East is he visited; and how
> soone is his infancy forced to an Egyptian
> peregrination? How restlesse and manifold were his
> after-peregrinations . . . . But my Pen is unworthy to
> follow his foot-prints.[4]

Deguileville had already written his <u>Pèlerinage Jhesucrist</u>
in which he traces the <u>vita</u> as if it were a pilgrimage.[5]
Gregory's <u>Moralia</u> permeated the Christian west and was
popular among pilgrims. We hear of Jerusalem pilgrims
carrying it in their luggage along with a Bible. It states
that the human soul is a <u>viator</u> who lodges at an inn, the
<u>stabula</u>, but who yearns to reach the heavenly city. Were he
to become too attached to bodily comforts at the inn--"The
chaumbres and the stables weren wyde, And wel we weren esed
atte beste"--he will lose his eternal reward. True pilgrims
consider themselves alien to the world and are eager to set
forth "ad coelestis patriae" [of thilke parfit glorious
pilgrymage/ That highte Jerusalem celestial].[6]   Chaucer,
the <u>Canterbury Tales</u> pilgrim, lingered all day long seeking
worldly companionship and was thus benighted at the Tabard.
The Inn's name, the "Tabard," recalls yet another such
classic, and not really Christian, commonplace, in which
clothing represents the body imprisoning the soul in its
bonds. The Gregorian allegory makes the concept of the inn,
the <u>stabula</u>, one that is negative and profane; the <u>vita
Christi</u> makes it positive and sacred. This contradiction
shapes pilgrimage's many paradoxes. It is central not only
to the Emmaus theme, but also to the <u>Canterbury Tales</u>.

Chaucer is aware of these traditions. In a lyric he
addresses to his friend, Sir Phillip de la Vache (whose
punning name, according to Edith Rickert, he uses in the
poem), we find a Chaucer who is the very opposite of our
pilgrim Chaucer seeking worldly <u>compaignie</u> at the Tabard Inn
with its wide chambers and stables and who lingers there all
day. In the "Balade to Truth" Chaucer tells us to "Flee fro
the prees," and declares:

> Her is no hoom, her nis but wildernesse:
> Forth, pilgrim forth! Forth, beste, out of thy stal!
> Know thy contree, look up, thank God of al;
> Holde the heye wey, and lat thy gost thee lede,

And trouthe thee shal delivere, it is no drede. (17-21)

"Vache" means cow. Chaucer in the Envoy humorously declares,
"Therefore, thou Vache, leve thyn old wrecchednesse,"
exhorting him to quit his stable and seek instead that
pilgrimage to Truth. It is probable that Chaucer wrote his
"Balade to Truth"'s Envoy to Wycliffite Vache at a time when
his friend was out of favor at court. Chaucer blends
together a wealth of classic commonplaces concerning inns
and stables and clothing as the body opposing the pilgrim
soul, likewise the body as beast, the soul as rider, with
Boethian patterns of consolation, Exodus imagery and I Peter
2.11. It ends with the punning promise of "hevenliche mede"
if this "vache" will follow "trouthe," a "mede" identified
by J.F. Ragan not only as "reward" but playfully also as
"meadow," in which Vache can graze forever.[7]

Dante's Commedia and Langland's Piers Plowman, both
vision poems, carefully contrast carnal pilgrimages to the
itinerarium mentis in deum, the quest within for St. Truth.
Chaucer, instead, presents carnal pilgrims journeying to a
"corsaint," Thomas Becket, as if in real space and time, at
Lenten tide; the night at the Tabard being, possibly, Maundy
Thursday, the Knight's Tale narrated on Good Friday, the
Parson's Sermon on Easter Sunday, and the pilgrimage going
from London to Canterbury, England's Jerusalem. We are
tricked into believing in the flesh and blood reality of
these "sondry folk." Yet we have evidence that the portraits
of the Canterbury Tales General Prologue are more absurd
than real, though they may caricature Chaucer's real
acquaintances in life.

Isidore defined ironia as "when we praise that which we
would blame, and we blame that which we would praise."[8]
Chaucer the foolish pilgrim in the Prologue blames in his
fellow pilgrims that which Chaucer the wise poet would
praise and foolishly praises that which he would wisely
blame. The Canterbury Tales begins at a profane inn and ends
with a sacred sermon. It begins with a distorted perspective
of ironia, that mirrors the folly of Luke at Emmaus, and
ends with one that is true. Like the Commedia and Piers
Plowman, it too is a Janus poem, a "twice-told tale," of a
world "up-so-doun" until its ending.

The Canterbury Tales is the greatest depiction of
medieval pilgrims we possess. By it we have falsely tended
to measure all others. Because we have done so we have
failed to see in it that medieval ironia that had already
fashioned the mock pilgrimages of the Roman de Renart and
the Roman de la Rose. Pilgrims gained no spiritual benefit

from their pilgrimages if they rode on horseback; nor were
friars, according to their rules, permitted to ride. Monks
and nuns, by council after council, were prohibited from
performing physical pilgrimages, theirs being the interior
one of the cloistered life of prayer and psalm. Further
problems are found in the text and, though they seem subtle
to us, the Ellesmere illuminators understood them well and
added to the portraits similar details, not even found in
the text yet part and parcel of Chaucer's outrageous joking
upon false pilgrimage.

The pilgrim Chaucer tells us that the Knight has just
returned from the Crusades, and that therefore his clothing
is travel-stained and shabby. He offers excuses for the
Knight's poverty of dress. However, though the world might
despise the Knight's simplicity, true pilgrims would not.
The Ellesmere illuminator captures that paradox by garbing
the Knight in somber clothes, yet having his cloth be cut
with elegance. Such a crusading knight realistically would
return to London by disembarking at the great seaport of
Dover. What is he doing riding from London to Canterbury
when Canterbury lay on the route from Dover to London? Nor
does our Knight, though St. Thomas was the Crusaders'
patron, need the Canterbury indulgence he seeks when he has
gained so many shedding Christian and heathen blood on
"straunge strondes" (I.13). The description of his Crusades
is filled with the oppositions of "As wel in cristendom as
in hethenesse" (I.49). At times he is a mercenary in the pay
of the "paynym," at others a true crusader. Similarly his
tale is of doubleness, of idolatrous "paynyms" enacting
Christian drama. The poverty of his dress is that of a
Lollard knight, who would take seriously the apostolic and
peregrinate injunctions concerning simplicity, though his
horse in text and illumination is magnificent. The Ellesmere
shows the beast as bearing the brand of a mitre as from a
London episcopal livery stable or as belonging to the Order
of St. Thomas of Canterbury's knights hospitallers.[9]
Joinville, friend of St. Louis, walked on his pilgrimage
barefoot when embarking on Crusade. Our Knight, upon his
return from Crusade, rides.

Professional crusading knights, in contrast to
Joinville, were generally of monastic, though military,
orders and therefore were vowed to celibacy. The English
Knights of St. Thomas of Canterbury were such an order. Only
the Spanish Knights of St. James were permitted to
marry.[10] Our Knight appears to be such a monkish crusader,
yet rides with his son. The young Squire, whose legitimacy
has been called into question, flouts the conventions of
pilgrimage as he rides to Canterbury, flauting love songs,

dressed in rich embroidery, upon a prancing steed.[11]
Pilgrims were, after all, meant to journey on foot to the
shrines, they sought to be dressed in simple and rough
clothing that set them apart from the world, and to abstain
from fleshly lusts that, Peter tells us, war against the
pilgrim soul. The Squire appears to think his pilgrimage is
to Venus, not to Christ, and that he inhabits the Roman de
la Rose and not the Canterbury Tales, yet Chaucerians have
noted parallels between his portrait and Chaucer's own
biography as such a young squire.[12]

The Monk and the Prioress similarly seem to think that
pilgrimage is to Venus rather than Christ. Both sport
worldly jewelry indicative of the lechery they ideally
should, as separately cloistered monks and nuns, especially
spurn. The General Prologue's ordering has the two ride side
by side. The Prioress' "brooch of gold ful sheene,/ On which
there was first write a crowned A/ And after Amor vincit
omnia" (160-162), couples her with the Monk's adornment, "of
gold ywroght a ful curious pyn;/ a love-knotte in the
gretter end" (196-197). Neither the Prioress nor the Monk
were permitted to journey on pilgrimage and certainly not
lecherously together. The Prioress' literary progenitors are
the Roman de la Rose' Papelardie and Abstynaunce, the latter
an anti-pilgrim who set forth in ecclesiastical garb with
her lemman, the friar Faussemblant, both sporting forbidden
scrips and staves (Plate IVa). The Monk's more spiritual
descendant is Daun John Lydgate of Bury St. Edmund's who,
in writing The Seige of Thebes as sequel to the Canterbury
Tales, must include himself upon that pilgrimage there,
though monks were forbidden to be pilgrims. He lamely
excuses his presence by describing himself as the opposite
of Chaucer's Monk; thin, where Chaucer's was fat from
eating the kingly fare of roast swan; poorly clad, where
Chaucer's was resplendent with lavish fur-lined sleeves;
pious, where Chaucer's was worldly.[13]

In contrast to the Prioress and the Monk, the Friar was
permitted to travel about. The mendicant and fraternal
orders revived peregrinatio after centuries of monastic
suppression of pilgrimage amongst the clergy. However,
Chaucer's Friar flaunts his lewd departure from the ideal.
The Ellesmere illuminator goes even further than does
Chaucer's General Prologue in placing in the Friar's hand
that pilgrim staff the angered Summoner will give to him in
his Tale (III.1737, and in which he is also awarded the
forbidden scrip) and upon his feet the illuminator paints
enormous shoes, while having him ride horseback. St. Francis
forbade his friars staves, scrips, shoes and horses.
Summoners, likewise, were forbidden to ride on
horseback.[14]

We then have the contrasting pair of the rich Merchant and the poor Clerk. The Ellesmere shows the one in flowered scarlet, the other in sober grey riding to Canterbury with books of black and red beneath his arm (Plate Xd). The Merchant can be envisioned upon such a pilgrimage, which the Shipman's Tale elucidates as an excellent device for avoiding paying out capital while it is gaining interest, though in contradiction to Chaucerian text canon law required that all debts be paid before making a pilgrimage and forbade usury (VII.233-234).[15]   The Clerk, were he to have interrupted his studies, would have walked to Canterbury in piety and thus saved his horse hire for books. They are of different worlds, of wealth, of poverty, yet the Wife's marriages to rich merchants and poor clerks link them together. The Pardoner and the Wife, the Friar and the Wife, the Summoner and the Wife, and Pardoner and the Summoner, the Summoner and the Friar, are each with the other full curiously "ywroght" with knots of lust and hate. The Physician, the Wife and the Parson seemingly ride together. The Wife and the Pardoner are professional pilgrims. Yet both, according to the Ellesmere, are garbed not in the white or undyed wool of pilgrimage, but in sinful scarlet. On them that color means the opposite than it had on the saintly Parson.

The Ellesmere shows the Physician in his furred red robes riding all the way to Canterbury examining a half-full glass urinal held aloft against the light (Plate XIb). One remembers, in the Canterbury Speculum Stultorum, Burnellus accidentally breaking the glass bottles of medicine he had procured from the Salerno doctors at great cost. Our London physician journeys to the "soules leche" of Canterbury, Thomas Becket. The Parson and his brother, the Plowman, represent the ideal of the clergy and the laity. Yet what are either of these men doing on pilgrimage to Canterbury when they ought to remain in their parish, their labor and their prayer being their true pilgrimage? The Ellesmere garbs the Parson in the medieval parish priest's scarlet dress. On him it is correct, representing the priestly imitatio Christi, who has taken upon himself the sins of his flock (Rev. 7.14); he is like Langland's Piers, "peynted al blody/ And come in wiþ a cros . bifore the comune peple,/ And ri3t like in alle lymes . to our lord Iesu" (B.XIX.6-8).[16]   The Ellesmere shows him riding to Canterbury with his hands not on his horse's reins but improbably crossed upon his breast, as if in a cavalier's version of pilgrimage's imitatio Christi. Our Parson, according to apostolic teaching, had no right to ride on horseback though he can, in imitation of Christ, ride an ass

into Canterbury (X.434). His presence on horseback on the
Canterbury pilgrimage, in realistic terms, is nonsensical;
in thematic terms his presence there will be essential and
since Chaucer mounts all his pilgrims, the good with the
bad, the false with the true, we find him thus rather than
as in his General Prologue portrait in which he visits "The
ferreste in his parisshe . . . /Upon his feet, and in his
hand a staf" as true pilgrim and true pastor (494-495).[17]
Moreover the portraits of the Parson and the Plowman are
strongly Wyclifite. Wyclif, like Piers the Plowman, saw
pilgrimage as honest labor.

The Miller and the Reeve are again a part of the
interlocking pattern of the General Prologue and the
Canterbury Tales. The Miller leads the pilgrims out of
London, not to Christlike Becket, but, with his bagpipes,
surely to Venus. Bagpipes had, in the Middle Ages, the same
connotation as had Amant's pilgrim scrip and staff with
which that doughty hero raped his Rose. The Reeve rides ever
the "hyndreste." In other aspects these figures are
carefully contrasted. The Miller is stout, the Reeve lean;
the Miller young, the Reeve old. The Miller appears by his
oaths to St. Thomas of Kent to be a southerner; the Reeve is
a northerner. The Miller tells a tale of Oxford and of a
carpenter; this angers the Reeve who was once a carpenter
and he tells a tale of Cambridge and of a cuckolded miller.
The symmetrical brawl is again unrealistic. We know that no
more than three horsemen could ride abreast to Canterbury.
The Reeve would not have even heard, at the tail end of the
cavalcade, the tale the Miller tells at its head ten horse
lengths away. The Ellesmere illuminator takes care to show
"Robyn" with the bagpipes and adds even the thumb of gold to
the illumination, while for the Reeve he adds the grim touch
of great keys to his belt that remind the reader of the keys
of the final Doomsday harvest, keys that lock the gates of
hell upon the damned. The Reeve is a saturnine figure in
contrast to the Miller's joviality in Chaucer's astronomy
and corresponding alchemy. Miller and Reeve, Pardoner and
Summoner, on secular and clerical planes, mirror patterns of
licentiousness and punishment.

We know from a fifteenth-century ecclesiastical
examination of a Lollard that medieval pilgrims sometimes
traveled to Canterbury to the accompaniment of bagpipes.
William Thorpe complained to Thomas Arundell, Archbishop of
Canterbury:

Also, Sir, I know well, that when divers men and women
will go thus after their own wills, and finding out one
pilgrimage, they will ordain with them before to have
with them both men and women that can well sing wanton

songs; and some other pilgrims will have with them
bagpipes; so that every town that they come through,
what with the noise of their singing, and with the
sound of their piping, and with the jangling of their
Canterbury bells, and with the barking of dogs after
them, they make more noise than if the King came their
way, with all his clarions and many other minstrels.
And if these men and women be a month out in their
pilgrimage, many of them shall be a half year after,
great janglers, tale-tellers, and liars. [18]

Thorpe in this statement attempts to blacken pilgrimage to
the greatest extent he can since, as a Lollard, he does not
hold with physical pilgrimages to shrines but instead with
"true pilgrims travelling towards the bliss of heaven,"
whose pilgrimages are their virtuous lives. Both Chaucer and
Thorpe draw upon an orthodox theological tradition that had
looked askance at superficial pilgrimage for centuries.

Opposing Thorpe is the worldly Archbishop whom
Thorpe--with damning _ironia_--describes as saying:

"Lewd losell! thou seest not far enough in this matter!
for thou considerest not the great travail of pilgrims;
therefore thou blamest that thing that is praisable! I
say to thee, that it is right well done; that pilgrims
have with them both singers and also pipers; that when
one of them that goeth barefoot striketh his toe upon a
stone and hurteth him sore and maketh him to bleed; it
is well done, that he or his fellow, begin then a song
or else take out of his bosom a bagpipe for to drive
away with such mirth, the hurt of his fellow. For with
such solace, the travail and weariness of pilgrims is
lightly and merrily brought forth."

The dialectical dispute continues between the two of them,
William stating that Paul asked Christians instead "to weep
with them that weep," the Archbishop replying that David
advocated minstrelsy, William, that Christ put "out the
minstrels, ere that he would quicken the dead damsel." The
Archbishop next states that the church's instruments and
songs sharpen men's wits better than do sermons setting
forth God's Word, to which William replies that Jerome said:
"Nobody may joy with this world, and reign with Christ."
Thorpe has placed within the Archbishop's mouth words which
are counter to Church doctrine; in his own, true teaching.

The problem is whether Chaucer or Thorpe truly describe
pilgrimage as it was enacted in the Middle Ages. Certainly,
granted the meaning bagpipes had in the Middle Ages, their

use in Chaucer's text augurs ill. They were not merely from their shape, and from the jokes played with that in manuscripts' marginalia grotesques, considered symbols of lust; to them was attached the opprobrium wind instruments merited in Boethius' De Musica, where, in contrast to the harp which represented reason, bagpipes represented folly. [19] The pilgrims' forbidden horses, likewise, from the Platonic commonplace, represented the body in contrast to the rider as soul. Illuminations of actual Compostela pilgrims in a fifteenth-century Book of Hours show most of them on foot, even barefoot; only two married couples together ride one horse and these may not be pilgrims. The Monk's jangling Canterbury bells upon his horse's bridle further condemn his figure. He is forbidden horse and hunt and pilgrimage, yet the Ellesmere shows his steed, his bells and his fair hounds.

Pilgrimage poetry is as a progress from folly to wisdom. The Emmaus pattern had Christ chide the two disciple pilgrims: "O stulti" [O fools] (Luke 24.25). To present that pilgrim folly Chaucer makes use of Ovid and Boethius. From Ovid he borrows the rhetoric of ironia, in which reader and poet collude. From Boethius he borrows the persona who is initially foolish in his responses to Philosophia's arguments; while Boethius proper with profound wisdom manipulates his reader towards consolation by means of this doubleness of persona and poet, of fiction and fact. Chaucer welds the apprentice in Philosophy that is Boethius' persona to the apprentice in Amor of Ovid's persona to create a persona who is an apprentice pilgrim, inept, in progress and not yet parfit. [20]

Chaucer gives us a satirical General Prologue that pretends to be as if written by the young, naive and poetic Squire, the apprentice to the crusading and "perfect" Knight. Such a courtly adolescent would measure men by their outward clothing, rather than by searching within for their true being. The Prologue's "poet" is not yet proficient in rhetorical protocol, praising seeming virtues, which Chaucer and the reader know to be vices, and despising seeming vices--such as poverty--which the reader and Chaucer know to be pilgrim virtues. (Similarly the Roman de la Rose banished poverty from her garden, showing her sculpted upon the outside of its wall.) Matthew de Vendôme noted that a man's attributes were to be described "according to the body and according to the soul," and that praise or blame was to be meted out "ab anima" [according to the soul]. [21] Gregory had already, in connection with the Emmaus pilgrim tale, spoken of the eyes of the body and of the soul. Chaucer's persona, who cannot yet "weel purtreye and write" (I.96),

metes out praise for supposed qualities of the soul which
are in reality mere outward, physical and material splendor.
The effect of this is that _ironia_ in which what is
praiseworthy is blamed and what is blameworthy is praised.
Of the Monk's desire for the pursuit of venery, rather than
of cloistered chastity, Chaucer _persona_ falls over himself
in declaring, "And I seyde his opinion was good" (183-187)
and more, in misguided approval of the Monk's great
worldliness. Yet some Christlike figures do break through,
just as with the foolish fabling pilgrims on the road to
Emmaus, recognition is almost achieved, "Nonne cor nostrum
ardens erat in nobis dum loqueretur in via?" [Did not our
heart burn within us, while he talked with us by the way?]
(Luke 24.32). The portraits of the ideal Knight, the Clerk,
the Parson and the Plowman are such recognitions, in which
the wisdom of the _oculis cordis_, of the heart's eyes,
perceives the truth though the folly of the _oculis corporis_,
the eyes of the body, would conceal it. The fabling on the
road to Canterbury will seem to be to the idol Venus, but
will be found to be to Christ.

The _Canterbury Tales_ begins at the Tabard Inn. We can
take this literally as would the young Squire. Or we can
take it allegorically as did Chaucer in his "Balade to
Truth." From this Inn the cavalcade sets forth as portrayed
by this Squirish pen. We watch it pass on its way to
Canterbury from the Tabard under the light of the sun. Then
we are suddenly jolted back with the realization that our
apprentice pilgrim poet of folly, stumbling over his
ill-learned rhetorical flourishes, has erred again. The
pilgrims are not pilgrims in the daylight journeying to holy
Canterbury as we had been led to believe. The _hysteron
proton_ has them still be slothful guests in the wide
chambers and stables of the Tabard at their ease, in stasis,
benighted from their goal, and no one has pilgrimly
progressed forth on the journey (I.715-724). "Che va col
cuore e col corpo dimora" [The heart may have advanced, but
the body has stayed] (_Purg_.II.11-12). Our suspicions,
aroused by the sophistries of the Ovidian rhetoric, are now
confirmed. We can either say this is due to Chaucer
persona's apprentice craft. Or we can say this is Chaucer
the pilgrim poet, in control of his material, though
seemingly not so, and showing how woefully inadequate these
pilgrims as pilgrims are. Even the work's title is
untrustworthy for they never do attain Canterbury. On the
morrow the Canterbury pilgrims are to be given another
chance--though it is with reprehensible fables and to
folly's bagpipes that they will sally forth. Luke, in the
medieval tradition, though the wise Gospeler, was thought to
show himself and Cleophas as foolish pilgrims.

J. Hillis Miller has written of the critic as host and
noted that that word meant not only host but also guest, not
only friend but also enemy. [22]   Chaucer's Host, likewise,
presents such ambiguities. He is the Host of the Inn in the
General Prologue who becomes the guest of his guests in
offering to guide their pilgrimage to Canterbury and in
their acceptance of his offer. He thereby makes of the
Canterbury pilgrimage a peripatetic Tabard Inn. Upon the
road the provisions are not so much cakes and ale as tales
told to wile away the journey. At their conclusion, in the
third part of this poem, is a sermon, as it were a "soper at
oure aller cost,' of bread and wine. Inns, pilgrimages,
tales, sermons and suppers are likewise characteristic of
the Emmaus patterning. In French versions of the play the
character of the Host assumed considerable dramatic
importance. [23]   At Emmaus, according to medieval tradition,
Christ had unbuckled his scrip and unstopppered his bottle to
give to his disciples bread and wine for their meal at an
inn. Similarly a major theme of the Canterbury Tales is that
of the unbuckling of pilgrim scrips from which first fables,
then sermons, emerge. The Canterbury Tales, like Piers
Plowman, seems to be a triad, in this case, of inn, then
pilgrimage, then cathedral, which proves instead to be a
unity, in which fables are sermons, Tabard and Inn and
taverns, temples and cathedrals, London, Canterbury, the
pilgrim road, "up-so-doun," that the pilgrimage not be by
feet, or horse, alone, but within. To the Emmaus patterning
Chaucer adds those of sickness and healing, another aspect
of pilgrimage, and one especially prevalent in fourteenth-
century plague-tide.

Chaucer's General Prologue lists the pilgrims as so
many dramatis personae. That tradition was extant in the
Middle Ages where manuscripts of the plays of Terence showed
the actors' masks hanging on racks and listed their names by
them. [24]   Then, in the Knight's Tale, Chaucer has Theseus
construct a classic pagan theatre replete with idols for
that tale's tragi-comic tourney. Chaucer's Tales begin with
an emphasis upon pagan idolatry while closest to London as
if to stress this as a region of poetic appearance rather
than pilgrim truth. It will end with a penitential sermon
from which lying poetry is banished when closest to Canterbury. Chaucer's Knight's Tale is a rewriting of Boccaccio's
Teseida, which in turn is a rewriting of Statius' Thebaid
XII, the vernacular Teseida metamorphosing the tragedy of
the Latin Thebaid into comedy. (Shakespeare will, in turn,
metamorphose all these works intertextually into his
Midsummer Night's Dream.) It is evident that Chaucer has
both works, the Latin and the Italian (the latter perhaps in
the French version) at his elbow as he writes. Statius'

Thebaid recounts the strife wrought by Eteocles and
Polynices in Thebes which is put down by Athenian Theseus.
Augustine in the City of God, linking Latin poetry and
Hebrew scriptures, saw parallels in the fraternal strife
between Eteocles and Polynices, Cain and Abel, Romulus and
Remus, and related all these to Babylon and Jerusalem, exile
and pilgrimage. Pseudo-Fulgentius wrote a brief allegory
upon the Thebaid in which Thebes was seen as "mankind,'
Theseus as "Theos," God. Thebes and Athens, Carthage and
Rome, were as analogies for Babylonian confusion and
Jerusalem's vision of peace, the visio pacis.[25] Dante used
the name of Theseus where he cannot use that of Christ in
the infernal pages to refer, "per speculum in aenigmate"
[through a glass darkly], to Christ's Harrowing of Hell.
Boccaccio in his sequel to Statius' Thebaid created the
figures of Arcites and Palaemon as types of Eteocles and
Polynices. All these concepts are present in Chaucer's text.
They are still to be present in Lydgate's Canterbury Tales'
continuation, The Seige of Thebes.

Chaucer gives to Theseus an enigmatic version of the
Oriflamme of the Crusades in describing him with a banner
and a pennant:

> The rede statue of Mars, with spere and targe,
> So shyneth in his white baner large,
> That alle the feeldes glyteren up and down;
> And by his baner born is his penoun
> Of gold ful riche, in which there was ybete
> The Mynotaur, which that he slough in Crete.
>
> (I.975-980)

These banners are neither in the Teseida nor in the Thebaid.
They are present in the version told by the crusading
Knight, who would have been familiar with the French banner
of the Oriflamme of St. Denis, of gold and red, and the
English banner of St. George, who slew the dragon, a red
cross upon a white ground, which was likewise the standard
Christ bore at the Harrowing of Hell and in the Officium
Peregrinorum. Here Mars' insignia recalls Dante's
condemnation of Florence's continued worship of that ireful
god, spoken of by Cacciaguida in Mars' sphere where the
spear and targe is metamorphosed to a white globe with a red
cross. Athens and Thebes were used by Dante and Boccaccio to
represent Florence and Pisa. The golden Minotaur is a
classical variant of the Golden Calf (Purg.XXVI.40-42). The
Chanson de Roland likewise mirrored the Christian Oriflamme
with an up-so-doun Saracen version of it. Chaucer thus gives
the pagan version foreshadowing the Christian and
enigmatically relates pagan wars and cities to Christian
ones.

Palamon's vision occurs through the prison window, foreshadowing Theseus' remark that life is "this foule prisoun" (3061), yet a further commonplace of the body's bondage of the pilgrim soul, similar to that of the inn and the traveler, and reminiscent of Boethius' Platonic Consolation of Philosophy and of its iconographic traditions in illuminated manuscripts which show the prisoner Boethius in a tower with thick bars over its windows:[26]

> And so bifel, by aventure or cas,
> That thurgh a wyndow, thikke of many a barre
> Of iren greet and square as any sparre,
> He cast his eye upon Emelya.   (1074-1077)

Arcite immediately blames Saturn for his cousin's sigh, though Palamon tells him it is from having seen, surely, Venus herself singing in the garden. Arcite also looks and declares the sight "sleeth me sodeynly" (1118). The cousins quarrel, Arcite saying that Palamon's love is as to a goddess, his as to a woman:

> "Thyn is affeccioun of hoolynesse,
> And myn is love as to a creature,"   (1158-1159)

and then lapses into Saturnine wanhope and despair. Throughout the tale these two figures will appear to be balanced. In fact Arcite will be portrayed negatively, Palamon positively.

The scene occurs in May and May will again be of importance to the text. Duke Theseus grants Arcite his freedom from prison, but he is nevertheless perpetually exiled from peaceable Athens. (It is of interest that Chaucer himself was once a young squire captured by the enemy, then ransomed by the King, returning to England in May 1360.) Arcite, defying Theseus' pronouncement, returns from Thebes in disguise and by guile becomes Theseus' squire that he might be near Emelye. The two cousins meet again in May on a Friday, Venus' day and Christ's, and battle. May the Third was the date upon which Helena was said to have razed the Temple of Venus and discovered beneath it the True Cross and the Holy Sepulchre. Medieval Europe played with that conflict between paganism and Christianity with its "women on top" maternity trays showing Tristan and other lovers worshiping Venus and with its May celebrations at which courtiers dressed in green and garlanded in hawthorn rode in cavalcades about the countryside as we see them do in the Très Riches Heures du Duc de Berry's illumination for

May. While Palamon and Arcite battle, Theseus and Emelye in
their May greenery come upon the pair. Theseus wishes them
promptly slain as traitors. The women of the court plead for
the lives of the noble pair, as Froissart describes they had
of Edward III and the Black Prince. Theseus at length
relents and arranges a tourney a year after for Emelye's
hand.

Chaucer's Theseus constructs a magnificent theatre for
the event. The form of the classic theatre was not forgotten
for we know not only sketches of such theatres in
manuscripts of this period, but also of Corpus Christi
dramas being acted in medieval Italy in such arenas, and of
Cornish dramas and the Castle of Perseverance touring play
building similar arena theatres representing mappae mundi
for Christian purposes. Theseus' theatre has temples to
Venus at the east at which Palamon worship, Mars at the west
at which Arcite worships and Diana to the north at which
Emelye worships. In the fifteenth-century Castle of
Perseverance analogous scaffolds housed God to the east, the
world to the west and the devil to the north.[27]   In
Chaucer's Knight's Tale the idols of the pagan deities [i
dèi falsi e bugiardi] are both worshiped and influence
events. Pagan Saturn, Jupiter, Mars, Venus, Diana and
Mercury still rule this pilgrimage rather than Christ
mirrored in Canterbury's St. Thomas. However, the
choreographed psychomachia enacted in this theatre teaches
the pilgrim that the eastern direction of Canterbury is of
salus, the western of London, of sickness and death. The
changes from Boccaccio's Teseida, which did not have
Theseus build the theatre nor did the theatre have in it
idolatrous temples, are wrought so that Chaucer's Theseus'
theatre can function as a shadowy, allegorical mappa mundi
to the "Book of the Tales of Canterbury" and to its
pilgrimage.

Chaucer reverses two aspects of Arcites and Palaemon in
his Arcite and Palamon. In the Teseida it was Arcites who
was called a pilgrim (IV.84). In the Knight's Tale it is
Palamon who steps into Watteau's Pèlerinage à Cytherea:

      With hooly herte and with an heigh corage,
      He rose to wenden on his pilgrymage
      Unto the blisful Citherea benigne,   (2213-2215)

while Arcite is spoken of as an exile (1221-1274,1344-1346).
Chaucer takes pains not to have Palamon associated with
sickness. He also carefully links exilic Arcite with gold,
who amasses it from Thebes and from Theseus (1441-1445), and
who is associated with it by the mourning Athenian women,

"And haddest gold ynough, and Emelye?" (2836), and whose
corpse at the funeral rites is covered with gold (2870-2873;
2937), while pilgrim Palamon is free from such golden,
deadly gleams. In Chaucer, Palamon worships first at the
white and eastern temple of Venus, Canterbury's direction,
an hour before the dawn. Emelye rises with the sun and goes
to Diana's temple of red and white at the theatre's north.
Arcite rises an hour after and worships at the grim red
temple of Mars at the west, in the direction of London, and
performs his sacrifice in "payen wyse" (2370). At the
tournament Arcite's prayer of worldly victory is first
granted; then Saturn (who had not so figured in the Teseida)
causes the mortal injury as Arcite triumphantly rides
towards Emelye's northern scaffold. Chaucer dwells
inordinately on his plague-like dying:

> Swelleth the brest of Arcite, and the soore
> Encreeseth at his herte moore and moore,
> The clothered blood, for any lechecraft,
> Corrupteth, and is in his bouk ylaft,
> That neither veyne-blood, ne ventusynge,
> Ne drynke of herbes may ben his helpynge.
> The vertu expulsif, or animal,
> For thilke vertu cleped natural
> Ne may the venym voyden ne expelle,
> The pipes of his longes gonne to swelle,
> And every lacerte in his brest adoun
> Is shente with venym and corrupcioun.
> Hym gayneth neither, for to gete his lif,
> Vomyt upward, ne dounward laxatif.
> Al is tobrosten thilke regioun;
> Nature hath now no dominacioun.
> And certeinly, ther Nature wol nat wirche,
> Fare wel phisik! go ber the man to chirche!
>   (2743-2762)

Aged and pagan Egeus gives his epitaph:

> "This world nys but a thurghfare ful of wo,
> And we been pilgrymes, passynge to and fro.
> Deeth is an ende of every worldly soore." (2847-2848)

Egeus' Stoic words will be countered at the end of the
Canterbury Tales by the Parson's Christian ones:

> And Jhesu, for his grace, wit me sende
> To shewe yow the wey, in this viage,
> Of thilke parfit glorious pilgrymage
> That highte Jerusalem celestial.   (X.48-51)

The roles Egeus and Theseus play in the drama correspond to
Saturn and to Jupiter; who shadow Satan who would devour man
and God who would save him. The roles Arcite and Palamon
play correspond to Cain and Abel in this pagan enigma of
Christian redemption. The Knight's Tale with its idols, gold
and death, translates Statius' pagan Latin poetry into an
English that denies Christ.

Another element added by Chaucer to Boccaccio and
Statius' versions is the use here and elsewhere in the
Canterbury Tales of figures representing the astrological
influences of Saturn, Jupiter, Venus and Mars. We are shown
that conjunction occurring within the tourney theatre which
Theseus (as Jupiter) has contrived; Arcite worships Mars,
Saturn, at Venus' request, engineers the accident, and
therefore Arcite is mortally wounded. It was this
conjunction of planets that occurred, tradition held, at
Noah's Flood, at Mahomet's birth and at the Black Death's
onset, 1348. [28]   To the traditional doom-filled conjunction
of Saturn, Jupiter and Mars, which occurred again in 1385,
Chaucer deliberately interpolates that of Venus. The Black
Death and the Flood were considered to be God's punishment
of man's lechery. Chaucer thus adds astrology to the
Boccaccian and Statian matter, then reuses it in the
Miller's Tale to allow lecherous Nicholas to prophesy
falsely that there will be a new Flood.

Later an alchemist and his apprentice join the
pilgrimage. The planets are also metals in correspondence:
"Sol gold is, and Luna silver we threpe, Mars iren, Mercurie
quyksilver we clepe, Saturnus leed, and Juppiter is tyn, and
Venus coper" (VIII.826-829). The Knight's Tale and Theseus'
theatre may represent, by means of the interactions of the
characters, not only astronomical conjunctions, but also
alchemical formulae: Palamon as Venus' copper, Arcite as
Mars' iron, Emelye as Diana's silver, Theseus as Jupiter's
tin, Egeus as Saturn's lead, Mercury, who appears to Arcite
in Thebes prompting Arcite's treacherous return in squire's
disguise to Athens, as the alchemists' quicksilver. But we
recall a detail in the worshiping of Diana, Emelye rising
with the sun (I.2273), which associates her not only with
Luna's silver but also with Sol's gold, not only with the
north but also with the south. Does she represent, then,
gold and silver which can be fashioned as a Golden Calf or
to adorn an Ark, bringing death in the first instance, salus
(health and salvation) in the second? She herself converts
from chastity to charity, from virginity to marriage.
However, the Knight, with his pagan temples in this first
tale, presents us with more of "hethenesse" than

"cristendom." His tale presents us with the hermeneutics of the "Book of the Tales of Canterbury." It is a riddle we must unravel. In so doing we will find it best to deal first, in this chapter, with the beginning and ending tales, then in chapter nine, with the central tales, observing the medieval chiasmus of the Tales, rather than modern linearity.

The Miller's up-so-doun Christian tale follows upon the Knight's pagan one, "unbokeled is the male" (I.3115), and is to be followed in turn by the bestial ire of the Reeve's Tale, in which Christian references are obliterated, though we hear of churches and of clergy's bastard progeny. The conclusion of the First Fragment is the Cook's Tale of Perkyn Revelour the apprentice, that rotten apple that is best removed from the hoard lest it rot the remnant (4406-4407). This tale, like the Squire's, is left half-told. Its teller is sick with what the Ellesmere shows as a gangrenous ulcerated leg (385-386; Plate XIa), the tale not worthy of the "soper at oure aller cost"--which the teller will have to cook. The rottenness that began with the Theban discord in the Knight's Tale and Arcite's bodily corruption and death, ripples out into the larger circle of the Miller and Reeve and Cook's Tales and has here ended in a putrid apple of sin and discord. This is the outcome of lechery, where bagpipes are opposed to pilgrimage and where plague reigns. "Wel bet is roten appul out of hoord" (4406). England's London of the plague and Canterbury of the thaumaturge St. Thomas are as a palimpsest upon Egypt and Babylon of bondage and plague in opposition to the freedom and salus of Israel and Jerusalem. The Knight's Tale's Thebes and Athens mirror their dichotomy in this hermeneutic mapping of moral values.

The Knight has just come from the Crusades in the east, the Miller is a southerner, swearing by St. Thomas of Kent, the Reeve is a northerner and the Cook, from London, is a westerner in relation to eastern Canterbury. The Miller tells a tale of an Oxford carpenter, the Reeve of a Cambridge miller. The Knight is in his prime and martial, the Miller is young, stout and jovial, the Reeve, old, slender and saturnine, and their astronomical conjunction necessarily results in the Book's bitter bale. Cooks were under Venus' sign, the Knight is of Mars, the Miller of Jove, the Reeve of Saturn. The First Fragment has regressed, not progressed, upon this pilgrimage, though its seeming disorder may be orderly mapped and diagramed. We are, again, back at the Tabard Inn and worse. The Cook's Tale's last line has us whoring in London still (I.4422).

Symmetrical Structuring of First Fragment and Canterbury Tales

Planets and Metals, Astronomy and Alchemy

S

Flesh ♃
Southern
Miller
Jovial
Young
Stout
Red-haired
Bearded
Sanguine
[Carpenter
Oxford]

Summoner's Tale
of Friar

[Palamon
Pilgrim/Abel
Venus/Copper
White ♀
Marriage

Emelye
Diana/Sol ☽☉
Silver/Gold
Red/White

Arcite
Exile/Cain
Mars/Iron ♂
Red
Sickness/
Death

Theseus/Prime
Jove/Tin
Red/White/ ♃
Gold

Egeus/Old
Saturn/ ♄
Lead

Mercury] ☿

[Oxford clerk's
"sickness"]

Cook/Young
London
Sickness
[Apprentice
Rotten apple]

[Sick Cambridge
manciple]

[Cambridge
Miller]
Choleric
Shaven
White-haired
Slender
Old
Saturnine
Reeve
Northern
Devil ♄
N

Friar's Tale of
Summoner

Eve
Wife ♀♂
Bath
Plague
Venus/Mars
W
World

Saturn
Gold/Lead
Plague
Pardoner ♄
Adam

Parson
Canterbury
St. Thomas
Gold ☉
E
God

Knight
Jerusalem
Christ/Mars
Red/White
♃♂

Chaucer's <u>Canterbury Tales</u> is concerned with sickness
and a pilgrimage to a healing saint. Giovanni Sercambi's
<u>Novelle</u>, in which the writer is present in the text and as a
pilgrim, is a frame tale of fables told by pilgrims and
guided by a host when fleeing the plague in Lucca. Sercambi
felt, and so did most learned men of his day, that the
pestilence was caused by man's idolatrous lechery, its only
preventive being the turning to God: "quella è la medicina
che salva l'anima e' corpo" [that is the medicine which
saves soul and body].[29]   Boccaccio wrote his tale
collection, the <u>Decameron</u>, against the backdrop of plague.
While Boccaccio escaped Florentine morbidity in a secular
pilgrimage, Petrarch passionately felt that the plague was
caused by man's lust, that it could be righted only by exile
from the world of the senses, and he became himself such a
peregrinate hermit upon the banks of the Sorgue. Boccaccio
and Petrarch were in contact with one another during the
plague years and Chaucer's use of their material, though he
perhaps did not know the <u>Decameron</u>, continues that context
of plague.[30] It is a theme in both the Knight and the
Clerk's Tales, borrowed by Chaucer from the two Italian
friends.

At the Tales' ending Chaucer clarifies his symbols and
properly apportions to them their positive and negative
meanings, which the youthful, naive persona of the General
Prologue confused. Themes throughout the Tales had been of
greed for worldly gold, and charity; of pagan idols, Saturn,
Jove, Mars, Venus, Diana, Mercury, and Christ; of astronomy,
alchemy, and medicine; of fables, and sermons. The pilgrims
journey, seemingly, to Canterbury to seek physical healing.
By canon law medieval doctors were forbidden to treat
patients without their first having made their confession to
a priest for their sins, so closely was sickness felt to be
connected with sinfulness. In turn medieval metaphors were
appropriated by theology, Christ (and St. Thomas) becoming
the "soules leche" (V.916), a concept Chaucer's Duchess
Blanche's father, Duke Henry of Lancaster, used in his
devotional treatise written in Anglo-Norman, <u>Le Livre de
Seyntz Medicines</u>, a concept found in Boethius' <u>Consolation
of Philosophy</u>, which Chaucer Englished.

A deliberate opposition is present in the Second Nun's
Tale and the Canon's Yeoman's, the one being sacred, the
other profane. That opposition of white lilies and red
roses, to infernal darkness, had been present in the tales
throughout, though often "ful curiously ywrought" as in the
garland of red and white flowers the Summoner sports upon
his black locks. The Second Nun finishes her tale to the
galloping horse hooves of the Canon and his Yeoman,

hastening to seek sanctuary with these pilgrims and to
escape retribution for their dark deeds. They are sweating
as if in hell. The Yeoman recounts that seeing them depart
he had advised his master that they join them to have sport
and dalliance. (So speak Luke and Cleophas of their new
companion in the medieval dramas of the Emmaus Pilgrims.)
The Yeoman proceeds to tell of his master that he is an
alchemist who has the power to pave the road on which they
ride to Canterbury all of gold (which the Janus tales have
taught us to associate with ensuing bodily corruption,
plague and death) and "up-so-doun" (which would return them
to profane London, the Tabard Inn and the plague, as has
rhetorically happened twice already, having them as if fail
their pilgrimage). The Host probes further, curious about
the Canon's dress, which is light, summery garb, though it
is a northern, cold, wet April, and which is blackened with
soot and whose tatters show evidence of a recent alchemical
explosion. He asks where the pair dwell and the Yeoman
answers that they lurk in the suburbs with thieves and
robbers (Tabard Inn country). He asks why the Yeoman's face
is black and burnt and the Yeoman recounts their latest
failure. The Canon is alarmed at the secrets thus given
away and flees. The sorcerer's apprentice is at last freed,
and proceeds to tell his Tale.

He has lived with the Canon for seven years, that
period of biblical bondage which an apprentice must serve
before becoming himself a master and free. Dante gives us
that ceremony where Virgil mitres and crowns Dante, Virgil
liberating him from discipleship. Other apprentices on this
pilgrimage have been the worldly Squire to the peregrinate
Knight to whom is juxtaposed the peregrinate Second Nun to
the worldly Prioress. The Cook's Tale gave us a further
opposition to this where Perkyn Revelour is released as a
good-for-nothing by his master long before his seven years
are up and where his liberation is libertine. Pilgrimage is
apprenticeship to God. The apprentice may fail, or succeed.
Or he may be apprenticed to the World, the Flesh and the
Devil; in which case, to become peregrinate, he must break
free, as does our Canon's Yeoman. Although the Second Nun
preached in favor of business, not "ydelness," the
contrasting Tale of the Canon's Yeoman gives us a business
that is infernal. In this cursed craft there is the deluded
hope that these metals may be balanced by alchemy into a
perfect harmony which will result in gold. The Knight's Tale
shadowily achieves that harmony; not in terms of Arcite's
exilic, worldly amassing of gold, but instead in terms of
pilgrimage with Palamon. The Canterbury Tales is the pagan
and idolatrous system rendered Christian and peregrinate,
which requires that the gold of the world be transmuted to

that of God by being scorned instead of sought. Christ said
to his pilgrim disciples: "Nolite possidere aurum neque
pecuniam in zonis vestris" [Provide neither gold, nor
silver, nor brass in your purses].

Chaucer in the General Prologue played a game of
appearance versus reality. His Canon's Yeoman picks up that
theme; and relates gold and apples as so much fool's gold
and Adam's apples:

> But al thyng which that shineth as the gold
> Nis nat gold, as that I have herd it told;
> Ne every appul that is fair at eye
> Ne is nat good, what so men clappe or crye.
>
> (VIII.962-965)

In the Cook's Tale we had heard, "Wel bet is roten appul out
of hoord/ Than that it rotie al the remenaunt" (I.4406-
4407). Now the Yeoman tells a tale of a canon (though
declaring this canon of the tale is not his canon as the
Prioress' Priest got his mistress likewise off the hook) and
declares that such an evil canon as his Tale's canon (and
really obviously his recent traveling partner) is like a
Judas best removed from the convent (1000-1009). Perhaps we
are meant, according to this advice, to remove the rotten
apples from the canon of the <u>Canterbury Tales</u>. Yet the
pilgrimage structuring requires that fables be there with
sermons in order to shape its truth by means of contraries.
In this instance the Canon's Yeoman preaches against the
vice which he has just relinquished, a refinement upon the
genre and an opposition to the Pardoner's obstinate
nonrepentence; the Pardoner confessed his sins, journeyed on
pilgrimage (considered as satisfaction) but showed no
contrition whatsoever. The Canon's Yeoman is now <u>parfit</u> in
confession, contrition and satisfaction.

The Yeoman ends with a sermon against gold and its
effect upon people, an effect we see upon Arcite, in the
Pardoner's grim tale and the Shipman's bawdy one and in the
Nun's Priest's pilgrim tale within the Tale of the two
travelers, one of whom is murdered for his gold, while the
Prologue gave us Monk and Prioress adorned with gold. The
Yeoman pleads that men not make God their adversary by
dabbling in alchemy contrary to his will. He ends with the
wish that all good men be healed of their illness--"God
sende every trewe man boote of his bale!" (VIII.1481). This
is an adaptation and translation of the Canterbury pilgrim
phial motto--"Optimus egrorum medicus fit Toma bonorum"
[Thomas is the best doctor for true men who are sick]. Gold,
Chaucer has decided, is not a plague remedy, nor, actually,

is mere physical pilgrimage lacking in contrition and reform, though his Physician treats his plague patients with and for gold.[31] The plague preventive of supreme efficacy, according to Chaucer and Petrarch and Sercambi, is that of the _imitatio Christi_, the pilgrimage within to restore man to the image of God the Creator.

The genre in which Chaucer writes the _Canterbury Tales_ requires that the false be juxtaposed to the true. Like the Physician, the Pardoner is a false "leche." He had spoken of himself as conveniently "the doctor in the house" where, if a pilgrim fell from his horse, he could pardon him all his sins while his soul was leaving his body, his neck broken "atwo" (936). His Tale had followed the Physician's. Now we have the Cook falling off his horse in a drunken stupor and another false physician ministering unto him, the Manciple. The Cook is too sick to tell his Tale in his turn, though the Manciple has come to the Cook's aid with a stiff drink of unsacramental wine to soothe the discord that has broken out once more in this quarrelsome _compaignie_. (We recall that in the Reeve's Tale we had had, not a sick cook, but a sick manicple [I.3993]). The Manciple's Tale that follows this incident concerns the birth of the pagan god of healing, Aesculapius, though it is told in pagan, bawdy, folk-tale terms. Pardoner and Manciple are as false physicians who must first heal themselves. Their contrary is the "soules leche," the Parson, St. Thomas and Christ.

The Tale of Aesculapius was well known to Chaucer. Ovid's _Metamorphoses_ contains the tale of his birth in Book II, his curing of the Roman plague in Book XV. On that occasion an embassy from Latium had sought out the god with the snake-twined staff, the caduceus, at Epidaurus, persuading him to take up residence in the _isola di Tevere_, the island in the middle of the Tiber shaped like a ship. To this day the island is a medical center. Ovid comments that Aesculapius did indeed stop the plague, but that he was a foreign god, and that Rome now deifies Caesar, not Aesculapius. The _Teseida_, telling of Arcita's mortal illness, stated that Aesculapius was helpless to heal him, only Jove having that power.[32] Chaucer's Christian and English pilgrims reject the pagan Aesculapius and deified Caesar in favor of Christ and their thaumaturgical martyr saint, Thomas Becket. Chaucer's Manciple, being himself a false physician, in telling the tale of that birth, suppresses Aescualpius' name and Christ's. However, as Ovid concluded the _Metamorphoses_ with that image of healing so also does Chaucer's _Canterbury Tales_.

Illuminations to Boethius' _Consolation of Philosophy_

show their author sick in bed, then healed by Philosophia.
The physician, on the other hand, shown with iconographic
similarity to that of the Ellesmere Physician who holds
aloft and inspects a jar of urine as he rides, had been
unable to bring about a cure (Plate XIb,c,d). Boethius has
Philosophia say to him:

> The physician, however, does not find such things at
> all strange, because he understands the nature of
> sickness and health. Now, what is the health of souls
> but virtue, and what is their sickness but vice? And
> who, indeed, is the preserver of the good and the
> corrector of the wicked but God, the governor and
> physician of men's minds.[33]

Here again, in a text Chaucer knew, translated and loved, is
the equation of physical sickness with sin. The
iconographical tradition shows Boethius _persona_ as the
patient treated by his own discourse with Philosophia while
Boethius the author heals himself by means of his book. The
reader who follows in that pilgrimage attains a like
consolation and healing.

In the Parson's Prologue we are told that the pilgrims
are "entryng at a thropes ende" (X.12), and that under the
opposing zodiac sign of the judgement scales of Libra to the
ram of Aries, evening has come. Chaucer glances down to
survey his shadow lengthening as they are approaching a
village (X.1-12). In the Gospel of the Physician, Luke 24.
28-29, we find also pilgrims drawing nigh to a village as
the shadows are lengthening: "et appropinquaverunt castello
. . . quoniam advesperascit, et inclinata est iam dies" [And
they drew nigh unto a village, whither they went: and he
made as though he would have gone further. But they
constrained him, saying, Abide with us: for it is toward
evening, and the day is far spent]. They have journeyed
the "stadiorum sexaginta" from Jerusalem--the "thropes ende"
would be about sixty miles from London--while telling
tales--_dum fabularentur_--and have now come to Emmaus. The
parallels between Chaucer's Parson's Prologue and Luke's
account of the Emmaus Pilgrims are verbally strong,
Chaucer's one interpolation being the Doomsday scales of
Libra. Yet this parallel has gone almost unnoticed save by
Frank Cook Gardiner in his dissertation on medieval Emmaus
Pilgrims' Plays. [34] The paradigm has the Host be as
Cleophas, Chaucer as Luke, the Parson as Christ.

We are told at the commencement that on their return
the pilgrim who has told the tale of "best sentence and
most solaas/ Shal have a soper at oure aller cost" (I.798-
799), seated at the Tabard Inn in Southwark. But instead the

pilgrimage ends with a spiritual feast near Canterbury under
a setting sun where the peregrinate Parson preaches a "myrie
tale in prose/ To knytte up al this feeste" (X.46-47). His
words to this compaignie will not be profane minstrels'
cakes and ale, but instead bread "benedixit ac fregit et
porrigebat illis" [blessed and broken and given to them]
(30) and wine. His Sermon is the response to the pilgrims'
fabling Tales. Under the sign of Libra it balances them and,
rather than condemning them, instead liberates them,
granting to them the salus they have sought by means of
pilgrimage. "Compaignie" means those who break bread with
one another. Chaucer gave the word a consistently profane
context throughout the Tales: the assembly at the Tabard Inn
(I.24); the Wife of Bath's lovers (I.461); the revelours of
the Pardoner's Tale (VI.672). Now, as in Piers Plowman, the
opposition of sacred and profane is revealed and yoked in a
startling way. The profane is blessed and broken and given
back to the givers, the compaignie, as in the supper at
Emmaus. We recall that in the medieval liturgical and
mystery drama much was made of the Vulgate paradox of
pilgrims telling profane tales, dum fabularentur (15), and
sacred sermons, hi sermones (17), on the road to Emmaus and
at the inn there. So here has Chaucer picked up that theme
for his purposes, becoming as if an English Luke, his role
fragmented into Physician, Pardoner, Parson, Clerk, and even
Canon's Yeoman, Manciple and perhaps Cook, the providers of
salus, of healing and salvation.

Canterbury is not attained in the text, as in the
Exodus Moses did not attain the Promised Land but viewed it
from afar, a characteristic of "pilgrims and exiles" (Iuxta
fidem defuncti sunt omnis isti, non acceptis repromissioni-
bus, sed a longe eas adspicientes et salutantes et
confitentes quia peregrini et hospites sunt super terram"
[These all died in the faith, not having received the
promises, but having seen them afar off, and were persuaded
of them, and embraced them, and confessed that they were
strangers and pilgrims on the earth] Hebrews 11.13), and as
in Luke where the pilgrimage is away from Jerusalem, not
towards it. The feast of tales told while in this viage
becomes the viaticum, fables transmuted into a sermon, the
Tabard's promised soper of cakes and ale metamorphosed into
the inn supper of bread and wine at Emmaus, Christ the
pilgrim disguised as the peregrinate Parson, whom Chaucer
recognizes not, his eyes being cast down upon the earth
(VII.696-698), as were those of Luke and Cleophas, "Oculi
autem illorum tenebantur, ne eum agnoscerunt" (16). As
pilgrim imitatii Christi the Parson and Chaucer can
counterfeit Christ and the Apostles though the Pardoner
would not (VI.447). The account of the physician Luke and
the pilgrim Christ at the Inn becomes a sovrasenso to

Chaucer's <u>Canterbury Tales</u>. The Knight has urged his
fellow pilgrims to tell such stories that they "shall the
soper wynne." All win the Emmaus supper of the Parson's
Sermon, though many upon the cavalcade are false pilgrims,
the Wife, the Pardoner, the Prioress, the Monk, among them.

Rodney Delasanta sees many references to the
"eschatological supper" in the <u>Canterbury Tales</u>, though he
omits that at Emmaus and that of Matthew. He draws attention
to the Parson's words:

> "He that openeth to me shal have foryifnesse of synne.
> I wol entre into hym by my grace, and soupe with hym,"
> by the good werkes that he shal doon, which werkes been
> the foode of God: "and he shal soupe with me," by the
> grete joye that I shal yeven hym. Thus shal man hope,
> for his werkes of penaunce." (X.288-290)

Delasanta's examples of the eschatological feast are the
solemn ones.[35]   One such is that of Maundy Thursday at
which Christ washed his disciples' feet (the night, perhaps,
of the scene at the Tabard, with Good Friday being the
telling of the Knight's Tale of Friday, Easter Sunday being
the most efficacious day for pilgrim miracles at Thomas'
shrine and it taking three days to attain Canterbury on
horseback). There were other suppers in the Gospels. Luke 5.
27-35 describes the banquet Matthew-Levi, the collector of
customs and gospeler-to-be, gave for his fellow sinners and
publicans and Christ. Luke 7.36-50, 15.1-2 and Mark 2.15-17
tell amusingly of the Pharisees and scribes murmuring
because Christ ate with sinners, publicans and tax
collectors and consorted with Mary Magdalen, the whore,
rather than with virtuous, self-righteous citizens. Christ's
rebuke to them was "Non egent qui sani sunt medico, sed qui
male habent. Non veni vocare iustos, sed peccatores ad
paenitentiam" [They that are whole need not a physician, but
they that are sick: I came not to call the righteous, but
sinners to repentance] (Luke 5.31-32). These are Chaucer's
themes of the Physician who heals the sick and the feast at
which sinners are present. Chaucer, the poet, is, we also
recall, an English Matthew-Levi, that Kittredgean monster,
the "naive collector of customs." (We recall that Nathaniel
Hawthorne noted in <u>The Scarlet Letter</u> that he shared the
same occupation as Matthew and Chaucer.) The <u>Canterbury
Tales</u> is such a banquet of tales and tellers (false pilgrims
such as the Pardoner and the Wife of Bath, the Monk and the
Prioress, the Friar and the Summoner; wordly citizens such
as the Physician, the Man of Law, the Merchant, the Shipman,
the Squire; and Christlike pilgrims such as the Knight, the
Clerk, the Ploughman and the Parson) gathered together and
invited by Chaucer the customs collector. It is the sort of

holy joke one senses Chaucer would relish--à la Sir Philip
de la Vache--where salus and merriment are combined.

The Host requests that the Parson now "Unbokele, and
shewe us what is in thy male" (X.26). He had used that word
in the First Fragment, after the Knight's Tale: "This gooth
aright; unbokeled is the male" (I.3115). That word was heard
of the Pardoner as the receptacle for his false relics: "I
have relikes and pardoun in my male" (VI.920). A male is a
pilgrim's scrip in which were carried bread, the viaticum,
and words, the documents required of all medieval travelers.
What the Parson, unlike the Pardoner, unbuckles from his
male is truth, not lies; the bread of salus, not poisoned,
death-dealing wine.[36]   We recall how the Ellesmere clothed
both Parson and Pardoner in the scarlet of the medieval
parish priest's garb. They seem to be alike but in reality
are not, as also seemed but were not the pilgrim and exile
figures of Palamon and Arcite, and the Levite brothers,
Moses and Aaron, of the Exodus. The Pardoner would have the
pilgrims purchase his worthless pardon, as if a latter day
Golden Calf; the Parson would have the pilgrims keep the law
of God.

Chaucer himself is poised between Parson and Pardoner.
He is Matthew-Levi, the collector of customs, who is called
and comes, who unlike the Pardoner, does the "apostles
countrefete" (VI.447); he is likewise the fabling pilgrim
Luke, who, as physician, first heals himself. The Canterbury
Tales began perhaps as the choice of the two ways under the
sign of Aries. It ends with the scales of Libra, of
Doomsday. Chaucer persona's choice and ours is to be made at
its ending. The tales told will influence it and so will
also the Parson's Sermon which judges all the tales and
their tellers. This will prompt Chaucer's pilgrim and
authorial confession. The Canterbury Tales shows forth the
penitential imitation of Christ by contraries and
similitudes. Thus can the Parson declare that his "myrie
tale"--a Sermon--will "knytte up al this feeste" (X.47) and
render the ending of the Canterbury Tales its beginning, its
Tabard an Emmaus and Bethlehem Inn.

Let us turn to the "hooly blisful martir." These
pilgrims journey not to the shrine of Aesculapius but to
Canterbury, to a shrine that combines the attributes of the
pagan deity with the Christian. The London plague doctor, by
his pilgrimage to St. Thomas, confesses that he is not the
"verray, parfit praktisour" (422) that Chaucer, the foolish
Prologue pilgrim, thought him to be. The powers of the
Canterbury shrine are greater than the remedies concocted
and paid for with the gold of mortality. Chaucer's sense of

the Saint is conveyed in the pilgrimage lines of the General Prologue.

> Thanne longen folk to goon on pilgrimages,
> And palmeres for to seken straunge strondes
> To ferne halwes, kowthe in sondry londes;
> And specially from every shires ende
> Of Engelond to Caunterbury they wende,
> The hooly blisful martir for to seke,
> That hem hath holpen whan that they were seeke. (12-18)

Though so obscure in the Tales he is yet central to the Pilgrimage. He functions as the English Christ and all the readers of the Tales in their minds, if not "by feet alone," converge upon his English Jerusalem of Canterbury. The pilgrim readers thus imitate their saint and attain Christlike salus.

"Physician, Heal Thyself!" Why does Chaucer confess contritely to his telling of fabliaux? Were he not to do so, his reader would remain as exilic as before. Because Chaucer confesses to attain salus his Canterbury Tales in turn can be a soules leche to us, albeit with laughter. Luke, the Pilgrim Physician, is healed and can heal in turn. Matthew-Levi, the collector of customs, is called and comes. Chaucer, like the repentant Canon's Yeoman who is given the motto of the pilgrim phial to declare to the compaignie, has opted, after all, not to be an evil Pardoner (whose drama, though seemingly comic, is idolatrous tragedy, a dance of death, at Doomsday),[37] but to repent and thereby be the true imitatio Christi, a Parson, a Physician and a Publican of a poet unrecognized until the Emmaus inn soper of a sermon, though fabling the while, with bagpipes and renarderie. The pilgrimage is no longer to the plaguey bills of London and Canterbury but to "Jerusalem celestial"; no longer to the World, the Flesh and the Devil, but to God; no longer to Venus, but to Christ.

CHAPTER SIX: EGYPTIAN GOLD

      Behind the Emmaus tale is the tale of Exodus. It is in
fact the pilgrim tale that Christ tells to his two disciples
as evening shadows are lengthening (Luke 24.27). Both these
tales shaped medieval pilgrimage, the one as the Old
Testament type, figure or shadow for the other New Testament
one. It is appropriate that Luke, or rather Cleophas, speaks
of evening tide's slanting light and shadow at the point
where Christ speaks of Old Testament prophetic types of the
New, the word <u>typos</u> itself meaning shadow.[1] Both Exodus
and Emmaus tales are as paradigms for the uses of poetry.
Both permit a Janus doubleness, seeing pilgrimage as
simultaneously sacred and profane. The Emmaus pilgrim tale
of the New Testament achieved that doubleness by seeming to
yoke fabling with sermoning, lies and truth, upon a road of
pilgrimage that led not to the famed Temple but away from
it, to a common inn. The Exodus tale of Egyptian gold used
first to fashion the profane Golden Calf, then used to adorn
the sacred Tabernacle of the Ark, progresses in the proper
direction, from the bondage of Egypt to the freedom of
Israel, from carnality to sanctity. The Emmaus tale was "up-
so-doun" in its regressing from the spirit to the flesh,
from the Temple in Jerusalem to an inn at Emmaus.[2] The
palimpsest of the one tale upon the other in medieval
pilgrimage and its literature lends itself to what Chaucer
terms "contraries" (<u>Troilus</u>, I.637,645) and which he sees as
essential to a proper definition or declaration of a
concept. Dante, in a similar way, uses the word "ambages."
The concept, "pilgrimage," is fashioned of such contraries,
oppositions and ambiguities, yoked together. It is both
shadow and substance at once.

      The Exodus tale of the Golden Calf and the Tabernacle
of the Ark was of great importance to medieval pilgrimage
poetry, as important as was Luke's Gospel concerning the

Emmaus pilgrims. Egyptian gold was used first to fashion the
Golden Calf; then the Tabernacle of the Ark was adorned with
these same spoils of the Egyptians converted and transformed
from an idolatrous use to a pilgrim one. These events
mirrored, in small, what the Exodus in its entirety showed
forth, the journey from an idolatrous Egypt to a godly
Israel. In Exodus 3.22 God told Moses to have the
Israelites borrow gold from the Egyptians: "every woman
shall borrow . . . jewels of silver, and jewels of gold, and
raiment . . . ye shall put them upon your sons, and upon
your daughters; and ye shall spoil the Egyptians." Aaron
fashioned the Golden Calf from this borrowed Egyptian gold
when the errant Israelites said: "Up, make us gods, which
shall go before us," during Moses' absence on Sinai. The
Israelites worshiped the Golden Calf with lecherous dancing:
"The people sat down to eat and drink and rose up to play,"
a phrase Paul, speaking against idolatry and lechery, echoed
(I Cor. 10.7). Moses, returning from Sinai, saw the
Israelites' idolatrous nakedness, broke the tables of stone,
burned the golden idol and put three thousand to the sword.
The account ends: "The Lord plagued the people because they
made the calf, which Aaron made." Paradoxically, Aaron
became the High Priest of the Ark of God and in that role
was to cure, rather than cause, a further plague outbreak
that afflicted the Israelites' pilgrimage (Numbers
16.46-50).

In Exodus 35-39, in penitential atonement at Moses'
bidding, rather than Aaron's, the Tabernacle was constructed
with the same offerings of gold and silver, jewels and
raiment which, according to God's command, had been first
spoiled of the Egyptians, then used to fashion the Golden
Calf. Thus borrowed Egyptian gold was used first for wrong,
idolatrous, lecherous purposes, and then for worshiping God.
Peter pleaded: "Dearly beloved, I beseech you as strangers
and pilgrims, abstain from fleshly lusts" (I.2.11). First
the creature was idolized, then the Creator worshiped. That
the idol "made with human hands" was Egyptian and in bestial
form made it even worse than were the idols of the Greeks
and Romans in human shape. Pagan philosophy taught that
men's lusts transformed them into beasts. Within the
Israelites' lavishly adorned Tabernacle and its Ark of
idolatrous gold, veiled with red, blue and purple cloth
brought from Egypt, were placed paradoxically humble
treasures, the tables of stone inscribed by God with the
Law, Aaron's wooden rod and the manna of the wilderness.
These treasures of godly stone, wood and bread were
perceived as of greater value than those of worldly gold,
silver and gems.

David and Solomon were to bring the Tabernacle and the
Ark into Jerusalem and the Temple. Depictions of Exodus' Ark
show it as like a reliquary chest while medieval
translations of relics were often carried out in ox-drawn
carts in memory of the Ark's translation into Jerusalem (II
Sam. 6; Plate VIIIb,c).[3]   Medieval shrines adorned with
gold, silver and cloth, often of pagan origin, were termed
"arcae santae" [holy arks]. Patristic and medieval
Christianity likewise thought of their richly bound and
illuminated scriptures as an Ark of the Word, as in the
fashioning of the Book of Kells which adorns Christian
words with pagan ornament. Christ was often painted or
mosaiced as holding the gold and jewelled Book, as the
Lawgiver of the New, just as Moses was the Lawgiver of the
Old Law. A fine example of such a book-holding Pantocrator
is at St. Catherine's Monastery at Mount Sinai where the Law
was given to Moses.[4]

The fourteenth-century saw the analogy between Exodus'
plague of the Egyptians and the Israelites and their own
devastating plagues which they considered to be God's
punishment for their sins, particularly for idolatry and
lust. One way to atone during pestilence was to pilgrimage
to the shrines of saints, among them St. Thomas' of
Canterbury, bringing gifts of gold, silver and jewels. St.
Roch, the pilgrim saint, was especially associated with
plague healing.[5]   Painting and poetry in that century of
the Black Death were often used to move viewers and hearers
to penance to prevent further affliction by the plague on
the parts of both the public and the artist. The Via
Veritatis in Santa Maria Novella, Florence (Plate XIII),
and the Triumph of Death in the Campo Santo, Pisa, have much
in common with poems such as Piers Plowman and the
Canterbury Tales.[6]   In them the sacred and profane are
mingled. They map the pilgrims' progress from the bondage of
lust to penance and salvation. They are as penitential
sermons in the guise of romances and fables, in which the
Golden Calf idolatry and lechery is metamorphosed into the
worship of God.

Psalm 113 (in the King James, Psalms 114 and 115), "In
exitu Israel de Aegypto" [When Israel went out of Egypt],
was composed for the Hebrew Jerusalem pilgrimage which God
commanded to commemorate the Exodus (Lev. 23.39-43). We
recall that there were three such mandatory pilgrimages to
the Temple, at Passover, Pentecost and Tabernacles. At the
Tabernacles' pilgrimage Jews singing this psalm with its
Alleluia or Hallel refrain came bearing palms to lay on the
horns of the Temple's altar. It was sung as well at the

pilgrimages to the Temple at Passover and Pentecost.
Christians used the psalm both in the Easter liturgy and
upon pilgrimage. Its Easter antiphon includes the Hebrew
"Alleluia" and its music derives from Hebrew usage. Psalm
113 is chanted at the Easter Vespers by the baptismal font
to a unique <u>tonus peregrinus</u>. It is used in the Easter
liturgy because Exodus' Passover is the type of Easter, the
Red Sea and the Jordan figures for baptism. Both bodies of
water were crossed in Exodus' pilgrimage, both are mentioned
in the pilgrimage psalm.[7]

Psalm 113

Alleluia.

1. In exi-tu Isra-el de Aegy-pto, * domus Iacob de popu-lo
   barbaro:

2. facta est Iudae-a sancti-fica-ti-o e-ius: * Isra-el
   pot-estas e-ius.

Flex: palpabunt:

3. Mare vidit, et fugit; * Iordanis conversus est retrorsum:
4. montes exsultaverunt ut arietes: * et colles sicut agni
   ovium.
5. Quid est tibi mare, quod fugisti? * et tu Iordanis, quia
   conversus es retrorsum?
6. montes exsultastis sicut arietes, * et, colles sicut agni
   ovium?
7. A facie Domini mota est terra, * a facie Dei Iacob:
8. qui convertit petram in stagna aquarum, * et rupem in
   fontes aquarum.
9. Non nobis, Domine, non nobis, * sed nomini tuo da gloriam
10. super misericordia tua et veritate tua. * Nequando
    dicant gentes: Ubi est Deus eorum?

11. Deus autem noster in caelo: * omnia quaecumque voluit fecit.
12. Simulacra gentium argentum et aurum, * opera manuum hominum.
13. Os habent, et non loquentur: * oculos habent et non videbunt.
14. aures habent et non audient, * nares habent et non odorabunt.
15. manus habent et non palpabunt: pedes habent et non ambulabunt, * non clamabunt in guttore suo.
16. Similes illis fiant qui faciunt ea: * et omnes qui confidunt in eis.
17. Domus Israel speravit in Domino: * adiutor eorum et protector eorum est.
18. Domus Aaron speravit in Domino: * adiutor eorum et protector eorum est.
19. Qui timent Dominum speraverunt in Domino: * adiutor eorum et protector eorum est.
20. Dominus memor fuit nostri * et benedixit nobis,
21. benedixit domui Israel: * benedixit domui Aaron.
22. Benedixit omnibus qui timent Dominum, * pusillis cum maioribus.
23. Adiiciat Dominus super vos, * super vos, et super filios vestros.
24. benedicti vos a Domino, * Qui fecit caelum et terram.
25. Caelum caeli Domino; * terram autem dedit filiis hominum.
26. Non mortui laudabunt te, Domine, * neque omnes qui descendunt in infernum;
27. Sed nos qui vivimus, benedicamus Domino * ex hoc nunc et usque in saeculum.

[Psalm 114

1. When Israel went out of Egypt, the house of Jacob from a people of strange language; 2. Judah was his sanctuary, and Israel his dominion. 3. The sea saw it, and fled: Jordan was driven back. 4. The mountains skipped like rams, and the little hills like lambs. 5. What ailed thee, O thou sea, that thou fleddest? thou Jordan, that thou was driven back? 6. Ye mountains, that ye skipped like rams; and ye little hills, like lambs? 7. Tremble, thou earth, at the presence of the Lord, at the presence of the God of Jacob; 8. Which turned the rock into a standing water, the flint into a fountain of waters.

Psalm 115

1. Not unto us, O Lord, not unto us, but unto thy name give glory, for my mercy, and for thy truth's sake. 2. Wherefore

should the heathen say, Where is now their God? 3. But our
God is in the heavens: he hath done whatsoever he hath
pleased. 4. Their idols are silver and gold, the work of
men's hands. 5. They have mouths, but they speak not: eyes
have they, but they see not: 6. They have ears, but they
hear not: noses have they, but they smell not: 7. They have
hands, but they handle not: feet have they, but they walk
not: neither speak they through their throat. 8. They that
make them are like unto them; so is every one that trusteth
in them. 9. O Israel, trust thou in the Lord: he is their
help and their shield. 10. O house of Aaron, trust in the
Lord: he is their help and their shield. 11. Ye that fear
the Lord, trust in the Lord: he is their help and their
shield. 12. The Lord hath been mindful of us: he will bless
us; he will bless the house of Israel; he will bless the
house of Aaron. 13. He will bless them that fear the Lord,
both small and great. 14. The Lord shall increase you more
and more, you and your children. 15. Ye are blessed of the
Lord which made heaven and earth. 16. The heaven, even the
heavens, are the Lord's: but the earth hath he given to the
children of men. 17. The dead praise not the Lord, neither
any that go down into silence. 18. But we will bless the
Lord from this time forth and for evermore. Praise the
Lord.]

Exodus itself, and Psalm 113 based upon it, sternly
forbade idolatry. The First and Second Commandments are
"Thou shalt have no other gods before me. Thou shalt not
make unto thee any graven image . . . Thou shalt not bow
down thyself to them" (Exod. 20.2-5); and the Psalm
proclaimed: "Their idols are gold and silver, the work of
men's hands. They have mouths, but they speak not: eyes have
they, but they see not: They have ears, but they hear not:
noses have they, but they smell not: They have hands, but
they handle not: feet have they, but they walk not: neither
speak they through their throat. They that make them are
like unto them; so is everyone that trusteth in them"
(115.4-8). This teaching concerning idolatry caused
conflict when the iconoclastic Hebraic world commingled with
the idol-worshiping Hellenic one. Christianity inherited
this conflict and saw the statues of pagan deities such as
Mars and Venus outwardly as beautiful idols which within
harbored devils.[8]   At the same time they attempted to
reconcile the clash of cultures by means of the allegory of
Egyptian gold.

This allegory, of the uses of pagan gold converted from
a profane to a sacred use, flourished in patristic and
medieval writings. In the De doctrina christiana Augustine
wrote of pagan poetry used in Christian sermons as such

Egyptian gold. It justified his use of the idolatrous <u>Aeneid</u>
as a scheme for his <u>Confessions</u> and his <u>City of God</u>.[9]
Peter the Venerable wrote in a letter to Heloise, breaking
to her gently the news of Abelard's death: "Now completely a
woman of wisdom, you chose the Gospels instead of logic, the
apostle in place of physics, Christ instead of Plato, the
cloister instead of the Academy. You snatched the spoils of
the defeated enemy, and passing through the desert of this
pilgrimage, with the treasures of the Egyptians, you built a
precious tabernacle of God in your heart."[10]   Dante,
throughout the <u>Commedia</u>, chided Florence for her retention
of the idol of her pagan patron, Mars, when she should
instead heed her Christian patron, St. John the Baptist,
and repent. In medieval and Renaissance love poetry the
woman to whom the lover pilgrimages, such as Tristan's
Isolde, such as Troilus's Criseyde, is as a Golden Calf, as
an idol of Venus; unless she converts her poet to God, in
Beatrice and Laura's manner.

Medieval art frequently showed golden calves and other
idols upon priapic pillars, remembering the practices of
antiquity in which forum statues of pagan deities and
emperors were so placed and worshiped with blood sacrifices.
The great thirteenth-century ironical pilgrimage poem, the
<u>Roman de la Rose</u>, precursor of those of the fourteenth,
had Amant's lady be placed upon a pedestal, Pygmalion's
Galatea upon a pillar, Pygmalion dancing before that idol in
the manner of the Israelites dancing before the Golden Calf
and David before the Ark.[11]   Siena in 1357, after a further
outbreak of the Black Death, fearfully dismembered her
statue of Venus by Lysippus which had been placed in her
shell-shaped piazza in 1334.[12]   In the square before St.
John Lateran was a pillar topped by the classical bronze
statue of a boy pulling a thorn from his foot, called the
Spinario. It was stoned by pilgrims who interpreted it as
man at the Fall, "Thorns also and thistles shall it bring
forth" (Gen. 3.18).[13]   The <u>Ship of Fools</u> shows male and
female Fools dancing about the Golden Calf, their antics
mirroring the Wife of Bath's "olde daunce" of lust.[14]
The carolling figures of the <u>Via Veritatis</u> who dance before
the allegorical personifications of the Senses and the
figures in the trees plucking fruit represent both folly and
lust (Plate XIII). Such idolatry was equated with the world,
the flesh and the devil; the pilgrim Tabernacle of the Ark,
mirrored in the shrines of saints, with God.

The books of the Old Testament centered upon the themes
of pilgrimage from bondage to freedom. The Egyptian
captivity was mirrored in time in the Babylonian diaspora.
That pattern was deepened for the medieval pilgrim by the

128

Figure 7 Twelfth-Century Pilgrim Map
    Robertus Remensis, *Historia Hierosolimitae*
    Joachim Lelewel, *Géographie du Moyen Age*

naming of the Soldan's Cairo in Egypt as "Babylon." Medieval
pilgrims deliberately journeyed from that city of "Babylon"
through the Sinai Wilderness to Jerusalem and therefore
doubly associated Saracen Cairo's mosques and minarets with
Egyptian and Babylonian perfidy.[15] The Song of Roland
mentions idolatrous Babylon when meaning Saracen Cairo.[16]
Other medieval texts, including Chaucer's Parson's Sermon,
speak of the worshiping of gold as the worshiping of a
"mawmet," of a Golden Calf, though Muslims condemn the
worshiping of idols with far greater severity than do
Christians.[17]   Medieval pilgrims thought the words chanted
from minarets were "Increase and multiply," a text the
lustful, Babylonian Wife chose for herself.[18]   These
fallacies largly arose because medieval Christians
associated the Egypt of Exodus and the Babylon of Apocalypse
with the Saracen Egypt and Babylon of their own day.

Pilgrims, singing Psalm 113 to its music of the tonus
peregrinus, made the Jerusalem pilgrimage in one of two
ways, the most arduous being to take ship, often from
Venice, landing at the Nile ports, traveling to the
Soldan's "Babylon" of Cairo, next crossing the Sinai
Wilderness and staying in St. Catherine's Monastery's guest
house at Mount Sinai, then journeying to the Jordan, bathing
there and plucking palm branches in the Garden of Abraham
before entering Jerusalem. At St. Catherine's Monastery they
donned the "sygne of Synay," the Catherine Wheel pewter
badge, to take its place beside their Jerusalem crosses.
Langland's far-traveled Palmer wears both Jerusalem cross
and Catherine wheel. The Sinai pilgrims consciously
patterned their journeying upon the Exodus, visiting the Red
Sea and the Jordan, visiting also the forty-two places named
in Numbers 33 and commenting upon these in the guides they
wrote. Dante, for this reason, gave his pilgrim Vita Nuova
forty-two parts, echoing in them the meanings of the names
of Exodus' forty-two stations.[19]

The easier way of pilgrimaging to the Holy Places was
to sail to Jaffa and then journey to Jerusalem, passing
through Emmaus on the way. Jerusalem was first seen from the
Mons Gaudii, Mount Joy, whose name became the battle cry of
the Crusaders, "Mon Joie!" Besides Jerusalem these pilgrims
also visited all the other sites named in the Gospels and
which were called by them the Loci Sancti, the Holy Places.
A manuscript History of Jerusalem shows as its colophon a
delightful map of Jerusalem upon which pilgrims with scrips
and staves converge (Figure 7).[20]   They would then, if they
were able, journey on to St. Catherine's Monastery at Sinai
and "Babylon" in Egypt. Such pilgrims performed both Exodus
and Emmaus pilgrimages upon

                those holy fields
        Over whose acres walk'd those blessed feet
        Which fourteen hundred years ago were nail'd
        For our advantage on the bitter cross.
                                (I *Henry IV* I.ii.24-27)

They sought in reality to retrace the *vita Christi* and the
events of the Old Testament which foreshadowed it. With
them they carried the knowledge of the legend in which,
when Christ came as a child into Egypt, all the idols
tumbled down from their pillars, a legend combining aspects
of Exodus and the Gospel. [21]

    Pilgrimage to Jerusalem became increasingly difficult
rather than easier. Acre (upon whose name Shakespeare may be
punning), the last Christian stronghold in Outremer, the
Jerusalem Kingdom, fell to the Saracen in 1291. Therefore
medieval Rome sought consciously to substitute itself as
Christendom's "Jerusalem." Dante's *Commedia*, set in the
Roman Jubilee year of 1300, carefully reflects this
substitution of the one city for the other.[22]   The pattern
of the translation from Jerusalem to Rome was strengthened
for medieval Christianity, though forgotten today, by the
concept of Egyptian gold. Dante, scholar of Virgil that he
was, used this pattern to translate pilgrim Jerusalem, as if
a New Troy, into "quella Roma onde Cristo è romano" [that
Rome whereof Christ is Roman] (*Purg.* XXXII.102).

    The gold and silver Egyptian spoils, used first by
Aaron to fashion the Golden Calf, then by Moses to adorn the
Tabernacle of the Ark and placed, through David and Solomon,
in Jerusalem's Temple, were captured by Babylon, then
returned (the Beauvais *Play of Daniel* celebrates this), and
were next spoiled from Roman Palestine by the Emperors Titus
and Vespasian. The Arch of Titus on the Via Sacra going into
the Forum shows in one relief the Romans bearing on their
shoulders the seven-branched candlestick, the table for the
shew bread and the Jubilee trumpets, in the other, the
Emperor Titus in an imperial quadriga (Plate VIIIa,b,c).
Following the Triumph the Jerusalem Temple's golden objects
were placed in the Roman Temple of Peace. It was at this
time that Statius lived and wrote his poetry. They were then
spoiled by Genseric and borne off to Carthage, and from
there by Belisarius and borne off to Constantine. There
they were recognized by the Jewish community and at their
prayers the Emperor Justinian sent them to Jerusalem. The
Temple treasures' pilgrimage had brought them from Egypt to
Israel, to Babylon, to Jerusalem, to Rome, to Carthage, to
Constantinople, and then all trace of their whereabouts is
tragically lost. [23]

However, the seemingly less precious objects of the
Jerusalem Temple, which the Egyptian gold had once served to
adorn, such as the veil, the chest and the writings,
Josephus tells us, were taken to the Palatine; Helena and
Constantine were said to have given these to the Lateran.
Roman pilgrim guides invariably stated that the Ark, or
chest, and its treasures, the tables of stone inscribed with
the Law, the manna of the wilderness and Aaron's rod, were
housed in the Lateran. However, pilgrim accounts repeat each
other. Though all the guide books spoke of them as there no
pilgrim said he saw them. Where in the Lateran they were
actually kept is uncertain. Logically they would have been
placed in the chapel called the Sancta Sanctorum which the
Pope entered only one day of the year and which mirrored the
Temple's Holy of Holies in which the Ark was originally kept
and which the High Priest entered only once a year. A Welsh
poem indicates this was so.[24] However, the Lateran
Basilica was sacked and destroyed many times. Today there is
neither evidence nor memory there of the Ark and its
treasures. The memory of the Lateran as "Tempio" and the
treasures of the Temple of Jerusalem linger, however, in
Dante's poetry.

A further Jerusalem substitution or rather palimpsest
of a Jerusalem upon a European city was Canterbury in
England. St. Thomas Becket, Archbishop of Canterbury,
murdered in his own cathedral in 1170, quickly became as if
England's Christ, Canterbury as if England's Jerusalem. The
iconography of Thomas' Christ-mirroring martyrdom is to be
found throughout Europe. On one side, usually, is the clerk
Grim, Thomas' crucifer, whose arm was struck by the sword
blows as he defended his archbishop (John of Salisbury
however sought safety in flight); on the other side are
three, sometimes four, knights who wield their heavy swords,
the armorial bearings clearly shown on their shields; in the
center St. Thomas is on his knees, raising his hands to God
in prayer. For this crime none of the knights was appre-
hended, though their king, Henry II, walked barefoot to
Canterbury as a penitent pilgrim and was scourged while
naked by the monks at its altar. Other kings from other
lands also journeyed barefoot on pilgrimage to the archbishop's tomb. [25] Henry VIII, however, walked barefoot not
to Canterbury but to Walsingham. [26]

London was the city of Thomas' birth, Canterbury the
site of the martyrdom, the one as if his Bethlehem, the
other as if his Jerusalem. The journey between the two
cities thus imitated the Saint's _vita et passio_. Chaucer's
Canterbury Tales' pilgrimage from a London inn to
Canterbury's cathedral reflects this. The archbishop in

turning from worldly pomp and secular power as the king's
favorite and becoming the man of God, servant of the Church
and sainted martyr, provided a "bri3t mirrour," a speculum,
as Langland put it, to all bishops (B.XV.435-443,551-555).
The medieval world saw bishops as types of Moses and popes
as types of Aaron. [27]   Thomas' martyrdom shaped Canterbury
as England's Jerusalem, upon which pilgrims, especially in
Jubilee years, converged; his birth in London made him the
patron saint of that city. [28]

Pilgrims journeying to Canterbury, like Chaucer's Monk,
showed their intent not with Jerusalem crosses, nor with
Roman keys, but with jangling Canterbury bells. The blood
shed at the martyrdom was cast into the water of St. Thomas'
Well and pilgrims were given this water in phials which were
reputed to be miraculous, especially against plagues. Some
of the ampulles were inscribed: "Optimus egrorum medicus fit
Toma bonorum" [Thomas is the best doctor for sick good
people] (Figure 8). These ampulles with St. Thomas' well
water and badges with St. Thomas' head or figure on them
were the signs of the completed pilgrimage. [29]   They were
Canterbury's answer to Jerusalem's palms, Rome's vernicles
and Compostela's shells. The Benedictine monks of
Canterbury's cathedral derived fat revenues from pilgrims.
The tomb of the Saint, like Jerusalem's Ark, was adorned with
gold, silver and precious gems that glinted in the light of
offering candles. Pilgrims slept overnight in its presence
seeking visions and miracles of healing in a practice
derived from the pagan world known as incubation which was
widely believed in by illiterate people. In time the
Lollards were to attack Canterbury's shrine and the
pilgrimage to it as so much Golden Calf idolatry. Henry VIII
was to obliterate the shrine and references to Thomas,
including those in Piers Plowman manuscripts, but not the
Canterbury Tales.

Stained glass windows at Canterbury, fabling sermons in
stone and light, celebrate the legends of St. Thomas'
healing miracles as well as episodes from the lives of Moses
and Aaron. One story in particular is of interest. Plague
breaks out in the house of Sir Jordan Fitzeisulf. The
children's nurse, Britonwy, dies. The others are healed by a
gift of St. Thomas' well water brought to them by Canterbury
pilgrims. However, the family fails to bring to the shrine
suitable offerings of gold and silver though St. Thomas
warns Gimp the Leper in a dream to remind them to do so.
Next St. Thomas is seen brandishing a drawn sword against
the negligent family (who were his friends while he was
alive) and the son is stricken with plague. Hastily they
make the promised pilgrimage bringing gifts of gold and

The Canterbury Ampulla.

Figure 9   Canterbury Ampulle
            Cutts

silver wire. [30] The tale, as also do many of those
connected with the Compostela pilgrimage, to St. James,
reflects aspects of Exodus.

There is yet another parallel between Canterbury's
cathedral and Jerusalem's Temple. The pilgrimage to Thomas
Becket's tomb became less popular than those to other
English shrines and so was artificially encouraged by
Canterbury's Jubilees of 1220, fifty years after the murder
in the cathedral, and of 1270. The Pope granted Jubilee
indulgences to Canterbury in return for a handsome payment
to his treasury in the years 1320, 1370, and every fifty
years thereafter until 1520. The Canterbury 1220 and 1270
Jubilees set the precedent for Rome's initial one of
1300. [31] Dante set his pilgrimage poem in the Roman Jubilee
year of 1300. The practice originated, however, not in Rome,
but first in Jerusalem in celebration of the Exodus, and
then at Canterbury in celebration of St. Thomas. Chaucer,
reader of Dante that he was, may well have contemplated
setting his Tales in 1370 when all converged upon holy
Canterbury seeking the Jubilee indulgence. Chaucer had been
in England that Eastertide, then had left for the Continent
on the king's business in June. [32] Kent and its capital,
Canterbury, lay on the busy road from London to Dover, the
route he would most likely have taken.

The Emmaus pattern sought to obliterate the need for
sacred places, having its pilgrimage take place in profane
regions, anywhere, rendering the entire world and all
people, sacred. The Exodus pattern demanded the progress
from the profane to the sacred. Consequently shrines in
Jerusalem, Rome, Compostela and Canterbury were inevitably
perceived as mirroring the Ark in the Temple. The Exodus
pattern, of the Old Testament, was the one most popular with
the common people, particularly those who were uneducated,
and the one appreciated by iconoclastic Puritans, though
they despised shrines and pilgrimages. The Emmaus pattern,
with its complex paradoxes lying at the very center of
Gospel teaching, was appreciated by the Fathers of the
Church and by Wyclifite Lollards. Learned lay poets of the
fourteenth century in France, Italy and England delighted in
imposing the two contrary patterns upon each other to create
and license their allegorical poems concerning pilgrimage.

The liturgical drama of the Officium Peregrinorum in
one version had already clearly linked Exodus and Emmaus
patterns. Manna in the form of communion wafers was dropped
from the ceiling upon the heads of the congregation below as
if they were pilgrimaging Israelites. In that play, that of
Padua, Christ had brought bread and wine for the supper at

the inn with him in his scrip and bottle. Moreover, Psalm
113 was sung at Easter Monday Vespers when the Officium
Peregrinorum was performed. The play thus dramatically
presented the New Law fulfilling, and not destroying, the
Old Law. [33]

While the Exodus and Emmaus patterns opposed each
other, they were thus also linked to each other. The one
wrote of the metamorphoses of Egyptian gold from the
idolatrous Golden Calf of Aaron to the sacred Tabernacle of
Moses. The other was written by the Gospeller telling of
pilgrims telling of fables and sermons and whose symbol from
the vision of Ezekiel, preceding his Gospel in such works as
the Book of Kells, was neither the Angel of Matthew, nor the
Lion of Mark, nor the Eagle of John, but the Bull of Luke.
Aaron's Golden Calf of the Exodus has merely progressed upon
a pilgrimage to become the Ox of the Physician Gospeller.
Both Exodus and Emmaus tales were about God's bread and
God's words. Medieval poets understood such patterns and
paradoxes as the "saumplerie" of God's poetry. Egyptian gold
and Emmaus inn, connected with actual pilgrimages, became
paradigms in poetry for the uses of poetic fables for
pilgrim sermons. They were as if "apologies for poetry."

CHAPTER SEVEN: "CHE D'EGITTO VEGNA IN IERUSALEMME"

In _Paradiso_ XXV, the pilgrim Saint James of Compostela says that Dante has been permitted to come upon a pilgrimage from Egypt to Jerusalem: "però li è conceduto che d'Egitto vegna in Ierusalemme" (55-56). This Exodus theme of pilgrimage is central to Dante's _Commedia_. Dante defined pilgrimage in _Vita Nuova_ XL, a work having forty-two chapters in order to mirror the forty-two stations of Exodus' pilgrimage from Egypt to Israel; then he recycled those definition of the different medieval pilgrimages in the _Commedia_'s pilgrimage similes, imposing the Exodus pattern upon the European landscape. He discoursed upon the pilgrim Psalm 113 in _Convivio_ II and the Epistola X to Can Grande and used it in the _Commedia_'s _Purgatorio_ II. His _Vita Nuova_ pilgrims and those of his _Commedia_ similes would have likewise sung its verses to its _tonus peregrinus_.

In _Convivio_ II.1 Dante gave the pilgrim psalm, which sermons against idolatry, as an example of theological allegory in opposition to poetic allegory:

. . . sì come vedere si può in quello canto del Profeta che dice che, ne l'uscita del popolo d'Israel d'Egitto, Giudea è fatta santa e libera. Che avvegna essere vero secondo la lettera sia manifesta, non meno è vero quello che spiritualmente s'intende, cioè che ne l'uscita de l'anima dal peccato, essa sia fatta santa e libera in sua potestate.

[. . . as it can be seen in the Prophet's psalm, saying that in the Exodus of the people of Israel from Egypt, Judah was made holy and free. Which is so according to the letter; it is not less true when taken spiritually, which is that the soul abandoning sin, is made holy and free in her influence.][1]

Augustine had discussed this psalm as prophecy, choosing
Psalm 113's account over the Exodus, because its poetry
departs from the other's history.[2] Dante, in the Convivio,
concurs, saying that Psalm 113 is both letter and spirit,
history and prophecy. Then he uses Psalm 113 in the
Commedia, a poem mirroring the psalm's pilgrimage and
prophecy.

In the Commedia the psalm is not merely written of, but
heard, being sung by a choir of a hundredfold Jubilee
pilgrim souls brought from Augustine and Monica's Ostia, the
seaport of Rome, to the shores of Purgatory (II.46). Hebrew
pilgrims had sung this psalm while entering Jerusalem
bearing palms to lay on the horns of the Temple's altar in
an annual celebration of the Exodus from Egypt's bondage.
Then for centuries it was sung by Christian pilgrims to the
tonus peregrinus in its Gregorian chanting, representing a
tradition from its Hebrew chanting.[3] From this practice
came the Christian name for Jerusalem pilgrims as "Palmieri"
[Palmers]. The psalm was sung in its entirety at the font in
the Easter Vespers litany as it is sung in its entirety
("con quanto di quel salmo è poscia scripto" [with what
follows after of that psalm as it is written] II.48) by
pilgrims on Purgatory's morning shores at the very hour when
in antipodal Jerusalem the Easter Vespers would be
celebrated. Casella's song is as its idle and idolatrous
contrefait.[4]

With the Commedia a letter, Epistola X, was written as
commentary for Can Grande della Scala, Dante's Maecenas and
patron. The letter discusses the allegory of Psalm 113 in
far greater detail than had the Convivio's passage
concerning it. It is become the Commedia's matrix. Dante
interprets the psalm with the scriptural fourfold allegory:
the first sense (literal) is of the historical journeying of
the children of Israel from Egypt at the time of Moses; the
second (allegoria) signifies the redemption wrought by
Christ of which the Exodus is the type; the third (moral)
signifies the conversion of the soul from sinful misery to a
state of grace; the fourth (anagogical) is the journeying of
the soul from the bondage of corruption to the liberty of
eternal glory.[5] It is in this letter that Dante speaks of
such allegory as "polysemous" [many-meaninged].

A debate has raged among Dante scholars as to whether
the Letter to Can Grande, Epistola X, is genuine or not, and
then as to whether Dante has used the fourfold "allegory of
the theologians" or merely the more simple "allegory of the
poets" for his poem.[6] This chapter will argue that Dante
uses both forms. The "allegory of the theologians" is

incarnate allegory, true in both letter and spirit, both flesh and word, the word becoming flesh; the "allegory of the poets" clothes its truth in beautiful lies ("una veritade ascosa sotto bella menzogna" says Convivio II.1 of this), and is structured not upon fact, but fantasy, and is admittedly a fable. Poets, imitating God's Creation, may write carnal allegories; but their words cannot become flesh, they cannot write incarnate allegories. Augustine notes that the psalmist wrote of both times past and future, both letter and spirit. Dante contrives a similar prophetic mode of writing (though he, Par. X.7 and 22, XXXIII.142, and his son Pietro Alighieri, speak of the poem as "alta fantasia" [high fantasy]), by having his pilgrim self, within the poem, journey, in 1300, amidst a landscape that is prescient of the events of his exile from Florence in 1302, while he writes after that event.[7] Thus the Commedia artfully mirrors the "allegory of the theologians" by incorporating as prophecy of the future Dante's past exile. The Aeneid similarly contained Sybilline prophecies. Joyce in Ulysses will borrow Virgil and Dante's contrivance. Dante, like Aeneid's Sinon, like Tristan's Isolde, lies truthfully.

Present and past, Florence and Egypt, coexist in the mental yet temporal and spatial aspects of the Inferno's vision. Dante equates the one with the other; both represent the bondage of the world and Cain-like exile from God's face.[8] The equation of Florence with Egypt and Babylon, the Crusaders' name for Cairo, and the poem's Tuscan language rather than Latin, grant Dante's Jeremiad a "local habitation and a name." Dante gave Psalm 113, "In exitu Israel de Aegypto," as the patterning of the poem. This Exodus pattern, celebrated by the psalm, was noted by a generation of fourteenth-century commentators to be the pattern of the Commedia, then forgotten until a handful of modern scholars rediscovered it.[9] It is still not entirely unfolded by modern commentators. It provides the poem's pilgrimage "allegory of the theologians," and thereby requires that the literal sense be no fiction. The Exodus once took place. Italian and Florentine Dante, as he writes, is in exile, his poem leading from despair's bondage to pilgrimage's freedom. The Commedia is as a typological mirroring of Exodus and Psalm 113, albeit adorned with the lying "allegory of the poets," with Egyptian gold. It is both fact and fiction.

Medieval pilgrimages to the Holy Places frequently commenced by disembarking at Alexandria, journeying to old Cairo, known as Babylon, and next setting forth to Sinai and Jerusalem to reenact the pilgrimages of history, the returns

from the exiles of Egypt and Babylon. The _Inferno_ is an
anti-peregrinate book, the book of exile from God; therefore
its landscape is of Egyptian bondage and Babylonian
confusion, and not of _Purgatorio_'s Sinai Wilderness of
pilgrimage, nor of _Paradiso_'s _visio pacis_, the city of
Jerusalem. Virgil and Dante enter the città dolente, Hell,
through what may be a Roman Janus arch with incised and
imperial inscription (the manuscript illuminations, however,
concur with Michelini's famous fresco in Florence's Duomo in
consistently showing it as a Florentine city gate, Plate
XII), and the two pilgrim exiles, Virgil and Dante, traverse
the gyring, labyrinthine circles; in the second of which
they find souls associated with Egyptian Babylon and African
Carthage.

The lustful sinners of _Inferno_ V are compared to
wheeling flights of birds migrating along the Nile:

> E come li stornei ne portan l'ali
> nel freddo tempo, a schiera larga e piena,
> . . . .
> E come i gru van cantando lor lai,
> faccendo in aere di sé lunga riga,

> [And as their wings bear along the starlings, at the
> cold season, in large and crowded groups . . . . And
> as the cranes go chanting their lays, making a long
> streak of themselves in the air,]   (40-48)

to be elucidated as Egyptian migrants, _gerim_, in _Purgatorio_
XXIV.64-66:

> Come li augei che vernan lungo 'l Nilo.
> [As the birds that winter along the Nile.]

The simile of cranes in Egypt is, again, borrowed Egyptian
gold. In Statius' _Thebaid_ XII.759, they were compared to
votaries: "before the Dome/ A Train of Pilgrims stood, but
all give Way. . . . Thus when a well-rang'd Host of
feather'd Cranes survey the _Pharian_ Coast,/ They stretch
their Necks, and clapping, as they fly. Such is their Joy to
scape the Winter's Reign,/ And share in Nile the summer
Heats again."[10]

The first lover of that band is the Empress of Babylon,
enemy of Jerusalem, Semiramis. Dante notes that she is ruler
of the land of the Soldan, of Egypt, "Babylon" being the
name crusaders and pilgrims gave old Cairo and which they
thought of as the city of the Apocalypse's Scarlet Whore.
Virgil's Dido of Carthage, for whom Augustine wept in

restless lustfulness, and Cleopatra, again of Egypt, follow
her. Tristan, lust's pilgrim, whose story crusaders enacted
at Acre before it fell, is of their band. Concerning such
figures are tragic lays composed, their poetry being as an
Egyptian Golden Calf, to be read in idleness.

When Dante comes to the city of Dis, John Demaray has
noted, he sees it as if he were a pilgrim viewing the
mosques and minarets of the Egyptian "Babylon" rather than
Jerusalem or Rome or Florence.[11]   He tells Virgil:

> "Maestro, già le sue meschite
> là entro certe ne la valle cerno,
> vermiglie come se di foco uscite
>   fossero."

["Master, already I discern its mosques distinctly
there within the valley, red as if they had come out
of fire."]   (VIII. 70-73)

The pilgrim cry upon seeing Jerusalem, Rome or Compostela
was "Mon Joie." At such places a Gothic stone cross was
raised, itself called a "Mon Joie."[12]   That cry is not
heard here of this città dolente, nor is there here such a
symbol of redemption. Satan's city as Babylon is an
inversion of Jerusalem. He, as Egyptian Pharoah against whom
Israelites strove, as Saracen Soldan against whom Crusaders
strove, is an inversion of God. His is "Mawmettrie's"
"up-so-doun" realm.

In Egypt, before Moses could accomplish the pilgrimage
of the Exodus, ten plagues were visited upon Pharoah's
people. Rhoda Ruditsky has suggested that the plague of the
rivers turned to blood, of frogs, of lice, of flies, of
boils, of hail, of locusts, of darkness and of death are
woven into the Infernal tapestry. Only the plague of the
cattle murrain, she says, is completely missing.[13]   To her
observations I should like to add others. Dante's time
connected Babylon with Egypt and viewed history as
Apocalypse. St. John in Revelation not only consciously
rewrote Ezekiel but also Exodus. He listed not ten, but
seven, last plagues. They were of sores, of living creatures
in the waters dying, of the waters turned to blood, of fire,
of darkness, of frogs, of hail. These were visited upon the
denizens of Babylon, rather than Jerusalem, upon those who
idolatrously worshiped the Beast rather than God. Babylon,
for medieval pilgrims, was Egyptian. Many of these seven
plagues and many of the other ten can be found in Dante's
Inferno.

The plague of hail Dante describes in Canto VI:

> Grandine grossa, acqua tinta e neve
> per l'aere tenebroso si riversa;
> pute la terra che questo riceve;

> [Large hail, turgid water and snow pour down through
> dark air, the ground that receives it stinks;] (10-12)

and the marsh that results:

> Questa palude ch 'l gran puzzo spira
> cigne dintorno la città dolente,

> [This marsh, which exhales the mighty stench, girds
> round the sorrowing city,]

is described in Canto IX.31-32. It recalls that of the
Exodus' "paludes Aegypti" [marshes of Egypt] (8.5); and it
reflects at the same time that marsh, the "livida paluda,"
Virgil described around the doomed city of Troy and in which
deceiving Sinon concealed himself. Dante delights in such
literary linkings of pilgrim tales, one with the other. From
that landscape Aeneas will depart upon a Roman pilgrimage,
just as from it Moses will depart upon a Jerusalem one, the
one prompted by the idol of the Wooden Horse, the other
associated with the idol of the Golden Calf, both images of
beasts.

In this same canto occurs the first Dantean frog
simile. An angel messenger with a wand at Dis' gate,
summoned by Virgil, disperses the evil spirits who scatter:

> Come le rane innanzi a la nimica
> biscia per l'acqua si dileguan tutte,
> fin ch'a la terra ciascuna s'abbica.

> [As frogs, before the enemy snake, all scatter through
> the water, till each piles itself up upon the land.]
> (76-79)

In the Exodus account, Aaron is instructed by Moses to
scatter the plague of frogs over the land from the rivers
and marshes by means of a wand or virga held "super aquas
Aegypti, et ascenderunt ranae operueruntque terram Aegypti"
[over the waters of Egypt, and the frogs came up and covered
the land of Egypt] (8.6). Aaron's rod, like Moses', Exodus
4.2-4, has the capacity of turning into a snake (7.10-12).
Yorkshire's St. Mary's Abbey shows Moses with the Tables of
the Law and Aesculapian caduceus.[14] The simile has similarly

turned the angel's rod into a snake that scatters evil
spirits turned into frogs up upon the land. Pharaoh
prevailed upon Moses to end the plague, the frogs died and
"computruit terra" [the land stank]. Dante had already
described "questa palude che il gran puzzo spira" [This
marsh, which exhales the mighty stench] (31) which results
from this pollution.

Aaron's rod was associated with the pilgrim's staff,
the Latin word for both being _virga_. Cesare Ripa notes that
Esilio's bordon or staff is borne in the right hand (Figure
1). Dante, likewise, takes pains to have the angel, summoned
by Virgil and sent by God, hold the disciplinary wand (_una
verghetta_) in his right hand, while brushing away the murk
with his left (82-84). This wand becomes, in the simile, the
serpent caduceus of Aaron's _virga_, associated with Exodus,
plague and pilgrimage. As for the frogs, the _Glossa_ for
Exodus 8.6, recalling Revelation 16.13 in which Antichrist
also spews forth frogs when misleading his worshipers,
interprets them as lying poetry.[15]   The figures of Aaron and
Virgil (whose name puns on the _virga Aaronis_) contain false
elements and true; Aaron's frogs and Aaron's Golden Calf,
like Virgil's poetry and Virgil's Wooden Horse, can punish,
but not reward; their pattern is tragic.

Dante does not allow these frogs to be forgotten. We
meet the barrators lying in pitch like frogs:

    E come a l'orlo de l'acqua d'un fosso
    stanno i ranocchi pur col muso fuori,
    sì che celano i piedi a l'altro grosso.

    [And as at the edge of the water of a ditch the frogs
    lie with only their muzzles out, so that they hide
    their feet and other bulk]   (XXII.25-27)

While still discussing this incident Dante mentions a fable
of Aesop concerning a frog who plays a similar deceptive
trick as does Ciampolo, XXIII.4-6, who has in the simile
already been compared to a frog. The _Glossa_ for Exodus 8.6
saw the singing of frogs as representing deceiving fables.
Dante here amusingly links deceit, fable and frog.

The frogs are now the sinners in Hell and in the ninth
circle we meet them glazed in ice where the Keatsian simile:

    E come a gracidar si sta la rana
    col muso fuor de l'acqua, quando sogna
    di spigolar sovente la villana,

[And as the frog to croak lies with his muzzle out of
the water, when the peasant girl often dreams she is
gleaning,]   (XXXII.31-33)

weaves that plague of frogs of the peregrinate Exodus once
again into the poetry of the Inferno; only this time its
loveliness, borrowed here from Ovid and not from Jerome or
Aesop, contrasts violently with the horror of the scene to
which it is compared. Ovid, another poet of exile, had
Lycian peasants, for their rudeness to a goddess, be changed
to the horrid posture of frogs, half in, half out of water.
The Inferno text, where sinners blaspheme against God as "la
nimica podesta" [the enemy power] (VI.96), punishes them
similarly. Dante has thus brought together a plague of frogs
out of the rivers of Hebrew, Greek and Latin writings, from
Jerome, Aesop and Ovid, and spewed them forth over that land
where Tuscan is so often spoken. The plague in the poem is
self-consciously, self-referentially, self-reflectively,
about poetry.

The plague of darkness is one omnipresent throughout
the Inferno since the sun fell silent on Dante's
journeyings, except for that penumbra of light about the
philosophers and poets of the classical world. The plague of
sores is encountered in Cantos XXIX.40-XXX as the punishment
for the falsifiers; for that Adam who falsified the florins
marked with St. John the Baptist and the lily of Florence,
for that Sinon who wrought Troy's Fall with the treachery of
the Wooden Horse contrived by means of his own true-seeming
lies (Aeneid II.65-198), both being thereby artificers of
false idols, of Golden Calves. Another of the plagues of
Egypt and Babylon, of Exodus and Apocalypse, was that of
rivers turned to blood. Indeed, the manuscript illuminations
of the Inferno in showing this are often derived from the
established iconography of the codices of Virgil's Aeneid
rather than from Biblical material, though these rivers of
blood are from both Exodus and Aeneid VI; just as,
poetically, Ovid, the poet of exile and conversion (the
Tristia, the Metamorphoses), is often echoed, yoked with
scriptural allusions. One senses that a further plague could
well be that of poetry. "Ranae significant carmina poetarum"
[the frogs signify the songs of poets] had said the Glossa
of that plague and went on to speak of their lying fables.[16]
Dante inflicts Egyptian and Babylonian plagues upon
Florentine, Italianate Inferno, punishing, in a fable, its
denizens. He writes in the realm of lies the lying "allegory
of the poets," using their Egyptian gold to do so,
though his Exodus and exile structuring is from the
"allegory of the theologians." Both truth and lie are
present in the text.

After the murk of the <u>Inferno</u> in which stars can be spoken of but not seen amidst the plague of darkness, Dante and Virgil, on the shores of <u>Purgatorio</u>, meet Cato whose face is illumined by the light of the four stars of the pagan virtues, Prudence, Justice, Fortitude and Temperance. The sun has not yet dawned this Resurrection day. The three stars, Faith, Hope and Charity, the Christian virtues, are yet to be seen. We are still in the realm of Oldness, rather than Newness. Cato's stars and those other three, which Dante says, were "non viste mai fuor ch'a la prima gente" [never yet seen save by the first people] (24), are of the southern hemisphere, the Southern Cross, a statement that makes of Ulysses a liar where he has said: "Tutte le stelle già de l'altro polo la notte, e 'l nostro tanto basso che non surgёa fuor vedea del marin suolo" [The night already saw the other pole, with all its stars, and ours so low that it did not rise from the ocean floor] (<u>Inf</u>. XXVI.127-129). Dante had fabricated a pilgrim fable for Ulysses and has him tell it in the realm of lies. However, in the Apocalypse all seven stars will be present (Revelation 1.20), John saying he saw them. In pilgrim poetry truth and lies are curiously interchangeable.

Stoic Cato is also a pagan, but, unlike Ulysses, he refused to transgress beyond the bounds and would not enquire beyond the <u>quia</u>. For Dante's orgulous Ulysses, whom the Stoics had seen as a hero and saint and whom the Third Vatican Mythographer termed the "Omnium Peregrinus," adding that "wisdom makes men pilgrims among all terrestrial things," <u>scientia</u>, knowledge, not <u>sapientia</u>, wisdom, was the primary goal, for which one cast aside the pagan virtues of Prudence, Justice and Temperance, while saying untruthfully one sought virtue thereby. Dante contrasts Greek Ulysses with Roman Cato. In the <u>Pharsalia</u> of Lucan, Cato is asked, upon his exilic pilgrimage into Africa from Rome, to consult the oracular idol of Jupiter Ammon. Labienus tells him, "I cannot think of any man for whom Heaven would be readier to reveal the hidden truths than your pure and virtuous self. It is clear that you have always lived in accordance with divine principles and are a follower of God." But Cato rebukes him, saying that the "author of the Universe told us at our birth, once and for all, as much as we are allowed to know" (IX.545-583).[17]   Cato's stern reticence contrasts greatly with Ulysses' <u>curiositas</u>. Ulysses had stolen Troy's Palladion, her goddess of wisdom, and substituted for it the idol of the Wooden Horse, of folly and lechery. Dante had sought, out of curiosity, through Virgil's sybilline pages of Latin (the <u>sortes virgilianae</u>), as Virgil had in turn through those of Homer in Greek, Virgil stealing lines from Homer, Dante from Virgil. Now Virgil and Dante quail before

Cato's severity who rejects, though he is a pagan, idols,
oracles, curiosity and poetry.

Dante describes Cato:

vidi presso di me un veglio solo,
. . . . .
Lunga la barba e di pel bianco mista
portava, a 'suoi capelli simigliante,
de' quai cadeva al petto doppia lista.

[I saw near me an old man solitary . . . . His beard
long and mixed into the white fleece he wore, which
matched his hair that fell upon his breast biforked.]
(I.31-36)

Bearded and solitary Cato, clad in fleece, is seen
corporeally as the true pilgrim of medieval iconography.
Most souls encountered in the Commedia are nude. Cato's garb
of sheepskin ("di pel bianco" [of white fleece]) is that
worn by the eremetical Thebiad and Sinaitic monks who
emulated those "strangers and pilgrims" who "wandered about
in sheepskins and goatskins . . . in deserts, and in
mountains, and in dens and caves of the earth" (Hebrews
11.37-38). His beard is that of the ascete of the desert,
and of the medieval pilgrim who allows no iron to touch hair
or nail; it is flowing and biforked; its white locks mingle
with the white sheepskin he wears.

Cato on Purgatorio's desert shore at the foot of Sinai
is placed amidst a pilgrim landscape. Yet his pilgrim aspect
is derived also from Lucan's classic portrait of him. The
stars illuminating his face are of the pagan virtues. Cato
in clean-shaven Rome, at his remarriage to Marcia, wore a
beard to mourn Civil War in the Roman world: "The husband
refused to remove the shaggy growth from his reverend face:
nor did his stern features grant access to joy. Even since
he saw the weapons of ill-omened war raised up, he had
suffered the grey hair to grow long over his stern brow and
the beard of a mourner to spread over his face; for he
alone, free from love and free from hate, had leisure to
wear mourning for mankind" (II.372-378). Beatrice will later
chide Dante for his lack of a beard, the classical badge of
the mourner, the Christian badge of the pilgrim (Purg.
XXI.67-75).[18] Dante, Florentine exile and pilgrim of Amor,
is by no means stoically "free from love and free from
hate."

Dante's treatment of Cato blends Hebraic and Hellenic,
Stoic and Christian elements. The same is true of the

Commedia's Virgil. It has become customary to note Cato's
likeness to Moses.[19] However, Cato and Virgil together can
be argued to be types of Moses and Aaron. After the Exodus
episodes of the Egyptian plagues the Israelites journeyed
through the Sinai wilderness. At the foot of Mount Sinai
they camped in tents while Moses communed with God. In his
absence they became restless and went to Aaron, Moses'
brother, saying, "Up, make us gods" (32.1). Aaron foolishly
advised them to fashion a Golden Calf out of the Egyptian
spoils of gold and silver they had brought with them into
the wilderness. Moses, returning, witnessed this idolatry
and rebuked the Israelites in great anger.

Dante at the commencement of the Commedia, in the
Inferno, was in a like state as were the pilgrim Israelites
in the wilderness. The selva oscura, which is described
there as "selvaggia e aspra e forte" [wild and harsh and
rugged] (I.5), was similarly a wilderness. Both Israelites
and Dante at this juncture lacked a leader and were exiled
from the face of God. The three beasts, symbolizing bodily
vices which impede the soul from pilgrimage, prevented
Dante's ascent of the sun-clad mountain, and his guide who
then appeared led him not to the light but to the infernal
darkness, in the bestial direction, while telling him of
that Rome of "li dèi falsi e bugiardi" [the false and lying
gods] (I.72). Medieval men knew that in classical times the
emperors and gods were worshiped as idols upon blood-stained
pillars; the Roman Wolf and likewise the Golden Calf being
iconographically shown as beasts atop such pillars.[20] The
Wilderness in which Dante is lost is pagan, whether of Rome
or Egyptian Sinai.

Virgil, whom Dante meets "nel gran diserto" [in that
vast desert], is not only the classic poet but also a type
of Exodus' Aaron. The Aeneid's poet's name had undergone a
change in the Middle Ages from "Vergilius" to "Virgil,"
after the word for wand, staff, rod, virga, because of his
roles as Roman magician and as pedagogue. Dante, ironically
in the light of Inferno XIII, where Dante plucks the tree
branch which bleeds and speaks, calls Virgil, "il dolce
pedagogo" [the gentle pedagogue] (Purg. XII.3). The Roman
paedagogus was really a slave who disciplined his young
master with the rod, the epithet here thus manifesting the
young master's fearful and flattering servility to the
slave. Virgil, like Aaron, is for a while a "false staff,"
a servile pedagogue, guiding his master astray into pagan
realms; not up Sinai's sun-clad slopes of liberty, but
down into the region of bondage, to Egyptian and Babylonian
plagues. Aaron, like the medieval Virgil, was a magician
(Exodus 7.8-12); Aaron, like the medieval Virgil, was a
prophet (7.1). Aaron used a rod or virga to bring about

Egyptian plagues, that _virga_ becoming a Roman pilgrim relic among the treasures of the Ark at St. John Lateran.

Singleton observed that the landscapes of the _Inferno_'s opening and the _Purgatorio_'s are the same, of Exodus. In the _Purgatorio_, amidst a landscape and seascape over which Cato as Moses dominates, in contrast to the _Inferno_'s over which Virgil as Aaron is vice-gerent, a hundredfold pilgrims disembark upon the shore singing Psalm 113's _tonus peregrinus_, which translates Exodus' Golden Calf into a condemnation of all pagan idols, of all "dèi falsi e bugiardi." Cato, who had been like Moses in the shining of his face (Exodus 34.35),

> Li raggi di le quattro luci sante
> fregiavan sì la sua faccia di lume
> ch'i 'l vedea come 'l sol fosse davante,

> [The rays of the four holy lights adorned his face so
> with brightness that I saw him as the sun were before
> him,]   (I.37-39)

has left the scene, again like Moses leaving the Israelites while communing with God on Sinai. Dante is greeted by one of the pilgrim souls. It is Casella. Dante asks him to sing solo one of Dante's own poems:

> "Se nuova legge non ti toglie
> memoria o uso a l'amoroso canto
> che mi solea quetar tutte mie doglie,
>   di ciò ti piaccia consolare alquanto
> l'anima mia, che, con la sua persona
> venendo qui, è affanato tanto"

> ["If a new law does not take from you memory or skill
> in the song of love which used to calm all my desires,
> may it please you with this to comfort my soul
> somewhat which with its body coming here is so
> labored."]   (II.106-111)

Robert Hollander has related this speech to its echo in Canto I of the _Inferno_, the ship-wrecked Dante "con lena affanata" [with laboring breath], and to the _Consolation_ of Boethius in which lust's poetry was false consolation.[21] It also is resonant with Virgil's own words of the _Inferno_'s Canto I:

> ché quello imperador che là sù regna,
> perch' i' fu' ribellante a la sua legge,
> non vuol che 'n sua città per me si vegna.

[For that Emperor who reigns above, because I was
rebellious to his law, wills not that I come into his
city.]   (124-126)

The infernal "legge" [law] is both Mosaic and Imperial,
Hebraic and Roman, the Old Law; the _Purgatorio_'s "nuova
legge" [new law] is Christ's, of Amor, of charity, and not
of cupidity and idolatry. Virgil's rebellion exiles him
perpetually. But it is Jerusalem from which he is exiled,
not Rome; it is the Mosaic law forbidding idolatry he has
broken, not the Imperial. His _Aeneid_ idolizes Mars, Venus,
Neptune and Augustus, bronze and marble statues upon pillars
requiring lustrations of blood, rather than Christ.

New and Old Laws alike condemn the self-centerdness of
Dante and Virgil's rapt listening to Casella's siren voice
singing the "amoroso canto." In their ears had been the
hundredfold choir singing of pilgrim liberty from Egypt's
idols. Now they have returned to the poetry of lust's
bondage. They worship the Golden Calf. The two songs, like
the two laws, are placed together, but their true order is
here reversed. Sometimes motets, in this manner, placed
sacred Latin texts, generally from the Psalms, together with
vernacular, profane verses. If the hearer only paid
attention to the profane words he missed the totality of the
music.[22] The two juxtaposed songs, however, exemplified the
old fulfilled in the new, the Golden Calf's Egyptian gold
and silver adorning the Ark of God. Here in _Purgatorio_ II
are found separated what ought to be joined: the Latin Psalm
113, "In exitu Israel de Aegypto" and the vernacular song,
"Amor che ne la mente mi ragiona" [Love that discourses in
my mind], as the pilgrim "Jesu, nostra redemptio, amor et
desiderium."

Cato, like Moses, in righteous anger comes upon the
tranced throng and chastizes them with "Correte al monte"
[Haste to the mountain]. Cato's severity at the pilgrims
staying from their journey to hear Casella sing Dante's song
is Moses' anger when he descended the mountain and found the
Israelites worshiping the Golden Calf. The poet Virgil
permitted Casella's singing of Dante's poem, Aaron the
Golden Calf worshiping. Aaron and Virgil are conjoined here
and associated with failed pilgrimage and cupidinous
artifices. Dante, with Virgil's cursed blessing, seems to
lapse once more into the prideful sin of the poet who uses
his artifice for the glorification of self, not God. He
abuses Egyptian gold--that his reader will not do so.

Cato had had Virgil baptize Dante with morning dew and
by Purgatory's shore gird him with a rush of humility

(I.118-136). That baptism too is part of the Exodus pattern, for Exodus was, liturgically, the type of baptism. Both the Red Sea and the Jordan had been crossed by the Israelite pilgrims.[23]   Psalm 113 was sung at the medieval Easter Vespers at the baptismal font at the same hour that it is heard here in the Antipodes and that psalm contains the words: "Quid est tibi mare quod fugisti? et tu Jordanis, quia conversus es retrorsum?" [What ailest thee, o thou sea, that fleddest? thou Jordan, that thou wast driven back?](5), stressing the parallels between the Red Sea and the Jordan. The Inferno's polysemous simile:

> E come quei che con lena affannata,
> uscito fuor del pelago a la riva,
> si volge a l'acqua perigliosa e guata,
>   così l'animo mio, ch'ancor fuggiva,
> si volse a retro a rimirar lo passo
> che non lasciò già mai persona viva,

[And as he, who with laboring breath has escaped from the deep sea to the shore, turns to the dangerous waters and gazes, so my mind which was still fleeing, turned back to gaze upon the pass that no one ever left alive,]   (I.22-27)

had referred both to a shipwrecked Aeneas landing upon Carthaginian shores and to saved Israelites gazing upon the Red Sea closing over the Memphian chivalry sent by Pharaoh. Baptism kills the old Egyptian self, saving the new Israelite self; it is a death into a new life. Therefore fraudulent, orgulous Ulysses, in the Commedia, must die by drowning and be met in Inferno (Plate VIa). He is the Greek threat to Troy and Rome; in Dante's catenary scheme of things the equivalent thereby of the Egyptian and Babylonian threat to Jerusalem and Rome, of the Saracen threat to Christendom. Dante has wedded Hellenic and Hebraic matter, Ulyssean lie and Christian truth.

Cato and Virgil, transplanted from a Classic world to one that is Judaeo-Christian by means of Dante's alchemy, become types of Aaron and Moses. Another type whom Virgil represents is St. John the Baptist. In a Neapolitan manuscript (London, BL Add. 19587, fol. 62; Plate IXa), Cato appears iconographically as Moses and as Christ, his head surrounded by a nimbus of light, while the gesture of Virgil is not unlike that of St. John the Precursor baptizing Christ. Dante genuflects to Cato as would the donor before his saints in medieval portraiture, such as is seen in the portrait of Richard II in the Wilton Diptych. Dante is then shown as if baptized by Virgil while in a Christlike stance.

The water is not shown as the Red Sea or the Jordan or as
dew upon the grass but as a small circular pool, the
traditional iconography for a baptismal well. This recalls
the singing of Psalm 113 in the Easter liturgy at the
baptismal font. That St. John baptized souls in the
Wilderness about Jordan and that Moses' journeying through
the Wilderness, crossing the Red Sea and the Jordan, were
traditionally interpreted as types of baptism as well as
being prototypical of pilgrimage, render this scene
polysemously: Cato is as a Moses and a Christ; Virgil as an
Aaron and a St. John the Baptist (all three, Virgil, Aaron
and John, it should be noted, prophets); Dante as an
Israelite and a Christian.

That Dante, the Florentine exile writing of the Roman
Jubilee, should make of his guide a type of St. John the
Baptist at this juncture, is especially apt. Florence's
patrons, old and new, were Mars ("Arma virumque cano" [I
sing of arms and the man]) and St. John the Baptist, whose
figure was stamped upon Florence's florins. Rome's Basilica
of St. John Lateran contained the rod of Aaron, the pilgrim
virga Aaronis and the pilgrim camelskin sclavin of the
Baptist (some accounts saying the Ark also held Moses'
caduceus virga).[24]   In Dante's Florence and in Dante's Rome,
the major ecclesiastical structures were dedicated to St.
John the Baptist. Virgil of Rome baptizing Florence's Dante,
is himself metamorphosed from Aaron to John, from old to
new.

The octagonal St. John the Baptist Duomo, Villani,
Dante's contemporary, tells us, mirrored Rome's Lateran
Basilica and its octagonal baptistery. Villani took pains to
note too that Florence was a "picciola Roma" [little Rome]
(I.42), being laid out after the plan of Rome by the Roman
Senate. This was done when, in order to put down the
Catiline conspiracy, Rome conquered Fiesole which had
harbored the traitors. In legend the Romans had built at the
city gate a temple, un tempio, to Mars who had given them
the victory over the treacherous Fiesolans. In Christian
times, Villani states, the sect at first "è dimoravano
ascesi in diverse montagne e caverne fuori della città"
[first dwelt hidden in mountains and in caves outside the
city] as "strangers and pilgrims." But with Constantine
Christianity triumphed and Florence's Temple of Mars was
converted to a Duomo dedicated to God and St. John the
Baptist, mirroring the Lateran's dedication. The idol of
Mars on its tall column at the center of that building was
taken to the other side of the city and set up looking over
the Arno by the Ponte Vecchio and in its place in the Duomo
was placed a large baptismal font. Its pillar is said to be

the one odd white one amidst the fifteen grey built into the
Christian edifice.[25]   According to legends Mars feuded with
St. John the Baptist for dominance of Florence. Similarly in
Jerusalem the Temple of Venus with its columned idol vied
with Calvary for dominance. The conflict between old and
new, idolatry and Christianity, the ancient admixture of
Fiesolan traitor and the sacred seed of Rome, was held to
give rise to the conflicts between Guelf and Ghibelline,
Black and White, which exiled Dante and many others from her
walls, and in this belief Pietro Alighieri's Commentary
concurs while Villani's History of Florence repeatedly
stresses this point. Similarly Augustine's City of God had
stressed the conflict between exilic Cain and pilgrim Abel,
idolatrous Babylon and godly Jerusalem, throughout history.

A map of Florence in Cacciaguida's time shows the
Baptistery of St. John to the north, the mutilated statue of
Mars to the south, close by the Ponte Vecchio. Dante
stresses this opposition of Mars and the Baptist first in
the Inferno, then in the Paradiso. A Florentine suicide in
Hell argues for Mars' hegemony:

> "I' fui de la città che nel Batista
> mutò 'l primo padrone; ond' ei per questo
>   sempre con l'arte sua la farà trista;
> e se non fosse che 'n sul passo d'Arno
> rimane ancor di lui alcuna vista,
>   que' cittadin che poi la rifondarno
> sovra 'l cener che d'Attila rimase,
> avrebber fatto lavorare indarno."

> [I was of that city that changed its first patron for
> the Baptist, on which account he with his art will
> always make it sorrowful; and were it not that at the
> passage of the Arno there yet remains some semblance of
> him, those citizens, who afterwards rebuilt it on the
> ashes left by Attila, would have worked in vain.]
> (XIII.143-151)

Dante, after this speech, "for love of his native place,"
gathers up the torn twigs. He has mutilated the suicide,
Pier delle Vigne, at Virgil's request (XIII.22-51); now he
attempts to undo that mutilation--which shadows Florence's
infernal act in still granting mutilated Mars dominance over
her. Florence still trusts in and placates "li dèi falsi e
bugiardi" [the false and lying gods]. The statue of Mars is
Florence's Golden Calf. The Inferno's verses are idolatrous
and filled with lies that seem truth, with fiction
masquerading as fact.

While the Florentine suicide's mutilated perspective
insists that Mars be honored, Cacciaguida's perspective is
the reverse and accords with the pilgrim psalm, 113, whose
liberating tonus peregrinus sings against idolatry. Dante's
crusading ancestor, encountered within the sphere of Mars
whose red spear and targe has been metamorphosed into a red
cross upon a white ground, speaks to Dante of Florence as
that city which geographically lay between Mars and the
Baptist: "tra Marte e 'l Batista" (Par. XVI.47), and later
refers to the mutilated statue and comments that it still
appears to require pagan lustrations of blood. A white-clad
bridegroom, Villani notes, V.38, had been slain at its foot
on Easter Monday in a rivalry that had commenced the
Florentine Guelf and Ghibelline vendetta. Cacciaguida
comments:

> Ma conveniesi, a quella pietra scema
> che guarda 'l ponte, che Fiorenza fesse
> vittima ne la sua pace postrema.
>
> [but it was fitting that to that mutilated statue which
> guards the bridge Florence should offer a victim in her
> last time of peace.]   (145-147)

His words are bitterly ironic. The Florence Cacciaguida
knew was a "visio pacis" [a vision of peace], the Latin of
the Hebrew word, "Jerusalem." Cacciaguida as knightly
crusader had fought for that vision of peace for Jerusalem
and Florence alike. It appears, amidst Florentine strife,
that now Mars is victorious. Dante must be Florence's Moses
bidding her to cease worshipping a Golden Calf, the idol of
Mars, lest God plague her. He does so as an exilic voice in
the Wilderness, a Jeremiah, a St. John the Baptist. The
message of his Commedia is prophetically Psalm 113's.

The present Duomo of Santa Maria del Fiore, domed by
Brunelleschi, was commenced in Dante's day but not completed,
and although it is shown in illuminations and frescoes
illustrating Dante (Plates VIIc,XII) it is there an
anachronism--unless his illuminators held that his Rose
prophesied that Duomo. It is the ancient octagonal structure
dedicated to the Baptist which is Dante's "bello ovile ov'io
dormi' agnello" [the fair sheepfold where I slept as a lamb]
(Par. XXV.5), and which mirrors the Lateran's octagonal
baptistery where Constantine was said to have been baptized;
and to this "bello ovile" Dante desires to return and be
absolved from the bitterness of the penitential exile. Or is
it to be crowned with laurel? The text is deliberately
ambiguous. The "capello" [chaplet] of which he speaks and
the "altro velle" [changed fleece] (7) are the distinctive

garb of the reconciled exile, where the Pope at the
Lateran,the Bishop in the Duomo, placed upon the penitent
the white robe and also bound his head with a white scarf or
stola, to represent a crown, in the manner of the saved in
Revelation. It liturgically echoed the baptismal rite;
pilgrimage and its return being spoken of in the Middle Ages
as a second baptism, a dying into a new life.[26]

Dante's language is baptismal:

> Io ritornai da la santissima onda
> rifatta sì come piante novelle
> rinovellate di novella fronde,
>   puro e disposto a salire a le stelle.

> [I came back from the most holy waters, born again even
> as new trees renewed with new foilage, pure and ready
> to mount to the stars.]   (Purg. XXXIII.142-5)

Baptisteries in their octagonal constructions,
especially those of Florence's Duomo and Rome's Lateran,
reflect Jerusalem's Holy Sepulchre in their architecture,
thus linking Christ's death with Christian rebirth.[27]   But
before Dante achieves that rebirth there is an arduous dying
to the world. Eight is the number of conversion from
oldness, to be followed by the vita nova, "nine" and "new,"
symbolizing Beatrice. Virgil states his bones were buried by
the Emperor Octavian: "fur l'ossa mie per Ottavian sepolte"
(Purg. VII.6). Virgil is not only as an Aaron to Cato's
Moses' role; he is also as if the Baptist, Beatrice as if
Christ; he is oldness, fulfilled by the new.

After the deadly landscapes of the Inferno Dante
performs a penitential pilgrimage upon the Mount of
Purgatorio. Similar pilgrimages with similar terraces and
gates were and are performed upon the Mountain of Sinai.[28]
In Canto IX Dante is admitted through a gate. An angel marks
upon his forehead seven P's. Father Dunstan Tucker has
suggested the parallels of this to the Ash Wednesday ritual
of the expulsion of the penitents who are at that time
marked upon the forehead with a cross formed from the oil
and ash of the previous year's palms. Edward Cutts suggested
that medieval pilgrims had the Jerusalem cross be so branded
or cut upon them with a sword. The Sarum Ritual's Benedictio
Peregrinorum states that canon law came to prohibit this
branding of the cross, or mark of Cain, upon the penitent
pilgrim, which indicates that such had once been the
practice.[29]   Dante in his poem has himself be marked upon
the forehead with the seven P's for "peccator" [sinner], cut
by a sword. He then ascends the seven terraces of the seven

sins, upon each one of which an angel with his wing feather
brushes away the P that is absolved by that terrace's
penance.[30]   When all seven are gone Dante attains Beatrice--
losing Virgil.

In Exodus the opposite of the Golden Calf is the
Tabernacle of the Ark, though both were fashioned with the
same gold and silver that had been spoiled of the Egyptians.
That Ark is in the Commedia. In Purgatorio X, on Pride's
terrace, the pilgrims view sculptures exemplifying humility.
In the first, Mary, the arca dei, is imaged with the angel
saying to her, "Ave." In the second, oxen draw the holy Ark
before which David dances, to Michal's scorn:

>   Era intagliata lì nel marmo stesso
> lo carro e' buoi, traendo l'arca santa,
> per che si teme officio non commesso.
> . . . .
>   Li precedeva al benedetto vaso,
> trascendo alzato, l'umile salmista,
> e più e men che re era in quel caso.
>   Di contra, effigiata ad una vista
> d'un gran palazzo, Micòl ammirava
> sì come donna dispettosa e trista.

[There, sculpted in the same marble, were the cart and
the oxen drawing the holy ark, because of which we fear
an office not given in charge . . . . There went before
the blessed vessel, the lowly Psalmist, dancing girt
up, and he was both more and less than king on that
occasion. Opposite, figured at a window of a great
palace, Michal was looking on, like a woman scornful
and sad.]   (55-69)

The final scene of the triad of humility is that of the
Emperor Trajan, round about him the great triumph of the
Roman army, depicted with "visibile parlare" [visible
speech]:

>   Quiv'era storiata l'alta gloria
> del roman principato, il cui valore
> mosse Gregorio a la sua vittoria;
>   i' dico di Traiano imperadore;
> e una vedovella li era al freno,
> di lagrime atteggiata e di dolore.
>   Intorno a lui parea calcato e pieno
> di cavalieri, e l'aguglie ne l'oro
> sovr'essi in vista al vento si movieno.

[There was storied the high glory of the Roman prince
whose worth moved Gregory to his great victory: I mean

the emperor Trajan. And a poor widow was at his bridle
in attitude of tears and of grief. Round about him
appeared a trampling and throng of horsemen, and the
eagles in gold above them moved visibly in the wind.]
(73-81)

Of these scenes, sculpted in marble, yet moving and
speaking, Dante states that neither Polycletus nor Nature is
their author. The implication is that God is; unless this be
Dante's _fantasia_ at work (Plate IXb). Later Dante further
compliments with artistry, God's artistry, while abasing his
own. He stoops beside the illuminator, Oderisi, who stoops
beneath his stone, speaking of the greater art than his of
Franco Bolognese, just as Giotto's excels that of Cimabue.
Above these mortal artists of paint and words is God's art
sculpted in stone, showing the Ark. Oderisi and Dante
together in this humble stance are compared to yoked oxen
drawing such a sacred Ark:

Di pari, come buoi che vanno a giogo,
m'andava io con quell' anima carca,
finché 'l sofferse il dolce pedagogo.

[Side by side, like oxen that go yoked, I went beside
that burdened soul, so long as the gentle pedagogue
allowed it.]   (XII.1-3)

It is as if Dante says he has yoked his mortal poesy
humbly to God's psalmistry, while Oderisi, the illuminator
of Bibles, and especially Apocalypses, speaks of mortal
artists' fragile fame. Dante no longer prides himself on
being numbered a sixth among the pagan poets (_Inf_. VI.102),
nor on his self-centered Golden Calf of an _amoroso canto_
(_Purg_. II); as much as Virgil can permit, Dante is now
harnessed to the choral music of Psalm 113's "In exitu
Israel de Aegypto," paradoxically disciplining himself to
the pilgrimage of liberation. With the apocalyptic symbol
for Luke as the ox and Luke being a writer and a painter
there exists the possibility that Dante sees himself as
metamorphosing his poetry, Oderisi, his accompanying
illuminations, from the Golden Calf of idolatry to an Emmaus
pilgrimage recognition of the Word become flesh. (Even
Cimabue's name, Oxhead, puns upon these associations.) Dante
and Oderisi in this scene are yoked as oxen to the poem as
sacred Ark.

However, Dante's artistry and _fantasia_ concerning God's
artistry and creation derive also from Roman pilgrim
reality. Pilgrims to Rome viewed not only Christian
monuments but also pagan ones. Trajan's Column and Trajan's

Arch would have been familiar to pilgrims. One tale current
is that Pope Gregory seeing the episode of Trajan and the
widow sculpted on these was moved to pray for the Emperor's
soul. The story of Gregory's prayer was widely told in the
Middle Ages, finding its way into Dante's Commedia (also
Par. XX.43-48, in which Trajan is paired with David before
the Ark again), and Langland's Piers Plowman, where Trajan
is "Troianus," linking Troy, Rome and London (B.XI.140ff).
But a quest through the sculptures upon the column, the arch
and the reliefs removed from it and placed on Constantine's
Arch is disappointing, only revealing crouched male Dacian
suppliants at triumphant Trajan's feet, not the widow in
question at his bridle.[31]

Another monument familiar to Roman pilgrims was Titus'
Arch over the Via Sacra which led into the Forum. It bridged
the triumphal route the Popes took when they performed the
Gregorian liturgical stations about Rome. On one frieze
within the arch is self-consciously, self-referentially,
sculpted the triumphal procession passing through that same
arch while bearing the Jerusalem spoils, the seven-branched
candlestick, the table with the shew bread and the Jubilee
trumpets. From this relief medieval Romans called the arch
the Arcus Septem Lucernarum, the Arch of the Seven
Candlesticks, or the Arcus cum Arca, the Arch of the Ark. On
its opposite frieze, Titus is shown in a quadriga, a chariot
drawn by four horses, a winged victory crowning him as he
rides and another female deity pulling at the bridle of the
fourth and most distant horse while her face gazes into
Titus' with an expression of sadness (Plate VIIIc). She is
iconographically closer to Dante's Gregorian widow, who
likewise pulled at an emperor's bridle, than are the male
suppliants crouched at Trajan's feet on his column and arch.
Jerusalem was sacked by Titus and Vespasian in A.D. 70; her
treasures, once the spoils of Egypt, became the spoils of
Rome and were housed by Titus in the Temple of Peace. These
two scenes, from Titus' Arch, sculpted in stone, the
Hellenic and the Hebraic commingling, could well have given
Dante the inspiration for his three scenes sculpted upon the
rocky walls of the Purgatorial mountain (Plate IXb).[32]

In Purgatorio XXIX.43-51, Dante will see what appear to
be seven trees of gold, which are in reality, seven golden
candlesticks (he had earlier done that in Inferno where he
mistook giants for towers and windmills, being Cervantes
and Quixote's precursor). He sees these in a landscape that
speaks as well of a triumphal chariot and of the trumpets of
Jubilee and Doomsday. The Purgatorial pageant's properties
are drawn from Revelation and from the arch Titus built
which Rome's Jubilee pilgrims saw, the Egyptian gold thus
become the artifice of stone and poetry. Dante has replaced

the oxen cart that drew the Ark into Jerusalem with the
imperial chariot of the Roman triumph, Beatrice thereby
becoming Ark and Caesar, the Florentine wedding Jerusalem
and Rome. Indeed, Byzantine translations of relics took
place in imperial quadrigas, the horses removed and the
members of the imperial family drawing the chariot, while
later translations in the west were carried out as in
Jerusalem, in carts drawn by oxen.

Popes passed through the Arch of Titus, the Arch of the
Ark, at their inaugural and were met there by Rome's Jewish
community who presented to them the Old Law which was
returned to them with the statement that there was now a New
Law.[33]   The ceremony would have made the arch seem a liminal
place, between Old and New. In the Commedia first Virgil is
the pilgrim guide and is associated with the Exodus and with
Aaron, with the virga and the Old Law, both treasures placed
in the Ark. Then Beatrice becomes Dante's guide as if she
were the New Law, and Dante's pedagogue, Virgil, no longer
stands at his side: "Prius autem quam veniret fides, sub
lege custodiebamur, conclusi in eam fidem quae revelanda
erat. Itaque lex paedagogus noster fuit in Cristo, ut ex
fide iustificemur. At, ubi venit fides, iam non sumus sub
paedagogo." [But before faith came, we were kept under the
law, shut up unto the faith which should afterward be
revealed. Wherefore the law was our schoolmaster to bring us
unto Christ, that we might be justified by faith. But after
that faith is come, we are no longer under a schoolmaster]
(Galatians 3.23-25). The Old Law is fulfilled by the New of
"l'amor che move il sole e l'altre stelle" [the Love that
moves the sun and the other stars], Virgil giving way to
Beatrice, Latin to Italian, punishment to benediction.

Time and again in the Commedia Virgil and Dante enter
through arches. In Inferno III they pass through a gate on
which is the dread inscription:

Per me si va ne la città dolente,
per me si va ne l'etterno dolore,
per me si va tra la perduta gente.
  Giustizia mosse il mio alto fattore;
facemi la divina podestate,
la somma sapienza e 'l primo amore.
  Dinanzi a me non fuor cose create
se non etterne, e io etterno duro.
Lasciate ogne speranza, voi ch'intrate.

[Through me is the way into the woeful city, through me
the way into eternal grief, through me the way among
the lost people. Justice moved my high maker; divine
power made me, supreme wisdom, and the primal love.

Before me no things were created if not eternal, and
eternal I endure. Leave all hope, you who enter.]
                                        (1-9)

A student of Professor Hollander suggested that this scene
is of a Roman triumphal arch.[34]   The illuminators of the
text instead tend to show it as the city gate of a medieval
town, and not of Rome but Florence. I suspect both the
student and the illuminations are right.

    A further arch or gate is encountered, then entered, in
the Inferno text. In Canto VII occurs the line that Browning
will rewrite (though he borrows it from Shakespeare's Lear):

    Venimmo al piè d'una torre al da sezzo.
    [we came to the foot of a tower at last.] (130)

From its top gleam the flames of a signal. When Virgil and
Dante come to it by the tower is a gate, barred against
their entry, yet illogically it stands within the earlier
confines, and Virgil notes its likeness to that first gate
inscribed with "scritta morta" [dead writing] (VIII.127; II
Cor. 3.7). Next, in Canto IX. we see upon the top of the
iron-walled tower the fierce Erinyes, Megaera, Alecto and
Tisiphone. These three threaten the pilgrims with the coming
of Medusa. Virgil hides Dante's eyes until the heavenly
messenger: "Venne a la porta e con una verghetta/ l'aperse"
[came to the gate and with a wand opened it] (89-90). The
tower is Egyptian gold, spoiled from Aeneid VI:

    stat ferrea turris ad auras
    Tisiphoneque sedens, palla succinta cruenta,
    vestibulum exsomnis, servat noctesque diesque.

    [the iron tower uprears itself, and Tisiphone sitting
    girt in blood-stained pall keeps sleepless watch at the
    entry by night and day.]   (VI.554-556)

The Sybil tells Aeneas that Tisiphone, armed with scourge
and snakes, punishes the sinners who enter with madness,
while calling upon her hideous sisters for aid. Dante is
"outdoing" Virgil. The iconography for this scene is
frequently taken directly from codices of the Aeneid.[35]
In the Commedia the Sybil's role is taken over by prophetic
Virgil, Aeneas' by Dante, but Dante adds to the classical
epic the Hebraic concept of the city gates, of Psalm 23.7's
"Atollite portas," held by Christians to be Hell's gates
closed against Christ by the Devil, and used as such
liturgically. These echo the gates of Troy insolently closed
against Jason and Hercules in Dares' History of Troy, and

Villani's of Florence.[36]   They echo, too, the gates of
Florence closed against the exiled Dante, an exile which
perhaps drove him close to madness and suicide. But perhaps
also Dante uses the Aeneid to show the grim truth and
tragedy of the Roman de la Rose's portal of idleness.
Chaucer's Parliament of Fowls (120-154) was to combine these
opposed Janus aspects of iron and gold.

   Beyond these literary and liturgical texts there is
more. The modern traveler to the Eternal City sees the Arch
of Titus as a classical triumphal arch. Triumphal arches
illogically are placed within cities and are free standing;
they are not city gates set into surrounding walls; they
function liturgically, rather than practically, denoting the
threshold, the limen, to cross which signified a conversion,
a public changing from one state to another. In the Middle
Ages the Arch of Titus was quite different in appearance. It
was sadly decayed though still possessing its two reliefs
amidst a mass of crumbling, shored-up brick, stone and
marble. At its side was a medieval tower, called by
pilgrims, "Virgil's Tower," because of the legend that in it
was the magician's study, a tale being told of a trick
played on Virgil by a woman who enticed him into a basket
that she let down from that study's window holding it
suspended for a day in the sight of all Rome. Another name
the pilgrims gave the tower was the "Turris Cartularia," or
"Turris Testamentum," the tower of documents, for it once
housed the Papal archives. The Frangipani family controlled
this part of Rome and used the Arch and Tower for their
fortifications. Such towers were later pulled down while
Pius VII restored the Arch to its present condition,
replacing the lost marble.[37]   An illumination of Inferno
VII-IX shows the tower and gate of that episode as were the
medieval Virgil's Tower of the Law and Arch of the Ark
(Plate VIIId,e).

   Just as Egyptian gold can be rendered a Golden Calf,
bringing death to its worshipers, or used to adorn the
Tabernacle of the Ark, bringing salvation, so is this the
case with Dante's poem. The Inferno gates of Canto III and
of Cantos VII-IX are as a Roman triumphal arch seen from the
perspective of the barbarian captive participating in a
triumph and going to his death blaspheming against God, "la
nimica podesta" [the enemy power] (Inf. VI.96). The
Purgatorio IX arch, which Michelini painted as being
identical with that of Inferno's gate (Plate XII), functions
similarly though here the perspective is reversed--from
despair to hope--in Boethius' manner. The Inferno's arches
are the exile's perspective, the Purgatorio's is the
pilgrim's. As Dante and Virgil pass through they see

sculpted on the stone walls of the terrace side the marble
reliefs exemplifying not so much humiliation, but humility:
Mary and Gabriel, David and the Ark, Trajan and the Widow.
Upon Titus' Arch are similar scenes: the Temple treasures
brought from Jerusalem to Rome and the Triumph of Titus
himself, though these scenes are less of humility than they
are of pride.

Penance is the fulcrum between the Janus perspectives,
of Virgil and Luke, the Aeneid and the Gospels, Hell and
Purgatory. We witness--and experience--in poetry the
liturgical expulsion and reconciliation of penitents and
pilgrims. If the arch is Florence's city gate, as
Michelini's iconography in his fresco in Florence's Duomo
states, to leave is exile and pilgrimage, to enter,
citizenry (Plate XII); if Titus' Arch it would be passed
through by pilgrims traversing that city in the Jubilee year
of pilgrimage, denoting their oldness become newness.
Dante's polysemum can encompass all these, Florentine and
Roman, pagan and Christian.

The reader can choose to descend into Inferno and read
its idolatrous poetry in idleness, thereby passing through
the gate, like the Roman de la Rose's Amant, in the wrong
direction of Egyptian and Babylonian iniquity, becoming an
exile in Hell, or ascend, passing through it in its opposite
direction, to Rome as Jerusalem, becoming a citizen of
heaven, of that Rome whereof Christ is Roman, an Augustan
primus inter pares. The poem of the Commedia itself is as a
Janus gate, one direction facing onto fratricidal war, the
other onto the "vision of peace." Ulysses attempting to
reach the hortus deliciarum of lost Eden, without penance,
is forced back, like Dante in Inferno I, to its opposite
realm, Hell. The reader has two ways before him and,
choosing aright, relinquishing sin, can return with his
"bordon di palma cinta" [pilgrim staff palm-wreathed] (Purg.
XXXIII.78). Dante has adorned the pilgrim tales of Exodus
and Emmaus with the idolatrous gold of Virgil and Ovid. He
has placed upon poesy's staff of folly the Temple's pilgrim
palm of wisdom. It is with such a pilgrim Golden Bough staff
of contraries and with such a pilgrim Golden (and Gideon's)
Fleece that Dante attains, in the words of the Officium
Peregrinorum's verses: "Jesu, nostra redemptio, amor et
desiderium" [Jesus, our salvation, love and desire].

CHAPTER EIGHT: "PIERS FOR PURE TENE . PULLED IT ATWEYNE"

    Piers Plowman tells of pilgrimage and story-telling--
whose paradigm derived from the Gospel of Luke--and
pilgrimage and education--whose paradigm derived from the
Old Testament's Exodus. Linking the two is the allegory of
agriculture. The poem has three documents within its text
that it presents to its reader: the first, a Pardon,
shadowing forth God's covenant, which Piers "for pure tene"
tears in two; the second a Charter, shadowing God's
Commandments, which Moses as Hope carries; the third,
shadowing the Word, a book who speaks to Will and to his
reader concerning the vita Christi. The opening of Piers
Plowman collates Abraham in Genesis and Moses in Exodus,
having them be shadowed in Piers the Plowman. The second
document, the Charter, will present Abraham and Moses as
encountering Will as the reader and Piers as Christ,
conflating Genesis, Exodus and Luke 24. The third document,
the speaking Book, is both the entire Bible, the Old and New
Testaments, and yet it focusses on the Gospels' unity of the
vita Christi of which the others were the shadowy types. The
Exodus typology is seen to be as crucial to the poem as is
the Emmaus paradigm.[1] Moreover, the two are linked to each
other, just as much as in Luke 24 where the two disciples
and the disguised pilgrim sermon and fable with one another
concerning Jesus and his shadowy types, beginning with the
Exodus and with Moses.

    In Passus XV.212, we are cryptically told of Piers the
Plowman, "Petrus id est Christus." The phrase echoes many
usages. The Glossa Ordinaria upon the Exodus makes frequent
use of the phrase, "Moses, id est Christus," to stress the
figural parallel between the salvation of Israel by Moses
from the bondage of Egypt, and the salvation of man by
Christ from the bondage of sin. The typological parallel had
been drawn by Paul in I Corinthians 10.4: ". . . petra autem

erat Christus," building upon Christ's pun, ". . . tu es
Petrus, et super hanc petram aedificabo Ecclesiam meam"
(Matt. 16.18). In Corinthians, Paul had discussed the
pilgrimage of the Israelites from Egypt who passed under the
cloud and through the sea, ate manna and drank from the
water of the rock which Moses struck. He interprets these
events as baptism and eucharist, the rock as Christ: "petra
autem erat Christus." He comments further concerning those
Israelites with whom God was not pleased and who perished in
the wilderness, that they were figures, types, of
ourselves.² Not only do we have these figural meanings
attached to Piers the Plowman and to the Field Full of Folk,
but we also have Christ's pun upon the name of Peter, seeing
Peter as the rock of the Church. Langland has Piers embody
these meanings, as he places Piers the Plowman in one
typological context after another, as Abraham, as Moses, as
Christ, as Pope. These figures exemplify, furthermore, the
roles of the laity and the clergy.

In the opening vision, Will sees a "fair feeld ful of
folk" poised on the plain between the Tower of Truth and the
Dungeon of Care. The Tower of Truth may be read as Mount
Sinai, the Dungeon of Care as the bondage of Egypt. Or they
may be read as Jerusalem versus Babylon. Lydgate's lines on
Deguileville's _Pèlerinages_ express these antitheses.³ Mede,
as the "scarlet whore of Babylon," then journeys with her
retinue to the king's court at Westminster. The types within
the landscape are drawn from Genesis, Exodus and Revelation,
though the setting is England's Malvern. The vices confess
and the folk, for satisfaction, elect to go on pilgrimage to
Truth rather than to Rome. But the thousands who throng
together for this pilgrimage blunder over hillocks and are
not able to find their way. The "paynim" pilgrim would guide
them into idolatry. He does not know Truth. Typologically
Piers is like Abraham and like Moses leading the people from
Chaldea and from Egypt toward the Promised Land. Yet Piers
paradoxically sees that pilgrimage as honest, stable
agricultural labor by the laity, that they may harvest wheat
for their bread, that they may garner heavenly manna.

At one point some of the field full of folk turn it
back into a Golden Calf scene:

Thanne seten somme . and songen atte Nale
And holpen ere þe half acre . wiþ 'how trolly lolly'.
'Now by þe peril of my soule!' quod Piers al in pure
tene,
'But ye arise þe raþer . and rape yow to werche
Shal no greyn þat here groweþ . glade you at nede.'
(VI.115-119)

At length a Pardon arrives, sent by Truth to Piers. It is the antithesis of the typical Papal bull granting indulgences, demanding instead that for salvation the people must do well; if they do evil they will be damned. Written in blood red, it reads:

> Et qui bona egerunt ibunt in vitam eternam;
> Qui vero mala in ignem eternum.   (VII.113-114)

The Douce manuscript has shown such a pardoner with his pardon as that in Chaucer (Plate Xa; Frontispiece). However, this Pardon, though not understood by these errant wanderers in the wilderness, is instead a summation of God's Covenant with Abraham, "For hym and for hise heires . euermoore after" (VII.4), and God's Law given to Moses, the "ten hestes," and in turn the basic teachings of Christ. The folk grumble and the priest, another type of Aaron, scorns.[4] Piers then, at their lack of appreciation, "for pure tene . pulled it atweyne" (VII.119).

The action is again analogous to the Golden Calf and Moses' breaking the tablets of the Law in anger at the idolatry of the Israelites that Aaron had permitted. Piers with the Pardon reflects the three figures, Abraham, Moses and Christ. Yet this is not made explicit in the Visio. As the Exodus prefigured what was to come "through a glass darkly," so does the Visio clothe itself in Malvern mists of enigma.

Will is in London, not on the Malvern Hills, when he describes himself as a penitent "wolleward" pilgrim, and his ensuing vision is not of the Egyptian wilderness but of the entry into Jerusalem with "Ramis-palmorum" on Palm Sunday. Like Dante, the movement Langland portrays in his poem is from Egypt and Babylon to Jerusalem. Like Dante, he palimpsests that patterning upon his native geography; here upon Will's journeying from Malvern to London. Like Dante he writes his poem in the language of his native land; instead of Florentine Italian _terza rima_, he writes his northern English alliterating verse. Both poets make the Exodus pattern immediate to their lives, rendering it into their own vernaculars.

The purpose of Christian education, Jaeger and Ladner note, was to achieve the _imitatio Christi_, to restore within the image of God, lost by Man at the Fall.[5] The Exodus pilgrimage was seen as God's education of man by Hebrew and Christian exegetes alike.[6] Pilgrimage in practice was related to _imitatio_. The pilgrim journeying to the shrine of St. James of Compostela and the iconography of that saint

in painting and sculpture were shown as like each other, the
saint and the pilgrim in each other's image. The pilgrim to
Rome viewed the Veronica veil which presented to him the
image of God, as Dante says, "de la nostra effige" [in our
image]. The pilgrim to Jerusalem was the viator who walked
in the steps of Christ, the via. Pilgrimage and education
are allied.

According to the typological structuring of the poem
(as in the Commedia), this section of Piers Plowman, the
Vita de Dowel, is the time under the Law of which Paul
spoke:

> But before faith came, we were kept under the law, shut
> up unto the faith which should afterwards be revealed.
> Wherefore the law was our schoolmaster to bring us unto
> Christ [Itaque lex paedagogus noster fuit in Christo],
> that we might be justified by faith. But after that
> faith is come, we are no longer under a schoolmaster.
> For ye are all the children of God by faith in Christ
> Jesus.   (Gal. 3.23-26)

This chapter in Galatians was incorporated in part in the
liturgy of the thirteenth Sunday after the octave of
Pentecost, whose Gospel is the parable of the Good
Samaritan. The Epistle to the Galatians (3.1) begins,
appropriately: "O foolish Galatians, who hath bewitched you,
that ye should not obey the truth, before whose eyes Jesus
Christ hath been evidently set forth." The text of Luke
concerning the Pilgrims of Emmaus likewise has the two
disciples, Luke himself, and Cleophas, be rebuked as "O
fools and slow of heart to believe all that the prophets
have spoken" (24.25) by the unrecognized Christ walking in
their midst. The iconography for this episode in medieval
art often took pains to show the disciples as under the
bondage of the Law, as Israelites rather than Christian.
Thus does Piers Plowman show Will's folly. It is a
pseudo-education, a time under the old Law. It is related
both to Exodus and Emmaus.

Pilgrimage and education can be shown to be related for
the one was anciently an allegory for the other; so can
ploughing and education be analogized in the ancient world.
Plutarch in the De liberis educandi had noted:

> The work of the farmer is an illustration of paideia.
> The natural ability of the child is like the earth
> waiting to receive the seed; the teacher is like the
> farmer; his words of admonition and instruction are the
> seed.[7]

Christ had made use of this metaphor in the parable of the
sower, and those concerning the laborers and the harvest.
There he had related preaching with ploughing, sowing and
harvesting, as had Plutarch, and had warned that "Nemo
mittens manum suam ad aratrum et respiciens retro aptus est
regno Dei" [No man, having put his hand to the plough, and
looking back, is fit for the kingdom of God] (Luke 9.62),
which was interpreted by Jerome and other exegetes as
applying to the role of the Church as preacher.[8] An example
of the metaphor occurs in a sermon, preached by Cyril of
Turov in medieval Russian:

> Today the plowman of the Word leads the oxen of the
> Word to the spiritual yoke, sinks the plow of baptism
> into the furrows of thought and deepening them to
> furrows of repentence plants in them the spiritual seed
> and rejoices in the hope of future returns.[9]

Both medieval analogies, in the Russian sermon, in the
English poem, have arisen from that sermon of Christ's,
reported in Luke 10, which enjoined the disciples to go
forth as preachers, rather than as pilgrim vagrants, and be
harvesters and laborers worthy of their hire. Langland uses
that text to shape his pilgrim figure of Piers the Plowman.

In the Visio the ploughing appears not to be metaphor
but reality. England has been ravaged by the plague. Famine
abounds. The poem undergoes a pilgrim's progress from this
carnal level to a spiritual one. In the Vita de Dobest Piers
Plowman once again describes a ploughing scene, this time as
an allegory. In Passus XIX Piers is God's ploughman. To till
and tell the Truth, he is given four oxen, Luke (whose
symbol is the ox), Mark, Matthew and John. He is also given
four bullocks, Augustine, Ambrose, Gregory and Jerome, with
which to harrow what he has ploughed. He is given grain, the
cardinal virtues, to sow in men's souls. He is to harrow
them with the old Law and the new. The text appears to speak
of a double harrow yet there is the possibility that the
scene describes what we find from the Très Riches Heures was
the common medieval practice, the placing of large stones on
the harrow to weight it down, which in this case could be
the stony tablets of the Law. Piers is also to make a barn
from the wood of the cross, to be called Unity, and to have
a cart called Christendom drawn by horses called Contrition
and Confession and having for hayward, Priesthood. The
allegory is of the Church's preaching.[10]

However, ploughing is not only an allegory for
preaching; it is also a scribal metaphor. Ernst Curtius in
European Literature and the Latin Middle Ages notes the

metaphor of ploughing as writing. Isidore in the <u>Etymologia</u>
had quoted the metaphor in a lost Roman comedy stating that
the Ancients had written furrow-wise, in Greek βουστροφεδον :
<u>boustrophedon</u>, turning like oxen in ploughing, writing from
left to right and from right to left alternately. A medieval
adage reads: "He urged on the oxen, ploughed white fields,
held a white plough, and sowed black seed."[11] Chaucer is
familiar with the scribal metaphor though he uses it in an
apparently oral tale. The Knight in order to excuse his
omission of a complete description of the wedding of Ypolita
to Theseus explains:

> I have, God woot, a large feeld to ere,
> And wayke been the oxen in my plough,   (886-887)

and Spenser borrows that scribal metaphor for his <u>Faerie
Qveene</u>:

> But now my teme begins to faint and fayle,
> All woxen weary of their journall toyle;
> Therefore I will their sweatie yokes assoyle
> At this same furrowes end, till a new day. (III.end)

Petrarch's sonnet CCXXVIII is "vomer di penna," ploughed by
his pen, watered with his tears.

This is the labor of the poet, William Langland, who
ploughs with his quill upon parchment, sowing in those
furrows words as seed of black and red. His own English is
in black; God's Latin words in blood red. He weds his native
alliterative line with its caesura to that of the Hebrew and
Latin antiphonal liturgical psalms. His text presents in an
English setting and in the English tongue a blending of
Psalm, Gospel and Patrology that men such as Haukyn may be
persuaded to cleanse themselves of sin and quest thereby
Piers' Pardon. The poet outside the poem, Piers Plowman
within, take upon themselves that task Christ had enjoined
upon his disciples, to preach and be laborers worthy of
their hire. Will is a self-portrait of William Langland. But
Piers is also his portrait. Will, by means of his fabling
and sermoning poem, has become not a Judas of a jangler but
a Peter upon whom the Church can be built. <u>Piers Plowman</u>
shows how the clergy and the laity, and even the minstrelsy,
can live the Christian pilgrimage upon earth.

The so-called Vita de Dowel concerns itself with a
false education in which Will's quest for Truth is a
failure. In contrast to Piers' cloistered monasticism, Will,
during this time, is a <u>gyrovagus</u>, a vagrant cleric, a
wandering scholar. He journeys from one teacher to the next,

ever discontent with what they have to teach him. In Passus
VIII, while wandering and roaming, he had met the two
Franciscans and he saw his relationship to these friars, the
great teachers of the medieval universities, in terms of
sterile, scholastic disputation. He falsely assumed that
they must surely know where Dowel lives since they have
peregrinately traveled everywhere. So had the folk thought
that the far-traveled palmer would surely have heard of St.
Truth.

Further in the vision Will meets Thought, similarly his
mirror image, as were the palmer and the two friars. Thought
tells him of Dowel, who sounds like the Piers of the Visio,
being any man who is truthful in word and deed and who is
worthy of his hire, honest and not sinning, and of Dobet,
who, like Piers, has retired to the life of the cloister,
entered an order, translated the Bible and preached to the
people upon Pauline texts. Dobest is bishop and king. Will
is not satisfied with this account and Thought directs him
to Wit who, again, is a mirror image of Long Will. In Passus
XI, Will asks Wit about Nature and this question leads Will
into many a digression, though in the midst of one
digression Wit mentions God's reasonable hatred of the waste
of time and the waste of words, both being sins which Wit
unconsciously commits, so pleased is he with his Wit and
learning as he displays it to Will.

In Passus X, Wit's shrewish wife, Dame Study,
interrupts harshly and amusingly since in the previous
passus many of Wit's digressions had centered on marriage as
a purgatory on earth. She presents Will with a tirade,
filled with scriptural examples, to the effect that Wit is
worthless. She is a combination of the Wife of Bath and the
Host's Wife and the merchant's rude discovery concerning
marriage; in other words Study is a stock medieval character
who characteristically busily defies yet exemplifies the
scriptural texts she cites.[12]   Will asks her forgiveness and
Study, mollified, directs him to her cousin Clergy who has
lately married Scripture but yet she holds him back by
describing her connections with the Seven Arts and her
difficulties with the dark mists of Theology, since she
finds bothersome contradictions between Cato's precepts and
those of Christ. (Part of the joke here, of course, is that
women were forbidden by Paul and the Church to preach and
by custom to be educated in universities. The Wife of Bath
and Erasmus' self-praising Folly are cut from the same
cloth.It is only in this century that this joke can now
mercifully go unobserved and unremarked.)

Will is welcomed by Clergy who explains that Dowel is

the lay life lived according to faith. Clergy quotes St.
Gregory to the effect that where human reason can grant
logical proof, faith has no merit. That question cancels out
the validity of Will's education into the meanings of Dowel,
Dobet and Dobest, showing it to be kin to the "paynym"
palmer's quest. Where Wit has served to criticize, to
deconstruct Wit, Study to deconstruct Study, Clergy now
criticizes Clergy. Learning, says Clergy, the
personification of learning, is not necessary for salvation.
He as much as tells Will that the mode of Will's quest is
folly. Yet Will fails to understand this and is driven
compulsively on.

Clergy hopes to see the king punish the religious
orders for their excesses. Will jumps to conclusions, seeing
kingship and knighthood as Dobest and Dobet to Clergy's
Dowel. Lady Scripture intervenes to point out that the
wealth and power of the kings and the knights will not get
them nearer to heaven. Will and Scripture dispute this point
and Will retires from the battle in confusion, deciding that
to be a good Christian it is not necessary to be learned in
theology and the Scripture, while paradoxically citing much
theology and many passages of Scripture to justify this
thesis. Langland uses this humorous technique throughout the
Vita de Dowel, having his characters preach against what
they are. Langland in the Vita de Dowel has written a
speculum stultorum et peregrinorum, a mirror for fools and
pilgrims in order to teach that Truth is to be found in
simplicity, not complexity; in honest labor or in cloistered
monasticism, but not by the questing of a wandering, idle
gyrovagus from one unversity doctor to another. Langland has
presented a false paideia, in order to educate against
education, to deconstruct it for both Will and the reader.

Nature then leads Will to the mountain of Middle Earth
from which Will views Creation and the government of Reason
amongst all beasts. The vision is like Achilles' shield
within which Homer placed war and peace. Here Langland
places within a vision within a dream the harmony of God's
Creation contrasted with man's loss of Reason. Will observes
this disparity and rebukes Reason for it, and wakes to find
Ymaginatif at his side who rebukes Will for his unreasonable
folly. Ymaginatif further explains that the outbreaks of
plague are God's chastisement of his people that they may be
brought to the true path. Ymaginatif chides Will for his
playing with poetry; his writing on the subject of Dowel,
Dobet and Dobest, when he ought to be reading his Psalter
and saying prayers for those who give him bread. Will
promises to reform if he could only find the answer first.
Ymaginatif replies that Dowel, Dobet and Dobest are Faith,

Hope and Charity. Ymaginatif also contradicts Will's
reproaches against learning by stressing its value.
Education, he states, leads ignorant man toward Reason.
Milton is to say, echoing patristic writers, that the
purpose of education is to restore from the ruins of our
first parents, Reason, the image of God in man.[13]   Used
for other ends, however, it is useless.

The Genesis and Exodus _figurae_ of the Visio, where
Piers is as Abraham and Moses, and in which Will is educated
under the "schoolmaster of the law," is fulfilled by
Langland's use of the parable of the Good Samaritan. Emile
Mâle in _The Gothic Image_ describes the exegetical treatment
of the parable at Sens and Ben Smith has noted its relevance
to _Piers Plowman_.[14]   The window is designed with three
central diamond panes, each presenting a scene from the
parable and each, in turn, surrounded by four medallions
presenting typological parallels to the central parable
scenes (Figure 9). The first set of medallions shows scenes
concerning the Fall of Man and the Expulsion from Paradise;
the second set shows scenes from the Exodus; and the last
relates to the Passion. Though these historical events at
first glance appear not to belong to the central design
which contains the parable, in the light of medieval
paradigms concerning history, and especially in the light of
the liturgy, the juxtaposition will be found to be suitable.

The traveler from Jerusalem to Jericho in the first
pane is beset by thieves, beaten, robbed and left for dead.
Surrounding this scene Adam and Eve sin and are driven from
Paradise. The beginning of the parable and the beginning of
biblical history, in the window's program, reflect the
condition of man as _homo viator_ in this world, in exile from
Paradise, journeying from Jerusalem, clad as a pilgrim. The
walled Jerusalem/Eden is shown at the top of the window.[15]
Mâle has noted that the _Glossa Ordinaria_ in this context
interprets the traveler journeying from Jerusalem to Jericho
as the type of fallen man leaving Paradise, that Jerusalem
is Eden, while Jericho in Hebrew signified the moon, which
in turn symbolized change, mutability, wrought by man's
sinfulness. Wyclif ably used this exegesis in a sermon.

The second central pane shows _homo viator_ as he lies
naked and wounded by the wayside. The priest and the Levite
pass him by. Four scenes from the events of the Exodus
surround the wounded _homo viator_, including one of the
worship of the Golden Calf. The juxtaposition spells out the
incompleteness, the inadequacy, of the Old Law of Moses to
heal sick humanity. Moses himself was destined not to attain
Israel. That task was left to Joshua, seen by the early

Figure 9
Sens. Samaritan
Window,
Giraudon

Church Fathers as the type of Jesus. The third pane shows
the Samaritan leading the wounded traveler (labeled
"[Per]egrinus") upon his beast toward the inn (stabula). In
Hebrew Samaritan means "keeper" and the scene thus becomes
one of Christ, an Abel rather than a Cain, binding and
healing the wounds of man, whom Moses had been unable to
cure, and leading the wounded traveler to the hostelry of
the Church. The scenes that surround the central pane are
those of the Passion where Christ restores fallen man to
salus and returns homo viator from the mutability and
mortality of Jericho toward the eternity of celestial
Jerusalem.

Three French cathedrals, Sens, Bourges and Chartres,
made use of this exegesis of the parable of the Good
Samaritan in stained glass. An English alliterative poem,
Piers Plowman, and Wyclif in his sermon also employ its
structure of figural parallels. This is not to say that the
fourteenth-century Englishmen have been influenced by
thirteenth-century French stained glass, but rather that
this is a mode of thought common to medieval Christendom
through its liturgy. Emile Mâle and Ben Smith point out that
such an interpretation was already formulated in the Glossa.
Robertson and Huppé applied the Glossa's exegesis to Piers
Plowman's text in a critical method already endorsed by R.W.
Chambers.[16] However, the depth and intensity of expression
of the formulation by stained-glass artisans and by
minstrel poet requires also a lay audience habituated to
such a mode of thought and capable of appreciating and
understanding it in the different media. Raymond St. Jacques
has traced the common source to the liturgy. In conjunction
with the Samaritan Gospel, which occurs in the same chapter
in Luke as does the tale of the young lawyer who asked, "How
may I save my soul?" the Mass for the thirteenth Sunday
after the octave of Pentecost made use of Galatians 3.16-22
as its Epistle. These verses discuss Abraham and the Law.
That juxtaposition led to homiletic exegesis which noted
these parallels.[17] The liturgy, with scripture and
resulting sermon, has engendered the gloss, the stained
glass and the poetry.

In Passus XVI Will awakens into another vision in which
he quests Piers. He meets a hoary Abraham upon the road who
calls himself Faith and a herald of arms, and who describes
Piers' blazon as that of the Trinity. He describes to Will
how once sitting in his porch in the spring three men came
to him and thus he can be herald of God as Three in One.[18]
Will notices the souls Abraham bears in his bosom and weeps
for their loss through sin, for Christ has not yet come.

Suddenly another figure comes forth upon the road and Will asks who he is:

> 'I am Spes, a spie,' quod he . 'and spire after a
> Knyght
> That took me a maundement . vpon þe mount of Synay
> To rule alle Reames wiþ . I bere þe writ riȝt here.'
> (XVII.1-3)

He is Hope and he is also Moses and we are full circle to the ending of the Visio. There Piers had received the Pardon from Truth. Will is as eager here as he was there to view the words of the parchment Charter:

> 'Is it enseled?' I seide . 'may men see þe lettres?'
> 'Nay', he seide, 'I seke hym . þat haþ þe seel to kepe,
> And þat is cros and cristendom . and crist þeron to
> honge.' (4-6)

The first three lines concern the Old Law, the second three, the New Testament. Will, at this point, loses his temper. Abraham, Faith, had told him of the Trinity; Moses, Hope, has spoken of the Law. Neither logically agrees with the other and Will despairs of learning which of the two is true.

At that point the vision becomes the tale of the Good Samaritan who tends the naked traveler abandoned by Faith and Hope. Will catches up with him and tells him of Faith and Hope neglecting the traveler. The Samaritan explains that only Christ can heal the traveler and that he himself journeys to joust at Jerusalem upon his allegorical horse Caro--who represents his carnal flesh. Where Piers the Plowman had preached on pilgrimage a true knight had vowed to follow him, though that pilgrimage was unchivalrous agriculture (VI.22-23). Now we meet Piers, no longer as a ploughman whose plough is his pilgrim staff, his scrip his hopper of seed, but who is himself a crusading knight, going to joust as Jesus in Jerusalem. Piers, like Spenser's St. George, has turned from ploughman to knight, a conversion that worldly romances scorned--yet employed.[19] Later he will become Piers as Pope, thus reflecting the ideals of the three estates of society, ploughman, knight and priest.

The Reims sculpture, perhaps of Abraham and Melchisadek, showed the one as a thirteenth-century crusading knight fighting to free Jerusalem, the other as a thirteenth-century priest.[20] So are Abraham, Moses and the Samaritan here translated into the world of fourteenth-century chivalry. Abraham is a tourney herald and can

explain Piers' arms, while Moses is a scout. Both belong on
the field of tourney and seige. In that tournament between
Life and Death, Moses and Abraham, Dowel and Dobet are
inadequate. The figure of Piers as Samaritan fulfills and
completes them and is their true champion in this Jerusalem
crusade. Allegorically Will has abandoned Faith and Hope as
in the parable homo viator is abandoned by the priest and
the Levite. Will is like one robbed and left for dead until
Christ and Charity can become his Saviour. Langland has
taken the typological parallels the Church saw in the
parable and has added to them further polysemous layers, the
Pauline triad of Faith, Hope and Charity, personified by
Abraham, Moses and the Samaritan, these rendered still more
complex by the addition of the romance apparatus of
tournament, seige and chivalry. The consonance of these
layers is testimony in the poet's mind, to their validity,
that "Samplarie" (XII.102) which the Holy Spirit imposes
upon all writers.

The influence of Joachim of Fiore upon figural thought
and upon Dante and Langland has been discussed by critics at
length.[21]   The general tendency has been to see Joachite
thought as apocalyptic and to stress its chiliasm. I am more
intrigued by its entire pattern which it imposes upon
mankind's history. Prophecy depends upon imposed symmetry
that appears to validate prediction. In both Langland and
Dante are found prophetic pronouncements. They write
pilgrimage poems which make use not only of the Exodus
pattern but also that of Emmaus in which Christ as an
unrecognized pilgrim expounded to Luke and Cleophas all the
scriptures concerning himself, beginning with Moses and, it
should be noted, the prophets (Luke 24.27). In Langland each
recension rewrites its prophecy. Unlike Old Testament
figurae reinterpreted after the event, these pronouncements
before the fact had no control over events to come. Dante's
Emperor dies; Langland is forced to revise and revise. Yet
the figural and apocalyptic structures, of parallels between
Bible and pilgrimage poem, are of value for the poem.

In Peter Brieger's account of the pictorial
commentaries to the Commedia he discusses the figural
diagram of Joachim of Fiore's Liber figurarum and the
marginal drawings in the Milan Commedia, dated not later
than 1355.[22]   Joachim's scheme saw historical events cast in
a paradigm, that paradigm being derived from the
Tetragrammaton, in particular that discussed and diagrammed
by Petrus Alfonsi. Joachim envisioned and diagrammed it as
one and three and four, as unity and trinity and quaternity,
by means of overlapping and entwining circles.[23]   Into this
pattern he places the history of the world. The first and
third circle represent the Old and New Testament and where

176

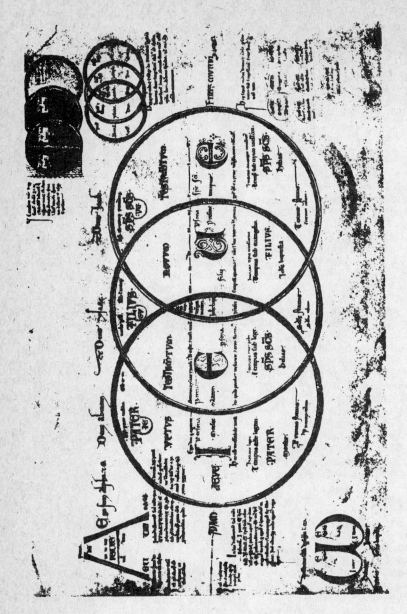

Figure 10   Joachim of Fiore, _Liber Figurarum_

they overlap at the Incarnation is written "Tetragrammaton" and the names, Jesus and John the Baptist. The first circle is "Pater," the second, "Filius," the third, "Spiritus Sanctus." The smaller divisions, four in all, are first, "Tempus ante legem," then "Tempus sub lege," then following the central Incarnation, "Tempus sub evangelio," and finally the present time. Alpha is Adam and Omega, the apocalyptic "Finis mundi." It is similar to the Sens' Samaritan window. The scheme is both naive and sophisticated. This borrowing from Dante scholarship, of material that is of use in explicating Piers Plowman, demonstrates that there is a mode, a matrix, a paradigm, of thought common to the poems and to the readers of that period. It is not even necessary to cite Joachim. The evidence from the twelfth through the fifteenth centuries is symptomatic of this mode of perception, governed by theological exegesis in general, rather than wrought by one practitioner upon his disciples. To comprehend these structures we must do paradigm shifts backwards through time; we must willingly, momentarily, suspend our disbelief, and even discomfort, concerning such differing modes of thought from our own, in order to feel comfortable with the structures of such poems.

Pietro Buonaccorsi's 1440 scheme in his "Il cammino di Dante," which Brieger also gives, is even more applicable to Piers Plowman than to Dante's pilgrimage poem. Buonaccorsi drops the Tetragrammaton scheme to portray the Trinity as central Unity. The exterior of this scheme presents the three persons of God, while the interior shows him as one, "Deus unus est" versus "Personae sunt tres." Buonaccorsi lists the attributes of the three persons, the Father being power, the Son, wisdom, the Spirit, will; the Father saying "sum" [I am], the Son, "scio" [I know], the Spirit, "volo" [I will]. This scheme, in medieval thought, belonged not to God alone, but to each individual created in God's image. In Piers Plowman Will learns that the many triads he encounters are to be in actuality the sum of incomplete parts, rather than a quest to a final third. He learns that the quest is centrally within and not fragmentarily external.

The construction to the whole poem corresponds to these patterns seen in history. Joachim's first circle, "Pater," encompassed the time before the Law and the time under the Law, the times of Abraham and Moses, Elijah and John the Baptist. This corresponds to Langland's Visio which began with Will as sleeping Adam, Piers as an Abraham and a Moses, while in what is traditionally considered to be the Vita of Dowel, Piers becomes a cloistered monk, his types being Elijah and John the Baptist. (In Dante's Commedia this would

correspond to Virgil's inadequate guidance.) The figure of
Piers as Christ the Knight in the Vita de Dobet accords with
the second circle, "Filius," which overlaps with the third,
the Pentecostal "Spiritus Sanctus," that extends from the
New Testament to the Omega of the Apocalypse. (In Dante this
corresponds with Beatrice's companionship.) However, this
poem, like the Commedia, does not end but recommences, being
circular. The original manuscripts of Piers Plowman, in
accord with this concept, did not divide up the Vitae, but
were one Vita, a unified trinity of Dowel, Dobet and Dobest.
The reader quickly realizes that the divisions are
fallacies, "Dobest" being of the Church's dismal failure
after the apostolic times. "Pater" and "Spiritus Sanctus"
alone are not enough. It is at the center, "Filius," that
all interweave and overlap in the pilgrimage schemes of
Langland, Joachim and Buonaccorsi.

Book's speech, like Piers' Pardon and Moses'
Maundement, is crucial to Piers Plowman. In between the
Crucifixion and the Resurrection appears this "wight . wiþ
two brode ei3en: Book highte þat beaupeere . a bold man of
speche" (XVIII.230-260), who narrates the story of Christ
from his sacred pages, of his Incarnation amidst the
elements which recognized him as their Creator and which
therefore trembled and raged at the Crucifixion, and how at
the Omega of Time, Book will be burned, since Book is both
the World and the Bible, and that then shall be meted out
to all people salvation and damnation according to their
desserts.[24]   Book's vita Christi is that internal Truth and
Charity, Holichirche (I.85-86) and Piers (V.606-607) saw in
men's hearts, that Pardon as Covenant and Law Piers received
for his pilgrimage (VII), and which Haukyn has bought of a
false priest as a "salue for þe pestilence" (XIII.246-248),
that "maundement vpon þe mount of Synay" Moses hears while
questing the Knight who will seal it with "cros and
christendom . and crist þeron to honge" (XVII.1-8). The
speech of Book is in small what Langland's entire vision is
in large. The poet forms his life as Will and as Piers upon
that of Christ, that he may, like an Apostle and a Gospeler,
by his poetic preaching bring others to imitate that which
is in his Book, the vita Christi, the via et vita et veritas
of pilgrims.[25]   The Book and Langland's Vision of Piers the
Plowman will then pass away, being self-consuming artifacts,
having fulfilled their tasks of guiding pilgrims and readers
in this world to the right path of salvation, not the
sinister of Mede and damnation.[26]   The book of Piers Plowman
is as the schoolmaster of the Law who brings the reader to
Christ.

CHAPTER NINE: "GARLEEK, OYNONS, AND EEK LEKES"

        Juan Ruiz in his fourteenth-century Spanish _Libro de_
Buen Amor, a work much like Chaucer's _Canterbury Tales_,
expressed the conflict between Venus and Christ as that
between Lord Carnal and Dame Lent. The _persona_ of the poem
is dining with Sir Shrove Tuesday when a messenger comes
with letters from Dame Lent, one of which, a challenge to
Lord Carnal, is open and bears a great seashell pendant,
"una concha muy grande de la carta colgada" (1074), an
inversion of a pardon with a bull attached. Sir Tuesday
rises from the table ready to joust with the doughty dame.
Lord Carnal also receives the letter and on the appointed
day surrounds himself with provisions upon which he royally
dines. Dame Lent comes upon the drunken rout that night and
she with her fish wreaks vengeance upon Lord Carnal in an
epic battle. Bacon and Beef are captured and brought before
Dame Lent who orders them hung, while Lord Carnal is thrown
in gaol to be visited by a friar and fed only once a day.
Dame Lent then spring-cleans all the houses and marks the
devout with the tau cross of palm ashes and oil. Meanwhile,
Lord Carnal, on Palm Sunday, talks Sir Fasting into letting
him out of prison to attend mass, and escapes. From the
mountains he challenges Dame Lent to another battle. She is
weakened by fasting, he strengthened by feasting. He sends
Breakfast ahead with the challenge written in letters of
fresh blood.

        Therefore Dame Lent . . . made a vow to go to
    Jerusalem; she put great effort into going across the
    sea. . . . On Good Friday she dressed in a pilgrim's
    cloak, a big, round hat with many scallop shells on it,
    a staff laden with religious images and on it a fine
    palm branch, a basket and beads so as to say her
    prayers rapidly, shoes that were round-toed and double-
    soled; she flung a big sack over her back, there she
    stored rolls and pieces of sacramental bread, pilgrims
    go equipped with these things.[1]

Juan Ruiz in his poem sets up the tension between Carnival and Lent. Geoffrey Chaucer also has his poem pivot upon the division between the Saturnalian and Carnival up-so-doun world and that of Lenten and Easter Christ and Thomas Becket. For the Golden Calf worship of Exodus Chaucer often substitutes the worship of the Roman "dèi falsi e bugiardi," [false and lying gods], such as Arcite's Mars, Palamon's Venus and Egeus' Saturn. Chaucer's pilgrim Wife is Martial and Venerian (III.609-613), his pilgrim Pardoner, I will show, Saturnine. Juxtaposed to them are the Clerk and the Parson. The division is between the pagan world and the Christian, the Old Testament and the New, Nature and Culture.

I

The Wife of Bath should, as a pilgrim to the Holy Places and other shrines, at least look like the allegorical Dame Lent and be dressed in undyed white wool, perhaps even the fleece-skin of a sheep or goat or camel. Margery Kempe, Dame Alys' real-life pilgrim contemporary, took pains to change her widow's black for pilgrim's white weeds.[2] Our saturnalian, carnival Wife, however, flouts these pilgrim customs and flaunts a very different dress. In the General Prologue she wears scarlet stockings: "hir hosen weren of fyn scarlet reed" (I.456). In the Prologue to her own Tale she speaks of her scarlet robes worn even in Lent so that the moth will not devour her dyed cloth (III.550-562), which is to twist to her own ends the scriptural: "Lay not up for yourselves treasures upon earth where moth and rust doth corrupt, and where thieves break through and steal: But lay up for yourselves treasures in heaven" (Matt. 6.19-20), and she protests against being told by the Apostle not to dress in pearls, gold and rich clothes (III.337-347; Peter 3.3; I Timothy 2.9). The good wife in Proverbs weaves such scarlet cloth for her household, not just for herself (31.10-31).

The Ellesmere illuminator paid heed to these words and shows the Wife resplendent in her scarlet cloth, belted in gold, astride her horse, a bright blue lap robe about her, spurs strapped on, goad in hand (like a new Phyllis astride the clerkly Aristotle), even on this pilgrimage to Canterbury at Lententide. Her clothing besides consists of many veils and kerchieves and a large traveler's hat. The hat is that of a pilgrim, though Chaucer endows it iconographically with martial and amazonian properties: "On hir heed an hat/ As brood as is a bokeler or a targe" (470-471). The meaning of these kerchieves will be revealed

in due course (if the reader will permit this academic
version of the strip-tease). The scarlet and gold link her
iconographically with the Whore of Babylon who "saith in her
heart . . . I am no widow" (Rev. 18.7), and also with the
Egyptian spoils used first for fashioning the Golden Calf
and then for adorning the Ark and Tabernacle. They do not
associate her with the black of widow's weeds or the white
of pilgrim's garb, colors which she ought to wear and which
Margery Kempe, her pilgrim contemporary in real life, does.
The Wife is a figure in a landscape, perhaps; but her garb
is ludicrously inappropriate to the landscape through which
she wanders.

The pilgrimages which the Wife performed involved
penance and healing. Bath, the Wife's home, through the
ages, from Roman Aquae Sulis to Jane Austen's fashionable
spa, was noted for its healing waters. Legal documents of
Chaucer's day refer to the various baths and a map of Bath
in the time of James I shows them as they would have been in
Alice's day and as they are still today. At the Priory of
Bath pilgrims venerated relics brought from Jerusalem.
Canterbury granted Bath a special pilgrim indulgence for the
annual September 14 feast of the Exaltation of the Holy
Cross.[3] The Wife, therefore, has no need to go on pilgrimage
from Bath, when Bath has become, as it were, an English
Jerusalem, with not one only, but three Bethesda pools of
healing: at the West Gate the Balnium Lepresorium, the
Lepers' Bath, today's Royal Baths; nearby the Balnium
Crucis, today's Cross Bath; in the center of the town the
Balnium Regium, today's King's Bath.

Bath is near Wells. Chaucer is playing a game in
associating the Wife of "biside Bathe" (I.445) with the
scriptural wife of "Biside a welle" (III.15). The General
Prologue states emphatically that the Wife has visited
Jerusalem not once but three times ("And thries hadde she
been at Jerusalem," I.463), on which occasions she would
have visited, too, the standard shrines of Cana in Galilee
and Jacob's Well at which Christ spoke with the Samaritan
woman in Sichem which she mentions in her Prologue. She
fails in her account to mention other, more sacred Holy
Land sights. However, these two are invariably included in
the pilgrimage narratives of Jerusalem palmers. Chaucer
makes use of their landscapes and the pilgrim narratives
concerning them in order to satirize the marriage argument
the Wife presents. The Wife refers first to the tale of the
marriage at Cana in Galilee of John 2, then to the tale of
Christ speaking with the Samaritan woman at the well of John
4, to justify her many marriages, both tales belying her
arguments, both places she would have visited.

John 4's narration of Christ speaking with the Samaritan woman "biside welle" (III.15) would traditionally have been read to pilgrims at Jacob's Well by friar guides. Samaritans, descended from Jacob, obeyed only the Covenant "to increase and multiply," and worshiped their gods in the mountains as idolatrous golden calves and, moreover, prohibited the pilgrimages to the Temple in Jerusalem which were performed at Passover, Pentecost and Tabernacles by faithful Jews. Samaria's Golden Calf worship mirrored that of the sinful Israelites in Exodus who yearned for the fleshpots of Egypt, the garlics, onions and leeks, and who danced naked about their Golden Calf. Their worship is that of the Wife's "olde daunce" (I.476).

Together Christ and the Samaritan woman at Jacob's Well discussed the "Fons aquae salientis in vitam aeternam" [well of water springing up into everlasting life] (14). Christ implies that he is the allegorical well of virginity in contrast to the carnal well of Jacob, that well being of lust. However, the Wife of Bath a few lines later in her acount will boast of how she flouts the "Crist, that of perfeccion is welle" (107), by being herself decidedly no virgin though she journeys to Cologne's Shrine of Eleven Thousand Virgins. The Wife here shadows Britain's and especially Bath's pagan deity, the Magna Mater, particularly associated with wells. Stones at wellheads in the British Isles often show her in her triple forms, as maiden, bride and crone.[4]

The Wife of Bath's Prologue centers upon this scene from John 4 between Christ and the Samaritan woman in such a way as to identify this lusty English Wife who has had five husbands with the Samaritan woman who likewise had had five husbands. Christ had confronted the Samaritan woman with her adultery and she had repented. Chaucer's pilgrim Wife, however, brazenly declares: "Housbondes at chirche dore I have had fyve" (III.6), and she speaks also of "oother compaignye in youth" and age, while vigorously defending such behavior on her part. John's account continues:

The woman saith unto him, Sir, I perceive thou art a prophet. Our fathers worshipped in this mountain; and ye say, that in Jerusalem is the place where men ought to worship. Jesus saith unto her, Woman believe me, the hour cometh, when ye shall neither in this mountain nor yet at Jerusalem, worship the Father.

Christ tells her there is no need for her to pilgrimage either to the Golden Calf or to the Temple, either to Sichem

or to Jerusalem, an argument that will be used by Lollards
and Protestants against the performance of pilgrimages.[5] The
Samaritan woman returns home to her people announcing to
them that the Messiah, the Christ, has come. The English
Wife will respond otherwise. She boldly journeys forth to
Cologne, to Compostela, to Canterbury.

Behind this new Testament text from John 4 lurks an Old
Testament one from Genesis 29, of which John had been aware,
concerning Jacob meeting Rachel at a well. Jacob sees
Rachel, rolls away the stone from the well's mouth so that
she may water her father's flock of sheep, kisses her and
then weeps. The echoes with Christ raising Lazarus from the
dead and Christ's own entombment would be obvious to the
medieval hearer of this tale. Jacob then worked seven years
to win Rachel as his wife, but Leah, her loathly older
sister with diseased eyes, was substituted. Their daughter,
Dinah, will be raped by Shechem for going "out to see the
daughters of the land." The Wife similarly pilgrimages "to
se, and eek for to be seye/ Of lusty folk" (552-553).[6]

Three times at that well the Wife would have heard
sermons preached at her by friars. At that same well Christ
spoke with the Samaritan woman. At the same well Jacob met
Rachel. Probably at that same well Abraham's servant had
found Isaac's bride, Rebekah. The Wife refers to their tales
(III.55-58). Interestingly, Abraham's words to the servant
sent to seek the bride were included in the Missa
Peregrinorum, the Pilgrims' Mass: "The Lord God of heaven,
which took me from my father's house, and from the land of
my kindred, and which spake unto me, and that sware unto me,
saying, Unto thy seed will I give this land; he shall send
his angel before thee, and thou shalt take a wife unto my
son from thence" (Gen. 24.7; Appendix I). These words must
have been said many a time over our errant Wife departing
from Bath upon her pilgrimages to Rome, Jerusalem and
Compostela. During the Benedictio Peregrinorum, the
Pilgrim's Blessing, she would have lain upon the church's
floor in the shape of a cross. We will find that the church
built over Jacob's Well is similarly cruciform. (William
Golding's The Spire gave us a masculine version of which
this church with its well at the center, instead of a
phallic spire, is the feminine form.)

Pilgrim accounts of Jacob's Well note the parallels
between Jacob, Rachel, Leah, Christ and the Samaritan, and
it is highly probable that Chaucer's audience would have
responded to the Wife's Prologue in this manner. The
landscapes of the Holy Places were as a Book of Memory,
known even to those had not traveled thither but who had

listened to the tales told by palmers returned from beyond
the sea. The Wife of Bath, in her Prologue, is consciously
as an English echo of the scriptural Rebekah, Rachel, Leah
and the Samaritan woman, and all five, whether they be
virgin or widow, at that well seek or find a spouse.
Medieval iconography showed Jacob and Rachel, Christ and
the Samaritan woman, as echoes of each other, at the well.
At Canterbury Cathedral these scenes of Jacob's Well were
placed with that of Moses smiting the Rock in the now
destroyed East Corona window. Rebekah, Leah and the
Samaritan woman are usually depicted with veils and hats to
represent their Glossa quality as "Synagoga," while Rachel
is "Ecclesia."[7] Chaucer makes much of the head kerchives the
Wife of Bath wears and of her large traveler's hat in the
General Prologue (I.453-455, 470-471), her red, and in the
Ellesmere, blue, garb reflects the Tabernacle's veil made
from borrowed Egyptian raiment, and she, in her own
Prologue, speaking of her comportment at her fourth
husband's funeral, says:

> I weep algate, and made sory cheere,
> As wyves mooten, for it is usage,
> And with my coverchief covered my visage, (III.588-590)

though she then callously adds, "I wepte but small." In
these scenes she is polysemously the literal English Wife of
Bath, the typological woman of Samaria of the Holy Places
and the moral abstraction, "Synagoga."

Pilgrim texts through time included descriptions of
Jacob's Well and of the events that took place there. Jerome
writes of Paula:

> She passed through Sichem . . . and entered the church
> built upon the side of Mount Gerizim, round about
> Jacob's Well; at the mouth of which the Lord sat,
> thirsty and hungry, and was filled by the faith of the
> woman of Samaria, who having had five husbands, the
> books of Moses, and the sixth . . . found the true
> Messiah and the true Saviour.[8]

Jerome and Paula emphasize the Samaritan woman's faith. She,
like Mary Magdalen, recognizes the Messiah with greater
celerity than do the male disciples. In the "up-so-doun"
revolution of Christianity it is these two, both fallen
women, who proclaim Jesus Messiah and who anoint him Christ,
not celibate priestly men. For these reasons the Meditations
of Pseudo-Bonaventure, written for nuns, stresses this
tale.[9] Augustine, however, will harshly castigate the

Samaritan woman's lust and cupidity.[10]

Other accounts of Jacob's Well fall into two groups.
The first gives a brief description on the order of:

> Shechem . . . two bow-shots from it is Jacob's Well
> . . . . On the right hand is Gerizim, which is thought
> to have been the place pointed to by the woman of
> Samaria, when she said, "Our fathers worshipped in this
> mountain,"[11]

as it is given in the twelfth-century account written by
Marino Sanuto. The more complicated versions, such as that
given by Anonymous Pilgrim VI (otherwise known as Pseudo
Beda), and also written in the twelfth century, state:

> Near the well of Sichem Jeroboam made the two golden
> calves, which he caused to be worshipped by the ten
> tribes which he had perverted and led away with him
> from Jerusalem . . . Jacob's sons destroyed this city
> of Sichem and slew Hamor, in their sorrow at the
> adultery of their sister Dinah. Sichem is at this day
> near the land which Jacob gave to his son Joseph. In it
> is Jacob's fountain, which also is the well, beside
> which, according to the Gospel, Jesus sat when weary
> with his journey and talked with the woman of Samaria.
> On this spot a church is now built.[12]

An interesting departure from the formulae of Samaritan
idolatry and adultery is to be seen in Arculf's narration to
Adamnan, when shipwrecked on the island of Iona, telling of
the church built over the site of Jacob's Well:

> Near that city he saw a church built beyond the wall,
> which is four-armed, stretching towards the four
> cardinal points, like a cross, a plan of which is drawn
> below [the manuscript contains a blueprint of a cross-
> shaped church, the well at its center]. In the middle
> of it is the Fountain of Jacob, which is often called a
> well, looking towards its four divisions, upon which
> the Saviour, wearied out with the toil of his journey,
> sat one day at the sixth hour, when the woman of
> Samaria came to that well at midday to draw water. As
> to the well, the woman, among other things, said in
> answer to the Lord: "Lord, neither hast thou anything
> to draw with, and the well is deep."

Arculf, who drank water from the well, relates its depth.

From this and other accounts we learn of pilgrims

drinking the water from Jacob's Well and that it also
wrought healing.[13] Both Arculf and the cruciform architecture of the Jacob's Well Church emphasize the hour when
Christ and the Samaritan woman spoke, the sixth hour of
daylight, noon, the time of the Crucifixion. This awareness
can be seen also in Cluny's music texts where the Gregorian
sixth mode of the total eight is "voluptuosus" and which is
illustrated by the sixth antiphon: "Sexta hora sedit super
puteum" [at the sixth hour he sat on the well] (John 4.6).[14]
A well, marked with crosses, in the cloister of St. John
Lateran is called a Jacob's Well.[15] Jacob's Well symbolizes
a conversion to Christ, from the five Old Testament books to
the sixth, the New Testament.

Jacob's Well called to mind, for the medieval pilgrim,
not merely the Old and New Testaments, but also the
opposition between Samaritan and Jew, between the idolatrous
and adulterous Golden Calf worshiper of Sichem and the
virtuous and Law-abiding pilgrim bearing palms to Jerusalem,
between Carnival and Lententide, between Nature and Culture.
The Wife of Bath, thrice a pilgrim to Sichem, should be
aware of this opposition. Yet, though she would have thrice
heard the sermons preached by friars at Jacob's Well, she
has obstinately failed to understand that intent. She
remains herself a Samaritan, worshiping a Golden Calf,
dancing to it an "olde daunce." Similarly the Ship of Fools
shows fifteenth-century mixed couples with the ass's ears of
folly, carolling and dancing lecherously about the Golden
Calf.[16] Instead of echoing the Samaritan woman's
recognition, "I perceive thou art a prophet," and who
returned to her people saying, "Is not this the Christ?"
the Wife first quotes and then foolishly rejects the truth:

> Herkne eek, lo, which a sharp word for the nones,
> Biside a welle, Jhesus, God and man,
> Spak in repreeve of the Samaritan;
> 'Thou has yhad fyve housbondes,' quod he,
> 'And that ilke man that now hath thee
> Is noght thyn housbonde,' thus seyde he certeyn.
> What that he mente therby, I kan nat seyn. (14-20)

She disregards Christ's Truth and Moses' Law and heeds only
God's ancient Covenant with Abraham, "God bad us for to wexe
and multiplye; That gentil text kan I wel understonde"
(28-29), a text Christian pilgrims thought Muslims recited
from their mosques.[17] This is certainly consistent with
lusty English Alys enacting the role of the woman of
Samaria, of a people descended from Abraham and Jacob, but
rejecting the Mosaic and Christian Law.

At Compostela Dame Alys had come to the shrine of the
martyred James, the New Testament's "Jacobus," leaving Bath
by the South Gate at St. James' Church, sailing from
Bristol, the seaport of "biside Bathe," and bathing in the
Galician "Lavamentula," in which pilgrims--as its name says
--washed their private parts before crossing the threshold
of the shrine.[18] In the Holy Land she had similarly bathed
herself in the Jordan and come to the shrine of Jacob's Well
of the Old Testament (one wonders, is "Jankyn," her spouse's
name, a domestication of "Jacob/James"?). Now, in English
Canterbury, she will come to the threshold of St. Thomas'
shrine and well, having crossed the "wateryng of Seint
Thomas" (I.826). Becket's bloody martyrdom mirroring
Christ's could likewise wash and bathe the penitent's sinful
scarlet garb as white as pilgrim wool.

If Alys of Bath can repent at the close of the Parson's
sermon she can be healed of her deafness and avoid the
plague, for Thomas is "the best doctor for sick people who
are good." She will come to Thomas' Well at Canterbury and
there be given the lead phial containing the water mingled
with his blood and stamped with this motto (Figure 8). It is
still possible for profligate Alys of Bath to change her
vestments from whorish scarlet (III.413-415), or even
widow's black, to bridal white as a penitent and reconciled
pilgrim whose sixth husband is a chaste and Christlike
Thomas. "Welcome the sixte" (III.45), she has declared. But
in her until now the Golden Calf has triumphed over
pilgrimage, lust over reason.

Clerkly Jerome declared: "Et de Ierosolymis et de
Britannia aequaliter patet aula coelestis" [One can just as
easily reach heaven from Britain as from Jerusalem]. Others
said: "Qui multum peregrinantur, raro sanctificantur" [Those
who travel much are rarely sainted].[19] Clerkly Chaucer's
gloss upon Jerome and the Wife could well read that to seek
heaven the Wife should cleanse herself of sin at home in
Bath, so noted through the ages for its healing waters,
rather than by impenitently pilgrimaging to "ferne halwes,"
Compostela, Cologne, Rome, Bologne and Jerusalem, or even
homespun Canterbury. But instead she will defiantly return
to Bath and its healing waters carrying with her the ampulle
of Canterbury's healing water and blood, rendered useless
because of her failure to repent of her lustiness. (Dylan
Thomas, in a letter, spoke of such acts as "carrying holes
to Sir Hugh's Castle.")

Her Prologue spoke of her marriages and her pilgrimages
and how she goes out "to see and eek for to be seye/ Of
lusty folk" (552-553). Her Tale tells of Jacob's Sichem

metamorphosed as the realm of Faerie whose Queene is a
version of the Celtic Magna Mater. In Sichem, Jacob's
daughter by Leah, Dinah, "went out to see the daughters of
the land. And when Shechem . . . prince of the country, saw
her, he took her, and lay with her, and defiled her" (Gen.
34.1-2). Though he loved her and desired marriage the sons
of Jacob were so angered that they treacherously slew
Shechem and all his kin in revenge after first circumcising
them. This tale the Wife would have heard from the friars at
Sichem. Her Tale begins with the "olde daunce" performed by
the elf-queen (in Chaucer's Tale of Sir Thopas that queen of
Fairye with her accompanying giant will be kin to the
Scarlet Whore of Babylon, VII.807-816), in the days before
the friars had blessed and exorcised the fairies into
oblivion (III.857-880). Next a young and lusty bachelor of
Arthur's court

>   Saugh a mayde walkynge hym biforn,
>   Of which mayde anon, maugree hir heed,
>   By verray force, he rafte hire maydenhed (III.886-887)

and does not even trouble to propose to his victim. The
queen of the land herself sides with him and has him
discover the answer to what women desire most, which leads
him to his marriage to the loathly lady, a Leah with veils
who becomes a Rachel: "Cast up the curtyn, looke how that it
is" (1249), the Magna Mater from crone metamorphosed to her
maiden state. This is an absurd, "up-so-doun," pagan
rendering of the Genesis tale of the rape of Dinah by
Shechem and the marriages of ugly old Leah and beautiful
young Rachel. The Wife has listened to the friars' fairy
tales with the ass's ears of folly and deafness that her own
Tale speaks of (950-982); and even that confessional
tell-tale has undergone a metamorphosis from Ovid's version
as Chaucer has her have the wife herself, rather than the
barber, betray the secret of Myda's "longe asses erys two."[20]

Chaucer has the Wife speak of the clerk Jerome, who
wrote of Paula's pilgrimages about the Holy Places with
approval, clerical marriage in the Adversus Jovinianum with
disapproval. The old Wife's Tale's Prologue includes the
sermons of friars preached at her at Jacob's Well and the
sermons her clerk husband preached at her at Bath, including
Jerome's "agayn Jovinian" (674). It is thus a Friar's Tale
and a Clerk's Tale that she tells, it is both sermon and
fable, and, above all, it is an old wive's tale, a woman's
tale that has enfolded into itself many men's tales.

Chaucer's conscious juxtaposition of the pilgrim,
book-carrying Clerk telling Petrarch's tale of a good wife

and the lusty Wife telling clerkly Jerome's tales concerning
bad wives is part of a pattern related to plague. The
Job-like tale the Clerk narrates of Grisilde's patience was
one considered efficacious against the Black Death.[21] He
even retells the tale of Jacob's Well (IV.290-294). By
telling Petrarch's tale the Clerk--and the clerkly
Chaucer--avoid plague. But the lusty Wife in her Tale's
conclusion absurdly declares she desires to embrace her
husbands dropping dead of the pestilence (III.1258-1264).
The Magna Mater in her triple form presided over the birth,
marriage and death of men and was most often encountered by
Celtic warriors about to die who would see her washing
their bloody clothing in running water. Both the Wife and
the loathly hag share these attributes.

The Tales of the Shipman, the Pardoner and the Nun's
Priest continue the themes of Chaucer's pilgrim satire. The
first two of the group stress mercantilism and pilgrimage, a
combination that ideally should not occur though it was
rampant in reality. The second two of the group, and they
overlap, are a diptych relating pilgrimage to beast fable.
The figures of the Wife and the Pardoner, the only two
professional pilgrims yet who are both inadequate and
perverse as such, function for the Canterbury Tales as an
errant and ancient Eve and an errant and ancient Adam, as
the first parents of mankind. The shadowy image behind them
is that of Christ, with his red and white banner which the
Canterbury Tales associates with the Knight and his Theseus,
who harrows the naked Adam and Eve from Hell, leading them
to "Jerusalem celestial" in the Parson's manner. The
Shipman's Tale shadows and interprets the figure of the
Wife; the Nun's Priest's Tale shadows and interprets the
figure of the Pardoner. These four Tales contain the most
references to pilgrimage, which Ralph Baldwin saw as the
sovrasenso of the Canterbury Tales, though here that theme
is given its Golden-Calf like parody that it may later be
rectified to the pilgrimage to the arca, the shrine of
Thomas Becket.[22]

A Tale the Wife may well have told and which reveals
much concerning the Wife is now assigned to the Shipman.
Just as the Wife is associated with up-so-doun pilgrimage so
is this Tale a worshiping of the Golden Calf of the World
and the Flesh, rather than of a true pilgrimage. It weds
gold and marriage, emmeshing mercantile contrivings with
marital infidelities. Merchants take off on pilgrimage to
avoid payments of debts (VII.224-234). In the palimpsest of
Tales upon tellers this has the Merchant of the Prologue,
according to the Wife's Tale, the Merchant's Tale and the
Shipman's Tale, be a pilgrim to avoid payment of both his

mercantile debt and his marriage debt (III.130), neither of which was allowed in canon law. What follows is a fabliau of usury and cuckoldry in which are scriptural echoes, as shadows that pass upon a wall (VII.9), that serve to heighten its outrageousness.

The Tale contains three characters, characters we meet in the General Prologue. One is a merchant, one is a wife, one is a monk. The fabliau as dramatic farce is about to begin. But first let us give its setting. No longer are we in England. No longer are we in the Holy Places. Instead we are in France, at St. Denis, and then in Flanders, at Bruges. St. Denis was the royal abbey in the suburbs of Paris which was dedicated to France's patron saint, Dionysius the Areopagite, mentioned by Luke in Acts, and considered to be the mystical Greek theologian who was said, in legends, to have suffered martyrdom at the hands of the Gauls and whose hagiography was embarrassingly disproved by the great and controversial scholar Abelard. Nevertheless, its Abbot Suger carefully rebuilt the Abbey to exemplify Pseudo-Dionysius' mystical writings and in so doing commenced the Gothic style. Crusades undertaken by the French kings were first blessed in the <u>Benedictio Peregrinorum</u> there and the famed oriflamme of red and gold presented by its Abbot to the King to signify the Church's indulgence to those who fought beneath that banner. Within its walls the kings of France were crowned and buried. But outside, as Victor Turner has described of pilgrimage festivals elsewhere, gathered a most worldly fair, the Lendit, famed far and wide for its chaffering and commerce.

Our merchant Peter has chosen a good town in which to live. Bruges in Flanders, to which he journeys, was another great medieval commercial center selling wool from England as cloth throughout Europe. That commerce would pay for the Van Eycks' splendid paintings, including the altarpiece at Ghent which shows Eve and Adam flanking the whole.[23]

Elizabeth Makowski has reexamined medieval canon law concerning conjugal relationships and has found, contrary to what might be expected, that in medieval marriages men and women had equal sexual rights.[24] The Wife of Bath refers to this principle, "That man shal yelde to his wyf hir dette" (III.130), though omitting the rest of the verse, "and likewise also the wife unto the husband" (I. Cor. 7.3). According to this teaching, both scriptural and canonical, each spouse was required to satisfy the other sexually. neither spouse could take a vow of chastity or set forth on pilgrimage, which required abstinence from lust (I Peter 2.11), without first obtaining the other's consent and

forgiveness of the marriage debt. St. Brigitta's husband
refused to give his consent to her taking the vow of
chastity until his last illness on their return from their
conjugal pilgrimage to Compostela, an irregular situation
which perturbed her greatly.[25] Were that consent not
obtained the marriage partner who did not pay the marriage
debt had no right to complain of the other's adultery and
indeed was culpable for it. Neither spouse was to indulge in
lust in Lent or on Fridays and other fast days. But even
then, if one spouse demanded payment the other was to give
it, the one requiring it being in a state of sin, the other
yielding to it, blameless. It is this principle of marital
equality and reciprocity, well known to Chaucer's
contemporary audience though not to us, that governs the
humor of the Wife's Tale, the Merchant's Tale and the
Shipman's Tale.

Our merchant in the Shipman's Tale is more married to
his money than to his wife and he enjoys his cousinage more
than he does his husbandry. He decides to go to Bruges on
business but first invites his "cousin," the monk John to
stay a day or two. On the third day the merchant Peter rises
and goes to his counting house. Daun John rises and goes to
the garden. So also does the wife. It has recently been
suggested that the scene in the garden is a perverse
shadowing of that of the Resurrection in which Mary Magdalen
meets Christ in the garden on the third day (Plate Vb).[26]
But in the biblical account and in the liturgical drama
Peter and John also on the third day rise and go to the
tomb, John arriving first but Peter entering in. Here, in
lieu of the Holy Sepulchre, is a counting house which is
this tale's Peter's "mawmettrie," that he enters in and
where he worships to the exclusion of all else. His wife
tells the tale's monk John who lingers in the garden that
her marriage brings no sexual gratification, her husband
spending all his energies upon this other form of Golden
Calf worship. (Lines 373-381, however, belie this.) Unlike
the chaste "Noli me tangere" of the scene in the garden
between the fallen, scarlet-clad Mary Magdalen and Christ,
here the respectable wife and the monk collude in obtaining
money and sex. He will pay a hundred franks for her favors,
multiplying Judas' coins. Christ is absent and the drama
only presents an avaricious Peter, an adulterous John and a
whoring Magdalen.

Our monk is breaking his Rule in countless ways. First
he has taken a vow of chastity, signified by his tonsure.
Chaucer amusingly tells us,

> The Sonday next the marchant was agon,
> To Seint-Denys ycomen is daun John,
> With crown and berd al fresshe and newe yshave,
>
> (VII.307-309)

to enjoy his bargain. Though Chaucer tells us the monk has
the license of his abbot to leave the cloister the
Benedictine Rule was strict about such matters. A monk, if
he had to leave the cloister for a journey that could be
done in a day, was not to eat any meal away from the
monastery on pain of excommunication (Rule 51). Our monk,
who has come from very near-by Paris, dines with great
sumptuousness and stays over for three nights, and returns
for yet another. Monks were not to possess personal wealth,
sharing everything in common. Our monk, it is true, shares
his host's wealth and possesses his wife in common, but that
was not the Rule's intent. Our monk has broken all vows of
chastity, poverty and obedience to his Rule.[27] He is a
"tredefowel" in the sense of the words that the Host
addresses to the Monk (VII.1945), words which are echoed in
the Shipman's Tale's lines 38, "as glad therof as fowel of
day;" and 51, "As fowel is fayn when that the sonne up
riseth." In this household he is "famulier" with both the
merchant and the wife, both being as members of his flock
of fowls of which he is the cock. The word "famulier" (31)
puns doubly with the French "femme" and the Latin "mulier,"
with whom he is decidedly too familiar.

The strictness of the Benedictine Rule, so flagrantly
violated by Daun John, was the monastic version of
peregrinatio of which pilgrimage was the secular form. While
Daun John violates pilgrimage's intent to obtain sexual
favors, the merchant Peter violates pilgrimage's intent to
obtain the increasing of his wealth. Emerging from his
counting house the merchant tells his wife how complex his
labor is, and includes among the guiles he lists for his
trade that of playing at pilgrimage (VII.233-234). He must
leave instantly for Bruges in Flanders (bourgeois and
mercantile Sir Thopas country in opposition to the St. Denis
of royal and peregrinate crusades) and a mass, a Missa
Peregrinorum (Appendix I), is said for the journey--and then
they bolt their dinner at which the monk wishes the merchant
"god-speed," but not without conning him of the hundred
franks with which he intends to pay the merchant's wife for
her favors.

The merchant agrees to the loan, announcing:

> But o thyng is, ye knowe it wel ynogh.
> Of chapmen, that hir moneie is hir plogh.
> We may creaunce whil we have a name;

<blockquote>
But goldlees for to be, it is no game.
Paye it agayn whan it lith in youre ese. (VII.287-291)
</blockquote>

The metaphors of the speech, of ploughing, of "creauncing,"
hold true for mercantile undertakings, yet they are
blasphemy. In the Roman de la Rose, a Golden Calf of a poem,
the plough metaphor applied to sex, "Plough, barons,
plough!" to man's seed sown for the harvest of a new
generation. In Piers Plowman the plough metaphor, as in
Christ's parables, applied to preaching, to words as seeds
to be sown in men's hearts. In the Shipman's Tale the plough
metaphor is applied to usury, to money loaned out at
interest and thereby increasing in value. That the Shipman's
Tale uses the metaphor of ploughing for usury is shown as
reprehensible in Dante's Inferno XVII which sees usurers as
betraying both nature and culture. Neither Florence's
florins, nor France's franks, nor England's angels,
according to medieval church doctrine, should be used for
such a purpose.[28]

The word "creaunce" immediately following upon the
plough metaphor with its sacred and profane meanings strikes
strange echoes. Exile could become pilgrimage because of
Christ's "creauncing" of Adam, by means of the Crucifixion,
"that boghte agayn mankynde" (VI.766). In that Passion he
restored man's credit, his imago dei, lost through sin in
the Edenic garden. Christ redeemed man's debt of death,
pledging instead himself. Here theology has taken over a
mercantile metaphor rather than the reverse. The merchant,
using it in its primary sense, strangely vulgarizes it,
restoring it to its original and profane meaning.

In Flander's Bruges, rather than dice and revel, the
merchant goes about his business; the word "faste" punning
upon pilgrim fasting.

<blockquote>
Now gooth the marchant faste and bisily
About his nede, and byeth and creaunceth.
He neither pleyeth at the dees ne daunceth
But as a marchaunt, shortly for to telle. (302-305)
</blockquote>

Again this seemingly sacred quality of his acts are not
really at all those of a pilgrim, but of the profane
contrary, the traffic of the world. Gold is here considered
the equivalent of Gospel preaching and the scriptural echo,
"I go about my father's business," is heard jarringly.

Meanwhile, the monk is lustily reveling in the
merchant's wife's bed all night. The monk tells the merchant
that the hundred loaned franks brought him such a bargain

and with such speedy profit that he has already returned the
sum to his wife. The monk should neither have slept with the
wife nor trafficked in usury. The merchant arrives home
joyous that by means of his Flanders pilgrimage he is now
entirely out of debt, for he has already paid back to the
Lombards with their three pawnbrokers' balls all that he
borrowed and more in return for his bond, yet he is puzzled
that his wife has not immediately told him of the monk's
return of the hundred franks. The wife replies that she has
already spent the sum. She agrees that she will return the
sum to him--in bed: "score it upon my taille" (VII.416)
being a pun upon the tally sticks used for accounting where
the credit has been granted by means of notches upon the
shank (the medieval check book and credit card in one), and
upon her.[29] The merchant sadly learns that this one is a bad
debt and "may nat amended be" (429). He consents to forgive
his wife her debt to him, a phrase that applies not only to
money but also to sex. However, he charges her to take
better care of their worldly goods in the future. His
concern is for her financial untrustworthiness rather than
for her sexual infidelity, which justifies her complaints to
the monk in the first place.

The emphasis of the Tale has been on the materialism of
the bourgeoisie, on the things of this world, though it
begins with a reference to the proverb that they "Passen as
dooth a shadwe upon the wal" (VII.9), used also by the
Merchant and the Parson in reference to the invalidity of
material possessions in this world (IV.1315;X.1068). The
Tale ends by making the pun quintuple:

Thus endeth now my tale, and God us sende
Taillynge ynough unto oure lyves ende. Amen. (433-434)

May we pay our marriage debts, have sex in our hosts' beds,
run up charge accounts, count money in our counting houses
and tell tales until our death. The multiplying of the word
into innumerable meanings is in turn a rhetorical version of
usury, referring back to the plough and seed metaphor. That
the fabliau is perverse, a Golden Calf, is shown only by the
passing shadow proverb which casts but a slight pall upon
the profane hilarity that follows. Yet the Tales the
pilgrims tell are their tally sticks in ernest, not only in
game, and at Doomsday they will account for their sins
revealed here in their confessions. The Shipman's pun is not
only on his Tale but on the entire Canterbury Tales at whose
ending Chaucer himself lists his credits and debits as poems
worthy and unworthy, those which turn their hearers to God,
those which tend to sin, in his tally stick of a confession.
There he pleads forgiveness for those fables of the debit

account desiring that they be creaunced by the sermons of
his credit account so that he "may be oone of hem at the day
of doom that shulle be saved" (X.1091).

The Shipman's Tale may have once been the Wife's. The
Pardoner interrupted the Wife's "sermon,"to speak of her as
a "noble prechour" (III.165), adding that he will not now
marry, though he had earlier decided on that course, due to
the effectivenss of her words. It would not matter to which
Tale he is responding, the Wife's or the Shipman's. Chaucer,
by this device, indicates that we should respond in a
similar manner and be warned rather than persuaded by the
Wife's or Shipman's precepts.

II

Chaucer's Diptych of Eve and Adam, of Wife and of
Pardoner, gives a careful chiastic bracketing, a panel
structure to the center of the Canterbury Tales. The Wife of
Bath commenced a Fragment (III). That which the Pardoner
concludes (VI) could easily have followed upon that
commenced by the Wife in an earlier ordering of the Tales.
In the Ellesmere ordering these two Fragments bracket those
of the marriage group (IV,V). The Pardoner's Tale with its
lengthy Prologue and its device of the tale that preaches
against the vice which the teller practices, echoes the
Wife's in structure and effect. The device requires a false
teller to speak true.[30] Chaucer pairs the Wife and the
Pardoner by means of their figures as false pilgrims, their
Prologues and their Tales. The one figure is under Venus'
influence, the other Saturn's. In both instances these
figures exemplify vices, the amazonian Wife as Flesh, the
emasculate Pardoner as the Devil. The conjunction of Venus
and Saturn was associated with the plague. The Wife and the
Pardoner, as pilgrims, ought to imitate Christ. Instead they
are a travesty of his teaching. They function as mocking
grotesques to the text, within it.

The Pardoner, like the Wife, is a "professional"
pilgrim:

A vernycle hadde he sowed upon his cappe,
His walet lay biforn hym in his lappe,
Bretful of pardoun, comen from Rome al hoot,
(I.685-687)

and the Ellesmere adds such details as robing him in
scarlet, placing the black and white vernicle upon a scarlet

though pilgrim hat, and slinging the pilgrim scrip about the horse's neck (Frontispiece). There is uncertainty whether Rouncivale is Roncesvalles upon the route to Compostela or the name of the corrupt London hospital. If the latter that name still subliminally recalls that other Roncesvalles of the pilgrimages and indeed the hospital was associated with a monastic house at Roncesvalles.[31]   This pilgrim quaestor, though he wears the black and white vernicle of the bearded Christ whom he should quest upon his red hat, definitely lacks that other badge of pilgrimage upon his chin, the beard flowing from a face serious and pale. "No berd hadde he, ne nevere sholde have" (689). Though he is singing for jolitee, "Com hider, love, to me," a very secular and lusty song, the words are addressed to the Summoner, not the Wife. The beardlessness would imply that he is a eunuch which renders the treble pun of the Summoner who "bar to him a stif burdoun," grotesque indeed (673). "Burdoun" is the bass accompaniment of the Summoner's male voice to the Pardoner's soprano; it recalls too the musical term, the "fauxburdoun"; and it is the pilgrim stave which Amant used in seducing the Rose; its qualifier, "stif," makes it even more sexual and perverse.[32]   Pardoner and Summoner oppose the Wife's natural lustiness; theirs, in the heterosexual medieval paradigm shift away from the homosexual classical one, is unnatural.

The Summoner, moreover, gives his Tale's friar a staff. Pilgrims bore staves, "burdouns," which Christ forbade. St. Francis in his Rule recognized that prohibition, having earlier discarded his pilgrim dress of staff and scrip for the russet robe with a belt of rope. John V. Fleming notes that in Bellini's painting of St. Francis the sandals, scrip and tau staff are shown cast side in the cell, the saint wearing none of them. Thus the Summoner with his friar in his Tale having "scrippe and tipped staf" (III.1737) mocks friars. The Summoner even adds to these forbidden artifacts by line 1776 a hat, forbidden to friars, expected of pilgrims.[32]   The medieval world was aware of these paradoxes concerning the friars' and pilgrims' garb, and attune to jokes played with them in these satires. The semiotics of pilgrimage, of monasticism, could be so disordered in a literary text because the readers of those satirical texts knew their true ordering and meaning. Laughter is evoked by that which is flagrantly inappropriate.

The Ellesmere portrait of the Friar therefore allots to him the Summoner's Tale's friar's forbidden pilgrim staff. The Ellesmere portrait of the Summoner places on his black locks a garland of red and white he has taken from an ale stake (a Renaissance painting of the Emmaus Inn clearly shows such a garland upon such a stake), while his buckler

is an ale cake, of which, it has been suggested, the
Pardoner partakes. The Summoner's mocking garland of red and
white echoes Emelye's and Cecilie's garlands of May,
matrimony and martyrdom. Medieval ivories, harking back to
Alexandrian conventions, showed such garlands being given to
each other by lovers.[33]

The Summoner's diet of "garleek, oynons, and eek lekes"
(634) is the diet desired by malcontent Exodus pilgrims,
yearning to return to the fleshpots of their Egyptian
bondage and to the worship of golden calves.[34] The
Ellesmere's Pardoner is, like the Wife, arrayed in glaring
scarlet. These figures are neither martyrs, nor pilgrims,
but instead sinners. The hellish three, Pardoner, Summoner
and Friar, travesty the Emmaus paradigm of the pilgrim
triad. The Wife plays the role in their group of an
impenitent Magdalen who, in the liturgical dramas, is garbed
as a whore in scarlet.

The Pardoner's Tale similarly parodies the Emmaus tale.
The Pardoner complies with the request for a Tale with a
sermon and a fable whose text is "radix malorum est
cupiditas" [the root of all evil is cupidity] and which
allows a pseudo-Jesse tree to flourish of all vices, sins
and iniquities with the ramification of catalogue and
accompanying exempla. A common theme in medieval iconography
is that of the two trees, shown on facing pages, the first
with its roots in cupidity, at its top, the old Adam, its
drooping leaves labeled with vices, the second with its
roots in charity, at its top the new Adam, Christ, its
flourishing leaves labeled with virtues.[35] The matching
figures of the Pardoner and the Parson in their scarlet
garb, preaching their ramified sermons, correspond to the
old Adam and the new, to Aaron and Moses, to cupidity and
charity, pride and humility, vice and virtue, the first tree
being a travesty of the second.

While downing his cakes and ale and intending to fleece
the pilgrims of their money with his fraudulent relics and
pardons, the Pardoner preaches against gluttony and
drunkenness and avarice. He knows he is, like the Wife of
Bath, a "noble prechour," and he is, unlike her, conscious
of his ability. She preached a "profane and old wives' fable"
(I Timothy 4.7). His sermon, based likewise on Timothy
("radix omnium malorum est cupiditas" 6.10), is really no
improvement upon her fable. He holds his audience's
attention with tales;

Thanne telle I hem ensamples many oon
Of olde stories longe tyme agoon.
For lewed pepel loven tales olde;

> Swiche thynges kan they wel reporte and holde.
>   (VI.435-438)

He defines his own genre (which is akin to Chaucer's in the
Canterbury Tales) in his Prologue's concluding words while
mentioning that he is now ready to begin fabling and
sermoning, having finished his draught of corny ale and
eaten of the cake:

> For though myself be a ful vicious man,
> A moral tale yet I yow telle kan.   (459-460)

The Tale begins--but it is no sooner begun than it
lapses into ramified sermoning once more concerning vice
after vice that flourish and interweave throughout the
Pardoner's words--with a compaignie--like those Chaucer took
up with at the Tabard--who hang out at taverns and such
places where folly has its haunts (463-482). The tree of
vices continues to flourish inexorably until at last the
reader is returned to the Tale so obscured by leafy sins.
They are still at the tavern, the "develes temple" (VI.470),
at line 661 (shades of Odysseus' scar) and this structural
device recalls the General Prologue where, after so many
figures on horseback were described as riding toward
Canterbury, we found they were still at that Tabard Inn at
their ease. Here while drinking, the revelours hear a bell
clap as a corpse is carried through the street to its grave.
This echoes John's words in the Miller's Tale: "I saugh
to-day a cors yborn to chirche/ That now, on Monday last, I
saugh hym wirche" (I.3429-3430). The riotours learn of the
serving boy that the dead man is one of their companions, of
their compaignie (VI.672-674):

> He was, pardee, an old felawe of youres;
> And sodeynly he was yslayn to-nyght,
> Fordronke, as he sat on his bench upright.

He has died of the pestilence, the Black Death that is
ravaging the countryside, and which has slain a thousand.
The child adds that his mother has taught him to prepare for
death. The host adds, "By Seinte Marie!" that the child is
right and that death indeed is stalking the land (685-689).[36]

They then meet an old man whom they treat, in their
pride, churlishly. The message which the child gave the
riotours, and which the host affirmed, that there was hope,
is now changed to the old man's despair. The three, the
child, the host and the old man, represent the stages of
man's life, much as had the Magna Mater shadow figure to the
Wife of Bath in her three forms as maiden, bride and crone.[37]

If the figure of the old man is Death, as some have thought, he is nevertheless Death presented benevolently, as a pilgrim with a staff who quests death within God's Providence, desiring himself that day when Death shall be dead. Yet the riotours hear him mention Death and rudely demand that he tell them where they may find that traitor that they may slay him. He answers truthfully that by turning up the crooked way (of sin, rather than the straight and narrow one of virtue) they will come to Death. His parting words spell out the promise of salvation if they will heed:

> "God save yow, that boghte agayn mankynde,
> And yow amende!"   (766-767)

Their subsequent damnation is of their own contrivance. The boy and the old man have been sent as messengers to persuade them to mend their ways. As in the plaguetide paintings of the "Trois Vivants et Trois Morts" in which a young man, a man in his prime and an old man meet with three corpses in differing stages of decay in three coffins, these three riotours meet with themselves; they quest death, not pilgrimage's via et vita et veritas, the "way, the truth, and the life." They wilfully choose the sinister "croked wey" of vice.

   At its ending they find that fortune of golden circled florins at the foot of the tree, at its tree roots, that could be but leafy, autumnal enchantment ("This is fairy gold, boy, and 'twill prove so," Winter's Tale), which leads us once again back to the flourishing of sin in all its selva oscura ramifications. This is the outcome. The Pardoner's cakes and ale are metamorphosed, within the tale, to poisoned sacramental bread and wine.[38] A pilgrim Abel is not slain by an exiled Cain but instead in this flimsy brotherhood of crime, through cupidity, each slays the other, leaving none alive. The three lie dead in a travesty of the Crucifixion at the roots of the great oak tree. Langland had presented a false revelour's argument of the Trinity as "how two slowe þe þridde" (B.X.54). The three parody the death of God. The golden treasure has been valueless (it could as well have been the fallen leaves of the damned of Dante's Virgilian simile, enchanted into gold, Inferno III.112-117). None here is a pilgrim, all are exiles. This is their fate, not salus. The Pardoner has told an "up-so-doun" Emmaus tale of three anti-pilgrims, complete with a tavern and with bread and wine, but with murder rather than with resurrection as its outcome.

The Pardoner ironically repeats the message of the boy, the host and the old man to these pilgrims, this compaignie from the Tabard of plague-ridden London:

      . . . Lo, sires, thus I preche
      And Jhesu Crist, that is oure soules leche,
      So graunte yow his pardoun to receyve,
      For that is best; I wol yow nat deceyve, (915-918)

and his tale making this point follows upon that of the exile figure of the Physician who, for all the gold in the world, cannot cure his patients of the pestilence that had raged in the city of London from whence these pilgrims journey, and whose tale is pagan and merciless, of suffering and death. The false Pardoner and the false Physician, associated with gold and pestilence in the Tales, echo the Exodus pattern of Aaron's association with the Golden Calf and plague.

Behind Chaucer's Pardoner and Wife lurk the figures of Faus-Semblant and La Vielle of the Roman de la Rose. The Roman de la Rose is a perverse pilgrimage poem and Faus-Semblant in its text, a false pilgrim. In the part of the Romaunt argued by Skeat to be Chaucer's translation, Faus Semblant and Dame Abstynaunce set forth on pilgrimage, though their guise is but guile.[39] They pretend to be "good and holy folke" (7360-7363), yet they murderously slit Male Bouche's throat while hearing his confession. Jean de Meun also associates Faus-Semblant with Sire Ysengrin the wolf wrapped in the skin of Balin the sheep of the Roman de Renart, another work that mocks pilgrimage. Faus Semblant states boldly that he is a hypocrite who avails himself of a papal bull as a pardoner to avoid real work:

      I wol both preche and eke counsaylen;
      With hondes wyl I not trauaylen,
      For of the pope I have the bull.   (6842-6847)

The Pardoner, in the Ellesmere illumination, is shown in scarlet robes and with a scarlet pilgrim's hat. Usually a pilgrim dressed in undyed wool and wore an undyed felt hat. The color change is glaring. De Meun's pilgrim Faus Semblant, in black and white Dominican garb but with the addition of scrip and staff, at least walked while Chaucer's Pardoner rides on horseback, his pilgrim scrip slung about the horse's neck (Plate IVa; Frontispiece). The scarlet color, worn by parish clergy not associated with an order as in the Parson's case, recalls in the figure of the Pardoner not Christ's redeeming blood but instead the red coat of a treacherous Judas fox. The Pardoner is modeled not only upon

Faus Semblant of the <u>Roman de la Rose</u> but also upon the hero
of the <u>Roman de Renart</u>, the wily fox who has a habit of
vowing pilgrimage--to save his neck--and who is frequently
depicted in medieval art disguised as a prelate and
preaching the while to barnyard fowl whom he will devour at
the sermon's conclusion.[40] The latter underlies the relation
of the Pardoner to his congregation of pilgrims--whom he
will fleece--the former the stance of the Pardoner himself
as seeming pilgrim--a "cock and bull" story.

Renart is a pilgrim in the <u>Roman</u> twice over. In <u>Le
Jugement de Renart</u> he has devoured Coupee, the sister of
Pintain and the sister-in-law of Chauntecleer, and for this
King Noble the Lion condemns him to death by hanging. But
Renart the fox gets off by vowing to sew the cross of
pilgrimage on his right shoulder, and to take up the scrip
and staff and set forth. Renart, however, arrives at no
pilgrim shrine; instead he dashes off to his chateau
stronghold of Maupertuis. In a further branche, IX. Renart
is moved to go on pilgrimage. He realizes that when he was a
gay young squire he devoured many a plump hen. Now he wishes
to confess and repent. The priest says that for such sins he
must seek repentence at Rome. The sins are too grave. Renart
dons pilgrim garb. However, he finds solitary pilgrimage
lonesome:

> Mout rensanble bien pelerin
> mout li siet bien l'escharpe au col,
> mais de si tint il por fol
> qu'il est meux sanz conpaignie. (8956-8959)

Instead of going up the right-hand path, Renart chooses the
left where he finds Bernart and Balin in an absurd Emmaus
echoing (8965-8968; Plate Vd). To them he narrates his
intent and explains that he has found in scripture that God
is happier over the sinner who repents than over the
ninety-nine who do not sin. But, alas, the <u>compaignie</u>
arrives at an inn at which point the pilgrimage falls apart
in a brawl. In the early Latin version it is at this point
that the fox, disguised as a pilgrim, wishes to devour the
cock. However, the cock, with great presence of mind,
suggests that the fox verbally defy the people who chase
them crying "Harrow!" The pilgrim fox does so, and loses his
dinner. After Chaucer's <u>Canterbury Tales</u>, Caxton will
translate the Dutch Renart tale into English and again
stress its pilgrimage motifs and will speak of Renart's
pilgrim scrip, as he also does of St. James' in the <u>Legenda
Aurea</u>, as a "malle," the same word Chaucer uses for the
pilgrim scrips of the Pardoner and the Parson (VI.920;
X.26).[41] It is clear that the Renart tale was already

well-known in oral and visual traditions in England as well
as on the Continent before the Caxton publication.
"Renarderies" were frequently sculpted in churches and made
use of in manuscript illuminations "in game" as grotesques
that mocked the "ernest" scriptural scenes.

Where we have the Pardoner as a Renart "prêchant aux
poules" [preaching to the barnyard fowl] and to the
Canterbury pilgrims, so nearly does this pilgrimage come
apart at its seams. The saturnine Pardoner desires that the
jovial Host kiss his relics. The Pardoner is an Aaron figure
insisting that the pilgrims buy his Pardon, with its leaden
bull, its Golden Calf grown up and transmuted with age. In
the Roman de la Rose Amant with his pilgrim staff had
reached into the cavity between the two pillars, the two
legs of the idol of the Rose to touch there the relics of
that shrine (Plate IVb,c). Such cavities were common to
saints' shrines and can be seen in depictions of Thomas'
tomb. Moreover, as Daniel Knapp has noted, pilgrims at
Canterbury kissed the hair shirt and breeches that Becket
had worn to mortify his flesh and which, at his death, were
found to be crawling with lice.[42] These were hung as sacred
relics above Thomas' tomb much as were the honors, the
tabard and the helm, of the Black Prince above his tomb.
That juxtaposition of the saintly and the worldly, the
ecclesiastical and the regal, side by side, must have been
satisfying to medieval pilgrims, though the kissing of the
breeches clearly displeased the heterosexual Host, who
reacts to the Pardoner's command as if anticipating the
gruesome Canterbury ritual:

> Thou woldest make me kisse thyn olde breech,
> And swere it were a relyk of a seint.   (VI.948-949)

It is at this point that a further element comes into
play. The Host speaks of castrating the already emasculate
Pardoner:

> I wolde I hadde thy coillons in myn hond
> In stide of relikes or of seintuarie.
> Lat kutte hem of,   (952-954)

and as he says so he swears by the Invention of the Cross on
May the third, "by the cros which that Seint Eleyne fond"
(951). Jove similarly castrated his father Saturn to prevent
that god's devouring of his progeny and the Roman de la Rose
both spoke of and illuminated that scene with great
explicitness. (It did the same for Origen and Abelard.) By
these means was Venus born and the Roman de la Rose
carefully shows her birth from the sea from Saturn's

genitalia. Yet here, at the same moment, the Host recalls
St. Helen's Invention of the Cross, who to do so razed the
idolatrous Temple of Venus upon the site of the Holy
Sepulchre.[43] This Invention of the Cross was celebrated on
May 3rd, immediately following May 1st's festival to pagan
Venus. The Host's angry words, similarly undo in Christian
terms the Pardoner's damage wrought upon this pilgrimage to
holy Canterbury, changing it from the worship of "St." Venus
to St. Truth. The anger recalls both Moses' at the
Israelites worshiping of the Golden Calf and Christ's at the
moneychangers in the Temple. The Pardoner had requested that
the pilgrims worship the saturnine lead bull of his pardon:
"Boweth youre heed under this hooly bulle" (909). The Host
refuses to bow to such a Golden Calf. The Pardoner is as an
Aaron, misleading the pilgrims to death and plague, the
Host, an angered Moses, rectifies the pilgrimage; the
Pardoner is a Saturn figure, the Host, a Jove; the Pardoner
is diabolical, the Host, Christian.

A further saturnine figure is found within the
Pardoner's Tale, the old man with his pilgrim staff and
beard. Burdoun and beard the Pardoner, as a eunuch from
birth, cannot have. Yet the aged man within the Tale who
says, "I knokke with my staf . . . And seye 'Leeve mooder,
leet me in'" (731), is like the figure of Saturn who became
Father Time with long white beard and scythe and hourglass.
Just as had the Wife and her Tale presented a figure that
blended the Roman Venus and the Celtic Magna Mater, with
three manifestations of maiden, bride and crone, so here
does the Pardoner and his Tale present a figure who shadows
the Roman Saturn, god of gold, plague and death, which
likewise is given three manifestations, child, host and old
man.[44] Together they are as an ancient Eve and an ancient
Adam, figures in need of a Christ to harrow them forth from
a realm of sin and death.

D.W. Robertson's Chaucer's London has noted how people
in the Middle Ages found wrongness comic. R.E. Kaske has
observed sculptures of virtues and vices in an English
church in which the words giving the vices have their
letters written backwards, those giving the virtues, the
right way round.[45] This is also Chaucer's humor in his
poetry, in which the world is turned "up-so-doun" until the
poem's rectification and ending. The animal fable in
medieval literature had much to do with this theme of the
world-upside-down, where beasts mirrored the actions of men
in apish mockery.[46] The Roman de Renart beast fabling
pilgrim theme pervades the Canterbury Tales. The General
Prologue's narrator describes Harry Bailly, the Host of the
Tabard, as a rooster: "Up roos oure Hoost, and was oure
aller cok, And gadrede us togidre alle in a flok" (823-824).

And the Host in turn refers to the Monk as a "tredefowel"
(VII. 1945-1948), that theme being echoed in the Shipman's
Tale's monk. Where the Nun's Priest tells a Renart tale of
Chauntecleer he is gathering together these remarks, and
perhaps he refers to his Prioress as Pertelote, the Monk as
Chauntecleer.

Dreams had been touched on in the Tale that preceded
the Nun's Priest's Tale where the Monk, in his final
tragedy, had narrated of Cresus. But these tragedies so
troubled the Knight and the Host that they protested against
such saturnine gloom and asked for something of jolitee, of
joviality (VII. 2767-2900), instead. The Nun's Priest in
reply tells of prophetic pilgrim dreams in a form that
delights rather than bores, and in so doing uncovers
Fortune's clouded bright face with a crowing Chauntecleer,
the emblem of priesthood and the Resurrection, rather than
trafficking with the gloomy Dame. The Monk's last line is
"And covere hir brighte face with a clowde" (2766),
concerning which the Host says, "He spak how fortune covered
with a clowde" (2782). The Nun's Priest agrees to tell a
"myrie" tale (2817) in lieu of the Monk's "greet disese"
(2771), which had had our Host so nearly fall into a
"slough" (2798) of despond. The hero of the Nun's Priest's
Tale is snatched from the jaws of death and lives to crow in
joy about it. From the Monk's worldly perspective pilgrimage
is worthless, men are fated to die and there is no
redemption. He reflects the pagan and saturnine perspective
of Egeus in the Knight's Tale. This attitude of despair, in
part, arouses the ire of the Knight and the Host. The
jovial-seeming Monk tells tales that are only saturnine
tragedies. However, from the Nun's Priest's perspective
pilgrimage is <u>salus</u>, rescuing the pilgrim from death, and
thereby, in Dante's sense, comedy.

Chauntecleer, the widow's cock, has a bad dream in the
dawning, that time Dante tells us at which dreams are
prophetically true (<u>Purg.</u> IX.13-18). He has dreamed of a
monster, whose appearance terrified him. But Chauntecleer's
wife chides him for his fears, calling him a coward and
warning him that dreams are not things of the soul at all,
but of the body, being caused by imbalanced humors,
digestive disorders and the like. Dreams, through incubation
rites, were, however, an important facet of pilgrimage in
the Middle Ages. The first tale Chauntecleer tells
concerning the veracity of dreams is, moreover, of two
pilgrims, on pilgrimage "in a ful good entente," who could
find no room at the inn for both. One is lodged in a stable.
The other man lodged at the inn dreams several times that
his fellow will be murdered. Three times he holds the dream
"but a vanitee." The third time he is told:

> 'I am now slawe,
> Bihoold my bloody woundes depe and wyde
> Arys up erly in the morwe tyde,
> And at the west gate of the toun,' quod he
> 'A carte ful of dong ther shaltow se,
> In which my body is hid ful prively;
> Do thilke carte arresten boldely,
> My gold caused my mordre, sooth to sayn.'
> And told hym every point how he was slayn,
> With a ful pitous face, pale of hewe.   (3014-3023)

The dream proves true. As in the Prioress' Tale (whose viciousness will out in her tale despite all her counterfeited gentility), "Mordre wol out." The pilgrim (a Palamon) finds a dead companion (an Arcite) amidst the dung in the cart at the town's western gate, his murder being caused by avarice for the gold he carried with him.

This tale within a tale is rich with implications.[47] It is analogous to the Knight's Tale, the martial western compass point of gold and death being clearly associated in both these tales, and it also adds to the complexity of the other Tale, this Arcite figure being paradoxically endowed with an _imitatio Christi_, the lodging in an ox's stall because there was no room at the inn, the beholding of the bloody wounds deep and wide. The Wife had said that in "dames lore" gold means blood (III.577-584). While the lodging in the ox's stall stressed the incarnation of God, here it appears to stress the opposition of the worldly body to the pilgrim soul, echoing the commonplace of stable and inn and traveler. It reflects back to Arcite as an allegory of the Body, Palamon as of the Soul, and echoes as well the Pardoner's Tale where gold likewise spells saturnine death.

The second tale Chauntecleer tells is of two travelers (again a pilgrim metaphor), of whom one dreams of a shipwreck. The other pays no heed, sails forth and is drowned, like the ship in Dante's _Paradiso_ Aquinas saw and like the _Inferno_'s Ulysses' bark that sailed beyond Hercules' western bounds:

> But casuelly the shippes botme rente.
> And ship and man under the water wente
> In sighte of othere shippes it bisyde,
> That with hem sayled at the same tyde. (3100-3104).[48]

Chauntecleer tells Pertelote many more tales. They are both applicable to his condition and to the pilgrim audience which includes the _Canterbury Tales_' hearers and readers. But then, like the Knight and the Host, Chauntecleer elects not to continue these tragedies, "Now let us speke of myrthe, and stynte al this" (3157).

But alas, amidst all Chauntecleer's pride, comes the fox. Hyperbole is piled up from epic and rhetorical handbook. City allegory is made use of (borrowed from Renart-le-Contrefait), Chauntecleer being a Troy betrayed by a Sinon, a Charlemagne betrayed by a Ganelon, a Christ betrayed by a Judas; a long digression is slipped in concerning destiny and free will, fitting to the tales previous to this concerning tragedy and Fortuna; and then the teller remarks that his tale is not of all this, but of a cock, his wife and foolish counsel. But he cannot resist adding, quitting the Wife of Bath (and the Prioress?):

Wommannes conseil broghte us first to wo,
And made Adam fro Paradys to go,
Ther as he was ful myrie and wel at ese, (3258-3260)

then hastily adds, "Oh, those words were Chauntecleer's, not mine!" But we still have not got to that fox. The fox is seen and Chauntecleer knows that he must flee. But the fox's flattery wins him over. Daun Russell's praises (he compares him to the cock who failed to wake Gandulfus in the Speculum Stultorum, that Canterbury masterpiece, thus causing him to lose his benefice), ravish Chauntecleer.[49]

It is Friday, May the Third (echoing again the Knight's Tale and also the Host's oath), and Chauntecleer is destined to be eaten by Daun Russell, Renart's son as friar. Epic invocation after epic invocation mourn the tragedy befallen the cock upon this fateful Friday of a May the Third. The hens of the barnyard carry on like ancient heroines. The whole neighborhood takes up the hue and cry and chase the pair, their clamor louder than that of the bands of fourteenth-century peasants marching on London and demanding Christian equality, yet killing Flemish weavers in a pogrom, resenting the competition they offered at labor. (Renart-le-Contrefait at this point had written of French social disturbance.)[50] But it is not all as fated as it seems, not all as darkly tragic as the Monk would have it, for Chauntecleer still has his wits about him and, like Christ, knows how to beguile the beguiler. The fox does his bidding and turns to boast aloud his triumph, at which moment the cock flies to the tree and perches in its branches, alive, not dead like Cresus and Kenelm and Christ. Chauntecleer is now immune to the fox's blandishments, having been by "fallacy surpris'd" and made aware through the experiencing of fallacy how to detect fallacy in the future.[51] Meanwhile the fox mourns that he has indeed been trapped in his own trap set for the cock, that of pride, and hence lost a good dinner. The original Latin version of this tale, we remember, had the fox be in pilgrim guise. The medieval beast fable satire upon pilgrimge, so frequently shown as grotesque marginalia about sacred wit, has here entwined itself amidst the <u>Canterbury Tales</u>.

The Nun's Priest concludes his pilgrim fable, metamorphosing it even into a sermon:

> But ye that holden this tale a folye,
> As of a fox, or of a cok and hen,
> Taketh the moralite, goode men.
> For seint Paul seith that al that writen is,
> To oure doctrine it is ywrite, ywis;
> Taketh the fruyt, and lat the chaf be stille.
>
> (3438-3443)

He states that the Tale, though so humorous, has a serious intent, that of the <u>salus</u> of its hearer. Grotesque <u>renarderies</u> playing bagpipes appear as diversionary mocking illuminations to sacred texts. Yet here, the marginal gloss has become the text, the grotesque the illumination, the Golden Calf the Ark. Chaucer will repeat these arguments at his conclusion to the entirety of his Tales, borrowing from Paul's Epistles to Timothy, which state that one should not listen to "profane and old wives' fables," yet which also state that all that is written is written for our doctrine (I. 4.7: II. 3.19). Chauntecleer the cock (a medieval symbol for the Resurrection, priesthood and more), is snatched from the jaws of death as will be the pilgrim who achieves the paradoxical mirroring of Christ, who "starf on rood." Chauntecleer mimes that death, to find it life. Daun Russell the fox is a shadow of the red-garbed emasculate Pardoner, Chauntecleer the cock, of the virile Host.[52] They also mirror the Devil and the Christian soul.

Chaucer himself, by his final confession following upon the Parson's sermon, becomes as an Aaron who repents having made the Golden Calf, as a Renart who takes upon himself a pilgrimage in penance for all the hens he has devoured and the lustful fabliaux he has told, as a trickster-saviour figure; his <u>persona</u> and his readers are as a Chauntecleer who learn to distinguish between <u>renarderie</u> and truth. The contrasting of the Pardoner and the Parson is reflected in that of the Monk and the Nun's Priest. Without that final confession Chaucer would be as the seemingly jovial but actually saturnine Monk and as the scarlet-robed, death-wishing, faussemblant, Falstaffian, pilgrim Pardoner. Mars, Venus, Jove and Saturn, the deities of plague of the Knight's Tale and of the pilgrim Wife and Pardoner are

metamorphosed into the _salus_ of Christ whom the Nun's Priest
and the Parson seek. All the pilgrims gathered together by
the Host, are as fragmentations of Chaucer's trickster-
saviour role towards his reader. The conclusion as
confession converts Chaucer from an Aaron figure who would
have the pilgrims listen to Saturnine tragedy and worship a
lead bull to being a Moses figure who can lead the pilgrims
not only "in this viage" to Canterbury, but also to
"Jerusalem celestial" (X.49-51). The _Canterbury Tales_ Parson
sermons on an English road, while "Harry" and "Geoffrey" are
as a Cleophas and a Luke, as if desiring a "soper" of fables
at the inn as evening shadows lengthen, beneath the Doomsday
scales of Libra. The Tales they tell are of lead and gold
used to fashion profane fables and true sermons, celebrating
the lust for life and the love of God, two halves of one
whole.

CHAPTER TEN: THE PILGRIM AND THE BOOK

        In the Genesis of this book the question was asked:
"Who was the pilgrim who was present in flesh and blood in
the medieval world and who is mirrored in the words of
medieval pilgrimage poems?" A question now needs to be posed
at this book's Apocalypse. "Why is the figure of the poet
present in these poems and as a pilgrim?" Pilgrimage poems
in the fourteenth century usurped the place of the epic.
Pagan Aristotle had stated that in the epic poem the figure
of the poet ought nowhere to appear. The Middle Ages had
Aristotle's Poetics but did not much consult that work.
However, rhetorical treatises of that period cited his
dictate, which came to them through other sources. These
fourteenth century Christian pilgrimage poems, Dante's
Commedia, Deguileville's Pèlerinages, Langland's Piers
Plowman and Chaucer's Canterbury Tales, and behind them
Guillaume de Lorris' and Jean de Meun's thirteenth-century
Roman de la Rose, blatantly defied that poetic and pagan
rule. The figures of the poets are present in their poems,
the creators within their creations, in their own image;
stern and bitter Dante in his eared cap and his long robe;
the lean and wild Will, looking like a Lollard; plump
Geoffrey in his sober garb and with his penner, each as a
pilgrim. Their other characters in their poems are as if
fragmentations of themselves: "Here is God's plenty."[1]
Why is this the pattern of pilgrimage poetry?

        This chapter will argue that there are two authorial,
intertextual paradigms at work in pilgrimage texts,
the first of Luke at Emmaus, the second, God himself, the
subject of Luke's Gospel; and that this doubleness of the
authorial paradigms create rich structures within the
thirteenth and fourteenth century pilgrimage texts that play
with the Old and New Testaments; that the mirroring of God's
writing in man's writing is of the essence of pilgrimage
imitatio Christi.

In Ezekiel 2.9-10 and in Revelations 5.1, in the Old
and New Testament, the two apocalyptic dreamers, Ezekiel and
John, who are present within their texts, both see held in
God's hand a scroll, "scriptus intus et foris" [written
within and without]. This scroll held by God in visions and
portrayed throughout Christendom as a bound codex lent
itself to the metaphor of the Book as being both Word and
World, Old and New.[2]

Dante in the Commedia, Langland in Piers Plowman and
Chaucer in the Canterbury Tales each made use of landscapes
mirrored within their texts and each self-consciously drew
an analogy between their poems as books of words and the
sensible world to that of the Creation of God as the book of
the Word and the World. Each in turn functions as a
"twice-told tale," an apocalyptic "duplex liber," written
with external and internal meanings.[3] Each poem speaks of a
Book. In the Commedia it is the Book God holds, Par. XXXIII.
In Piers Plowman it is Boke's speech, B.XVIII. Within the
Book of the Tales of Canterbury the Wife is shown to both
hate and destroy her Clerk's book (III.669-815). These are
literary works that yoke poetry to theology, old wives'
tales to parsons' sermons, lying fables to Gospel truth, and
which can do so because of pilgrimage's paradoxes and the
self-awareness of apocalypses as books, of books as
apocalypses, which save or damn their readers and their
poets. Chaucer, even, twice self-referentially quotes Paul,
"Al that is writen is writen for oure doctrine" (VII.3441-2;
X.1083; II Tim. 3.16).

Dante consummates his poem with the image of the Book
of God's Creation as gathered up and bound in one volume. By
analogy the sacred and apocalyptic Book within the poem
mirrors the poem that Dante writes and which the reader
completes, from alpha to omega. With the poet as pilgrim the
reader sees:

> Nel suo profondo . . . ch s'interna,
>   legato con amore in un volume,
>   ciò che per l'universo si squaderna:

> [Within its depth . . . ingathered, bound by love in
> one volume, the scattered leaves of all the universe].
>   (XXXIII.85-87)

The books are bound, the one with the other, in that great
and universal ingathering of particulars, Dante's Commedia
with that other Book, the Creation of God, of which it is a
counterfeiting, an encyclopedic mirroring.

Illuminations of the Commedia are aware of Dante's
analogy of the book with the Book. While the initials N and
P of the Inferno and the Purgatorio often show Dante's
author portrait busily engaged in writing the Commedia
within his study, the L of the Paradiso instead often
presents Christ as Creator who holds the Book of the World
open to the reader, the alpha and the omega clearly marked
upon its pages.[4] No longer does Dante carry through Hell
Virgil's pagan Aeneid as lie-filled guidebook of inversions.
Instead both Dante in the poem and the reader confront the
true pilgrim guide, God's Book. Such a deliberate analogy
within Dante's text (Par. XXXIII.85-87) and within the
Paradiso's illuminated initial demonstrates the writer's,
the illuminator's and the reader's awareness of the Commedia
as likewise an ingathering of God's Book of the Word and the
World, even including among its many pages the Aeneid's
idolatry and the Roman de la Rose's. The Commedia's
apocalyptic ending ingathers pagan materials; the borrowed
simile from Virgil's Aeneid I.430-436 of Carthage as built
by bees is used to inseminate, fulfill and adorn Dante's
celestial city of the Rose (Par. XXXI.7-12); the borrowed
simile from the Roman de la Rose of Jason's Argo questing
the Golden Fleece and admired by the pagan idol, Neptune,
is used to convey the pilgrim's worship of God (Par.
XXXIII.94-96).[5] Dante has taken the Egyptian gold from these
Golden Calf poems and used it for his "poema sacro."

Langland's vast and rambling poem whose ending is its
beginning envelopes the brief speech of Book. That speech
is, as it were, an Achilles' shield within an Iliad; it is
both microcosm and macrocosm of the poem that contains it.
"Boke's" speech, and here I use Skeat's spelling and
capitalization in lieu of Donaldson's mere "book," narrates
the vita Christi, the life and death of Christ, and closes
by saying that, at Doomsday, "I, [Boke], wole be brent"
(XVIII.255), though that narrated vita will save those that
"bileue" on it.[6] That "Boke" narrates only the life of
Christ reduces all the Doubting-Thomas-like verbiage of Will
Langland in Piers Plowman and all its fair field full of
folk, to the one figure who created all and whom they quest,
St. Truth. Piers Plowman's per speculum in aenigmate is
rendered facie ad faciem; no longer does the reader see
"through a glass darkly," but is "face to face" with "Boke."

Thanne was þer a wight . wiþ two brode eiȝen;
Book highte þat beaupeere . a bold man of speche.
(XVIII.230-231)

"Boke," with his two broad pages, of Alpha and Omega, Old
and New, tells of the birth of Christ, the World's Creator

whom all the elements obey, fire, air, water and earth, and of his death. He concludes by saying that at Doomsday "Boke" will be burnt: "And I, [Boke], wole be brent . but Iesus rise to lyue" (255). He is the World that has been created and that will pass away; all books that mirror him, including Langland's own poem, Piers Plowman, sharing in his fate, "Boke" having saved those who have pilgrimaged upon its via et vita et veritas, its way, life and truth. Langland's and God's Books will be burnt at the Apocalypse; they both are, if used rightly in this world and time, merely instrumental in presenting the vita Christi and his salus to their readers.[7] Then they deconstruct. The speech of Boke in little thus mirrors what Langland does with all Piers Plowman.

With Chaucer, whose genre is not that of the apocalyptic dream visions of Dante or Langland but is instead a tale of tales told by pilgrims on a pilgrimage, the theme of Book is less obvious. Yet it does occur. We are shown Book abused by the Wife of Bath, who pilgrimages throughout the external world but is deaf to the internal word. She echoes pagan Trajan's "Ye, baw for bokes!" She appears not to heed Francesca's courtly pornographic romances. Her destruction of her clerkly husband's book damns her as a teller yet her lustiness attracts her readers to her point of view. She celebrates the senses. She discards that internal "auctoritee," derived from the Word, that consonance between all texts which served to convey to the medieval reader the godly wisdom of the soul rather than the fallen knowledge of the eyes. "Experience, though noon auctoritee/ Were in this world, is right ynogh for me" (III.1-2). She opts for the carnal, not the spiritual, for Oldness, not Newness, for the Golden Calf, not the Ark of the Word, for "profane and old wives' fables" and not for sermons, for a foris world that is "up-so-doun." Yet, paradoxically, her old wives' tale serves as preface to friars' and clerks' sermoning tales, and even includes their sermons within her fable.

The Clerk of the General Prologue and in the Ellesmere illumination to his Tale possesses and carries books of black and red like a latter-day Emmaus Luke (Plate Xd). The Wife's clerkly husband is also a lover of books, one of which is such a summa as that which Dante describes in Paradiso XXXIII.

> And alle thise [tales] were bounden in o volume
>   (III.681)

echoes

Nel suo profondo vidi che s'interna
legato con amore in un volume
ciò che per l'universo si squaderna,

[Within its depths I saw ingathered, bound by love in
one volume, the scattered leaves of all the universe.]
(XXXIII.85-87)

Jankyn's book, from which the Wife states first that
she wrenches one leaf, then three, then burns all its pages,
had gathered together tales against wicked wives. Jankyn's
book began, she says:

Of Eva first, that for hir wikkednesse
Was al mankynde broght to wrecchednesse,
For which that Jhesu Crist hymself was slayn,
That boghte us with his herte blood agayn.(III.715-720)

It contains the work of Cardinal Jerome, the translator of
the Bible:

And eek there was somtyme a clerk at Rome,
A cardinal, that highte Seint Jerome,
That made a book agayn Jovinian.   (III.673-675)

And it even includes, the Wife mentions, Chaucer's own work,
that of "the leon" (692), of which Chaucer will repent in
his retraction at the conclusion of the Canterbury Tales
(X.1086). Her Tale thus is a commentary on God's Book, and
even on Chaucer's book, the book of the Lion, the Canterbury
Tales. How will they be read? Like an old wives' fable? Like
a sermon? Will the readers tear the pilgrim Tales out of
context, revel only in those parts which are chaf, not
fruyt, foris not intus? Or will they heed the Tales' yoking
of experience with authority, Egyptian gold as both Golden
Calf and Ark; the totality of the work, and not a fragment.
Chaucer, by means of his Wife, both laughs with and at the
reader who will heed only the outward sense. But the Wife in
her Oldness is too deaf to hear the Tales' sermon fable that
could save her when the Book of the World is burnt.

Pilgrimage poems thus stress the "Book," both negative
and positive. There are other likenesses between these
fourteenth-century poems, likenesses which cannot be caused
by direct borrowing. They are instead commonplaces of
Christendom, which bridge barriers of language and clime.
Beatrice tells Dante that "Qui sarai tu poco tempo silvano"
[Here shall you be short time a forester] (Purg. XXXII.100).
the Samaritan announces to Will that "An þanne shal Feiþ be
forster here. and in þis Fryth walke" (XVII.115), and that

in this world and time Faith will aid pilgrims to attain
Jerusalem, while Hope will be their innkeeper tending those
too sick to journey further until they are strengthened and
placed once more in their guide's hands. Before Dante met
Beatrice in the Commedia he was guided by Matilda, noted in
reality for the hospital she built for pilgrims.[8] In both
Dante and Langland these injunctions that Dante, the pilgrim
in the poem, and Faith, who is also Abraham, be as pilgrim
guides appear to be strictly temporal. In Langland that time
is to be until Death is dead, until Dante will become "cive/
di quella Roma onde Cristo è romano" [citizen of that Rome
whereof Christ is Roman (101-2)]. That short time, poco
tempo, in both instances is apocalyptic time, the "silvano"
and "forster" of the time in this world anticipating its
near ending. Similarly in Chaucer the Tabard Inn's Host so
places the pilgrims into the Parson's hands at the
Canterbury Tales' ending beneath Libra's Doomsday scales;
and among Chaucer's pilgrims, too, is the Knight's Yeoman, a
forester dressed in Lincoln green. He, of course, is
countered by the false guide, the devil as forester in the
Friar's Tale of a damned summoner, a Tale which interestingly speaks of Dante's Commedia.

Books and guides and forests are found not just in
pilgrimage poems but also in pilgrimage paintings; in Andrea
da Firenze's Via Veritatis (Plate XIII) and Francesco
Traini's Triumph of Death, all of the fourteenth century. In
these frescoes, painted following the Black Death, gaily-
clad processions traverse sinister, shadowy woods in which
are enthroned personifications of the Senses, then pilgrims
in simple garb journey up the narrow stony paths where they
confess their sins to hermits and friars.[9] In the Via
Veritatis it is Thomas Aquinas the Dominican who is shown
as guiding pilgrims from the world of the senses, foris,
to the world of the soul, intus, which he does by means
of a book held open to them. It is his Summa contra
gentiles and it mirrors the Book God holds in his hand at
the top of the fresco. In the Triumph of Death a hermit
holds out an unrolled scroll to a worldly cavalcade, much as
will Chaucer's Parson his Sermon to the gaily-clad
Canterbury pilgrims. The implication is that the Book held
in the hand of God, of which Aquinas' Summa and the hermit's
scroll are reflections, binds up both World and Word, intus
et foris, as in Ezekiel and John. Not only are Aquinas' book
and the hermit's scroll reflections of that Book, but so
also are fourteenth-century pilgrimage poems books guiding
their readers to the via et vita et veritas.

At the extreme left hand side, however, of God in
Andrea da Firenze's pilgrimage Via Veritatis is a seated

figure clad in scarlet who refuses to heed Thomas Aquinas'
sermon preached at him from a book (Plate XIII). In his own
hands is a book that mirrors that other. He is busily
wrenching out its pages, destroying it as wilfully as does
the Wife her clerkly husband's omnium gatherum. Another
figure stops up his ears. He iconographically echoes the
stoners of Stephen before the martyrdom (Acts 7.57-58). He,
likewise, is a commentary within the painting as to how not
to respond to its sermon.[10] Trajan, in Piers Plowman, the
pagan thumbing his nose at books, is related to them (Plate
Xc). The poems and the paintings are as mirrors of each
other, partaking in commonplaces that cluster about the
concept of pilgrimage in the fourteenth century.

    In the paintings, the Florentine Via Veritatis, the
Pisan Triumph of Death, the life of this world, of the
senses, is portrayed as a forest, as indeed it was in
Dante's poem opening in which he was lost in "una selva
oscura" [a dark wood]. Yet now these foresters, Dante
Alighieri, Langland's Faith and perhaps even Chaucer's
Yeoman in Lincoln green, are guides to others; as
twice-journeyers they can aid other pilgrims in their
travails. Dante's Italian reads: "Nel mezzo del cammin di
nostra vita/ mi ritrovai per una selva oscura" [In the
middle of the journey of our life I found myself again in
a dark wood]. Though translators fail to render "ritrovai"
completely it means "I refound," "I found again." It is as
if Dante had intended the poem's first reading to be obscure
and foolish, while the second journeying is with knowledge
and wisdom. It is as if Dante intended the reader to turn
from the Paradiso's omega to the Inferno's alpha again, as
in a twice-told tale, "si come rota ch'igualmente è mossa"
[rolled--even as a wheel that moves equally] (Par. XXXIII.
144). Though Dante's poem is not God's "In Principio erat
Verbum" [In the Beginning was the Word], being instead the
pagan epic's "in medias res," "Nel mezzo" [In the middle];
nevertheless it implies the other, bringing its "In
Principio" into the midst of Dante's world, translating it
from Jerome's Latin into Francis' Italian, and from the
first century of Christendom to the fourteenth.

    Dante wrote a "twice-told tale" in the Commedia, a
Janus poem. Singleton had noticed that quality in the Vita
Nuova:

    He is the protagonist of the action, moving forward
    along the line of events in their first occurrence. And
    then he is that same person who, having lived through
    all these happenings, looks back upon them and sees
    their meaning now as it was not possible for him to do
    at the time. As the first of these persons he knows

> nothing before it happens. But as one reading in a book
> of memory he knows the end, the middle and the
> beginning of all that happened.[11]

Dante the author is therefore a "silvano," a forest guide to
the reader. But Dante the pilgrim is still lost in the
forest and as such he is ourselves. That is the pattern also
of Piers Plowman. Boethius had made the dual strategy
popular with his Consolation of Philosophy, Augustine with
his Confessions. More was to continue it in the Utopia,
Erasmus in the Praise of Folly. Today it is found in the
detective novels of Dorothy Sayers and Agatha Christie. The
strategy requires the twice-telling, of folly, then wisdom,
of Oldness, then Newness, of the pilgrim Israelites and the
Christian pilgrim, to be contained within one Janus text.
Much of the paradigm, of course, comes from the dual
authorship of Luke 24, by both Gospeler and God, by both
Luke and Christ; and lurking behind that the dual authority
of Aaron and Moses. These partnerships are uneven, yet their
inadequate member is ultimately forgiven and honored despite
the Emmaus folly, the Exodus Golden Calf fabrication. Such
sacred authorial paradigms become apologies for pilgrim
poetry--and for pilgrim poets.

Domenico Michelini's fresco celebrating Dante and his
Commedia is much like Andrea da Firenze's Via Veritatis
(Plate XIII) and Francesco Traini's Triumph of Death. Like
them also it was painted in time of plague (Plate XIV). It
shows Dante in his red doctor's robes with his open book
upon which is clearly stated, "Nel mezzo del cammin di
nostra vita," as if mirroring God's Book's "In Principio
erat Verbum." Dante holds his book in the same manner as
Thomas Aquinas holds his Summa in the Via Veritatis and as
the hermit holds the scroll in the Triumph of Death. Dante's
free hand shows the Florentines who view this fresco the
Inferno, before it the bannered procession of those who
never chose, as if to equate that band of dead souls with
these living Florentines who stand before his painted
figure. The intent of his held book is clearly to prompt
Florentine Christians to choose and to choose aright. Behind
him, beyond marshes, rises the mountain of Purgatory, above
which are the seven spheres of Paradise. At his left is the
city of Florence with the new Duomo, within which this
fresco is painted. Dante bitterly stands outside the city
walls, as Florence's Jeremiah, as Florence's salus noster,
while she denies her gates to him as did Hell her gates to
the Creator. The gates of Florence, Inferno and Purgatorio
all mirror each other and are the same. The fresco's

landscapes, with its dungeon and mountain is not only that
of the Commedia, but also of Piers Plowman's field full of
folk poised between the Castle of Care and the Tower of
Truth, and of the Canterbury Tales' cavalcade of pilgrims
poised between secular London and sacred Canterbury. These
pilgrim poems localize the landscapes of Exodus' pilgrimage
upon Italy and England.

For pilgrims the Book was indeed written both "intus et
foris," within and without; it was the Bible and the World.
Egeria, a fifth-century nun, emphasized that monks read to
pilgrims the appropriate passages from the Bible at each of
the pilgrimage sites of the Exodus and in Jerusalem and she
in turn linked text and landscape within the guidebook that
she wrote for other pilgrims, who could either actually make
that pilgrimage--or experience it vicariously through
reading of it in her book. Bunyan was later to say, "This
book will make a traveller of thee." Dame Margery Kempe, on
her return, dictated her experiences of the Holy Places and
of other pilgrimage shrines. These experiences were shaped
for her by sermons preached by friars upon the correct
biblical texts at each Holy Place. Sir Richard Guylforde's
chaplain also noted that at each site the friar guardians
preached upon the appropriate texts, linking sacred history
with sacred geography. From the anonymous Bordeaux pilgrim
to Sir Richard Guylforde, for a thousand years and more,
pilgrims carefully described their journeys to and from the
Holy Places and linked the pilgrimage to both landscape and
Bible.[12] Such books in turn acted as guides to other pilgrims
and, to judge from their surviving numbers, were in great
demand in the medieval world, both for actual travelers to
the Holy Places and for those who performed that journey
only in imagination through reading such books. Anglo-Saxon
Bede, in his isolated monastery in the eighth century, wrote
a famous "Description of the Holy Places," without ever
having traveled from the British Isles. Instead he consulted
and edited the account dictated by ship-wrecked Gaullish
Bishop Arculf to Iona's Abbot Adamnan in the seventh
century.[13] Fourteenth-century Dante in turn, perhaps,
consulted Bede's "Description of the Holy Places." In such
cases the book could substitute for the world, the
pilgrimage through a book being considered as a mirroring of
the other. What would not have been adequate would have been
the reverse, to have traveled, like Dante's Ulysses,
Langland's Palmer, and Chaucer's Wife, through the World
without paying heed to the Book.

Pilgrims were eminently "People of the Book." Their
essential guidebook was the Bible. They traveled light,
except for books which they either placed in their scrips or

carried in their hands. The Vercelli manuscript, which contains sermons and legends, the "Dream of the Rood," the "Andreas" and the "Elene," concerning the Holy Places, was possibly brought to Italy from England by an Anglo-Saxon pilgrim on his way to Rome or Jerusalem. Irish manuscripts are found scattered throughout Europe, brought by pilgrim monks from that western isle. In the fourteenth century Italian pilgrims describe their sailing to the Holy Places with a Bible and Gregory's _Moralia_ in their luggage. A Middle English poem describes pilgrims sailing to Compostela, likewise with books to read.[14] Pilgrims wrote guidebooks, recounting their travels, upon their return. Compostela's _Codex Calixtinus_, itself such a pilgrim guidebook, is illuminated with St. James the pilgrim saint who holds in his hand a self-referential book. So does the Luttrell Psalter include an illumination of St. James holding a book. A manuscript of Lydgate's translation of Deguileville's _Pilgrimage of the Life of Man_ for frontispiece shows the Cistercian author in white monastic garb, rather than the Benedictine translator in black, presenting the Book of the Pilgrim personified as an actual pilgrim in fleece sclavin, "cockle hat and staff," and scrip, who offers in turn his book _The Pilgrim_, as if it were his guidebook to the Holy Places, to Lydgate's noble patron (Figure 11). The medieval world clearly associated pilgrims with books and this is graphic evidence of that fact.

Both in Ezekiel and in Revelation those who are to be saved are recorded by means of writing: in the earlier prophetic book, by a man clothed in linen, with a writer's inkhorn at his side, "who set a mark upon the forehead of those who feared God" (Ezek.9.2-4, shown in illuminations as a Tau); in Revelation it is declared, "he that overcometh, the same shall be clothed in white raiment; and I will not blot his name out of the book of life" (Rev. 3.5). Medieval monasteries kept such books of names of the deceased for whom they offered masses, in return for funds for them to do so, which they called "Books of Life."[15] The books of Ezekiel and Revelation, books that in turn contained the Book held in God's hand, gave rise to patristic and medieval works, such as the _Pastor_ of Hermas and the _Commedia_ of Dante, in which the poets include their names and those of others within their poems from this desire that they be numbered amongst the saved. Books, thus, could even be as chantries for their writers' souls.

These poems mirror the Book, in space as _mappae mundi_, in time from Genesis to Apocalypse. Moreover, within them their poets are pilgrims, in their own image, first as a

Figure 11   Lydgate/Deguileville presents
            The Pilgrim MS Harleian 4826

fallen Adam, then becoming Christlike. The task of the
pilgrim is to imitate Christ. The task of the pilgrim poet
is to imitate Christ the Creator. This they do. Both Exodus
and Emmaus patterns stressed not only pilgrimage but also
authorship. Moses as God's scribe was considered to have
written the biblical books concerning Genesis and Exodus; he
had, moreover, brought down the stony tablets of the Law
that God had written upon Mount Sinai; Luke was considered
to be the foolish pilgrim at Emmaus, a tale of which he was
the wise Gospeler portraying with words the life of Christ
who was the Word. Dante, Langland and Chaucer, in a fictive
form, become also as God's scribes portraying Exodus and
Emmaus patterns within their fourteenth-century vulgates,
Italian and English, and upon the landscapes of those
landscapes, Italy's and England's. Their task is to be as if
Jerome translating Moses and Luke; they similarly translate
the Word into their words. (We recall that Dürer prefaced
Erasmus' edition of the Letters of Jerome with a portrait of
Jerome translating the Bible from Hebrew and Greek into
Latin, in his Bethlehem study cave, that place were the Word
was made flesh and dwelt among us, and gave to Erasmus, the
Bible's editor, another engraving of that scene, thereby
giving the visual form of the imitatio, translatio studii
and intertextuality of these mirrored events twice over.)

The Commedia and Piers Plowman have their pilgrim
selves be named within the texts as their poets. Thus they
"incarnate" themselves within their creations. Beatrice
names Dante in Purgatorio XXX. 55-64, where she recalls him
from his bitter grief at the loss of Virgil to an awareness
of her presence:

> "Dante, perché Virgilio se ne vada,
> non pianger anco, non piangere ancora;"

> [Dante, because Virgil goes away, do not weep yet, do
> not weep yet.]

Will names himself while debating with Anima, who is also
Amor, that he has never met Charity or Christ: "'I have
lyued in londe', quod I . 'my name is longe wille,/ And fond
I neuere ful charite . bifore ne bihynde" (XV.152). It
should be noted that that figure of Charity, the image of
God, who speaks to him parallels Beatrice. Will's pilgrim
self adds that:

> Clerkes kenne me þat Crist . is in alle places
> Ac I sei3 hym neuere sooþly . but as myself in a
>   Mirour:
>   Hic in enigmate, tunc facie ad faciem.   (XV.161-162)

and in so doing speaks more truly than his <u>persona</u> of folly
realizes.

Dante had at the same point unabashedly gazed at his
feet, only to see himself mirrored there "nel chiaro fonte"
[in the clear fount] like a new Narcisuss, and drew back
from the reflection in shame. Narcissus' sterile self-love
echoed the Golden Calf's idolatry. To recognize that
idolatry and to turn instead to Charity and Beatrice is to
find in them the echoing of God's image in man, thereby also
loving oneself, being likewise in that image of that Word.
Beatrice then holds up to Dante a verbal mirror, a <u>speculum</u>
of words, of his faults. These have misguided him:

> e volsi i passi suoi per via non vera,
> imagini di ben seguendo false,
> che nulla promession rendono intera,

> [and he turned his steps by a way not true, pursuing
> false images of good, that pay no promise in full.]
> (XXX.130-132)

When corrected and baptized, Dante is led to Beatrice's
eyes, which in turn reflect the Griffon as Christ upon which
she gazes. She is not Golden Calf, but Ark.

These poems are each as a <u>speculum</u>. Each mirrors the
naming by Amor and by Anima. In Langland's patterning the
naming dialogue between Will and Anima described Charity as
a russet-clad pilgrim, mirroring Will. Deguileville's
<u>Pèlerinage</u> similarly named the author; Dante and
Deguileville both taking pains to have that naming be only
the Christian names of "Dante" and "Guyllyam," not the
mortal patronyms, Alighieri and de Deguileville, though
Langland is considered punningly to allow his patronym its
presence also. Deguileville's naming is by Grace Dieu (1308,
1328) as she baptizes him; Langland's comparable figure is
"Holichirche"; the early <u>Pastor of Hermas</u> had himself be
named by Rhoda and by Ecclesia. All these figures mirror
Beatrice's. As for the <u>Roman de la Rose</u>, at a similar point
Amore tells Amant that the poem is a "Miroer aus Amoreus"
and then names its dual authors, Guillaume de Lorris and
Jean de Meun, as being its <u>persona</u>.[16]

The <u>Commedia</u>, the <u>Pèlerinages</u> and <u>Piers Plowman</u>, like
the <u>Roman de la Rose</u>, are <u>speculum peregrinorum</u> poems,
mirrors for pilgrims. In their texts the equation is made of
the poet as "Dante," "Guyllyam," "Wille longe londe" as
flesh and blood and particular, and the Adamic pilgrim as
allegorical and universal. All three pilgrim protagonists

come--with the reader--to a mirroring of Christ, their
Creator who created them in his mirror image, though that
mirroring has been darkened by their folly. At first such
poems are as <u>per speculum in aenigmate</u>, as seen through a
glass darkly, and are thereby as a <u>speculum stultorum</u>, a
mirror for fools exiled from God's face. Yet each <u>persona</u>
progresses by means of pilgrimage from idle and idolatrous
narcissism to restoration, from the folly of self-love to
the love of the Creator, becoming <u>facie ad faciem</u>, face to
face with him.[17] Paradoxically because Dante, Will, Guyllyam
and Everyman are created in the Creator's image, that love
can now also be self-love. It embraces the opposites and
proves them the same.

Mirroring and painting are invoked, "mi parve pinta" in
the <u>Commedia</u>, "peynted al blody" in <u>Piers Plowman</u>, in
phrases that are so alike yet in poems written without an
awareness of each other, which surely indicates a common
patterning in fourteenth-century pilgrimage poetry. Dante's
poetry "paints" the face of God as "ours," Langland bloodily
"peynts" Piers, whom Will quests, as Christ. Dante, perhaps,
describes such a mosaiced Pantocrator as at the two St.
John's, in Florence and Rome; Langland presents a priest
painted with wounds on his hands, feet and side with
sanguine coloring as in the <u>Officium Peregrinorum</u> play
performed at Easter Monday Vespers and the <u>Visitatio
Sepulchri</u> drama enacted on Easter Sunday itself. Thus on the
plane of human art both poets strive to express, by
deliberately inadequate and mortal means, a paradox that
cannot be shown, save for the fact that it existed imprinted
upon men's souls and could therefore be tremblingly and
inadequately expressed by man the artist, causing its
pilgrim viewers to both doubt and marvel, to be as if both a
Thomas and a Luke, in the <u>Officium Peregrinorum</u>.

That Dante and Langland borrow from another art,
painting, to convey shadowily what poetry "fails" to do,
emphasizes the loss through translation, the reduction of
reality to mere imitation, the inadequacy of portraying
flesh and blood with paint or poetry. Paradoxically this
deepens the intensity of the metaphorical statement. It does
not diminish it at all. And neither does it lie. (Interestingly, Luke was both writer and painter.) With Chaucer the
pattern alters. We do not see Chaucer's poem self come face
to face, <u>facie ad faciem</u>, with Christ, nor with Piers the
Plowman as Christ. He listens instead, on a literal level,
to a sermon preached by a Christ-like Parson--yet that
pattern shadowily is as of Luke listening and yet not understanding as the pilgrim Christ fables and sermons on Emmaus'
road.

Gerhart B. Ladner discusses the concept of the image of God in man and its corresponding influence upon art and literature. He gives examples to demonstrate the theology and iconography of Adam's creation by the Word, in which Adam is shown as like Christ, concluding with Chartres Cathedral's sculpture of Christ with the newly created Adam upon his knee, each in the other's image.[18] In that act there is a mirroring both ways and that reflection, the one of the other, God in man's image who is in God's, results in the salvation of man. "But we all, with open face beholding as in a glass the glory of the Lord, are changed into the same image from glory to glory" (II Cor. 3.18). For this reason that imitation and reflection in Dante and Langland where the poet pilgrim views God face to face and in his image ("mi parve pinta de la nostra effige" [seemed to me painted in our image]), denotes the salvation of that particular pilgrim poet, restored to the primal likeness, and with him that of the Everyman reader. Dante's transposition of the imaging is powerful, seemingly daring to the point of blasphemy, yet correct and true to the theology of the Incarnation. Blake similarly depicted God and Job in each other's image.

The Exodus and Emmaus patterns of pilgrimage are paradigms for education. Exodus was spoken of by Jewish and Christian theologians and exegetes as God's education, his paideia, of his people. Each of the three pilgrim poems is also a paideia. The purpose of Christian paideia is to attain to the image of God in which one is created; pilgrimage, likewise, is the imitatio Christi. Dante's Commedia shows the progress of its pilgrim protagonist, first under the guidance of pagan Virgil, then under that of Christian Beatrice. He first learns the trivium and the quadrivium, and then partakes of the knowledge of the queen of sciences, theology. Langland's Piers Plowman is also a poem about education. Piers and Will are taught their ABC, study the trivium, the quadrivium and theology. Chaucer's Canterbury Tales is less overtly an education poem. However, its General Prologue is an exercise in grammar, rhetoric and somewhat faulty logic. Its Tales make use of the liberal arts, geometry and astronomy in the Knight's Tale and elsewhere, arithmetic in the Shipman's Tale, music in the Second Nun's Tale, and the servile arts of alchemy in the Canon Yeoman's Tale, law in the Physician's Tale and medicine in the Manciple's Tale. The Parson's Sermon crowns the work with thorny Theology.

These poets have their poem selves pilgrimage from Adam to Christ. They have their poems mirror Creation and Resurrection. Dante and Chaucer begin their poems at

Eastertide; Langland centers his poem upon Easter, though
beginning it at Pentecost. Dante's <u>Inferno</u>'s Good Friday is
dated March 25. That was the traditional date for the
Creation of the World and the Fall of Man, for the
Annunciation to Mary and the Crucifixion of Christ.[19] In both
the calendar of the pagan Zodiac and the calendar of the
Christian Church it was considered to be the beginning of
the year's cycle, of the world's creation--and re-creation.

Dante states:

   Temp'era dal principio del mattino
e 'l sol montava 'n sù con quelle stelle
ch'eran con lui quando l'amor divino
   mosse di prima quelle cose belle;

[The time was at the beginning of the morning; and the
sun was rising with those stars that were with him when
divine love first set those beautiful things in
motion.]   (I.37-40)

He furthermore states that his poem's "Nel mezzo" was
nevertheless also of "Il Principio," that it was of "l'ora
del tempo e la dolce stagion" [the hour of the time and the
sweet season]. One almost sees and hears the angel enter
Mary's chamber to announce the Word made Flesh, "Verbum caro
factum est," while she reads in a held book, perhaps of Adam
and Eve's Expulsion from Eden upon that day (Plate IIa,b;
<u>Purg</u>. X.34-45). Fra Angelico's painting in the Prado
portrays the paradox of "Eva" become "Ave." Panofsky has
noted Flemish Annunciation paintings which play with the
Oldness of the Romanesque upon the Virgin's left, the
Newness of Gothic upon her right.[20] Dante's poem opening
likewise heralds that Newness though his poem self is so
soon to be despairingly guided by pagan Virgil from the
sunlit mountain into the exilic realm of "scritta morta"
[dead writing], of the Old Law, rather than of the Word
become flesh.

Chaucer also draws attention to both Creation and
Resurrection. His first lines,

Whan that Aprill with his shoures soote
The droghte of March had perced to the roote, (I.1-2)

are unfolded in the Nun's Priest's Tale, when we are told of
the fall and redemption of Chaunticleer, that it occurred,

Whan that the month in which the world bigan
That highte March, whan God first maked man,
Was compleet . . . (VII.3187-9)

March, Creation and the Fall of Man, April, Easter and the
Redemption of Man are embodied in the poem's first couplet.
Rhetoricians recommended this to poets, in view of the
analogy of the creation of the poem to the Creation of the
World, and recommended as well that the beginning consist of
yoked oppositions, nature and culture, chaos and order,
creature and Creator.[21]

It was common in the Middle Ages to compare artists and
authors to the deus artifex and deus auctor, not in order to
honor mortal art and poetry, said Panofsky, but in order to
make it easier to understand the nature and working of the
divine mind.[22] Auerbach in his essay, "Figura," observed a
similar concept, both Auerbach and Panofsky here speaking of
the way the artist first conceives the idea of his completed
work, then brings it to fruition through imposing the form
of the idea upon matter. Like Panofsky, Auerbach stated:
"The question of the imitation of nature in art roused
little theoretical interest in the Middle Ages; but all the
more attention was accorded to the notion that the artist,
as a kind of figure for God the Creator, realized an
archetype that was alive in his spirit."[23] Joseph Anthony
Mazzeo in "The Analogy of Creation in Dante" states that:
"The image of the Deus Pictor or Deus Artifex in medieval or
patristic thought is not intended as a glorification of the
artist. It is rather an attempt to understand the divine
creation by using the artist as an analogue . . . .The
divine act of creation, the conferral of existence, came to
be considered the act of creation in the proper sense of the
word while other forms of what we would call creation were
analogically or mimetically related to it."[24]

Mazzeo notes that Dante makes use of this analogy,
though, at the same moment, of its disparity. He cites
Purgatorio as demonstrating the limitations of mortal art.
That had been foreshadowed where Cato in Purgatorio II
chided the pilgrims for singing the amoroso canto of
Dante's own composing rather than God's pilgrim psalm: "In
exitu Israel de Aegypto. Then, on the terrace of pride,
God's workmanship far exceeds that of man, where sculptures
of David before the Ark, Mary and the Angel, Trajan and the
Widow, move and all but speak and where the pride of earthly
artists, Cimabue and Oderisi, is humbled. Dante's pride is
likewise corbelled as he stoops to hear Oderisi's words,
walking side by side as if the poet and the illuminator,
both artificers of apocalyptic books, were two yoked oxen
drawing God's sacred Ark; Dante's and Oderisi's art thereby
being metamorphosed from Golden Calf to Luke's Ox. Of
interest is that in the medieval tradition Luke was not
only a gospeler of words but also a painter of icons.

Cristofero Landino said that Dante was a prophet poet
and that "although the feigning of a poet is not entirely
out of nothing, it nevertheless departs from making and
comes very near to creating. And God is the supreme poet,
and the world is his poem." These words appeared in his
"Commentary on Dante" in 1481.[25] They represent a Renaissance
interpretation of a medieval text, presenting, instead of
the required humility the speculum Christi demands, artistic
pride. Dante in the Commedia showed his persona progressing
from the Inferno's pride to the Paradiso's humility, the
Purgatorio as fulcrum between the two. Nevertheless
Landino's words correctly portray the analogy between the
creation of the poem by Dante as poet and the Creation of
the World by God as Author. The Creation, according to
theology, was created by the Word. Further the Word then in
an inn, upon a pilgrimage, took upon himself flesh, "Verbum
caro factum est," becoming in the flesh in his own image, in
which he had created man, in order to save him. It was due
to this tautology that medieval theologians viewed Christ as
the Creator and showed him as such at Sinai, Chartres and
elsewhere.

Ladner not only traced instances where the image of the
Creator, Adam and Christ mirrored one another in art, but
also noted that the figure derived from classical
philosopher and author portraits: "A motif much favored on
third and fourth century sarcophagi was that of the sage or
philosopher shown in the act of reading or teaching."[26] He
adds: "They not only foreshadowed certain types of the image
of the Christian saints, especially of evangelists, apostles
and prophets, but also contributed to the formation of the
earliest iconography of Christ himself."[27] He comments that
it is frequently impossible to disentangle the figure as to
whether it is Christian or pagan since this "motif of the
reading, teaching, or pondering philosopher on these
Christian and pagan sarcophagi is an adaptation of an old
classical scheme used for portraits of philosophers, poets,
and authors in general."[28] He notes that with the
Lindisfarne Gospels, the fourth evangelist, St. John, is
shown frontally holding an opened scroll, no longer engaged
in the act of writing, in the iconography of the Pantocrator
rather than of the author portrait tradition. He sees in art
a new dignity in man where, by the exercise of free will, he
may govern his body in accord with his soul and thereby be
restored to his image-likeness to God, exemplifying in
himself the central tenet of Christianity, the Incarnation.

God in the Old Testament created Adam in his image:
"And God said, Let us make man in our image, after our

likeness" (Gen. 1.26). God then in the Gospels took upon
himself that image to save Adam: "In the beginning was the
Word, and the Word was with God, and the Word was God . . .
And the Word was made flesh, and dwelt among us" (John 1.1 &
14). The Word became Flesh within Creation. Pilgrimage
poetry plays, so to speak, a "god-game" with this
patterning.[29] The pilgrim poet further desires to mirror the
Gospelers and God in creating a poem that is analogous to
God's Janus Book, the Word and the World, then to incarnate
within it a pilgrim in the poet's own image, who is as
fallen and foolish Adam, who is as Luke who walks by
Christ's side, the _viator_ by the _via_, and who is to be
restored to a pilgrim Christ-likeness. Luke fleetingly
comes _facie ad faciem_, face to face with Christ at the inn
at Emmaus, mirroring and counterfeiting him. Similarly the
reader is for the duration of his reading of the text the
viator, the _via_ the poet's poem self as a pilgrim.

Just as the Word created the World, then became within
that World the Word made flesh in his own image to save man,
so has the pilgrim poet created a poem, within which he has
his flesh become words, in his own image, that he might save
his reader. The pilgrim poet thus is analogous to the
pilgrim gospeler Luke but also to the pilgrim Creator who
walked at his side on the Emmaus road, the Truth who
paradoxically seemed to tell fables. As the shadows
lengthened the pilgrim Christ told pilgrim tales of his
types, his shadows, in time past, beginning with Moses. The
type, the shadow of the past pilgrim of folly, in contrast
to the pilgrim of wisdom, was Moses' brother Aaron, who
permitted the fabling fabrication of the Golden Calf. Where
the poem's pilgrim self is lost in Exodus and Emmaus folly
the reader is not saved. Where the poem's pilgrim repents of
his sins, casting pride aside and donning humility, then has
the pilgrim poet himself achieved the pilgrim mirroring of
the Truth, and become, not so much as like Luke the Gospeler
as like Christ the Creator. He can then guide his readers to
God and thus can himself be saved. Fourteenth-century
pilgrimage poetry, written in Dante's case in the bitterness
of exile, in Langland and Chaucer's in fear of the plague,
sought in the vernacular to give fallen man a pilgrim
pattern by which to return himself from exile and regain the
salus Adam lost. Wyclif, as had Jerome before him,
translated the Bible. The _Commedia_, _Piers Plowman_ and the
Canterbury Tales are likewise as Bibles of fabling sermons
telling of Emmaus and Exodus. They are pilgrimage poems
written for Italy and England that save their readers--and
by doing so, also save their poets.

Dante described a pilgrim from Croatia viewing Rome's

Veronica in <u>Paradiso</u> XXXI. In Canto XXXIII he has pierced
through that Tabernacle and Veronica veil and he himself, in
the fiction of the poem, comes "face to face" with the face
of God which: "Mi parve . . . pinta de la nostra effige"
[seemed to me as if painted in our image] (131). For a brief
moment the reader responds to the statement with shock,
sensing it to be blasphemous; for Dante has humbled God by
portraying him in man's image. Yet, because this is a
<u>speculum peregrinorum</u>, a mirror of pilgrims, this is both
poetically and theologically justifiable. God created man in
his image, then according to theology humbly took upon
himself that image that was his own in order to become man.
Man and God mirror each other. This image Dante sees of God,
moreover, holds a Book:

    Nel suo profondo vidi che s'interna,
    legato con amore in un volume,
    ciò che per l'universo si squaderna;

    [Within its depths I saw ingathered bound by love in
    one volume that which is scattered through all the
    universe]   (85-85)

Gathered into that Book God holds is also Dante's book,
including his <u>Inferno</u> of exile along with his <u>Purgatorio</u> of
pilgrimage and his <u>Paradiso</u> of citizenship. Gathered into
that book is fabling poetry side by side with Christian
sermon, such as that which Paul preached and Luke wrote down
on Athens' hill of Mars, the Areopagus.[30] This is why the
poet is in the poem as both foolish pilgrim and wise
author, intertextually mirroring both Luke and God.

    The poems of Dante, Langland and Chaucer, the <u>Commedia</u>,
<u>Piers Plowman</u> and the <u>Canterbury Tales</u>, are as if lies
wrought of prideful gold, silver, jewels and raiment, yet
which adorn the truth of humble stone, wood and bread; they
are as fables and sermons told on the road to an inn under
the setting sun by three humble figures clad in cockle hats
and staves and sandal shoon; they are of Exodus and Emmaus.
The pilgrim reader can open the pilgrim book, illuminated
with sacred scenes yoked to grotesque <u>renarderies</u>, and read
to its ending, its Apocalypse, then turn back to its
Genesis, going contrarily from <u>omega</u> to <u>alpha</u>, and
recommence the pilgrim reading, the tale twice-told. He can
read it as if a worldly Cain, exiled from God's face, and as
if a pilgrim Abel, face to face with God; he can read its
pages carnally and up-so-doun, as if Aaron's Golden Calf, or
penetrate its purple veils of allegory, of Moses' Tabernacle
of the Ark; he can perceive with the eyes of the body alone,
the <u>oculi corporis</u>, or with the heart, the <u>oculi cordis</u>, as
well; he can read it in the penitential garb of fleece of

Genesis, or in the white linen of Apocalypse--or in
Babylonian scarlet silk. All these oppositions are
ingathered and made one. Then, as in a pilgrimage to St.
James in which the pilgrim comes to mirror his book-holding,
cockle-hatted pilgrim Saint, so does the reader of Dante,
Langland and Chaucer and their speculum peregrinorum come
"face to face" with himself, mirrored in that book-holding
image of God, in his own hands that ingathered pilgrim book
and is, thus, "oon of hem at the day of doom that shulle be
saved" (X.1091, Plates XII,XIII).

EPILOGUE

　　At the Reformation the Canterbury pilgrimage abruptly
stopped. Under Henry VIII's decree all references to Thomas
were to be erased. Several manuscripts of Piers Plowman have
his name expunged.[1] All statues of him were to be destroyed.
Tancred Borenius' frontispiece to St. Thomas Becket in Art
is of two saintly archbishops flanking a third, now empty,
niche. All frescoes were to be painted over. His shrine was
dismantled. Churches dedicated to him were rededicated to the
other Thomas, the Doubting Thomas of the Pilgrims' Plays.
In 1536 and 1537 a rebellion against Henry VIII's decree to
dissolve the monasteries was mustered in northern England and
called the "Pilgrimage of Grace." It was rigorously put
down.[2] Henceforth in Protestant countries poets who used
pilgrimage and of their number were Ralegh, Shakespeare,
Blake and Byron, did so only as metaphor. Ophelia's song in
Hamlet, "How shall I your true love know/ From another one?
/By his cockle hat and staff,/ And his sandal shoon," is
tragic. She can neither quest a Hamlet in pilgrim guise nor
wed a Christ in Emmaus garb. In Elizabethan England, both
pilgrimage and monasticism are of the past.

APPENDICES

APPENDIX I: THE <u>BENEDICTIO PEREGRINORUM</u>

The text given here generally follows that of a
fourteenth-century manuscript fragment of an English Manual,
which represents what would have been used during the time
of Langland and Chaucer, and which is in the possession of
Leo Arons of Princeton who kindly allowed me to transcribe
it. <u>Caveat lector</u>: I did so before adequately studying
paleography. The text has been compared with other Pilgrim
Blessings in the Henry Bradshaw Society publications of
rare liturgical English texts. An English translation is
given in the Sarum Missal. The manuscript is vellum, 5 3/4"
X 4", written in red (here italics) and black.

[First psalms are said over the prostrate and
confessed pilgrims who lie in front of the altar.]
Kyrieleison. Christeleison, Kyrieleison. Pater
noster . . . . Dominus vobiscum.
<u>Oremus</u>: Deus qui ad vitam ducis et confidentes
in te paterna protectione custodis: quesumus ut
presenti famulo tuo a nobis egredienti angelicum
tribuas comitatum: ut eius auxilio protectus nullius
mali concuciatur formidine, nullo comprimatur
adversitatis angore, nullis irruentis inimici
molestetur insidiis et spaciis necessarium itineris
prospero cursu peractis propriisque locis fideliter
restitutis, universos repereat sospites, ac debitas
exsoluat tuo nomini gracias. P
<u>Oremus</u>: Deus qui diligentibus te misericordiam tuam
semper impendis et a serventibus tibi in nulla es
regione longinquus dirige viam huius famuli tui in
voluntate tua ut te protectore te preduce per
iusticie semitas sine offensione gradiatur. P

Benedictio pere et baculi [Blessing of the Scrip and
Staff, the pilgrims now standing]: Domine ihesu
christe qui tua ineffabili miseratione ac patris
iussione spiritus que sancti cooperatione de celo
descendere ovemque perditam a diabolica seductione
voluisti querere, atque propriis humeris ad celestis
patrie gregem referre [who came from heaven to seek
the sheep lost through the devil's wiles, and bore it
on your own shoulders to the sheepfold of heaven],
quique precepisti filiis matris ecclesie orando
petere, bene vivendo querere, ac pulsando perseverare,
ut citius invenire valeant salutaris premia vita, te
humiliter invocamus quatinus sanctificando benedicere
[+] digneris hanc peram vel baculum ut qui ea pro tui
nominis amore instar humilis armature lateri suo
applicare, atque collo suspendere sive in manibus suis
gestare, sicque peregrinando suffragia sanctorum humili
comitante devotione studuerint querere: dextere tue
protectus munimine pervenire mereantur ad gaudia
mansiones eterne. Q. vi.
Hic impone [   ] collo pera ita dicendo [Here the
scrip is sprinkled with holy water, then placed about
the pilgrim's neck while saying]: Accipe hanc peram
signum peregrinationis. In nominis patris et filii et
spiritus sancti. Amen. Dabis etiam baculum dicens
[Here you give the pilgrim the staff]: Per hunc
baculum accipiens benedictionem et misericordiam a
deo salutari tuo. Amen.
Si quis eorum ierosoliman profecturus est benedictes
cruce dices [If some of the pilgrims are going to
Jerusalem bless the cross saying]: Benedic [+] domine
hanc crucem per qui erupuisti mundum de potestate
inimici et passione tua superasti suggestorem peccati
qui gaudebat in prevaricacione primi hominis per
vetitum lignum sanctifica domine istud signa. Orem.
Proculum passionis tue, ut sit inimicis tuis
obstaculum et credentibus in te, et sepulchrum
petentibus perpetuum perfice vexillum. Q. vi.
Deinde dabis vestrem signatum cruce dicens [Then
you give the raiment with the cross saying]: Accipe
vestimentum cruce domini salvatoris signatum: ut per
illud salus, benedictio, et virtus prospere
profisciendi ad sepulchrum ipsius tibi comitetur. Qui
cum patre.

The Mass for Pilgrims, the Missa Peregrinorum, follows,
its lesson being Genesis 24.7:

The Lord God of heaven, which took me from my father's
house, and from the land of my kindred, and which
spake unto me, and that sware unto me, saying, Unto

thy seed will I give this land; he shall send his
angel before thee, [and thou shalt take a wife unto my
son from thence,]

this being the passage in which Abraham sends his servant to
Jacob's Well to seek there a wife, Rebekah, for Isaac. The
Gospel of the Mass is Matthew 10.7-15:

And as ye go, preach, saying, the kingdom of heaven is
at hand. Heal the sick, cleanse the lepers, raise the
dead, cast out devils: freely ye have received, freely
give. Provide neither gold, nor silver, nor brass in
your purse, nor scrip for your journey, neither two
coats, neither shoes, nor yet staves: for the workman
is worthy of his meat. And into whatsoever city or
town ye shall enter, inquire who in it is worthy and
there abide till ye go thence. And when you come into
a house, salute it. And if the house be worthy, let
your peace come upon it: but it if be not worthy, let
your peace return to you. And whosoever shall not
receive you, nor hear your words, when ye shall depart
out of that house or city, shake off the dust of your
feet. Verily, I say unto you, It shall be more
tolerable for the land of Sodom and Gomorrah on the
day of judgement than for that city.

[Post missam dicat sacerdos has orationes sequentes
super peregrinos coram altari prostratos: sive
profecturi sint hierusalem: sive ad sanctum iacobum:
vel ad aliam peregrinationem.] Deinde dic canones
istas super eos in terra prostratos: Deus infinite
misericordie et maiestatis immense, quem nec spacia
locos nec intervalla temporum ab hiis quos tueris
abiungunt: adesto famulis tuis ubisque in te
confidentibus, et per omnem viam quam ituri sunt dux
eorum et comes esse dignare, nichil eis noceat,
nichil difficultatis obsistat. Cunta eis salubria
cuncta sint prospera, et sub ope dextere tue quicquid
iusto expecierint desiderio celeri consequentur
effectu. Per. cristum. Oro. Omnipotens deus qui est
via, et veritas, et vita iter vestrum in beneplacito
suo disponat, et angelum sanctum suum raphaelem in
hac peregrinatione vestram custodem adhibeat, qui ad
loca desiderata cum pace vobiscum eundo perducat et
cum salute iterum ad nos redeundo reducat. Sit
interventrix per vobis beata dei genitrix maria cum
omnibus angelis et archangelis, patriarchis, et
prophetis sint intercessores vestri sancti apostoli
petrus et paulus, cum ceteris sanctis apostolis,
martyribus, confessoribus et virginibus,
obtineantque vobis sancti illi quorum suffragia

queritis iusta desideria et properitatem, remissionem
que peccatorum, et vitam eternam. Amen.[1]
[Deinde communicentur et ita recedant in nomine
domini.]

The Sarum Rite in English adds: "The branding of a cross
upon the flesh of pilgrims going to Jerusalem has been
forbidden by canon law," indicating this was an earlier
practice.

APPENDIX II: PILGRIMAGE AND FALCONRY

The classic world had not known the art of falconry.
The medieval world avidly practiced it. The names of the
different types of falcons derived from the Arabic world.
Two names should especially interest us, one being the
"peregrine," the other, the "gerfalcon" (this pronounced
with the Arabic soft "g" rather than the hard of Hebrew, yet
meaning the same). Both names refer to the pilgrim, the
wanderer. Cesare Ripa's figure of Esilio as a Pilgrim holds
in its hand a falcon, perhaps in allusion to this. The
Vocabolario degli Accademici della Crusca speaks of their
nomenclature ("Pellegrino . . . una spezie particolare di
Falcone") being such because they are homeless, as if in a
pilgrimage, and that they eat little as if piously fasting.
Dante ambiguously refers to the soul ("anima") as
"peregrina." His doing so refers both to the pilgrimage of
the human soul to its creator, and to the trait of the
trained falcons to return to the lure of their master. So
had Ripa had his pilgrim figure of Esilio hold a peregrine
in his fist (Figure 1).

In the Inferno we are treated to a falcon (in the
Inferno Dante never mentions the word "peregrine") who has
seen neither prey nor lure and descends to earth dispirited
and sullen as he gyres down, refusing to obey his master's
call.

Come 'l falcon ch'è stato assai su l'ali,
che sanza veder logoro o ucello
fa dire al falconiere "Omè, tu cali!"
discende lasso onde si move isnello,
per cento rote, e da lunge si pone
dal suo maestro, disdegnoso e fello;

[As the falcon that has been long enough on the wing
--that without seeing lure or bird, makes the
falconer say, "Ah, you're coming down!" descends

slothfully, through a hundred gyres, to where it set
forth swiftly, and alights far from its master,
disdainful and sulking.]   (XVII.127-132)

Langland makes use of the same image, not to describe
fraudulent Geryon, but wilful Sloth who says:

> For I haue and haue had . somedel haukes maneres;
> I am no3t lured wiþ loue . but þer ligge au3t vnder
>   þe þombe.   (V.431-432)

In the _Purgatorio_ Dante had been lured by the flesh,
represented by the Ulyssean Siren witch. Virgil bids him
spurn her and instead:

> . . . "batti a terra le calcagne;
> li occhi rivolgi al logoro che gira
> lo rege etterno con le rote magne."
>   Quale 'l falcon, che prima a' piè si mira,
> indi si volge al grido e si protende
> per lo disio del pasto che là il tira
>   tal me fec' io;

> ["Strike your heels on the ground; turn your eyes
> to the lure which the eternal king gyres with the
> great spheres." Like the falcon that first looks
> down, then turns at the cry and stretches forward,
> through desire of the bread that draws him there,
> so did I.]   (XIX.61-67)

That image is repeated again in _Paradiso_ XIX. 34-36,
where Dante compares himself to the falcon liberated from
its hood, preening its feathers on head and wing.

A similar use of the image occurs in a Middle English
poem M.D. Anderson cites from the fifteenth-century British
Library Additional Manuscript 37049. In it the falconer
lures the hawk toward him with "red flesh to see" who is
also Christ bleeding on the tree to win back man's soul,
"The whilk fro hym by sin does flee away."[1] In the _Commedia_
it is the "anima peregrina," the pilgrim soul, who journeys
not to the lure of woman's flesh but to that other lure, the
eternal king who became man (a _logoro_ of flesh and of bread)
in order to liberate mankind and who gyres the great
spheres. This lure or "logoro" in falconry is a bait of
flesh upon which feathers are stuck and which is whirled
about in the air by the falconer to attract his falcon back
to him.[2]

Dante's first two falcon similes involved fraud, the

first, the comparison to Geryon's fictional flight, the
second to the spurning of the at first beautiful, but then
vile, Siren. The pilgrim lure is not to be to the flesh of
the lady but of God, not lust, but Incarnation. This was a
commonplace. A Flemish manuscript gives the pun between
the lure of falconry and that of lust.[3] It shows the
falconer being to his lady, the falcon, bringing to her
the game that he has caught as if she were, in turn, his
lure. Dante's similes play upon this pun in order to spurn
it in one context, that of the world, the flesh and the
devil, and seek it in another, that of God. The difference
between the soaring peregrine of the _Purgatorio_ and the
sullen falcon of the _Inferno_ is immense; the one ascends to
the heavens where his king lures him towards the spheres,
the other descends to the earth spurning his master,
gaining no reward. They reflect in turn the hope of the
pilgrim book, the despair of the book of exile.

NOTES

CHAPTER ONE: PILGRIMS AND EXILES

[1] Erich Auerbach, "Odysseus' Scar," _Mimesis_, trans.
Willard Trask, New York, 1957, pp. 1-20, demonstrates how
the opposing concepts of time held by the Hellenic and
Hebraic world shaped their literatures; Fredric Jameson,
"Metacommentary," _PMLA_, 86 (1971), 9-17, notes that the
convergence of opposing Hebraic and Hellenic historical and
literary modes in patristic and medieval material led to
polysemous allegorization, the four senses, or ways of
reading a text: literal; allegorical; tropological;
anagogical.

[2] Homer, _The Odyssey_, trans. Albert Cook, New York,
1974. See also David Belmont, "Early Greek Guest-Friendship
and its role in Homer's Odyssey," PhD thesis, Princeton,
1962.

[3] Aeschylus, "Eumenides,' _Oresteia_, 90-93; Sophocles,
"Oedipus Rex," 451-456 (Oedipus murders his father, with his
pilgrim staff, 810-813); Hubert J. Treston, _Poine: A Study
of Greek Blood Vengeance_, London, 1923, pp. 107-126; F.J.M.
de Waele, _The Magic Staff or Rod in Graeco-Italian
Antiquity_, Ghent, 1927; W.B. Stanford, _The Ulysses Theme_,
Ann Arbor, 1968, pp. 324-327; with J.V. Luce, _The Quest for
Ulysses_, New York, 1974, p. 200, he gives a Pinturucchio
painting of Penelope and the disguised Ulysses--who is as a
pilgrim with hat, beard and pommelled staff.

[4] _Petri Allegherii super Dantis ipsius genitoris
Comoediam Commentarium_, Florence, 1846, p. 125.

[5] Ovid, _Metamorphoses_, XV; pilgrimage incubation
discussed, E.R. Dodds, _The Greeks and the Irrational_,
Berkeley, 1951, pp. 102-134; C. Kerenyi, _Asklepios:_

Archetypal Image of the Physician's Existence, Princeton,
1959, pp. 12,35,41; William Durandus, The Symbolism of
Churches and Church Ornaments, trans. John Mason Neale,
London, 1906, pp. 114-115; Daniel Rock, The Church of our
Fathers, London, 1903, III, 287-416; Bernard Kötting,
Peregrinatio Religiosa: Wallfahrten in der Antike und das
Pilgerwesen in der alten Kirche, Regensberg, 1950; Jonathan
Sumption, Pilgrimage: An Image of Medieval Religion, Totowa,
1976, pp. 211-216. For a hypothesis explaining such
practices in connection with relics see Julian Jaynes, The
Origin of Consciousness in the Breakdown of the Bicameral
Mind, Boston, 1977.

[6] William H. Matthews, Mazes and Labyrinths: A General
Account of their History and Development, New York, 1922, p.
60 and passim (on p. 193 he notes that the Spanish
fifteenth-century poet Juan de Mena wrote El Laborinto in
imitation of Dante's Commedia; a Vatican Commedia, MS Lat.
4776, has a labyrinth drawn on its end paper); W.F. Jackson
Knight, Cumaean Gates: A Reference of the Sixth Aeneid to
the Initiation Pattern, Oxford, 1936, pp. 12-27; Donald R.
Howard, The Idea of the Canterbury Tales, Berkeley, 1976, p.
72, takes the labyrinth as pilgrimage idea from D.W.
Robertson, Jr., Preface to Chaucer, Princeton, 1962, p. 373,
as the argument of his book; Durandus, p. 52, notes that
bishops walked on tapestries to trample on worldliness.

[7] TDNT, V, "ξένοι," 1-36, "πάροικοι," 841-843;
Du Cange, Glossarium Mediae et Infimae Latinitatis, Niort,
1883-7, VI,307-308; X,54-55, "De l'escarcelle et du bordon
des pèlerins de la terra sainte"; James A. Brundage,
Medieval Canon Law and the Crusades, Madison, 1969, pp.
3-16; Gerhart B. Ladner, "Homo Viator: Medieval Ideas on
Alienation and Order,"Speculum, 42 (1967), 223-259; Juergan
Hahn, The Origins of the Baroque Concept of Peregrinatio,
Chapel Hill, 1973, pp. 15-22; Edmond-René Laband, Cahiers de
civilization medièvale, 20 (1977), 286, claims that
"peregrinus" did not retain biblical meaning; Edward L.
Cutts, Scenes and Characters of the Middle Ages, London,
1922, pp.157-194; Lucien Rudrauf, Le Repas d'Emmaus, Paris,
1955, fig. 5, Pembroke College, Cambridge, MS 194; fig. 22,
Pierpont Morgan MS 44; fig. 29, Fitzwilliam Museum; fig. 59,
St. Albans Psalter, Hildesheim.

[8] Lausiac History, trans. W.K. Lowther Clarke, London,
1918, XXII,3, p. 113; Institutiones Cénobitiques, trans.
Jean-Claude Guy, Paris, 1965, I,i-ii, pp. 34-55; Hebrews
11.37-38; J. Quasten, "The Garment of Immortality,"
Miscellanea liturgica in onore di sua eminenza il cardinale
Giacomo Lercaro, Rome, 1960, I,391-401, on wool as

signifying death, linen life. Christian practices reflect
those of the Essenes.

[9] Langland, Piers Plowman: Prologue and Passus I-VII
of B Text, Bodleian MS Laud. Misc. 581, ed. J.A.W. Bennett,
Oxford, 1972, p. 80; Oxford English Dictionary notes W.W.
Skeat's error in assuming Will is as a shepherd, rather than
as clad in a hermit's sheepskin garb. The C Text has Will as
a shepherd, on the basis of one manuscript, but not A or B.
Barbara Nolan, p. 212, like Skeat, speaks of Will's garb as
a "shepherd's shroud."

[10] The Rosenbach Pèlerinages MS, Philadelphia, which is
carefully illuminated throughout, shows the text visually in
this manner; Nathaniel Hill, The Ancient Poem of Guillaume
de Guileville entitled Le Pèlerinage de l'Homme compared
with the Pilgrim's Progress of John Bunyan, London, 1858;
Siegfried Wenzel, "The Pilgrimage of Life as a Late Medieval
Genre," Medieval Studies, 35 (1973), 370-388; Rosemond Tuve,
Some Medieval Books and their Posterity, Princeton, 1966;
illuminated manuscripts of Dante's Commedia likewise show
the souls as naked.

[11] Missale Sarum, ed. Francis Dickinson, Oxford, 1883,
pp. 850-859; "Benedictio super Capsella et Fustes et super
eos qui cum his limina ac suffragia Sanctorum Apostolorum
petituri sunt" of Vienna, Nationalbibl. cod. lat. 701, fol.
3^V, 134. Cyrille Vogel, "Le pèlerinage penitential,"
Pellegrinaggo e culto dei santi in Europa fino alla I^a
Crociata, Todi, 1963. pp. 93-94; Luis Vasquez de Parga, José
Maria Lacarra, Juan Uria Riu, Las Peregrinaciones a Santiago
de Compostela, Madrid, 1949, III,145-146; John Henry Feasey,
Ancient English Holy Week Ceremonial, London, 1925, pp.
30-42; John W. Tyrer, Historical Survey of Holy Week, Alcuin
Club, 29, Oxford, 1932, pp. 71-92; Fr. Dunstan Tucker,
O.S.B., "Dante's Reconciliation in the Purgatorio," American
Benedictine Review, 20 (1969), 75-92; Appendix I, giving
fourteenth-century English pilgrim blessing, transcription
from manuscript; Tau mark, Gen. 4.15; Exod. 12.7; Exek. 9.4;
Rev. 7.3; 14.9; Silvio Calzolari, Arnolfo Gengaroli, Lucia
Parigi, Daniela Naldi, Donella Sottili, Viaggatori e
pellegrini italiani in Terrasanta fra trecento et
quattrocento: Ricerca seminariale, Florence, 1975, I,
107.

[12] The cuts are removed from Dante's brow by means of an
angel's wing feather, Purg. XII,98,121-123. I saw patients
at Casamaris Abbey near Rome being treated for cuts with
healing lotion applied with a feather.

[13] Augustine was influenced by Philo, "On the Posterity
of Cain and his Exile," trans. F.H. Colson, London, 1929;
City of God, trans. John Healey, London, 1945, XV, I and
passim.

[14] Hakluytus Posthumus or Purchas his Pilgrimes,
Glasgow, 1905-7, I.138.

[15] Sumption, pp. 101,110; J.J. Jusserand, English
Wayfaring Life in the Middle Ages, trans. Lucy Toulmin
Smith, London, 1889, 1961, pp. 192-240, and passim; P.L.
Henry, The Early English and Celtic Lyric, London, 1966,
passim; Frank Allen Patterson, The Middle English
Penitential Lyrics: A Study and Collection of Early English
Verse, New York, 1911.

[16] Nova Iconologia, Padua, 1618, p. 166.

[17] "Profunda illa paenitentia est, cum laicis deponit
arma et peregrinatur longa lateque, nudus pedes, qui bis non
pernoctatur loco uno . . . qui ieiunet multum et vigilat,
qui dies et noctes ardentur orat . . . et qui adeo est
incultus ut nec crines nec ungues ferro tetigit," Canones
sub Edgaro rege, in Vogel, Pellegrinaggi, p. 57.

[18] Edmond-René Labande, "Recherches sur les pèlerins
dans l'Europe des XIe et XIIe siècles," Spiritualité et vie
littéraire de l'Occident, X^e-XIVe siècles, London, 1974, pp.
339-349; Sumption, pp. 127-128; Durandus, pp. 135-136;
Joinville, Memoirs of the Crusades, trans. Sir Frank T.
Marzials, New York, 1958, p. 166. Crusaders could, as
apocalyptic "milites Christi" [knights of Christ] (Rev. 6.2;
19.11-16), scripturally justify their use of horses. Dante
in the Vita Nuova is on horseback, pilgrim Amor on foot, in
contrast to each other. See Parson's Tale, X.434, "This folk
taken litel reward of the ridynge of Goddes sone of hevene,
and of his harneys whan he rood upon the asse, and ne hadde
noon oother harneys but the povre clothes of his disciples;
ne we ne rede nat that evere he rood on oother beest."

[19] Theresa Coletti, "The Pardoner's Vernicle and the
Image of Man in the Pardoner's Tale," 1,10-12; Hope Phyllis
Weissman, "The Pardoner's Vernicle, the Wife's Coverchiefs,
and Saint Paul," 2,10-12, The Chaucer Newsletter, I (1979).

[20] Vogel, Pellegrinaggi, pp. 39-40; J.A.W. Bennett, pp.
201-202; Le Pèlerinage Jhesucrist, p. 305, has Christ on the
cross make his Testament which John writes down, his
executors being his disciples and their successors; The Book
of Margery Kempe, ed. Sanford Brown Meech, EETS 212, London,

1940, p. 60; Sumption quotes the London preacher, Richard Alkerton, saying in 1406, "He that be a pilgrim oweth first to pay his debts, afterwards to set his house in governance, and afterwards to array himself and take leave of his neighbours, and so go forth," p. 168.

[21] Whitley Stokes, "Lives of Saints from the Book of Lismore," _Anecdota Oxoniensa_, Oxford, 1890, p. cviii, cites _Lebar Brecc_, p. 23b, of seven Egyptian monks on pilgrimage in Ireland; P.L. Henry, pp. 29-39; E.G. Bowen, _Saints, Seaways and Settlements in the Celtic Lands_, Cardiff, 1969, pp. 77-79,132,196-200; G. Hartwell Jones, _Celtic Britain_ and _the Pilgrim Movement_, London, 1912, p. 62, cites the _Islendinga Sogur_, 1843, I, pp. 23-24, _Islendinga Bok_, p. 4, as to the presence of Irish hermits at the time of the Norse colonists' arrival there in 870, and the _Landnama Bok_ on Irish objects being discovered by Norse settlers, Bowen noting these were bell, book and pilgrim staff, p. 78; _Njal Saga_ ends with protagonist and antagonist, after pagan vengefulness, on Christian pilgrimage to Rome; Paul Riant, _Expéditions et pèlerinages des Scandinaves en Terre Sainte au temps des Croisades_, Paris, 1865.

[22] The Benedictine Rule begins with a discussion of monastic _stabilitas_; Brundage, p. 16 and passim; Ladner, "_Homo Viator_," pp. 240,245; Leclercq, "Monachisme et peregrination du IXe au XI^{e}siècle," _Studia Monastica_, 3 (1961), 44; Giles Constable, "Opposition to Pilgrimage in the Middle Ages," _Studia Gratiana_, 19 (1976), 123-146; "Monachisme et pèlerinage au Moyen Age," _Revue historique_, 258 (1977), 3-27; George Williams, _Wilderness and Paradise in Christian Thought: The Biblical Experience of the Desert in the History of Christianity and the Paradise Theme in the Theological Idea of the University_, New York, 1962.

[23] Thomas of Celano, "The Second Life of St. Francis," _St. Francis of Assisi: Writings and Early Biographies: Omnibus of Sources_, ed. Marion A. Habig, Chicago, 1973, p. 375. St. Francis was a rich merchant's son.

[24] E.H. Gombrich, _Art and Illusion_, Princeton, 1961, pp. 68-69, notes a woodcut appearing four times in one text, being in turn, Damascus, Ferrara, Milan and Mantua, thus representing "cityness"; Emile Mâle, _The Gothic Image: Religious Art in France in the Thirteenth Century_, trans. Dora Nussey, New York, 1958, p. 2, notes medieval iconography represented a town by a tower pierced by a doorway, if an angel was added it was Jerusalem; Canterbury's Cathedral in the Middle Ages had such a golden angel on it, as did also Rome's Castel Sant' Angelo.

[25] Lines 2699-2708.

[26] Trans. Archimandrate Lazarus Moore, London, 1959,
Step I, p. 7; Marjorie Reeves and Beatrice Hirsch-Reich, The
Figurae of Joachim of Fiore, Oxford, 1972, pp. 1-2; trans.
Philotheus Boehner, O.F.M., New York, 1965, I,13, p. 45;
John Demaray, The Invention of Dante's Commedia, passim. On
Exodus typology see C. Spicq, Esquisse d'une histoire de
l'exégèse latine au Moyen Age, Paris, 1944; Henri de Lubac,
Exégèse mediévale: les quatre sens de l'Ecriture, Paris,
1959-63, 4 vols; "Figura," Scenes from the Drama of European
Literature, trans. Ralph Manheim, New York, 1957, pp. 49-51;
Johan Chydenius, "The Typological Problem in Dante,"
Commentationes Humanarum Litterarum, 25 (1958); A.C.
Charity, Events and their Afterlife: The Dialectics of
Christian Typology in the Bible and Dante, Cambridge, 1966;
Robert Hollander, Allegory in Dante's Commedia, Princeton,
1969; Ruth M. Ames, The Fulfillment of the Scriptures:
Abraham, Moses and Piers, Evanston, 1970; Frederic Jameson,
"Metacommentary," pp. 9-17; David Aers, Piers Plowman and
Christian Allegory, New York, 1975.

[27] Ruth Melinkoff, The Horned Moses in Medieval Art and
Thought, Berkeley, 1970, p. 128, notes the "Judenhut" or
"pileum cornutum" required 1216, 1267; Erwin Panofsky,
Renaissance and Renascences in Western Art, New York, 1972,
p. 102, observed that it appeared in art nearly a century
earlier; Rudrauf, fig. 43, Leiden Library, St. Louis
Psalter, has Christ at Emmaus wear the Judenhut of pilgrims.

[28] Mâle, Religious Art from the Twelfth to the
Eighteenth Century, New York, 1958, pp. 26-28; Otto Pächt
and Francis Wormald, The St. Albans Psalter, London, 1960,
pp. 73-79; Pächt, The Rise of Pictorial Narrative in
Twelfth-Century England, Oxford, 1962, pp. 33-59; Rudrauf,
Repas d'Emmaus, surveys art of Emmaus supper; G. McN.
Rushforth, Medieval Christian Imagery as Illustrated by the
Painted Windows of Great Malvern Priory Church, Oxford,
1936, pp. 78-91.

[29] Roland de Vaux, Ancient Israel: Its Life and
Institutions, trans. John McHugh, New York, 1961, pp.
495-502; G.W. McRae, "The Meaning and Evolution of the Feast
of Tabernacles," The Catholic Biblical Quarterly, 22 (1960),
272.

[30] Rev. 7.9; "Pèlerinage à Rome," DACL, 14,45 and
passim; mosaics at Sant' Apollinaro Nuovo, Ravenna, show
white-clad, palm-holding martyrs.

[31] Isidore, Etymologiarum, VII, PL, 82,282: "Inde

propter visionem Dei Israel appelatus est, sicut et ipse
ait: 'Vidi Dominum et salva facta est anima mea'" [The
vision of God is called Israel, as he himself said, "I
have seen God and my soul is saved"]

[32] The Scallop: Studies of a Shell and its Influence
upon Humankind, ed. Ian Cox, London, 1957, pp. 36-93 and
passim; Vasquez de Parga, I,129-131, note that the Venus
shells are pagan in origin and symbolize death and rebirth;
the Codex Calixtinus states that the bivalves are the two
charities, to God and to neighbor, Marilyn Stokstad,
Santiago de Compostela in the Age of the Great Pilgrimage,
Norman, 1978, p. 105. Pilgrims dying on pilgrimage, though
excommunicate, were considered saved; Figure 2 is redrawn
from a photograph of a pilgrim tomb effigy at Llandyfodwg
Church sent by its vicar, Rev. K.J. Gillingham; Hartwell
Jones noted a pilgrim grave at St. Mary's Haverfordwest, p.
261, and the Pilgrim's Church graves, Llanfihangel,
Carmarthenshire, pp. 372-337; Edward Cutts, of these and
others, pp. 169-170; a particularly fine one is at Ashby
de la Zouche.

[33] Joseph Bedier, Les légendes épiques: recherches sur
la formation des chansons de geste, Paris, 1913; 1921, vol.
III; Arthur Kingsley Porter, Romanesque Sculpture of the
Pilgrimage Roads, Boston, 1923; Mâle, L'art religieux du
XIIe siècle en France, Paris, 1922; Sir Steven Runciman, A
History of the Crusades, Cambridge, 1951, I,28-29,89-92,
106-107; Ramon Menendez Pidal, La Chanson de Roland et la
tradition épique de France, Paris, 1960; Walter Starkie, The
Road to Santiago: Pilgrims of St. James, New York, 1957;
Stokstad, p. 17; Vasquez de Parga, I, 177-179, claims that
the Codex Calixtinus is not a Cluniac MS. Hartwell Jones,
p. 252, notes the popularity of the name for the Milky Way
"Campus Stellae," "field of stars," in different languages
as "Camin de St. Jacques," Provençal," "Chemin de St.
Jacques," French, "Hynt St. Ialm," Welsh, Dante noting its
Italian form, Il Convivio, as "via de Santiago," while in
English it was called "Watling Street," after the Roman road
that led to Canterbury. However, Edmund Waterton, Pietas
Mariana Britannica, London, 1879, p. 112, notes that
"Compostela" most probably derives from "Giacomo Apostolo."

[34] Mirks Festial, ed. Theodor Erbe, EETS 96, London,
1905, pp. 212-213; Christian K. Zacher, Curiosity and
Pilgrimage: The Literature of Discovery in Fourteenth-Century
England, Baltimore, 1976, p. 97, on parallel in this tale to
Chaucer's number of pilgrims on the road to Canterbury;
Paolo Caucci, Las Peregrinaciones Italianas a Santiago,
trans. Camilo Flores Varela, Compostela, 1971; Vera and

Helmut Hell, *The Great Pilgrimage of the Middle Ages*, New York, 1966, pp. 180-197; William Caxton, *The Golden Legend*, London, 1900, pp. 97-111. Music also traveled along the pilgrimage roads, tunes being transmitted from Sephardic to Ashkenazic Jewry by Christian pilgrims, Abraham Z. Idelsohn, *Jewish Music*, New York, 1929, p. 143.

[35] John Williams, *Early Spanish Manuscript Illuminations*, New York, 1978; Starkie, pp. 22-25; Hell, pp. 16,18,43; Rev. 19.11-16; Shakespeare names the Moor Othello's destroyer, Iago. On Cairo as "Babylon," Malcolm Letts, *Mandeville's Travels: Texts and Translations*, London, 1953, p. 24, notes that "Babylon" was falsely derived from the Egyptian Pi-Hapi-n-On, th Nile City of On, which the Arabs later dropped because of the confusion; Demaray, pp. 33-34,75-76.

[36] Stokstad, pp. 84-85; Runciman, III,41-42.

[37] Bernard McGinn, "*Iter Sancti Sepulchri*: The Piety of the First Crusade," *Walter Prescott Webb Memorial Lectures: Essays on Medieval Civilization*, ed. Bede Karl Lachner, Kenneth Roy Philip, Austin, 1978; Desmond Seward, *The Monks of War: The Military Religious Orders*, London, 1972, pp. 22-27,52,66,84,223; Du Cange, "De la bannière de St. Denis et de l'Oriflamme," X,59-63; Anthony Luttrell, "The Hospitallers' Hospice of Santa Caterina at Venice, 1384-1451," *Studi Veneziani*, 12 (1970), 369-371;   Joseph O'Callaghan, *The Spanish Military Order of Calatrava and its Affiliates*, London, 1975, p. 172; A.J. Forey, "The Military Order of St. Thomas of Acre," *English Historical Review*, 364 (1977), 481-503.

[38] Hartwell Jones, pp. 104-105; M.D. Anderson, *Drama and Imagery in English Medieval Churches*, Cambridge, 1963, p. 48 and fig. 21a, of Ludlow Palmers' Guild founded 1284.

[39] Hartwell Jones, p. 569; *Conciliorum Oecumenicorum Decreta*, Bologna, 1972, Lateran II, 1139, 11, p. 199; *Dives and Pauper*, ed. Priscilla Heath Barnum, EETS 275, Oxford, 1976, pp. 51-220. Victor Turner, "The Center Out There: Pilgrim's Goal," *History of Religions*, 12 (1973), 191-203, notes how pilgrimage is yoked to its opposite, vast commercial fairs growing up side by side with sacred shrines and concurring with their feast days. An example is the Lendit, the great medieval fair at St. Denis. The Second Council of Nicea, A.D. 787, decreed relics were necessary for churches' consecrations. See Patrick Geary, *Furta Sacra: Theft of Relics in the Central Middle Ages*, Princeton, 1978, on the commercialism and even thievery of relics.

40 John Ryan, S.J., _Irish Monasticism: Origins and Early Development_, London, 1931, pp. 318-321; Celano, "Second Life," pp. 414-415; "_De Hospitibus Suscipiendis_. Omnes supervenientes hospites tamquam Christus suscipiantur, quia ipse dicturus est: _Hospe fui, et suscepistis me_. Et omnibus congruus honor exhibeatur, maxime tamen domesticis fidei et peregrinis," _Rule of St. Benedict_, ed. Dom Paul Delatte, London, 1959, p. 330; _Guide_, Sumption, p. 198, who also cites an eighth-century text stating that all pilgrims were entitled to shelter, fire, wholesome water and fresh bread. _TDNT_ and Ladner, "_Homo Viator_," discuss paradox of words "xenos" and "hospes," meaning both guest and enemy.

41 In _Purgatorio_ XIII,94-96, Dante asks if any soul on that terrace is Latin, Sapia gently rebuking him: "O frate mio, ciascuna e cittadina/ d'una vera città; ma tu vuo' dire/ che vivesse in Italia peregrina" [O my brother, each one here is a citizen of a true city: but you mean one that lived in Italy while a pilgrim]. Victor Turner discusses _communitas_ and pilgrimage, _The Ritual Process: Structure and Anti-Structure_, Chicago, 1969, pp. 95-971. A marginal note in Nathaniel Morton's _New England Memoriall_ reads: "About this time, Mrs. Susanna White was delivered of a son, who was named Peregrine; he was the first of the English that was born in New England." Eden's tale was twice-told. The Pilgrim Fathers' first-born, Peregrine White, was read out of Meeting--for the sin of lust.

CHAPTER TWO: EMMAUS INN

1 Fray Justo Perez de Urbel, _El Claustro de Silos_, Burgos, 1975, pp. 191-200 and Plates on pp. 96,98,100,101, 103-105,153-154.

2 It is clear that literary materials on medieval pilgrimage manifest Janus aspects, for which see Mikhail Bakhtin, _Rabelais and his World_, trans. Hélène Iswolsky, Cambridge, Mass., 1968, pp.1-58,437-474; Turner, _The Ritual Process_; _The Reversible World_, ed. Barbara Babcock, Ithaca, 1978; Maria Corti, "Models and Anti-Models in Medieval Culture," _New Literary History_, 10 (1979), 339-366. For material concerning "reader response," "reception theory," see Hans Robert Jauss, _Toward an Aesthetic of Reception_, trans. Timothy Bahti, Minneapolis, 1982, pp. 3-45,76-109.

[3] "The Examination of Master William Thorpe, Priest, of Heresy, Before Thomas Arundell, Archbishop of Canterbury, the Year of Our Lord, M.CCC. and Seven," Fifteenth-Century Prose and Verse, ed. Alfred W. Pollard, New York, 1905, p. 121,140-142; Professor William Hecksher notes Magister Gregorius' comments on pilgrims, Narracio de mirabilis urbis Romae, ed. R.B.S. Huygens, Leiden, 1970: "vanas fabulas . . . peregrinorum," line 77; "peregrini mentiuntur," line 503, etc. On other uses of "fabula" see Peter Dronke, Fabula: Explorations in the Use of Myth in Medieval Platonism, Leiden, 1974.

[4] A Golden Treasury of Irish Poetry, A.D. 600 to 1200, ed. David Greene, Frank O'Connor, London, 1967, p. 112. [Accents should be acute, not grave, here.]

[5] Un guide du pèlerin de Terre Sainte au XVe siècle, ed. Regine Pernoud, Mantes, n.d., pp. 62-63. This is a most interesting pilgrim manuscript: its tiny dimensions make it ideal for carrying in a scrip; it tells of the pilgrimage to Jerusalem; the languages of the nations one passes through; the liturgies carried out at the shrines at the Holy Places; even a lengthy history of the Crusaders' Kingdom of Jerusalem or Outremer, from the Council of Clermont, 1096, to Acre's Fall, 1291.

[6] Mâle, Religious Art, pp. 26-238; Pächt and Wormald, The St. Albans Psalter, pp. 73-79; Pächt, The Rise of Pictorial Narrative in Twelfth-Century England, pp. 33-59; Rudrauf, Le Repas d'Emmaus, gives art of Emmaus supper; Rushforth, Medieval Christian Imagery, pp. 79-91

[7] I am here influenced by my former colleague, Gail McMurray Gibson, who is influenced in turn by V.A. Kolve.

[8] Benedicti Regula, ed. Rudulphus Hanslik, Corpus Scriptorum Ecclesiasticorum Latinorum, Vienna, 1960, I.1-13, condemns the gyrovagus, the wandering monk, in favor of cloistered stabilitas.

[9] Paris, 1861. See also Frank Cook Gardiner, The Pilgrimage of Desire; "Una rappresentazione inedita dell'apparizione ad Emmaus," Rendiconti della Reale Accademia dei Lincei, 5th ser., 1 (Rome, 1892), 769-782; Karl Young, "A New Version of the Peregrinus," PMLA, 34 (1919), 114-129; Young, The Drama of the Medieval Church, Oxford, 1933, 2 vols; Otto Schüttpelz, "Der Weltlauf der Apostel und die Erscheinungen des Peregrinispiels im geistlichen spiel des Mittelalters," Germanistische Abhandlungen, 62,57-59; William Smoldon, Peregrinus

(Beauvais MS), Oxford, 1965; Fletcher Collins, The
Production of Medieval Church Music-Drama, 1972, Medieval
Church Music-Drama: A Repertory of Complete Plays, 1976,
Charlottesville; Sacre rappresentazione nel manoscritto 201
della bibliothèque municipale di Orléans, ed. Giampiero
Tintori, Cremona, 1958; Robert Edwards, The Montecassino
Passion and the Poetics of Medieval Drama, Berkeley, 1977,
notes the relationship of Passion Plays and pilgrim texts;
The Fleury Playbook: Essays and Studies, ed. Thomas P.
Campbell and Clifford Davidson, Kalamazoo, 1985. Gerard
Farrell and Dunstan Tucker, O.S.B., guided the music
research and the production of Princeton University's
Officium Peregrinorum, Easter Monday, 1976. Two secular
plays involving pilgrims are "The Pilgrim," overture to
"Robin et Marion," and Heywood's "4PP."

[10] It is of importance that the medieval drama stressed
Christ's entrance at the line "tuo vultu" [thy face] as the
drama consciously saw pilgrimage as a progression first
"through a glass darkly, then face to face." See Young, p.
693, reproducing the Rouen Ordinarium. The verses, Tintori,
p. lxxi, are:

I. Jesu, nostra redemptio
   amor et desiderium
   Deus, creator omnium
   homo in fine temporum.

II. Quae te vicit clementia
    ut ferres nostra crimina
    crudelem mortem patiens
    ut nos a morte tolleres?

III. Inferni claustra penetrans
     tuos captivos redimens
     victor triumpho nobili
     ad dextram Patris residens.

IV. Ipsa te cogat pietas
    ut mala nostra superes
    parcendo, et voti
      compotes
    nos tuo vultu saties.

V. Tu esto nostrum gaudium
   qui es futurum praemium
   sit nostra in te gloria
   per cuncta semper
     saecula.

[11] Du Cange, VI, 270-271; Young, I, 693. Mandeville
described the Holy Sepulchre: "And there is a full fair
church . . . in the midst is a tabernacle as it were a
little house made with a low little door, and that
tabernacle is made in manner of half a compass, right
curiously and richly made of gold and azure and other rich
colours." Similarly the schola cantorum in Paris' Notre Dame
(sculpted with the Emmaus Pilgrims) is ornamented with blue,
gold and red, the scriptural colors of the Ark's Tabernacle.

[12] Celano, "First Life," pp. 246-247.

[13] Gregory, Homily XXIII, PL, 76,1182.

[14] Ladner, "Homo Viator," pp. 235-236,238; PL, 75, 857,858. Walter Kaiser, Praisers of Folly, Cambridge, Mass., 1963, notes: "At one moment, for example, the curtains part to reveal a pilgrim moving along a road. He is middle-aged, and the season is spring; and whether he descends the winding path to the earth's infernal core or climbs the craggy mountain of virtue or rides the fabled roads eastward to Canterbury, or south to Compostela, it is the same man, from the same time, on his way to God. He is Everyman, the symbolic protagonist for his age. Many scenes later, the curtains part again . . . " to usher in not so much the medieval pilgrim but the Renaissance fool; Ladner, "Homo Viator," pp. 257-259, links pilgrimage and folly, omitting the Emmaus paradigm.

[15] Rudrauf reproduces the Jacopo da Ponte painting of the Emmaus pilgrims at supper at an ale house complete with stake and garland and host, fig. 185; Brueghel's "Numbering at Bethlehem" also shows an inn, with ale stake and garland at the door; Young, I, 476, notes the use of the figure of the Inn's Host in later plays; Blake's poem, "The Little Vagabond," Songs of Experience, of the child who wishes cold churches were warm ale-houses, gives the same paradox.

[16] D.A. Bullough, "The Continental Background of the Reform," Tenth-Century Studies, ed. David Parsons, London, 1975, p. 27; Leslie Webber Jones, The Miniatures of the Manuscripts of Terence, Prior to the Thirteenth Century, Princeton, 1930-1933.

[17] Thomas W. Ross, Chaucer's Bawdy, New York, 1972, p. 8; Caroline Spurgeon, Five Hundred Years of Chaucer Criticism and Allusion, Cambridge, 1925, I,xxi. My former colleague, Jonathan Arac, notes the trial of a Lollard who claimed that the Canterbury Tales was his Bible.

[18] Pp. 121, 140-142; Gregorius, lines 77,503, etc.

[19] William Stubbs, Seventeen Lectures on the Study of Medieval and Modern History, Oxford, 1900, p. 1347, tells of a Canterbury pilgrim writing home while crossing the Alps, his beard frozen into a long icicle, likewise the ink in his scrip; Alan Kendall, Medieval Pilgrims, New York, 1970, p. 49.

[20] Young, I, 482.

[21] Specimens of Pre-Shakespearian Drama, ed. John M. Manly, New York, 1967, I,xxxiii-xxxvii.

[22] "Peregrini," The Towneley Plays, ed. George England, EETS, E.S. 71, London, 1897, 325-337.

[23] Sir Steven Runciman, "The Pilgrims to Palestine Before 1095," A History of the Crusades, ed. Kenneth Setton, Madison, 1969, I, 68-69; DACL, 14,69, discuss Venus and Calvary.

[24] Fleming, The Roman de la Rose: Allegory and Iconography, passim.

[25] Minnesänger Vierundzwauzig farbige Wiedergaben aus der Manessischen Leiderhandschrift, ed. Kurt Martin, Aachen 1974, I,10, fol. 371.

[26] Thomas of Britain, The Romance of Tristan and Ysolt, trans. and ed. Roger Sherman Loomis, New York, 1967, pp. xxv-xlvi; Ladner, "Homo Viator," pp. 247-249.

[27] Seward, The Monks of War, p. 80; Runciman, A History of the Crusades, III,397; see also Jaroslav Folda, Crusader Manuscript Illuminations at Saint-Jean d'Acre, 1275-1291, Princeton, 1976.

[28] Francis P. Magoun, Jr., "Hymselven Lik a Pilgrym to Desgise: Troilus V, 1577," MLN, 59 (1944), 176-178; B.J. Whiting, "Troilus and Pilgrims in Wartime," MLN, 60 (1945), 47-49, noting that medieval pilgrims were able to penetrate' enemy lines owing to the right of sanctuary held by their persons.

[29] Mirks Festial, pp. 212-213; Zacher, p. 97, notes one tale of a miracle of St. James which concerns a band of pilgrims, who number the same as do Chaucer's.

[30] Carl Jung, "On the Psychology of the Trickster-Figure," The Archetype and the Collective Unconscious," trans. R.F.C. Hull;, New York, 1959, pp. 255-272.

CHAPTER THREE: " COME NE SCRIVE LUCA"

[1] William S. Hecksher, Sixtus IIII aeneas insignes statuas romano populo restituendas censuit, The Hague, Utrecht University, 1955; Panofsky, Renaissance, pp. 88-90,

112,151,155; Millard Meiss, Painting in Florence and Siena after the Black Death: The Arts, Religion and Society in the Mid-Fourteenth Century, New York, 1951, p. 157.

[2] F.J.M. de Waele; Ferdinand Gregorovius, History of the City of Rome in the Middle Ages, trans. Annie Hamilton, London, 1894, IV,278,691; John Webster Spargo, Virgil the Necromancer: Studies in Virgilian Legends, Cambridge, Mass., 1934, pp. 136-197,256; Domenico Comparetti, Virgilio nel Medio Evo, Florence, 1896; the Welsh poet Merlin was similarly changed into a magnician.

[3] Fleming, p. 18 and passim; Henry Martin, Le Bocace de Jean sans Peur, Brussels, 1911, p. 11; Earl Jeffrey Richards, "Dante's Commedia and its Vernacular Narrative Context," Ph.D. thesis, Princeton, 1978, pp. 141-142, 219-220, reproduces Arsenal MS 5193, 394^V-395; Karl Uitti, "Relevance of the Romance of the Rose," Machaut's World: Science and Art in the Fourteenth Century, ed. Madeleine Pelner Cosman, Annals of the New York Academy of Science, 314, pp. 209-216, discusses Roman as a "defense of poesy."

[4] Ronald C. Finucane, Miracles and Pilgrims: Popular Beliefs in Medieval England, Totowa, 1977, p. 89, figs. 4-7.

[5] Meiss, Painting in Florence, p. 37 and passim; Carmelo Capizzi, S.J., "ΠΑΝΤΟΚΡΑΤωρ: Saggio d'esegesi letterario iconografica," Orientalia Christiana Analecta, 170, Rome, 1964; André Grabar, La sainte face de Laon: le mandylion dans l'art orthodoxe, Prague, 1931; Hartmann Grisar, History of Rome and the Popes in the Middle Ages, trans. Luigi Cappadelta, London, 1812, III,300-302 and fig. 22; Durandus, p. 40; Henry Charles Thurston, The Holy Year of Jubilee: An Account of the History and Ceremonial of the Roman Jubilee, London, 1900, p. 91-95; Hartwell Jones, p. 185; Demaray, p. 90, on the Lateran portraits; Coletti, Weissman, The Chaucer Newsletter, I,1,10-12,2,10-12.

[6] Thurston, p. 87; Robert Davidsohn, Storia di Firenze, Florence, 1960, III, 275-282.

[7] Josephus, The Jewish War, VII,162, trans. G.A. Williamson, Harmondsworth, 1970, pp. 372-373; Joannis Diaconi, Liber de Ecclesia Lateranensi, PL, 194,1543-1549; Mandeville's Travels, p. 64; Gregorovius, I,210-213; Grisar, I,97-98.

[8] Thurston, pp. 30-42; Grisar, III,315-336; Tyrer, pp. 71-92; the entering through a gate and the caroling is encountered perversely in the Roman de la Rose; I am influenced here by John Leyerle's arguments concerning the

Rosa/Rota symbolism; for related Flagellants' penitential
rituals see Norman Cohn, The Pursuit of the Millennium, New
York, 1961, p. 133.

[9] Dunstan Tucker, O.S.B., "In exitu Israel de Aegypto:
The Divine Comedy in the Light of the Easter Liturgy,"
American Benedictine Review, 11 (1960), 43-61; "Dante's
Reconciliation," 75-92.

[10] Thurston, passim; Grisar, III,291-336.

[11] Davidsohn, IV,186.

[12] Macaulay, "Dante's similes are the illustrations of a
traveler . . . ." Edinburgh Review, 42 (1825), 316; Leigh
Hunt spoke of the Commedia as a Pilgrim's Progress; Francis
Fergusson, Dante's Drama of the Mind: A Modern Reading of
the Purgatorio, Princeton, 1953, of Dante as knowledgeable
author and progressing "Pilgrim," p. 10. Dream visions were
sought by pilgrims in incubation at shrines. Dante may be
influenced by the tale of the knight Owain who dreamt of the
Otherworld's labyrinthine bridgy chasms in the island cave
of St. Patrick's Purgatory, Hartwell Jones, pp. 39-49;
Richard II signed and sealed a passport for a noble Catalan
pilgrim journeying to St. Patrick's Purgatory; Bede, History
of the English Church and People, III,19, gives a similar
dream vision.

[13] Las Siete Partidas del Rey don Alfonso el Sabio, Real
Academia dela Historia, Madrid, 1807, I,497-500; Raccolta di
Rime Antiche Toscane, Palermo, 1817, II,32.

[14] DACL notes tombs marked with pilgrim palms, 14,45,
and passim; Starkie, pp. 36-41,85-89; Singleton, The Divine
Comedy: Inferno, Princeton, 1970, p. 141, Plate 3; the
photograph Singleton gives is of the reconstructed road
evenly edged with stone sarcophagi; closer to the church is
an area where the sarcophagi, which are clearly Roman, were
used by monks for burying the Christian dead and here they
are placed in such a way as to "make the ground all uneven,"
and exactly in the manner shown in Dante manuscript
illuminations of this scene. Pilgrim roads in England were
bordered with funereal yew trees; Caedwalla pilgrimaged to
Rome and was baptized there, A.D. 689, Sergius I inscribing
on his tomb at his death shortly after: "Candidus inter oves
Christi" [white-robed among the sheep of Christ].

[15] The angel on the castle iconograpically makes Rome as
if Jerusalem, Mâle, Gothic Image, p. 2; the gate by the
bridge was called St. Peter's Gate, Grisar, I,266; many

pilgrims died from overcrowding on this bridge at the 1450
Jubilee, Thurston, pp. 26-27; Singleton, _Inferno_ commentary,
pp. 315-316, Plate 4.

[16] _Pylgrymage of Sir Richard Guylforde to the Holy Land_,
ed. Sir Henry Ellis, London, 1851, p. 7; Hartwell Jones, pp.
267-268; Bernard von Breydenbach, _Peregrinatio in Terra
Sancta_, 1484, fol. 13, shows Jerusalem ships in Venice being
repaired; Luttrell, "The Hospitaller's Hospice of Santa
Caterina at Venice, 1348-1451," 369-371.

[17] Mâle speaks of west in medieval thought as meaning
death, pp. 5-6; Phillip Damon, "Dante's Ulysses and the
Mythic Tradition," _Medieval Secular Literature_, ed. William
Matthews, Berkeley, 1965, speaks of the Galaxy as Soul Road
in mythology; Hartwell Jones, p. 252, notes the popularity
of the name for the Milky Way in different languages as St.
James' Road.

[18] "Mount Sinai and Dante's Mount Purgatory," _Dante
Studies_, 89 (1971), 1-18; Demaray, passim.

[19] Joinville, p. 166.

[20] Ladner, "_Homo Viator_," pp. 235-236,238,258; _Moralia_,
VIII,54,82, _PL_, 75,857-858.

[21] Denise Heilbronn, "The Prophetic Role of Statius in
Dante's _Purgatory_," _Dante Studies_, 95 (1977), 61, sees
Virgil and Statius as Justice and Peace embracing, Psalm
84.4, the same verse which shaped _Piers Plowman_'s Four
Daughters of God and the N Town Annunciation Play; Statius'
Thebaid, Boccaccio's _Teseida_ and Chaucer's Knight's Tale
allude to Titus' Temple of Peace at Rome, built to house the
treasures of the Jerusalem Temple, as Theseus' Temple of
Clemence at Athens.

[22] There is an iconographical joke upon this matter in
Inferno XI.8, in which the Pope Anastasius (whose name
associates him with the Sant' Anastasia, the Holy Sepulchre
in Jerusalem) is encountered in his sepulchre, his
punishment for denying the Incarnation—and Resurrection.
The illuminations inscribe his name upon the tomb, show him
with the papal crown, mocking the empty Holy Sepulchre in
Jerusalem with the full one in Rome. Pietro Alighieri, p.
128, notes the punishment in the Decretals for idol-makers
is to be placed living in tombs surrounded by fire. In _Piers
Plowman_ a false Palmer will quest "corsaints," B.V.520-543.

[23] That text also proclaims: "And you shall eat the

flesh of your sons." Such did indeed occur in Jerusalem
where a Jewish Mary ate her child, Josephus, The Jewish War,
VI, and Dante, Purg. XXIII.29, and in Pisa, Inf. XXXIII.

[24] Petrocchi, IV,520. Meiss, Painting in Florence, p.
37, discusses the Pax, the liturgical instrument, in some
cases painted with the face of Christ and with the words,
"Pacem meam do vobis" (his fig. 42), used to transmit the
kiss of peace at the Mass, and he relates this to Holy Faces
and Veronicas; a Middle English lyric speaks of the
instrument as a "pax-brede"; in these instances an
equivalence is being made between the face of God and the
bread of the Mass; Dante also speaks of the Rose/Holy Face
as a "pacifica orifiamma," an oriflamme paradoxically not of
war and crusade but of peace and pilgrimage (Par. XXXI.127).

[25] Pp. 128-130.

[26] Pylgrymage of Sir Richard Guylforde, p. 7.

[27] Hartwell Jones, pp. 267-268; Joinville, p. 167;
Deguileville, Pilgrimage, lines 21691-22068, on allegory of
ship as church, most manuscripts being illuminated with
Grace Dieu in the Ship of the Church which is marked by a
Dove and a Cross; Paul A. Underwood, "Drawings of St.
Peter's on a Pilgrim Staff in the Museo Sacro of the Vatican
Library," JWCI, 3 (1939-1940), 147-153, notes the analogy
between Noah's Ark, Peter's Ship and St. Peter's, Rome;
Spain sent her Conquistadors to the New World in ships
flaunting the Jerusalem cross of crusade and pilgrimage.

[28] Shipwrecked Arculf dictated his account of the Holy
Places to Abbot Adamnan on Iona, Bede repeating it in The
History of the English Church and People, The Pilgrimage of
Arculfus in the Holy Land, trans. James MacPherson, PPTS,
London, 1895, III,v-91; The Pilgrimage of Saewulf, PPTS,
London, 1896, IV,6-8; Durandus gives instructions for the
burial of a pilgrim dying at sea, p. 81; Joinville, pp.
137-138,294.

[29] Peter Brieger, Millard Meiss, Charles Singleton,
Illuminated Manuscripts of the Divine Comedy, Princeton,
1969, Plates 24b, formerly Geneva, Bodmer 247, fol. 95;
25a, Perugia, Augusta B.25, fol. 46.

[30] Pietro Alighieri, pp. 236-237, states that the
Ulysses material derives from Isidore and Augustine, Isidore
speaking of the Pillars of Hercules, like columns of idols,
as set on the isles of Gades in Oceanos. Pietro says of
Ulysses: "He came to the wilderness islands of Gades by

Spain in the west . . . there where the threshold of the
Ocean is first opened . . . But there Hercules placed
columns to signify that that was the end of inhabited land."
He quotes the City of God: "Nothing is more absurd than to
say of that part as some men do, that Ocean being such a
vast track, that it is possible to sail and come to it; yet
from one man there came all mankind." He adds that beyond
Oceanos the land "that is beneath us, is uninhabited." He
omits in Isidore: "Paradise is a place in the eastern part
of Asia, which word from Greek translated into Latin is
'garden,' in Hebrew it is 'Eden,' which in our language is
'delight,' from which comes the 'garden of delights,'"
PL,82,495. Brunetto Latini, Il Tesoretto, also discusses the
Pillars of Hercules. The voyages of Ulysses and the pilgrim
Saint James, through the Straits of Gibralter, parallel each
other.

[31] Hugo Rahner, Greek Myths and Christian Mystery,
London, 1963; Ladner, "Homo Viator," pp. 237,241; W.B.
Stanford, The Ulysses Theme, passim; Damon, "Dante's
Ulysses," p. 37; Sister M.C. Pohndorf, "Conceptual Imagery
Related to the Journey Theme in Dante's Commedia," Ph.D.
dissertation, University of Denver, 1965; David Thompson,
Dante's Epic Journeys, Baltimore, 1974. Leslie Fiedler has
observed that Ulysses' voyage was to America before
Columbus.

[32] Guillaume de Lorris and Jean de Meun, Le roman de la
Rose, ed. Felix Lecoy, Paris, 1975-1979, II,39, lines
9479-9486; E.R. Curtius, "The Ship of the Argonauts," Essays
on European Literature, Princeton, 1973, pp. 465-496; E.J.
Richards, pp. 189-194.

[33] Pohndorf, pp. 178-187, discusses the Ulysses, Jason
episodes.

[34] T.K. Swing, The Fragile Leaves of the Sybil,
Westminster, Maryland, 1962, p. 299; Renato Poggiolo,
"Tragedy or Romance? A Reading of the Paolo and Francesca
Episode in Dante's Inferno," PMLA, 72 (1957), 313-358, sees
Francesca as representing French romances; Hollander,
Allegory, pp. 108-114. One of my students compared Francesca
da Rimini to Emma Bovary.

[35] A punning tradition that Shakespeare will continue
with Juliet's speech to her Romeo: "saints have hands that
pilgrims' hands do touch / And palm to palm is holy palmer's
kiss" (I.v.101-102).

[36] Dante's text implies that his despair drove him close
to suicide: Inf. II.61-66; XIII.139-151; XV.49-51; Purg.

I.58-60. Dorothy Sayers/Barbara Reynolds note the
parallels of Romeo and Pier dell Vigne to Dante's
autobiography in their translation of the Paradiso.

[37] Alpignano, 1967, p. 12. The opening of the poem
states that it would be preferable to have its pages burnt
in hell than to have it be misunderstood. Earl Jeffrey
Richards suggests that this is the reason why Dante has
jokingly placed its author in hell flames. I note that its
leaves will be gathered up and bound in the one volume God
holds, Par. XXXIII.

CHAPTER FOUR: "WITNESSE IN YE PASK WYKE"

[1] On the circularity of Piers Plowman see R.W.
Chambers, p. 165, and W.P. Ker's lecture on the Commedia and
Piers Plowman, p. 405, Man's Unconquerable Mind: Studies of
English Writers, London, 1939; Raymond St.-Jacques,
"Conscience's Final Pilgrimage in Piers Plowman and the
Cyclical Structure of the Liturgy," Revue de l'Université
d'Ottowa, 40 (1970), 210-233; William Matthews, The Tragedy
of Arthur: A Study of the Alliterative Morte Arthure,
Berkeley, 1960, likened the structure of Troilus and
Criseyde to Fortune's Wheel; John Leyerle has discussed
relation of Commedia and Fortuna.

[2] Nathaniel Hill, Le Pèlerinage de l'Homme compared
with Pilgrim's Progress; G.R. Owst, Literature and Pulpit in
Medieval England: A Neglected Chapter in the History of
English Letters and of the English People, Cambridge, 1933,
pp. 77-109, notes their common source in sermon conventions;
Allan H. Bright, New Light on Piers Plowman, Oxford, 1928,
reproduces Corpus Christi, Oxford, MS 201, fol. 1, which
shows the Prologue's sleeping, slothful Will of Piers
Plowman; Elizabeth D. Kirk, The Dream Thought of Piers
Plowman, New Haven, 1972.

[3] Both Henry W. Wells, "The Construction of Piers
Plowman," pp. 5,6,12, and Nevill K. Coghill, "The Character
of Piers Plowman Considered from the B Text," pp. 75-77,
Interpretations of Piers Plowman, ed. Edward Vasta, Notre
Dame, 1968, tended to interpret the text with such diagrams.
St. Bonaventure, Itinerarium mentis in deum, ed. Henri
Dumery; Pietro Cali, Allegory and Vision in Dante and
Langland: A Comparative Study, Cork, 1971, p. 23, notes that

the relationship between Wyclif and Langland was Crowley's
concept; The Vision of Pierce Plowman: now fyrst imprinted
by Robert Crowley, 1550, ed. J.A.W. Bennett, Cambridge,
1976; John M. King, "Robert Crowley's Edition of Piers
Plowman: A Tudor Apocalypse," MP, 73 (1976), 342-352, notes
that Crowley suppressed the very moving and beautiful
passage in praise of the life of a Benedictine monastery,
B.X.305-310; during the persecution of Lollards much
emphasis was placed by authorities upon physical
pilgrimages, including offerings to shrines, Lollards
insisting at their trials that the better pilgrimage was
the inward quest, which was in fact according to the
orthodox teachings of Augustine and Jerome.

[4] Owst, p. 393, notes that medieval sermons saw Lent
and May as time of tension between lust and Christ.

[5] Lausiac History, xxxii,3,p. 113; Cassian, I,i-ii,pp.
34-55; M.R. Clay, The Hermits and Anchorites of England,
London, 1914, p. 20, notes famous hermits of the Malvern
Hill; Barbara Nolan, p. 212.

[6] The general tendency among Piers Plowman critics,
following Skeat, is to interpret "as I a sheep were" as
meaning "as if I were a shepherd." The C Text, from one
manuscript, so states it. See on this the discussion by
David Mills, "The Role of the Dreamer in Piers Plowman,"
Piers Plowman: Critical Approaches, ed. S. S. Hussey,
London, 1969, pp. 185-186. The OED, under "Shep," argues for
hermit's dress, "sheep's clothing," from linguistic
evidence. Turner, Ritual Process, p. 46, like Cassian, notes
that such garb signifies a dying to the secular structure,
membership in the sacred.

[7] M.A. Rothe, Les Romans du Renard, Reinardus Vulpes,
III, p. 48; Kenneth Varty, Reynard the Fox: A Study of the
Fox in Medieval Art, Leicester, 1967, passim.

[8] D.W. Robertson, Jr., and Bernard Huppé, Piers Plowman
and the Scriptural Tradition, Princeton, 1951, pp. 33-34.

[9] Chambers, p. 124.

[10] St. Athanasius, The Life of St. Anthony, trans. Robert
T. Meyer, Westminster, Maryland, 1950, pp. 19-20; St.
Augustine, The Confessions, VIII,2,12; Celano, "Second
Life," p. 375.

[11] The Vision of William concerning Piers the Plowman in

three parallel texts, Oxford, 1886: 1924, II,31; Haldeen
Brady, "Chaucer, Alice Perrers and Cecily Chaumpaigne,"
Speculum, 52 (1977), 906-911.

[12] Bright, p. 41; Edwards, Montecassino Passion, p. 64,
notes a monastic verse drawing the parallel between the
Benedictine Rule and the Mosaic Law, Monte Cassino and Mount
Sinai.

[13] Preface to Bright, p. 12; R.E. Kaske, "Piers Plowman
and Local Iconography," JWCI, 31 (1968), 160, notes that the
photograph in Bright is taken from the other side of the
valley from where Will would have viewed that landscape.

[14] Meiss, Painting in Florence, p. 94 and passim; J.J.
Jusserand, Piers Plowman: A Contribution to the History of
English Mysticism, New York, 1884, conveys the sociology of
Piers Plowman though better to consult is his English
Wayfaring Life; Langland, Piers Plowman, ed. J.A.W. Bennett,
pp. 187-189; Cutts, p. 174; G. McN. Rushforth, pp. 46,95-96;
Lucie Polak, "A Note on the Pilgrim in Piers the Plowman,"
N&Q, 215 (1970), 282-285, which give information as well
about his pilgrim staff.

[15] J.A.W. Bennett, p. 85, notes that Palmers were
hireling pilgrims; I have only found evidence that Palmers
were those who had returned from the Holy Places. However,
wills did set aside sums of money for pilgrimage to be
performed.

[16] David C. Fowler, "The 'Forgotten' Pilgrimage in Piers
Plowman," MLN, 87 (1952), 324-326, considers that the
pilgrimage is obviated by the need to stave off famine; T.P.
Dunning, Piers Plowman: An Interpretation of the A Text,
London, 1937, p. 133; E. Talbot Donaldson, Piers Plowman:
The C-Text and Its Poet, London, 1966, p. 162; A.C.
Spearing, "The Art of Preaching and Piers Plowman,"
Criticism and Medieval Poetry, London, 1964, p. 71;
Elizabeth Salter, Piers Plowman: An Introduction, Cambridge,
Mass., 1963, pp. 98-99; Mary Carruthers, The Search for St.
Truth, Evanston, 1973, p. 65; David Aers, Piers Plowman and
Christian Allegory, p. 116, contends that Piers does not
understand the first ploughing as an allegory, but he does
the second, while Robertson and Huppé interpret both
ploughing scenes as equally allegorical and unrealistic. I
place the ploughing, as does Aers, in the context of a
progress in understanding.

[17] Odo of Deuil, De Profectione Ludovici VII in
Orientem, ed. Virginia C. Berry, New York, 1948, pp. 8-11,
gives the ceremony for pilgrims and crusaders.

[18] J.A.W. Bennett, p. 201. Bennett's editorial notes throughout are worth consultation. He here observes that though the format of the Testament is that of an allegory it also corresponds closely to real pilgrim Testaments. He notes that in the Visio Piers is illiterate and has to have his Will written for him and the Pardon read to him but that he makes his own dispositions, exemplifying in this section the ideal lay Christian. See also Vogel, Pelegrinaggi, pp. 39-41; Le Pèlerinage Jhesucrist, p. 305; The Book of Margery Kempe, p. 60; Sumption, p. 169.

[19] Singleton, Inferno Commentary, p. 370, Plate 5; Giovanni Fallani, Dante e la cultura figurativa medievale, Bergamo, 1971, p. 77.

[20] Roberts, Chronicle of the Kings of Britain; E.M.W. Tillyard, Myth and the English Mind, New York, 1962, pp. 43-48; the material goes back to Geoffrey of Monmouth's eponymous use of Dares Phrygius, nor was this regional for European histories in general followed this pattern: see Villani, Istorie Fiorentine; Fallani, pp. 89-91, discusses Trajan and the Widow.

[21] L.A. Hammond, The Ancient Windows of Great Malvern Priory Church, London, 1947, pp. 51-68; Rushforth, pp. 789-81.

[22] Jusserand, Piers Plowman, p. 43; Kaske, "Piers Plowman and Local Iconography," pp. 158-169.

[23] Robertson and Huppé, p. 217.

[24] Grisar, III,302-303, the legend dating from the thirteenth century, the portrait itself supposedly from Constantine's era; The Vernon Manuscript "Stacions of Rome," F.J. Furnivall, EETS 25, "In þe Rof . ouer þe popes se. A saluator . þer may þou se. Neuer I. peynted . with hond of Mon. As men I. Roome . tellen con. Whon Seluestre halwed þat place . Hit apeered þer . þorw godes grace" (297-302). For Easter Sunday liturgy see Raymond St.-Jacques, "Langland's Bells of the Resurrection and the Easter Liturgy," English Studies in Canada, 3 (1977), 124-135; Rock, IV,288; Dives and Pauper, p. 87.

[25] See Chapter II, Officium Peregrinorum text; David Fowler, Piers the Plowman: Literary Relations of the A and B Text, Seattle, 1961, argues for the author's identity as the Cornish John of Trevisa partly on the basis of the likeness to the Cornish dramas, which speak of Christ as coming from

Edom, dyed with vestments from Bosra (Isaiah 63.1-3), and
these lines in <u>Piers Plowman</u>, without realizing that these
lines, which are not present in English Corpus Christi
plays, are present in the Latin liturgical drama which was
international; Hartwell Jones gives a pilgrim map of Rome
from the British Library print collection showing the
pilgrims and their titular saints at each of the seven
churches.

[26] Skeat, II,201. The shrine of the heads of Saints
Peter and Paul is still to be seen today at the Lateran
Basilica in a Gothic structure erected over the altar.

[27] Skeat, II,202,204.

[28] Walter J. Ong, "Wit and Mystery: A Revaluation in
Medieval Latin Hymnody," <u>Speculum</u>, 22 (1947), 316-317; C.S.
Lewis, "The Genesis of a Medieval Book," <u>Studies in Medieval
and Renaissance Literature</u>, Cambridge, 1966, p. 21, notes
how Geoffrey of Monmouth gave to Merlin the prophecy that
Arthur's deeds were "cibus narrantibus," bread as narration
and payment, while La3amon prophesied of Arthur: "Of him
scullen gleoman godliche singen/ Of his breasten scullen
eaten aþela scopes/ Scullen of his blode beornes beon
drunke" (18856-18861).

[29] Swing, p. 299; Deguileville, lines 11195-11212.

[30] Barbara Nolan, p. 139, notes that Deguileville's
presence in such a garden, <u>Pèlerinage Jhesucrist</u>, pp. 2,360,
frames his third vision--of Christ as a pilgrim.

[31] Elizabeth Salter, "Medieval Poetry and the Figural
View of Reality," <u>Proceedings of the British Academy</u>, 54
(1968), London, 1970, p. 86: a "glass held before us--one of
many in <u>Piers Plowman</u>--in whose flawed and cloudy depths we
glimpse, fleetingly, and 'darkly', the image of Christ,"
and, p. 91, that the different representations of Christ
are as perfected in Piers, in Will as still stumbling;
Barbara Raw, "Piers and the Image of God in Man," <u>Piers
Plowman: Critical Approaches</u>, pp. 143-179.

[32] Jerome, <u>Epistola LVIII ad Paulinum</u>, <u>PL</u>, 22,581,
stressed that "et de Hierosolymis et de Britannia aequaliter
patet aula coelestis" [Heaven could be reached as well from
Britain as from Jerusalem]; Alan Kendall, <u>Medieval Pilgrims</u>,
p. 11.

CHAPTER FIVE: "UNBOKELED IS THE MALE"

[1] Frederick Tupper, "Saint Venus and the Canterbury Pilgrims," The Nation, 97 (1913), 354-356; Chauncey Wood, Chaucer and the Country of the Stars; Poetic Uses of Astrological Imagery, Princeton, 1970, argues for a General Prologue Taurus dating. I sense that Chaucer, in speaking of April coming to March, and of the Ram's half-run course, like Dante, intends Aries.

[2] Gregory, Homily XXIII, PL, 76,1182.

[3] José Maria Lacarra, "Espiritualidad del culto y de la peregrinación a Santiago antes de la primera cruzada," Pellegrinaggi, p. 121; Jerome, Epistola LVIII ad Paulinum, PL, 22,581; Meiss, "Scholarship and Penitence in the Early Renaissance: The Image of St. Jerome," The Painter's Choice: Problems in the Interpretation of Renaissance Art, New York, 1976, pp. 189-202; Liber Sancti Jacobi, I,v,p. 39; xv. p. 36.

[4] Hakluytus Posthumus or Purchas His Pilgrimes, I,138-139.

[5] A fine MS of all three Pèlerinages in one volume is at the Rosenbach Collection, Philadelphia, and it shows Christ as a boy, garbed as a pilgrim, in the Temple doctors' midst. It is of interest that Dante's Commedia consists of three canticles, Inferno, Purgatorio, Paradiso; that Deguileville's work likewise is the Pèlerinage de la vie humaine, Pèlerinage de l'âme and Pèlerinage Jhesucrist; that Langland's Vision of Piers Plowman consists of the Vita de Dowel, Vita de Dobet and Vita de Dobest; Chaucer's triadic structure being Prologue, Fables, Sermon. Kane and Donaldson omit the division headings of Piers Plowman.

[6] Ladner, "Homo Viator," pp. 235-236; Moralia, VIII, 54,92,PL,75,857-858. Ladner notes that his image is gnostic. Augustine gives a milder version in the travel imagery of the De Doctrina Christiana. Lionardo Frescobaldi, Visit to the Holy Places, 1384, p. 35, notes the purchasing of a Bible and Gregory's Moralia.

[7] Ed. F.N. Robinson, pp. 860-961; Alfred David, "The Truth about Vache," CR,11 (1977), 332-337, notes that the envoi occurs only in one MS; an Anglo-Irish lullaby concludes with this pilgrimage theme:

Child thou ert a pilgrim   Child, thou nert a pilgrim.

In wikidnis ibor;   Bot an uncuthe gist;
Thou wandrest in this fals   This dawes beth itold;
  world;   Thi iurneis beth icast.
  Thou loke the bifore.   Whoder thou salt wend,
Deth ssal come with a blast   North other est
  Ute of a wel dim horre,   Deth the sal bitide,
Adamis kin dun to cast,   With bitter bale in brest.
  Him self hath ido befor.   Lollai, lollai, litil
  Lollai, lollai, litil   child!
    child!   This wo Adam the wrogth,
  So wo the worth Adam   Whan he of the appil ete,
In the lond of Paradis   And Eve hit him
Through wikidnes of   betacht.
  Satan.

Early English Lyrics: Amorous, Divine, Moral and Trivial,
ed. E.K. Chambers, F. Sedgewick, New York, 1967, pp.
166-168. Elsewhere E.K. Chambers suggested that this poem is
as sung by the Virgin to her child and that its pessimism is
pre-Redemptive, English Literature at the Close of the
Middle Ages, Oxford, 1961, p. 80.

8 Etymologiarum, II,21,42: "Ironia est, cum per
simulationem diversum quam dicit intellegi cupit. Fit autem,
aut sum laudeamus eum quem vitupere volumus, aut vituperamus
quem laudare volumus. Utriusque exemplum erit si dicas:
Amatorem reipublicae Catilinam, hostem reipublicae
Scipionem" [Irony is to appear to say the contrary to that
which is desired to be understood. Such occurs where we
praise that which we would blame, and blame that which we
would praise. An example would be if one said: I would love
the Republic of Catiline, hate the Republic of Scipio], PL,
82,139. the effect is to create a "World Upside Down,"
Curtius, pp. 94-98; Rosalie L. Colie, Paradoxia Epidemica:
The Renaissance Tradition of Paradox, Princeton, 1966; The
Reversible World, ed. Barbara Babcock; the researches of
Victor Turner, Leonard Biallas, William LaFleur especially
show this quality in pilgrimage. Erhenpreis on "Personae"
notes: "In such a literary structure, the author's
fundamental tone also reverses itself; what sounded sober is
transformed to mockery. For the device to succeed, the
reader must be tricked during the early stages of the work
and be undeceived during the later"; for Dante understood
this way, see Swing, pp. 329-330; a more modern term is
"Deconstruction."

9 D.W. Roberston, Jr., Chaucer's London, p. 59; Theo
Stemmler, The Ellesmere Miniatures of the Canterbury
Pilgrims, maintains it is an M.

[10] Memoirs of the Crusades, p. 166; Seward, Monks of War, passim; the Anglo-Norman Mandeville's Travels describes a crusading knight who, at times, is in the pay of the Sultan of Babylon; the brutality of Peter Lusignan's Cyprus crusade to Alexandria caused Moslems to close the Holy Sepulchre to Christian pilgrims for three years, Runciman, III,446-449; Terry Jones, Chaucer's Knight: The Portrait of a Medieval Mercenary, London, 1980.

[11] James Sledd, "The Clerk's Tale: The Monsters and the Critics," Chaucer Criticism, ed. Richard J. Schoeck and Jerome Taylor, I,174.

[12] Rosemary Woolf, "Chaucer as Satirist in the General Prologue to the Canterbury Tales," CQ, 1 (1959), 150-157; Robert S. Haller, "Chaucer's Squire's Tale and the Uses of Rhetoric," MP, 62 (1965), 285-295; Arthur W. Hoffman, "Chaucer's Prologue to Pilgrimage: The Two Voices," ELH, 21 (1954), 1-16; Ralph Baldwin, "The Unity of The Canterbury Tales," pp. 15-110.

[13] A similar problem exists for Deguileville who, though a monk, presents himself within the poem as a pilgrim, the illuminations absurdly showing him with robe and tonsure, scrip and staff. A late frontispiece to Lydgate's translation of this work shows Deguileville in his monk's garb presenting his Pilgrim as such, who in turn holds forth the presentation copy of the Pilgrimage of the Life of Man (Figure 11). Monks and Puritans, forbidden to be pilgrims, write of pilgrimage as allegory; lay poets, such as Dante and Chaucer, could write with much greater realism for they could themselves be pilgrims.

[14] Peter S. Taitt, Incubus and Ideal: Ecclesiastical Figures in Chaucer and Langland, Salzburg, 1975, p. 104.

[15] The Benedictio Peregrinorum and its Mass (Appendix I) required the reading of Matthew 10.7-15, including the verse: "Provide neither gold, nor silver, nor brass in your purses." The Shipman's Tale's merchant ignores this command of Christ's.

[16] Cutts, pp. 243-251, discusses the dress of the secular clergy (those not in monastic or mendicant orders), and finds that several are in scarlet though he also notes Grosseteste's annoyment at a curate who "dressed in rings and scarlet like a courtier." He observes the will of the rector of Arncliffe, Yorkshire, bequeathing not only the type of clothing Langland says priests ought not to wear but also an "English book of Piers Ploughman."

[17] Portraits of Wyclif give him the pilgrim staff with its two pommels.

[18] "Examination of William Thorpe," pp. 140-141.

[19] D.W. Robertson, Jr., A Preface to Chaucer, Princeton, 1962, pp. 128,130,133,482; Edward A. Block, "Chaucer's Millers and their Bagpipes," Speculum, 29 (1954), 239-243: Julia Bolton Holloway, "The Asse to the Harpe: Boethian Music in Chaucer," Boethius and the Liberal Arts, ed. Michael Masi, New York, 1980.

[20] Robert Durling, The Figure of the Poet in the Renaissance Epic, Cambridge, Mass., 1965, pp. 66-80. John M. Fyler, Chaucer and Ovid, New Haven, 1979, p. 126

[21] J.W.H. Atkins, English Literary Criticism: The Medieval Phase, New York, 1943, p. 104; Baldwin, p. 37.

[22] "The Critic as Host," Deconstruction and Criticism, New York, 1979, pp. 220-221. See also William LaFleur, "Inns and Hermitages."

[23] Young, I, 476, speaks of a mute actor at Fleury who acts the role of the inn's Host; on p. 455 he notes that the Saintes play text has Christ distribute the hostia, the communion host or wafer, to those present.

[24] Mary L. Richmond, Terence Illustrated, Williams College, 1955; The Abbaye de St. Benoit-sur-Loire, which perhaps performed the Officium Peregrinorum, owned an illustrated Terence, copied from one at Winchester. The concept of the staging of Christ's disappearance behind a curtained rack probably came from these illuminations of scenes of pagan plays.

[25] Fulgentius, Opera, ed. Rudulfus Helm, Leipsic, 1898, p. 186; Lydgate with Chaucer, associates Thebes, Babylon and London, in contrast to Athens, Jerusalem and Canterbury, in his Pilgrimage of the Life of Man:

       Ye worldly folk, avyse yow betymes
       Wych in thys lyff ne ben but as pylgrymes
       Lyk straungerys ffere fro youre Cuntre
       Vnfraunchysed and voyde off lyberte;
and
       Ryght so, pylgrymes to-ward Ierusaleem
       Haste on her way in thys world, & echone
       To-ward that cyte, or to Babylone,   (1-60)

and in his continuation of the <u>Canterbury Tales</u> in which he
has himself be as a pilgrim who is also a cloistered monk he
tells the pilgrims the tale of <u>The Seige of Thebes</u>; Joseph
Westlund, "The Knight's Tale as an Impetus for Pilgrimage,"
<u>PQ</u>, 43 (1964), 526-527, discusses paganness of Knight's
Tale; Terry Jones, <u>Chaucer's Knight</u>, likewise questions the
figure of the Knight.

[26] Pierre Courcelle, <u>La Consolation de Philosophie dans
la tradition littéraire</u>, Paris, 1967, Plate 12.2, Boethius
weeping behind prison bars in illuminated initial; Plate 21,
Boethius judged and Boethius imprisoned in tower, writing
<u>Consolation</u>; Plates 60-61, Boethius enchained, in bed, to
the theatre harlots. Plate VIIc is a Dante illumination that
borrows from <u>Consolation</u> iconography. Courcelle, p. 97,
notes that MS Cambridge, Trinity Hall, 12, fol. 6^v, remarks
of Socrates' imprisonment, "Le duc d'Athenes le fist prendre
et le fist en prison mourir." Theseus in myth escaped the
prison of the Cretan labyrinth; Chaucer's Theseus,
constructing his theatre, assumes a task worthy of Daedalus;
Howard, <u>Idea of Canterbury Tales</u>, omits this association.
There was a duke of Athens who was tyrant of Florence at the
time Boccaccio penned the <u>Teseida</u>.

[27] Roberto Weiss, <u>The Renaissance Discovery of Classical
Antiquity</u>, Oxford, 1969, Plate 5, of Vatican Library, MS.
Chig, I.vii,fol. 13, of a drawing of a classical arena;
Francesco de Sanctis, <u>History of Italian Literature</u>, trans.
Joan Redfern, New York, I, 96, discusses the <u>Passione</u> acted
by the Company of the Gonfalone in the Colosseum, Good
Friday, 1264, and the <u>Ludus Christi</u> in Cividale, May, 1298;
Richard Southern, <u>The Medieval Theatre in the Round</u>, London,
1957; Merle Fifield, "The Arena Theatres in Vienna Codices
2535 and 2536," <u>Comparative Drama</u>, 2 (1969), 259-280; <u>The
Cornish Ordinalia: A Medieval Dramatic Trilogy</u>, trans. Mark
Harris, Washington, 1969; <u>The Macro Plays: The Castle of
Perseverance, Wisdom, Mankind</u>, ed. Mark Eccles, Oxford,
1969, EETS 262; Henri Rey-Flaud, <u>Le cercle magique: essai
sur le théâtre en rond à la fin du Moyen Age</u>, Paris, 1973.

[28] Jean Seznec, <u>The Survival of the Pagan Gods: The
Mythological Tradition and its Place in Renaissance
Humanism and Art</u>, New York, 1953; Chauncey Wood, "Chaucer
and Astrology," <u>Companion to Chaucer Studies</u>, ed. Beryl
Rowland, Toronto, 1968, pp. 176-191, and <u>The Country of the
Stars</u>; Douglas Brooks and Alastair Fowler, "The Meaning of
Chaucer's Knight's Tale,'" <u>Medium Aevum</u>, 39 (1970), 123-146.

[29] <u>Sources and Analogues of Chaucer's Canterbury Tales</u>,
ed. W.F. Bryan, Germaine Dempster, New York, 1958, p. 37;

Mircea Eliade, <u>Aspects du Myth</u>, Paris, 1963, pp. 41-48,
notes that the telling of tales which include the patient's
name is curative; <u>The Seven Sages of Rome</u>'s theme is of
tales told to ward off death, likewise the <u>Arabian Nights</u>.

[30] Meiss, <u>Painting in Florence</u>, p. 159.

[31] Meiss, <u>Painting in Florence</u>, p. 75, notes that
Gentile da Foligno, the physician, prescribed gold in a
potable emulsion as a plague preventive and cure; Petrus
Alfonsi, <u>PL</u>, 157, states that sickness is an imbalance of
elements brought about by sin and that God as Creator
restores that balance, "Dialogus Petri cognomento Alphonsi,
ex Judaeo et Moysi Judaei"; gold was considered to be the
harmony of elements and humours.

[32] X, 11-14.

[33] Boethius, <u>The Consolation of Philosophy</u>, trans.
Richard Green, Indianapolis,1962, pp. 93-94.

[34] "Medieval 'Pilgrim Plays' and the Pattern of
Pilgrimage," Ph.D. dissertation, University of Oregon, 1966,
published as <u>The Pilgrimage of Desire</u>; Rodney Delasanta
notes the theme of an eschatological supper but not that of
Emmaus, "The Theme of Judgement in <u>The Canterbury Tales</u>,"
<u>MLQ</u>, 31 (1970), 300, "Penance and Poetry in the <u>Canterbury
Tales</u>," <u>PMLA</u>, 93 (1978), 240-247; see also Bernard McGinn,,
"<u>Iter Sancti Sepulchri</u>," p. 37, who notes that penitentially
"with bared feet, chanting litanies of forgiveness, the
whole Christian people were to recapitulate the pilgrimage
to Jerusalem, to repeat in ritual form the great <u>iter</u> that
in itself was a type of the pilgrimage of life."

[35] Delasanta, "Penance and Poetry," noting that after
the Parson's Sermon the pilgrims would assume a similar
penitential attitude, walking the remainder of the way to
Canterbury.

[36] William Caxton, the <u>Golden Legend</u>'s "Life of St.
James the More," p. 105, uses the word "malle" of the
pilgrim's scrip into which the wicked innkeeper places the
silver cup, his <u>Reynard the Fox</u>, p. 48, of Reynard's pilgrim
scrip.

[37] Hans Holbein, <u>The Dance of Death</u>, ed. Werner L.
Gandesheimer, New York, 1971, p. xiv; examples of "trois
vivants, trois morts," Bernardo Daddi diptych, Accademia,
Florence, beneath the Annunciation and Crucifixion, and in
Psalter of Bonne of Luxembourg, Countess of Normandy,

Cloisters, New York; The Dance of Death, ed. Florence
Warren, London, 1931, EETS, O.S. 181; Phillip Damon
suggested that the Canterbury Tales is a Dance of Death. I
should also like to compare it to a Ship of Fools. Pisa,
whose Camposanto's Triumph of Death could illustrate the
Knight's, Pardoner's and Parson's Tales, was for Dante a
type of Thebes.

CHAPTER SIX: EGYPTIAN GOLD

[1] Auerbach, "Figura," pp. 49-51.

[2] Dante, "Epistola X," to Can Grande, speaks of Egypt's
bondage, Israel's freedom. The diagram of the two patterns,
Exodus and Emmaus, reveals interesting transformations:

	Profane		Sacred
Exodus	Egypt		Israel
	Aaron		Moses
	Bondage	⟶	Freedom
	Golden Calf		Ark
	Carnival		Lent
		✕	
Emmaus	Jerusalem		Emmaus
	Cleophas/Luke		Christ
	Temple	⟶	Inn
	Sermon		Fable
	Friday		Monday
	Death		Life

[3] Durandus, pp. 115-116; Starkie, pp. 16-18, Plates
between pp. 22-23; Pedro de Palol and Max Hirmer, Early
Medieval Art in Spain, New York, n.d., figs. 74-75, of
reliquary, "Arca Santa," given in 1075 by Alfonso VI and
Dona Urraca to Orviedo Cathedral's Camera Santa; D.J. Hall,
English Medieval Pilgrimage, London, 1966, p. 102, notes St.
Cuthbert's body was wrapped in rich cloths from Byzantium
and Sicily, one embroidered with "There is no God but God,
and Allah is his prophet," as if Egyptian gold, and was
placed in a wood coffin with the Lindisfarne Gospels. After
an initial resistence, Revelation 6.4 was used to justify the
quasi-pagan practice of placing relics of the dead "beneath
the altar" and parts of Roman martyrs' bodies were sent
throughout Europe for the consecration of churches.
Miracle-working relics of saints, both local and brought

from afar, as well as the Holy Places, became the pilgrims'
goals; Rock, III,287-416; Durandus, p. 107; Finucane, pp.
17-38; Geary, Furta Sacra.

[4] Kurt Weitzmann, The Monastery of Saint Catherine at
Mount Sinai: The Icons, Princeton, 1976, I,13-15, Icon B.1.

[5] Mâle, Religious Art, pp. 129-132, notes St. Roch of
Montpellier's iconographical likeness to St. James, but with
the dog who fed him with a loaf of bread a day while he lay
ill of plague at Piacenza. He sometimes bears the crossed
keys of the Roman pilgrimage he never completed, being
delayed tending the plague sick. His figure is found in
Germany and Spain, rather than in France and Italy, along
the pilgrimage routes.

[6] Meiss, Painting in Florence, passim.

[7] John F. Mahoney, "The Role of Statius in the
Structure of the Purgatorio," 79th Annual Report of the
Dante Society (1961), p. 22; Idelsohn, Jewish Music; Gustave
Reese, Music in the Middle Ages, New York, 1968, p. 10;
Erich Werner, The Sacred Bridge, London, 1959, pp. 419-421.

[8] Hecksher; Panofsky, Renaissance, pp. 89-90,112,151,
155; Meiss, Painting in Florence, p. 157; Pseudo
Bonaventure, Meditations, fig. 59; the Penguin cover,
Augustine's Confessions, shows nude idols on pillars, each
with a devil, being worshiped by idolators.

[9] De Doctrina Christiana, XL, trans. D.W. Robertson,
Jr., Indianapolis, 1958, pp. 75-76.

[10] The Portable Medieval Reader, ed. James Ross, Mary
McLaughlin, New York, 1949, p. 332; see also the Contra
Amatores Mundi of Richard Rolle of Hampole, trans. Paul F.
Theiner, Berkeley, 1968, pp. 9-10.

[11] Fleming, p. 235.

[12] Meiss, Painting in Florence, pp. 71,157; Panofsky,
Renaissance, pp. 151-152.

[13] Hecksher.

[14] Alexander Barclay, The Ship of Fools, Edinburgh, 1874,
I,291.

[15] Malcolm Letts, Mandeville's Travels: Texts and
Translation, p. 24, notes that "Babylon" was falsely derived

from the Egyptian Pi-Hapi-n-On, the Nile City of On, which
the Arabs later dropped because of the confusion; Demaray,
pp. 33-34,75-76.

[16] The poem has the Saracens worship statues of Apollo,
Mohammed and Termagent; The Song of Roland, trans. Patricia
Terry, Indianapolis, 1965, lines 8,417,611,853,2580-2591,
2696-2697,2710-2717,3267-3268,3490-3494,3637-3639,3661-3665.

[17] Chaucer's Parson's Tale, X,748-750: "And certes,
every floryn in his cofre is his mawmet. And certes, the
synne of mawmettrie is the first thyng that God deffended in
the ten commaundementz, as bereth witnesse in Exodi capituli
vicesimo 'You shalt have no false goddes bifore me, ne thou
shalt make to thee no grave thyng'"; Panofsky, Renaissance,
pp. 111-112; the Bible Moralisée equates the worship of the
Golden Calf with the amassing of gold as it were a saint's
shrine (I.i); the Livre de Merveilles' illuminations show
the worship of idols as of golden calves upon pillars; idols
fall off pillars in Egypt when the Holy Family travels
there.

[18] "Pilgrimage of Lionardo di Niccolo Frescobaldi to the
Holy Land," p. 41, "Pilgrimage of Simone Sigoli to the Holy
Land," p. 167, Visit to the Holy Places of Egypt, Sinai,
Palestine and Syria in 1384, trans. Theophilus Bellorini,
O.F.M. Eugene Hoade, O.F.M., Jerusalem, 1948.

[19] On the 42 stations of Exodus: Demaray, passim;
Hartwell Jones, p. 214; St. Gregory the Great instituted
similar station upon Rome's topography, PL,78,866; last of
all, friars in Jerusalem created the "Stations of the
Cross"; Professor Fleming remarked to me that the Vita Nuova
has 42 chapters, mirroring Exodus' 42 stations. Egeria's
Travels, trans. John Wilkinson, London, 1971; Early Travels
to Palestine, ed. Thomas Wright, London, 1848; PPTS
publications, passim; Mag. Thietmari Peregrinatio, ed.
J.C.M. Laurent, Peregrinationes Medii Aevi Quatuor, Leipsig,
1873; Un guide du pèlerin, ed. Pernoud; R.J. Mitchell, The
Spring Voyage: The Jerusalem Pilgrimage in 1458, New York,
1964, pp. 131-161, notes the Exodus journeying of pilgrims,
the earliest being the nun Egeria's in the fourth century.
Lionardo Frescobaldi and Giorgio Gucci speak of Mount
Sinai's ancient frescoes and paintings in their fourteenth-
centiry pilgrimage account of the Holy Places and even
retell stories that derive from John of Climacus' Ladder of
Divine Ascent written centuries earlier concerning Moses'
ghostly presence at the monastery, Visit to the Holy
Places, pp. 61,116.

[20] Figure 7 is from Joachim Lelewel, Géographie du Moyen

Age, Brussels, 1852, 3 vols. I have compared it to the
original in the Brussels MS of the Historia Hierosólomytae
by Robertus Remensis and found it remarkably exact. See also
Jürgan Schulz, "Jacopo de' Barbari's View of Venice: Map
Making, City Views and Moralized Geography before the Year
1500," Art Bulletin, 60 (1978), 446-453

[21] Pseudo Bonaventure, p. 70, fig. 59. Meiss, French
Painting in the Time of Jean de Berry: The Limbourgs and
their Contemporaries, New York, 1974, II, Plates, 378,415.

[22] Thurston, pp. 30-67; Richard FitzRalph, Archbishop of
Armagh, noted that the Hebrew Jubilee required charity
towards one's neighbor, but not pilgrimage abroad, Sumption,
p. 241.

[23] Josephus, The Jewish War, VII,162, pp. 372-373;
Joannis Diaconi, Liber de Ecclesia Lateranensi, PL,
194,1543-1549; Mandeville's Travels, p. 64; Gregorovius,
I,210-213; Grisar, I,97-98.

[24] Joannis Diaconi, 1547-1548; Hartwell Jones citing
Welsh pilgrim lyrics, pp. 165,187; Durandus, pp. 32-33;
Vernon 'Stacions of Rome,' pp.8-12; Descritione de le
Chiese, Stationi, Indulgenze & Relique de Corpi Sancti, che
sonno in la Citta de Roma, Rome, 1554, A vii^v, printed in
Five Early Guides to Rome and Florence, ed. Peter Murray,
Farnborough, 1972, Gregorovius, I,90; Bishop Zacharius in
the time of the Emperor Justinian speaks of the virga
aaronis and the arca foedoris as at the Lateran; the Lateran
Basilica also had seven altars and seven candles, in order
to mirror the Jerusalem Temple and the Apocalypse.

[25] Howard Loxton, Pilgrimage to Canterbury, Newton
Abbot, 1978; Tancred Borenius, St. Thomas Becket in Art,
Fort Washington, 1970, passim; Guernes de Pont-Sainte-
Maxence, La vie de saint Thomas Becket, ed. Emmanuel
Walberg, Paris, 1964; Lydgate, "Prayer to St. Thomas," Minor
Poems, ed. Henry N. McCracken, London, 1962, I,140-143;
Raymond Foreville, Le Jubilé de saint Thomas Becket du XIIIe
au XVe siècles, Paris, 1958; Materials for the History of
Thomas Becket, Archbishop of Canterbury, Rolls Series,
London, 1875-1883.

[26] Sumption, p. 264; Adair, p. 116.

[27] Melinkoff, The Horned Moses; Deguileville, lines
1576-1896.

[28] D.W. Robertson, Jr., Chaucer's London, New York,
1968, pp. 39,75-77; Loxton, p. 145, shows the thirteenth-

century common seal of the City of London with St. Thomas with pallium and cross.

[29] Cutts, pp. 170-173.

[30] D. Ingram Hill, _The Stained Glass of Canterbury Cathedral_, Canterbury, n.d., Window VI, Panels 25-33, pp. 14-15.

[31] Foreville, pp. 3-81.

[32] F.N. Robinson, p. xxi.

[33] Young, I,482.

CHAPTER SEVEN: "CHE D'EGITTO VEGNA IN IERUSALEMME"

[1] _Il Convivio_, II.i.6.

[2] "When we read in the psalm, 'In exitu Israel de Aegypto, domus Jacob de populo barbaro, facta est Judea sanctificatio eius . . . ,' let us not suppose that history is being retold but that the future is being foretold. When this miracle happened to the Jewish people, it happened as fact, but a fact with a future significance. But the purpose of the man who prophesied through his psalmistry was to show that he was doing with words what was done with Exodus with facts. And the same spirit caused both the facts and the words in order that the things which were to be fully manifested only at the end of the world should be announced by the concurrence of both figural history and figurative language. And so the psalmist did not remain entirely faithful to history, but departing in certain respects from the account found in Exodus, lest he should be thought to be writing of things done instead of things to come," trans. Phillip Damon, "The Two Modes of Allegory in Dante's _Convivio_," _PQ_, 40 (1961), 144-149.

[3] Mahoney, "The Role of Statius," p. 22; Idelsohn, _Jewish Music_; Reese, _Music in the Middle Ages_, p. 10; Werner, _The Sacred Bridge_, pp. 419-421.

[4] Hollander, _Allegory_, pp. 124-125; "_Purgatorio_ II; Cato's Rebuke and Dante's _Scoglio_," _Italica_, 52 (1975), 355-356; John Freccero, "Casella's Song: _Purg._ II.112," _Dante Studies_, 91 (1973), 73-80.

[5] Hollander, _Allegory_, pp. 44-45, the relevant text given in Chapter V with the Psalm's _tonus peregrinus_. Dante punningly flatters Can Grande della Scala with a scheme popularized by John of Climacus' Sinaitic _Ladder of Divine Ascent_ (Climacus=Ladder=Scala).

[6] Hollander, _Allegory_, pp. 15-56; Richard Hamilton Green, "Dante's 'Allegory of the Poets' and the Medieval Theory of Fiction"; Singleton, "The Irreducible Dove," _Comparative Literature_, 9 (1957), 118-135.

[7] _Petri Allegherii super Dantis ipsius genitoris Comoediam_, ed. Lord Vernon, Florence, 1846, p. 739; Vincenzo Cioffari, "Guido da Pisa's Basic Interpretation," _Dante Studies_, 93 (1975), 3,9; Gioacchinao Paparelli, "La definizione dantesca della poesia come 'fictio,'" _Dante e la critica_, ed. Carlo Salinari, Bari, 1968, pp. 62-77; Touchstone to Audrey: "The truest poetry is the most feigning," _As You Like It_, III.iii.19 and John Bunyan's Apology to _Pilgrim's Progress_,

> "But it is feigned." What of that? I trow
> Some men, by feigned words, as dark as mine,
> Make truth to spangle and its rays to shine,

state the argument.

[8] Domenico Michelini painted a fresco in the Duomo, which shows Dante standing beyond the city walls in the stance of exile while holding towards Florence the book of his poem, his right hand pointing to _Inferno_'s gate of despair. Behind him is the gate of _Purgatorio_'s hopefulness. Above are "Il sole e l'altre stelle" [the sun and the other stars] of the _Paradiso_. The three gates of the painting, of the city of Florence, of the despairing _città dolente_ of exile, of the hopeful and penitential city of pilgrimage, mirror each other. Dante's poem is a Jeremiad directed not at Jerusalem but at Florence (Plate XII).

[9] Pietro Alighieri, p. 289; Guido da Pisa, _Expositiones et Glose super Comoediam Dantis_, ed. Vincenzo Cioffari, Albany, 1974, pp. 49-50; Benvenuti de Rambaldis de Imola, _Comentum super Dantis Aldighierij Comoediam_, ed. Lord Vernon, Florence, 1887, III,62-66; Singleton, "_In exitu Israel de Aegypto_," _78th Annual Report of the Dante Society_ (1960), 1-24; Dunstan Tucker, "_In exitu Israel de Aegypto_: The _Divine Comedy_ in the Light of the Easter

Liturgy," American Benedictine Review, 11 (1960), 43-61;
Carol Kaske, "Mount Sinai and Dante's Mount Purgatory,"
Dante Studies, 89 (1971), 1-8; Demaray, passim; Rhoda
Ruditzky, "Those Infernal Plagues: A Proposal," Italica,
50 (1973), 222-241. Deguileville's Pèlerinage Jhesucrist,
p. 118, calls on his hearers as people of Egypt to receive
Christ with joy in verses that spell out that poet's name
in acrostics. Typical pilgrim guides of Sinai: Egeria's
Travels, pp. 91-112; "Pilgrimage of Giorgio Gucci to the
Holy Places," Visit to the Holy Places, p. 117 and passim.

[10] Trans. W.L.Lewis, Oxford, 1757.

[11] P. 75.

[12] Mandeville's Travels, ed. M.C. Seymour, London, 1967:
"Also from Jerusalem two miles is the Mount Joy, a full fair
place and a delicious . . . . And men clepe it the Mount Joy
for it giveth joy to pilgrims' hearts because that there men
see first Jerusalem," pp. 71-72; nineteenth-century scholars
decided that John Mandeville was a fake, Jospehine Waters
Bennett, The Rediscovery of Sir John Mandeville, New York,
1954, exonerating him; DACL, 14,91-110; Starkie, pp.
257,305-306. While Rome and Compostela had their Mon Joies
be called so, Canterbury's was Harbledown from which
pilgrims first saw Canterbury and, if they were on
horseback, now dismounted. Henry II walked from here,
barefoot and in sackcloth. Elizabeth Home Beatson has told
me of the "Mon Joies" as Gothic stone crosses and structures
set up at crossroads.

[13] Ruditzky, p. 230. Joyce, who spoiled the Egyptian
gold from Dante for his Ulysses, for his Exodus patterning
used the cattle murrain of Foot-and-Mouth disease instead of
all the other plagues. There was no actual Foot-and-Mouth
outbreak in Ireland that Ulysses year.

[14] " . . . che con la destra mano tiene vn bordone," p.
166; Pietro Alighieri associates it with Mercury's caduceus,
Aaron's rod, and comments that Mercury was the god of
eloquence, commerce and fraud; he also speaks of Aaron's rod
as placed in the Arca Santa, p. 125; Alexandrian
commentators allegorized the staves of Exodus as paideia,
discipline wrought by educations, TDNT, V,614.

[15] PL, 113,205. See Beatus Apocalypse illuminations of
frogs.

[16] Ibid. Even Wordsworth in the nineteenth century was
associating poets with Exodus' plague of frogs.

[17] Lucan, *Pharsalia*, trans. Robert Graves, Baltimore,
1957, p. 211, Tacitus speaks of Moses, Pharaoh and the
oracle of Ammon Jupiter, in a similar manner to Lucan's and
Dante's handling of Cato and connects Moses with the seven
stars while Dante allots four to Cato. It is possible that
Dante noted the parallels. Cato, like Ulysses, is
enigmatically a pilgrim. His terrible flight after
Pharsalia, through the snake-infested deserts of Libya (a
type of Exodus in which snakes are routed by Moses'
snake-twined staff, Numbers 21.9;*Inf*. XXIV.82-90), he
declares to be still the path to liberty. Dante borrows his
speech (IX.400) for thieving Ulysses, stealing for it also
Aeneas' speech to the shipwrecked Trojans on the Libyan
shores and Christ's speech to his disciples on Galilean
shores, that last borrowed from that of God to Abraham.
Cato's exile is analogous to Dante's. Zacher, pp. 18-41,
discusses Ulysses as the type of curiositas.

[18] Dunstan Tucker, "Dante's Reconciliation," relates
this to the penitent's unshavenness, pp. 91-92.

[19] Hollander, *Allegory*, pp. 124-126. Pilgrim tales at
Sinai are told of Moses' appearance there, John of Climacus
and *Visit to the Holy Places*.

[20] I make use of Professor William Hecksher's research
on idols on pillars in Venice and at the medieval Lateran;
Fleming, pp. 226ff.

[21] Hollander, "*Purgatorio* II," p. 350.

[22] See *Polyphonies du XIIIe siècle: le Manuscrit H 196
de la Faculté de Medicine de Montpellier*, ed. Yvonne
Rokseth, Paris, 1936, vol. II. "Sing cuccu" with its Latin
"Perspice christicola" is similar in its juxtaposition of
profane vernacular verses with sacred Latin ones.

[23] Singleton notes that the rushes allude to the Red
Sea's other name, Yam Suf, the Sea of Rushes, "*In Exitu
Israel*," p. 12; *Mandeville's Travels* states that Christ's
crown of thorns preserved in the Sainte Chapelle was of such
"jonkes of the see" as are Dante's baptismal "giunche" (95)
or rushes, p. 9.

[24] *The Jewish War*, VII,162, pp. 372-373; Joannis
Diaconi, *Liber de Ecclesia Lateranensi*, *PL*, 194,1543-1549;
Mandeville's Travels, p. 64; Gregorovius, I,90,210-213;
Grisar, I,97-98; Hartwell Jones citing Welsh pilgrim lyrics,
pp. 165,187; Durandus, pp. 32-33; *Vernon 'Stacions of Rome*,'
pp. 8-12: *Descritione de le Chiese*, V vii[v].

[25] Augustus Hare, _Florence_, London, 1896, pp. 124-125; Villani, _Istorie Fiorentine_, Milan, 1802, I,xlii,lx; V,xxxviii, concerning Mars as Florence's idol and mounted on a column, whether in the Temple or at the Ponte Vecchio.

[26] Grisar, III,331-332; Villani,I,lx; Tyrer, p. 169; Sumption, p. 128.

[27] Richard Krautheimer, "Introduction to an 'Iconography of Medieval Architecture,'" _JWCI_, 5 (1942), 1-33.

[28] Demaray, pp. 154-168, notes purgatorial pilgrimages up the terraces of Mount Sinai, which include a gated arch at which a monk with the rank of "angel" heard confessions. _Inf_. XVIII.28-33 had been the bridge of the angel Michael and the gate of St. Peter's, at which, in traditional Jerusalem iconography, as in Plate XIII, pilgrims' confessions are heard; _Purg_. IX,73-145 is therefore modeled on Sinai's gate but also on the Lateran whose Tarpeian Gates of sanctuary were in Christian times rendered as Jubilee doors of pilgrimage, a concept that was to be transferred to the Vatican after the papal return from the Babylonian Captivity, Thurston, pp. 39-40. The Arch of Titus, interestingly, has two angels on it.

[29] Dunstan Tucker, "Dante's Reconciliation," pp. 76-78; penitents at the expulsion waited dressed in rough garments, barefoot, their eyes held to the ground (in the manner of Adam and Eve, Plate IIa,b, and of the Emmaus Pilgrims), until they were led to the bishop seated in the nave who marked them with the cross of ashes, blessed their sackcloth garments with holy water, compared them, as they lay prostrate on the floor, to Adam and Eve, then led them forth, each penitent holding hands with the other in a chain, out the church's door, Cutts, pp. 167-168.

[30] At Casamaris Abbey near Rome the Cistercian dispensary still tends the sick. I saw there a man's cut treated with healing lotion applied with the gentleness of a bird's wing feather. It is in this manner that Dante's cut P's are dressed and healed. John Freccero in a paper read at Western Michigan University, May 1978, suggested a play upon "pen" and "sword." I observe that here the very "pen" is reversed in erasing the diacritic.

[31] Fallani, _Dante e la cultura figurativa medievale_, pp. 89-91.

[32] Ralph P. Elliott, _Runes: An Introduction_, Manchester, 1959, pp. 100-102, Fig. 44 of the Franks Casket, itself a treasure chest, the inscription being both Runic and Latin:

"Her fegtaþ titus end giuþeasu" [Here fight Titus and the
Jews]; "hic fugiant Hierusalim afitatores" [here the
inhabitants flee Jerusalem]; the words "dom" [judgement],
and "gisl" [hostage]; Adelheid Heimann, "A Twelfth-Century
MS from Winchcomb and its Illustrations," JWCI, 28 (1965),
86-109; Christian reliquaries were shaped like the Hebrew
Ark; Gregorovius, I,210-213, discusses history of the "arca
foedoris"; a Renaissance painting at the Lateran shows bad
priests crushed beneath an oxen cart at the Arcus cum Arca,
I. Samuel 4.11-22, II Samuel 6.6-11; Purg. X.57, "per che si
teme officio non commesso" [because of which men fear an
office they have not earned]; Piers Plowman, B.X.280-284,
C.I.104-124.

33 Augustus Hare, Walks in Rome, New York, n.d., pp.
167-169.

34 Gregory Curfman's observations are in Hollander,
Allegory, pp. 297-300, suggesting Hell Gate as being
Trajan's Arch; Grisar tells of attempts at copying the
inscription on Titus' Arch preceding it with the cross of
Christian epigraphy, I.226; its inscription is
"SENATUSPOPULUSQUEROMANUSDIVOTITODIVIVESPASIANOAUGUSTO";
Freud, like Dante, used the landscape of Rome as an analogy
to the landscapes within the mind, then too quickly
dismissed the idea as "absurd phantasy," Civilization and
its Discontents, trans. James Strachey, New York, 1962, pp.
16-18; Paul Piehler, The Visionary Landscape: A Study in
Medieval Allegory, London, 1971, attempted to discuss
Dante's mentally traveled landscapes without their anchorage
in physical pilgrimage sites. Dante uses real landscapes as
a "Book of Memory"; Frances Yates has studied that aspect in
the Renaissance with her Theatre of Memory; V.A. Kolve's
study of the Canterbury Tales makes use of these concepts.

35 Curtius, European Literature, pp. 162-165. Brieger,
Meiss, Singleton, I,86, note that in 1198 Giovanni Alighieri
illustrated a now lost Aeneid in gold and color; Grisar,
III,192, notes that St. Paul in medieval legend is said to
have wept at Virgil's tomb, desiring both to embrace him
living and to convert the greatest poet to Christianity, an
analogue both to Statius' and Virgil's embraces and to
Gregory's prayer for Trajan's soul.

36 Dares Phrygius in Roberts, The Chronicles of the
Kings of Britain, pp. xxiv-xxvi; Istorie Fiorentine,
I,xii,15-16.

37 Gregorovius, IV,278,691; Spargo, Virgil the
Necromancer, pp. 136-197,256, noting Italian engraving of

the fifteenth century of Virgil in the basket hanging from
the Frangipani Tower by the Colosseum, the lady standing
near the Arch of Titus; Hare, Walks in Rome, p. 169;
Chaucer, Parliament of Fowls, 120-168, gives such a Janus
arch. The landscape serves further to link Virgil and Dante,
since Dante's ancestors, the Elisei, were descended from the
Roman Frangipani whose tower this was.

CHAPTER EIGHT: "PIERS FOR PURE TENE . PULLED IT ATWEYNE"

[1] Auerbach, "Figura," pp. 11-76; Singleton, "In Exitu
Israel," speaking of the Exodus paradigm in the Commedia.
pp. 1-24.

[2] "Figura," pp. 49-51; Ames, Abraham, Moses and Piers.
Mildred E. Marcett, "Uhtred de Boldon, Friar William Jordan,
and Piers Plowman," New York, 1938; Huppé, "Petrus, id est
Christus: Wordplay in Piers Plowman, B Text," ELH,
17 (1950), 163-190; Maureen Quillinan, "Langland's Literal
Allegory," Essays in Criticism, 28 (1978), 95-111.

[3] Lines 58-63, p. 2.

[4] Howard Meroney, "The Life and Death of Longe Wille,"
ELH, 17 (1950), 18; John Lawlor, Piers Plowman: An Essay in
Criticism, London, 1962, p. 157, on parallels of Moses and
Piers, the Pardon and the Law; Carruthers, p. 71, and also
in her article, "Piers Plowman: The Tearing of the Pardon,"
PQ, 49 (1970), 10, notes that the priest is a type of Aaron.

[5] Early Christianity and Greek Padiea, Cambridge,
Mass., 1961; Ad Imaginem Dei: The Image of Man in Medieval
Art, Latrobe, 1965, and The Idea of Reform: Its Impact on
Christian Thought and Action in the Age of the Fathers, New
York, 1967.

[6] TDNT, "παιδεία," V,620-1.

[7] 4,11,2b; TDNT, V,599.

[8] Robertson and Huppé, pp. 18-19.

[9] Medieval Russia's Epics, Chronicles and Tales, ed.
Sergei A. Zenkovsky, New York, 1964, p. 85.

10 David Jeffrey, "Bosch's Haywain: Communion, Community and the Theatre of the World," Viator, 4 (1973), 311-331.

11 Pp. 313-314.

12 E.K. Rand, Founders of the Middle Ages, New York, 1928: 1957, p. 31, discusses Gregory's Moralia where Job is Christ, his wife, the temptations of the flesh.

13 Tractate on Education, 1664: "The end then of Learning is to repair the ruines of our first Parents by regaining how to know God aright, and out of the knowledge to love him, to imitate him, to be like him, which being united to the heavenly grace of faith makes up the highest perfection"; Jaeger notes that the Christian paideia was the imitation of God.

14 Pp. 196-197; Traditional Imagery of Charity in Piers Plowman, The Hague, 1966, p. 82, f.n. 16; Samaritan exegesis, Select English Works of John Wyclif, ed. T. Arnold, Oxford, 1871, I,32-33.

15 D.W. Robertson, Jr., "The Doctrine of Charity in Medieval Literary Gardens," Speculum, 26 (1951), 24-49; Fleming, Roman de la Rose; Stanley Stewart, The Enclosed Garden; The Tradition and the Image in Seventeenth-Century Poetry, Madison, 1966; Deguileville, Pèlerinage Jhesucrist.

16 Gothic Image, p. 196; Scriptural Tradition, pp. 204-216; Traditional Imagery, pp. 74-93; Man's Unconquerable Mind, p. 119.

17 "The Liturgical Associations of Langland's Samaritan," Traditio, 25 (1969), 217-230; J.F. Goodrich's notes to his translation of Piers the Ploughman, Harmondsworth, 1959:1966, are valuable for their identification of antiphons in the text derived from the liturgy with which Langland would have been very familiar; Robert Adams, "Langland and the Liturgy Revisited," Speculum, 73 (1976), 266-284, finds fault with liturgical studies of Langland through mistakes he uncovers in Greta Hort's Piers Plowman and Contemporary Religious Thought, London, 1938; however, these studies should not be discarded.

18 Ravenna's San Vitale gives this scene in mosaic and with it those of Abraham and Melchisadek, Abraham's Sacrifice of Isaac, Abel's Sacrifice of the Lamb, above the altar, as all are liturgical and iconographical types of the Eucharist; Pernoud, Guide du pèlerin, pp. 58-59, gives the

dialogue between friars and pilgrims at the Holy Place of
Mambre where the three and one appeared to Abraham: "V. Tres
vidit, R. Et unum adoravit"; the Glossa Ordinaria preserved
the living continuum of sermon commentary; literature
reflected that yoking of liturgy and sermon.

[19]   Judith H. Anderson, The Growth of a Personal Voice:
Piers Plowman and The Faerie Queene, New Haven, 1966.

[20]   Mâle, Gothic Image, pp. 154-155; Rita Lejeune and
Jacques Stiernon, La legende de Roland dans l'art du Moyen
Age, Brussels, 1966, I,204-205, challenge Mâle's figural
interpretation and state that the priest is the Archbishop
Turpin of Reims, the crusading knight, Roland.

[21]   Morton Bloomfield, Piers Plowman as a Fourteenth-
Century Apocalypse, New Brunswick, 1961; Marjorie Reeves,
The Figurae of Joachim of Fiore; Barbara Nolan, pp. 205-258;
see also Brieger, Meiss, Singleton, p. 112 and fig. 130.

[22] Brieger, p. 112, figs. 129,130.

[23] It is also of interest that Petrus Alfonsi was
associated with Malvern Priory. He visited its Prior Walcher
and taught him Arabic eclipse computation methods in 1120,
Sententia Petri cognomento Anphus de dracone quam dominus
Walcerius prior Malvernensis ecclesie in latinam transtulit
linguam, published by José Millas Vallicrosa, Sefarad, 3
(1943), 65-105. The Dialogus Petri cognomento Alphonsi ex
Judaeo Christiani et Moysi Judaei, in PL 157, contains the
diagrammatic scheme of the Tetragrammaton Joachim will use.

[24]   R.E. Kaske, "The Speech of 'Book' in Piers Plowman,"
Anglia, 77 (1959), mentions Joachite beliefs that the Old
and New Testaments will be consumed in flames, p. 139;
Richard L. Hoffman, "The Burning of 'Boke' in Piers
Plowman," MLQ, 25 (1964), 57-65, argues against this
interpretation, though medieval thought, beyond Joachim,
considered that the Book held by the Pantocrator represented
the Books of God's Word and of God's World, the Creation at
Doomsday being consumed in flames. This iconography of Book
came from Ezekiel 2.9 and Revelation 5.1. Not understanding
this J.F. Goodrich mistranslates this line and Donaldson and
Kane write 'book' in lower case.

[25]   William Empson, Some Versions of Pastoral, New York,
1960, "Piers Plowman is the most direct case of the pastoral
figure who turns slowly into Christ and ruler," p. 84.

26 Fish, Self-Consuming Artifacts, pp. 224-264.

CHAPTER NINE: "GARLEEK, OYNONS, AND EEK LEKES"

1 Ed. Raymond S. Willis, Princeton, 1972, pp. 294-330;
pilgrimage images abound in this work, which is Spain's
equivalent to England's Canterbury Tales.

2 The Book of Margery Kempe, p. 32 and passim; Cutts,
pp. 152-156; "The Good Wife Wold a Pylgrymage," The Good
Wife Taught her Daughter, ed. Tauno Mustanoja, Helsinki,
1948, pp. 173-174: "Do3ttor, seyd þe good wyfe, hyde thy
legys white, And schew not forth thy stret hossyn, to make
men haue delytt, And men wyll say of þy body þou carest but
lytt . . . 'The bocher schewyth feyr his flesche, for he
wold sell hit ful blyth'"; Malory, Works, ed. Eugene
Vinaver, London, 1954, pp. 481-482, gives the figure of a
sexually forward Alys le Beall Pylgryme; Lewis Carroll's
Alice is associated with pilgrimage, her tale being "Like a
pilgrim's wither'd wreath of flowers/ Pluck'd in a far-off
land"; Vogel, "Le pèlerinage penitentiel," Pellegrinaggi, p.
75, notes Boniface's complaint to Cuthbert of Canterbury
that English women pilgrims tended to become whores on the
Continent.

3 Ancient Deeds Belonging to the Corporation of Bath:
XIII-XIV Centuries, ed. Rev. C.W. Shickle, Bath, 1921;
Vernon P. Helming, "Medieval Pilgrimage and English
Literature to A.D. 1400," Ph.D. dissertation, Yale, 1937,
discusses the pilgrim sites of Bath.

4 John Sharkey, Celtic Mysteries: The Ancient Religion,
London, 1976, p. 7, plates 14,23-25; John Adair, The
Pilgrim's Way: Shrines and Saints in Britain and Ireland,
London, 1978, p. 95; Loomis, Arthurian Literature in the
Middle Ages: A Collaborative History, Oxford, 1959, p. 43.

5 James Norhnberg, The Analogy of The Faerie Queene,
Princeton, 1976, pp. 222-260 and passim.

6 Owst, p. 119, notes that the rape of Dinah was a
popular sermon topic; Zacher, p. 26, relates Dinah and the
Wife but omits the Jacob's Well pilgrimage that links the
two figures to one place; George Eliot will continue this
tale with her Adam Bede's heroine Dinah.

[7] Robertson, <u>Preface to Chaucer</u>, pp. 319-320, discusses marriage at Cana, Samaritan woman at well, <u>Glossa Ordinaria</u>, <u>PL</u>,114,573, and Canterbury stained glass, Index of Christian Art; for pilgrims and friars see Pernoud, <u>Guide du pèlerin</u>; Beatrice Dansette, "Les pèlerinages occidentaux en Terre Sainte: une pratique de la "Devotion Moderne' è la fin du Moyen Age? Relation inédite d'un pèlerin effectué en 1486," <u>Archivum Franciscanum Historicum</u>, 72 (1979), 106-133.

[8] <u>The Pilgrimage of Holy Paula, by St. Jerome</u>, PPTS, London, 1896, I,31.

[9] Pp. xxvi, 170-173.

[10] He states that her water pot is cupidity and the five husbands are the Old Testament, the sixth, the New; or they are the five senses which, without the sixth, Reason, represent fallen man, <u>PL</u>, 114,571-573.

[11] <u>Marino Sanuto's Secrets for True Crusaders to Help them to Recover the Holy Land</u>, PPTS, XII,19.

[12] <u>Anonymous Pilgrims</u>, I-VIII, PPTS, VI,59. The formulaic quality of these accounts can be seen in a comparison with <u>Mandeville's Travels</u>, pp. 81-82: "And after men go to Shechem, sometimes cleped Sichar, and that is in the province of Samaritans . . . And from thence is a journey to Jerusalem. And there is the well where Our Lord spake to the woman of Samaria, and there was wont to be a church but it is beaten down. Beside that well King Jeroboam let make two calves of gold and made them to be worshipped (I Kings 12.28), and put that one at Dan, and that other at Bethel . . . . And nigh beside is the tomb of Joseph, the son of Jacob, that governed Egypt, for the Jews bore his bones from Egypt and buried them there. And thither go the Jews often time in pilgrimage with great devotion. In that city was Dinah, Jacob's daughter, ravished, for whom her brothers slew many persons and did many harms to that city. And there beside is the hill of Gerizim where the Samaritans make their sacrifice."

[13] <u>Arculf's Narrative about the Holy Places, Written by Adamnan</u>, PPTS, III,42; George Bain, <u>Celtic Art</u>, New York, 1973, pp. 120-128, suggests the Kells Quoniam page represents Christ and the Samaritan woman each holding water vessels.

[14] Kathi Meyer, "The Eight Gregorian Modes on the Cluny Capitals," <u>Art Bulletin</u>, 34 (1952), 75-94, esp. 81-82.

[15] Augustus Hare, Walks in Rome, p. 462, notes the twelfth-century cloister at St. John Lateran enclosing a tenth-century "Well of the Woman of Samaria" adorned with crosses; the Hortus Deliciarum iconography, Rosalie Green notes, gives Jacob's Well a cross or font shape; Victor Guérin, La Terre Sainte, Paris, 1882, I,254-268; the Pardoner's Prologue echoes the Wife's in discussing wells in connection with Jacob's increasing and multiplying of Laban's flock, VI.350-365.

[16] I,291; Fleming, p. 235 and passim; The Dance of Death, ed. Florence Warren, relates the "olde daunce" to the plague, pp. xiv-xv; the Israelites were afflicted with plague for dancing lecherously about the Golden Calf, Exodus 32.35; the Wife's Tale begins with an "olde daunce"--of the fairies (III.860-861 & 990-998) which the friars banished; however, see David L. Jeffrey, The Early English Lyric and Franciscan Spirituality, Lincoln, 1975, pp. 132-142, on friars' dances. The Wife hankers for Samaritan idolatry and adultery.

[17] Frescobaldi thought the chant from the minarets was "increase and multiply," p. 50; Sigoli, likewise, p. 167.

[18] Starkie, p. 305; Liber Sancti Jacobi, V.vi.354, discuss the Lavamentula in which pilgrims washed their private parts before attaining their shrine; Bristol's connections with Compostela are noted in Book of Margery Kempe, pp. 106-111, The Pilgrims Sea Voyage, ed. Furnivall, EETS,25,37; parallels between St. James of Compostela and Jacob, PL,113,153, Berchorius, Opera Omnia, 1731,III,298-299, noting that Jacob is the prototype pilgrim, "similiter Christus,' in abandoning his family and journeying to the east to find a bride.

[19] Epistola LVII ad Paulinum, PL, 22,581; Thomas a Kempis, Imitatio Christi, I,i.23-24. Mary Carruthers in her recent PMLA article noted the relationship between the Wife and Jerome. Pilgrim accounts stress Jerome's Bethlehem cave, Mandeville, p. 53; Frescobaldi, p. 69, notes "first is where St. Jerome did penance, and where he translated the Bible from Hebrew to Latin, and he is buried in the same place," adding that pilgrims chipped off pieces of stone to give to scholar friends; Pernoud, Guide du pèlerin, p. 60, notes liturgy used by pilgrims at cave: "Ant. O doctor optime," then in cave of Nativity: "V. Verbum caro factum est." This shaped Renaissance paintings of Jerome as scholar/cardinal. See Meiss, "Image of St. Jerome," The Painter's Choice: Problems in the Interpretations of Renaissance Art, New York, 1976, for Jerome as penitent: "Nudus nudum Christum sequor" [Naked I follow the naked Christ.]

[20] Robertson, _Preface to Chaucer_, p. 331, f.n. 96;
Holloway, "The Asse to the Harpe."

[21] Meiss, _Painting in Florence_, p. 68.

[22] Baldwin's "Unity of the _Canterbury Tales_," Hoffman's
"Two Voices," between them come closest to the "idea" of the
Canterbury Tales.

[23] _Abbot Suger on the Abbey Church of St.-Denis and its
Art Treasures_, ed. and trans. Panofsky, Princeton, 1946;
Turner, "The Center Out There," pp. 191-230; Panofsky, _Early
Netherlandish Painting: Its Origin and Character_, Cambridge,
Mass., 1966, 2 vols.

[24] "The Conjugal Debt and Medieval Canon Law," _Journal
of Medieval History_, 3 (1977), 101,111.

[25] Johannes Jørgensen, _Saint Bridget of Sweden_, trans.
Ingeborg Lund, London, 1954, II,259-260.

[26] Gail McMurray Gibson notes the parody in the
Shipman's Tale of Corpus Christi Resurrection drama.

[27] He has broken Rules I against being a _gyrovagus_, II on
obedience, III against adultery, theft and false testimony,
XXII on sleeping singly in a single bed, "Singuli per
singula lecta dormiant," LIIII, against relationships with
one's relations, LXVII, against listening to evil
conversation while absent from the abbey, and countless
others.

[28] Charles-Joseph Hefele, H. Leclercq, _Histoire des
conciles d'après les documents originaux_, Paris, 1914,
VI.641; however, Kenneth S. Cahn, "Chaucer's Merchants and
the Foreign Exchange: An Introduction to Medieval Finance,"
Studies in the Age of Chaucer, 2 (1980), 81-119, argues that
the merchant's way of making money from money is not
technically usury; though he does admit the merchant is
trafficking in money. See also Paul Stephen Schneider,
"'Taillynge Ynogh': The Function of Money in the Shipman's
Tale," _CR_, 11 (1977), 201-209; David H. Abraham, "Cosyn and
Cosynage: Pun and Structure in the Shipman's Tale," _CR_, 11
(1977), 319-327; Kenneth Rexroth, "_Canterbury Tales_,"
Classics Revisited, New York, 1969, pp. 141-145

[29] Maurice Hussey, _Chaucer's World: A Pictorial
Companion_, Cambridge, 1967, p. 94.

[30] Maria Rosa Lida de Malkiel, Two Spanish Masterpieces: The Book of Good Love and the Celestina, Illinois Studies in Language and Literature, 49 (1961), notes this characteristic in Spanish medieval poetry; the Roman de la Rose's Faus Semblant exhibits it in French medieval poetry (a later manifestation is Tartuffe); Ann Kernan, "Chaucer's Archwife and Eunuch," ELH, 41 (1974), 1-25, also pairs the two tellers and their tales.

[31] The hospital of "Rouncivale" near Charing Cross was a cell of the convent of Nuestra Senora de Roncesvalles in Navarre, one of its patrons was John of Gaunt, and it was notorious for its sale of false pardons, Robinson, p. 667.

[32] Reese, pp. 389-406; Jewish and Christian law forbade the priesthood to those who were physically incomplete; Reversible World, ed. Babcock, p. 22; Roman de la Rose stresses Amant's staff and scrip and the Rose's corresponding relics while also discussing Saturn's, Origen's and Abelard's castrations; Ross, Chaucer's Bawdy, pp. 49-50; Ann S. Haskell, "The St. Joce Oath in the Wife of Bath's Prologue," Essays on Chaucer's Saints, The Hague, 1976, pp. 70-71.

[33] The papers of Laila Gross demonstrate the relationship between medieval ivories and literature.

[34] R.E. Kaske, "The Summoner's Garleek, Oynons, and eek Lekes," MLN, 74 (1959), 481-484; C.S. Lewis has the Narnian Chronicles villains share this diet.

[35] Index of Christian Art; Robertson, "The Doctrine of Charity in Medieval Literary Gardens," pp. 29-49; Ladner, "Medieval and Modern Understanding of Symbolism: A Comparison," Speculum, 54 (1979), 223-256.

[36] Robert P. Miller, Jr., "Chaucer's Pardoner, the Scriptural Eunuch and the Pardoner's Tale," Speculum, 30 (1955), 180-199, notes the christological aspects of this passage.

[37] Robert E. Todd, "The Magna Mater Archetype in 'The Pardoner's Tale,'" Literature and Psychology, 15 (1965), 32-40; Erich Neumann, The Great Mother: An Analysis of the Archetype, trans. Ralph Manheim, Princeton, 1972.

[38] Robert E. Nichols, Jr., "The Pardoner's Cakes and Ale," PMLA, 82 (1967), 498-504; Rodney Delasanta, "Sacrament and Sacrifice in the Pardoner's Tale," Annuale Medievale, 14, 43-50.

[39] Ronald Sutherland, The Romaunt of the Rose and Le Rome de la Rose: A Parallel Text Edition, Berkeley, 1968, p. x.

[40] C.G. Sedgewick commented of the Pardoner: "The 'lost soul' whom Chaucer inflicts on the Pilgrimage fairly reeks of the medieval pulpit: he is the supreme example of the Preaching Fox," in "The Progress of Chaucer's Pardoner, 1880-1940," Chaucer: Modern Essays in Criticism, ed. Edward Wagenknecht, Oxford, 1959, p. 130. Hussey, p. 145; Kenneth Varty, Reynard the Fox; G. Ward Finley, "Faus-Semblant, Fauvel and Renart le Contrefait: A Study in Kinship," RR, 23 (1932), 323-331, notes Faus-Semblant's relationship to Renart: Pierre de Saint Cloud, Ysengrinus (ca. 1150) has the fox in pilgrim guise capturing the cock. Illuminations of Renard as pilgrim have him strike down a hare with his staff, or bribe a pilgrim lion with a money bag and a dead goose. In Gorleston Psalter, fol. 47, Renard holds a crozier in one hand, a duck by the neck in the other, while preaching. Varty, p. 58, speaks of a game in which a man dressed in a fox skin and surplice preached to people as if they were geese. Le roman de Renart le Contrefait, ed. Gaston Reynaud and Henri Lemaitre (Paris, 1914), I,2, has the author, a former cleric, state that he adopts the fox skin in order to preach truths concerning society's ills; Arnold Clayton Henderson, "'Of Heigh or Lough Estat': Medieval Fabulists as Social Critics," Viator, 9 (1978), 265-290. Robert Torrance, The Comic Hero, Cambridge, Mass., 1978, pp. ix, 83-110, and Jung see Renard as trickster-savior and hero.

[41] Le roman de Renart, ed. Mario Roques, Paris, 1957-1960, V, Branche III, "Et vos Renart le pelerin, l'escharpe au col, bordon frainin" (4420-4421); William Caxton, The History of Reynard the Fox, ed. N.F. Blake, EETS 263, London, 1960, p. 48; Caxton, Renart the Foxe, a. iii^V-iiii, London, 1976; Charles Dahlberg, "Chaucer's Cock and Fox," JEGP, 53 (1954), 77-290, notes that Russel is Renart's Franciscan son, Renardiel, his Dominican brother; M.A. Rothe, Les romans du Renard, Renardus Vulpes, III, p. 49; Varty, passim.

[42] Canterbury stained glass windows of the shrine show these openings, frequently with a figure who may either be sleeping, in incubation, in the church or dreaming of Thomas and his shrine while at home. "The Relyk of a Seint: A Gloss on Chaucer's Pilgrimage," ELH, 39 (1972), 1-26.

[43] Runciman, "Pilgrims to Palestine," I.68-69. It is not

without interest that the alchemical and astrological symbol
for Venus, ♀, merely needs reversing to symbolize instead
the orb of the world with Jerusalem's Calvary at its top, ♁.
The Old English <u>Elene</u> brings in the references to Troy as if
to have its Roman (and English) Christian Helen undo the
damage done by the Greek and pagan Helen, Jerusalem thereby
being a "Vision of Peace," in contrast to the Trojan War.

[44] Panofsky, <u>Studies in Iconology</u>, New York, 1962, pp.
69-91; the iconography of Saturn ultimately becomes Goya's
frightful picture, which is also that of Dante's Ugolino
devouring his sons, and both as types of Satan devouring
his progeny, in Dante, Judas, Brutus and Cassius.

[45] "<u>Piers Plowman</u> and Iconography," p. 162 and Plate
59c.

[46] H.W. Janson, <u>Apes and Apelore in the Middle Ages and
the Renaissance</u>, London, 1952; Babcock, <u>Reversible World</u>;
Bakhtin, <u>Rabelais</u>; <u>New Literary History</u>, 10; Curtius on
"<u>adynata</u>," <u>European Literature</u>, pp. 94-98.

[47] Ernest Jones in a footnote, <u>Hamlet and Oedipus</u>, New
York, 1955, p. 101, remarked that dreams within dreams
express that which is true but which the dreamer wishes
were not; it is the uncensored part, reversing its
censored surrounding dream; he draws the parallel to plays
within plays in Shakespeare. The point is equally valid in
other literary forms, including tales within tales.

[48] Frescobaldi, p. 36, described an ancient pilgrim
ship, laden with pilgrims returning from the Holy Sepulchre,
sinking as it enters the harbor of Venice within sight of
his own outgoing pilgrim ship.

[49] St. Ambrose's Hymn at Cockcrow, "Gallo canentes spes
redit/ aegris salus refunditur/ mucro latronis conditur/
lapsos fides revertitur," <u>The Oxford Book of Medieval Verse</u>,
ed. F.J.E. Raby, Oxford, 1959, p. 9; Durandus, pp. 153-154,
notes the church's weather vane, the cock on the cross and
ball, represented the Christian preacher, waking up his
flock to save them from doom; <u>Nigel de Longchamps' Speculum
Stultorum</u>, ed. John H. Mozely, Robert B. Raymo, Berkeley,
1960; <u>The Book of Daun Burnel the Ass: Nigel Wireker's
Speculum Stultorum</u>, trans. Graydon W. Regenos, Austin, 1959.

[50] II, lines 30819-30858, compares Renart's flight from
the peasants to the persecution of lepers and Jews in Troyes
in 1320.

[51] Stanley Fish, <u>Surprised by Sin: The Reader in Paradise Lost</u>.

[52] Lorrayne Baird-Lang has written on "Cock Iconography in the Nun's Priest's Tale."

CHAPTER TEN: THE PILGRIM AND THE BOOK

[1] "Admirable as he is in so many other respects, Homer is especially so in this; he is the only poet who recognizes what part he ought to play in his poem. The poet should speak as little as possible in his own person, for it is not in that way that he represents actions. Other poets appear in their own character throughout their poems, and little of what they write" is of worth, <u>The Art of Poetry</u>, trans. T.S. Dorsche, Baltimore, 1965, pp. 67-68; Curtius, "Mention of the Author's Name in Medieval Literature," <u>European Literature</u>, pp. 515-518; Dante excuses his presence within his work, citing Augustine and Boethius' examples, <u>Convivio</u>, I,23,13-14. Breughel's "Sermon of St. John the Baptist" shows a sixteenth-century pilgrim figure to the Holy Places, who represents ourselves, listening to the first-century penitential sermon; (see also Jan Van Eyck, "Adoration of the Lamb," with pilgrims with cockle hats and scrips); W.H. Auden, "Musée des Beaux Arts," understood the principle; in oriental scrolls the viewer identifies with a figure placed within the landscape. The pilgrim figure in these texts is both author and reader.

[2] Singleton, <u>Essay on the Vita Nuova</u>, pp. 38-39; Hugh of St. Victor, <u>Eruditiones didascalicae liber septimus</u>, <u>PL</u>, 176.814: "Universus enim mundus iste sensibilis quasi liber est scriptus digito Dei . . . . Quemadmodum autem si illiteratus quis apertum librum videat, figuras aspicit, litteras non cognoscit: ita stultus et animalis homo qui non percipit ea quae Dei sunt in visibilibus istis creaturis foris videt speciem sed intus non intelligit rationem. Qui autem spiritualis est ed omnia dijudicare potest, in eo quidem quod foris considerat pulchritudinem operis, intus concipit quam miranda sit sapientia Creatoris" [the world is as a book written by the finger of God, which the fool, as if an illiterate, sees only outwardly, without understanding, but which contains the Creator's wisdom]; Curtius, pp. 302-347; Josipovici, <u>The World and the Book</u>; Demaray notes the theme of pilgrimage and the book in Dante,

Zacher and Howard in Chaucer; Elizabeth R. Hatcher, "The
Moon and Parchment: Paradiso II.73-78," Dante Studies, 89
(1971), 55-60; Astrik L. Gabriel, "The Significance of the
Book in Medieval University Coats of Arms," Medieval and
Renaissance Studies, ed. O.B. Hardison, Jr., Chapel Hill,
1966.

[3] Singleton, Essay, p. 39; St. Bonaventure,
Breviloquium, pars II,11: "Et secundum hoc duplex est liber,
unus scilicet scriptus intus, qui est Dei aeterna ars et
sapientia, et alius scriptus foris, scilicet mundus
sensibilis" [And it follows that the book is duplex, one
written within, which is the eternal art and wisdom of God,
and the other written without, which is the sensible world].

[4] Brieger, Meiss, Singleton, II,28a,29b.

[5] Dante links John's vision of the City of God with
Virgil and Aeneas' of Dido's Carthage: the angels about the
rose of Paradise are like a swarm of bees which alight on
flowers, "Si come schiera d'ape che s'infiora," recalling

> qualis apes aestate nova per florea rura
> exercet sub sole labor, cum gentis adultos
> educant fetus, aut cum liquentia mella
> stipant, et dulci distendunt nectare cellas,
> aut onera accipiunt venientum, aut agmine facto
> ignavum fucos pecus a praesibus arcent:
> fervet opus, redolentque thymo fragrantia mella.
>   (Aeneid I.430-436)

Milton, Paradise Lost, II.768-775, employs the simile in the
infernal Carthaginian context of building Pandemonium.
Curtius discusses the Jason simile, Essays, pp. 465-496;
Roman de la Rose, II,39, lines 9479-9486.

[6] I depart from Richard L. Hoffman, "The Burning of
'Boke' in Piers Plowman," and agree with R.E. Kaske, "The
Speech of 'Book' in Piers Plowman," who saw the Book as
consumed in Apocalypse's flames.

[7] Fish, Self-consuming Artifacts, observes a similar
poetic in seventeenth-century writings.

[8] Matilda's pilgrim hospice, Riant, p. 59; Sapia, Purg.
III, likewise did so, both hospices neighboring Siena.

[9] The identification of the throned allegorical figures
as the Senses was made with the aid of the Longthorpe Tower,
Wheel of Senses' fresco, and was discussed with Millard
Meiss. The Wheel shows Reason as a crowned man surrounded by

a monkey symbolizing Taste, as in da Firenze, a vulture
symbolizing Smell, as in Traini, the spider web's delicate
tracery of Touch (in da Firenze and Traini the figures who
touch their cheeks), the boar's keen Hearing (in da Firenze
and Traini, the figures with the viol and lyre), and the
cock's Sight (in da Firenze and Traini represented by
falcons).

[10] Stephen preached while the priests "stopped their
ears," then stoned him, Acts 7.57; Mâle, Gothic Image, p.
44, fig. 18, Honorius of Autun, the adder, "lays one ear
close to the ground, and stops up the other with its tail,
so that it can hear nothing . . . . The adder is the sinner
who closes his ears to the words of life"; the Parson's
Sermon's text: "Stand ye in the ways, and see, and ask for
the old paths, where is the good way . . . But they said, We
will not walk therein . . . . We will not hearken," Jer.6.
16-17; John M. Steadman, "The Book-Burning Episodes in the
Wife of Bath's Prologue," PMLA, 74 (1959), 521-525; Mary
Carruthers, "The Wife of Bath and the Painting of Lions,"
PMLA, 94 (1979), 209-222.

[11] Singleton, Essay, p. 8; this quality in pilgrim poets
is also discussed in Fergusson, Dante's Drama of the Mind,
pp. 9-10; Donaldson, "Chaucer the Pilgrim," PMLA, 89 (1974),
97-104, republished in Speaking of Chaucer, New York, 1972,
p. 1; Josipovici, "Chaucer: the Teller and the Tale," The
World and the Book, pp. 52-99; Bertrand Bronson, In Search
of Chaucer, Toronto, 1960, pp. 25-31; William R. Crawford,
Bibliography on Chaucer, 1954-63, Seattle, pp. xxiv-xxviii;
several recent PMLA articles; Cali, Allegory and Vision in
Dante and Langland, Cork, 1971: "First, I am convinced that
critics of Piers Plowman have not yet made up their minds as
to what extent the experience of its hero--the 'Fool' or 'I'
of the poem--are to be related to the experiences of the
life and the mind of its author," adding that study of the
Commedia would aid with Piers Plowman, p. 188; Barbara
Nolan, The Gothic Visionary Perspective, "These willing but
ineffectual narrators introduced in the prologue offered
poets perhaps their most flexible device for innovation and
experimentation. Through the fallible 'I' they could provide
one point of view--one way of "seeing" the visionary world.
Then using their art and their audience's judgement, they
could also suggest alternative perspectives, juxtaposing
them with the pilgrim's in order to underscore the
difficulties of perceiving divine meaning aright," p. 140;
Durling, The Figure of the Poet; William Calin, "The Poet at
the Fountain: Machaut as Narrative Poet," Machaut's World,
ed. Cosman, pp. 176-187; "Persona" as a critical term is
discussed by Irvin Erhenpreis, "Personae," Restoration and

Eighteenth Century Literature: Alan Dugald McKillop
Festschrift, Chicago, 1963, pp.25-37; Satire News Letter, 3
(1966), symposium on "Persona"; Mary Hatch Marshall,
"Boethius' Definition of Persona and Medieval Understanding
of the Roman Theatre," Speculum, 26 (1950), 471, notes
Boethius' awareness that the word meant "actor's mask"
(sound through) and person of the Trinity.

[12] Egeria's Travels, pp. 93,95-98,108; Book of Margery
Kempe; Itinerary from Bordeaux to Jerusalem, A.D. 333, PPTS,
London, 1896, I,1-35; Information for Pilgrims unto the Holy
Land, ed. E. Gordon Duff, London, 1893; Howard, Idea of
Canterbury Tales, erroneously claims pilgrims did not
include their return journeys, p. 28, when it was standard
practice to also recount these. However, later printed
editions of these texts did frequently omit this material.

[13] Adamnan, Arculf's Narrative about the Holy
Places,v-91; Adamnan's De Locis Sanctis, ed. Denis Meehan,
Dublin, 1958; A History of the English Church and People,
trans. Leo Sherley-Price, Harmondsworth, 1955, pp. 300-303.

[14] The Vercelli Book, ed. George Philip Krapp, New
York,1932; Frescobaldi, p. 35; The Pilgrims Sea Voyage;
Pernoud, Guide du pèlerin, frontispiece of miniature book.

[15] Rock, II, 277-284; Bernard von Breydenbach names his
companions and himself "utinam sunt scripta in libro vitae,"
Peregrinatio in Terra Sancta, fol. 103. The Jerusalem map in
the Taylor copy, Princeton University Rare Books Collection,
is worn from being constantly touched, its paths traced by
"fingers doing the walking," not so the Venice one.

[16] Deguileville, Pilgrimage, lines 9438-9439; Roman,
10439-10680; Le Pasteur d'Hermas, ed. Auguste Lelay, Paris,
1912, I,2; Theodore Bogdanos, "The Shepherd of Hermas and
the Development of Medieval Visionary Allegory," Viator, 8
(1977), 33-46; Mircea Eliade, Aspects du Myth, pp. 33-70,
notes that for healing rituals the patient must become
God-like or origin of the world be recounted incorporating
patient's name.

[17] Sister Ritamary Bradley, "Backgrounds of Title
Speculum," pp. 100-115; Marcia L. Colish, The Mirror of
Language: A Study in the Medieval Theory of Knowledge,
New Haven,1968; Wimsatt, Allegory and Mirror; Susan K.
Hagen, "The Pilgrimage of the Life of Man: A Medieval
Theory of Vision and Remembrance," Ph.D. dissertation,
University of Virginia, 1976; Heinrich Schwarz, "The
Mirror of the Artist and the Mirror of the Devout:

Observations on Some Paintings, Drawings and Prints of the
Fifteenth Century," <u>Studies in the History of Art Dedicated
to William E. Snida</u>, London, 1954, pp. 98-100.

[18] <u>Ad Imaginem Dei</u>, p. 4; Kurt Weitzmann, <u>Late Antique
and Early Christian Illumination</u>, New York, 1977, p. 11;
Durandus, p. 48; Graham Hough applies the same term,
"Incarnation," to Shakespeare's art, <u>Preface to The Faerie
Queene</u>, London, 1962, p. 107.

[19] Brunetto Latini, <u>Il Tesoro</u>, Venice, 1839, I.vi.12,
129, discusses the world as created by God on March 25 in
the sign of Aries; Tyrer, p. 11, notes March 25, date of
Crucifixion; Aries and Mars were associated in pagan
thought; in Christian thought the Ram recollects the
"hills leaping like rams" of Psalm 113, John the Baptist's
"Behold the Lamb of God," and the Paschal Lamb of the
Apocalypse.

[20] <u>Early Netherlandish Painting</u>, I,133

[21] Matthew of Vendôme, citing Ovid's commencement of
the <u>Metamorphoses</u>, spoke of poems, like the Creation, as
requiring a <u>zeuma</u>, Edmond Faral, <u>Les Arts poétiques du XIIe
et du XIIIe siècles</u>, Paris, 1924, p. 111.

[22] <u>Idea: A Concept in Art Theory</u>, New York, p. 40.

[23] <u>Scenes from the Drama of European Literature</u>, p. 62;
Boethius' <u>Consolation</u>, trans. Chaucer, Robinson ed., p. 368.

[24] <u>Speculum</u>, 32 (1957), 706-708.

[25] M.H. Abrams, <u>The Mirror and the Lamp: Romantic Theory
and the Critical Tradition</u>, New York, 1958, pp. 272-273.

[26] <u>Ad Imaginem Dei</u>, p. 4.

[27] P. 5.

[28] Pp. 5-6.

[29] I borrow John Fowles' <u>The Magus</u>' concept.
Interestingly, he revised the novel for a second
edition omitting this powerful, blasphemous analogy.

[30] Milton, <u>Areopagitica</u>, is written with this
consciousness and as a defense of books.

EPILOGUE

[1] Skeat, II,234; Finucane, plate 16, shows the defacement and mutilation of a manuscript naming Becket.

[2] Madeleine Hope Dodds and Ruth Dodds, _The Pilgrimage of Grace, 1536-1537_, Cambridge, 1915.

APPENDICES

I

[1] _Missale Sarum_, Dickinson; "Benedictio super Capsella et Fustes et super eos qui cum his limina ac suffragia Sanctorum Apostolorum petituri sunt" of the Vienna, Nationalbibl. cod. lat. 701, fols. 3^v, 134, in Vogel, pp. 93-94, differs interestingly from the Sarum version in being explicitly conscious of typology, seeing the pilgrim as an Abraham, his pilgrim staff as an Aaron's rod to flower with almonds in the sight of his enemies and with angels to guide him as they had Tobit; see also Vasquez de Parga, I,137-143, III,145,148; John Henry Feasey, _Ancient English Holy Week_, pp. 54-55, for Palm Sunday's ritual antecedants, pp. 96-97, for reconciliation of penitents, p. 120, for ceremony of "Creeping to the Cross," p. 212, for liturgical use of Aaron and Moses' caduceus.

II

[1] M.D. Anderson, _Drama and Imagery in English Medieval Churches_, p. 1.

[2] Charles Singleton, _Inferno Commentary_, p. 309; Frederick II's _De arte venandi cum avibus_, in its scientism, gives no allegory to falconry; however, see Brunetto Latini, _Li Livres dou Tresor_, ed. P. Chabaille, Paris, 1863, pp. 202-4.

[3] Bodleian MS Douce 219, fols. 47-73.

INDEX

I. Primary

II. Secondary

PLATES

Ia   Pilgrim Figure, Detail, <u>Via Veritatis</u>, Alinari
b   Palmer, <u>Piers Plowman</u>, Bodleian Library, MS Douce
104, fol. 33

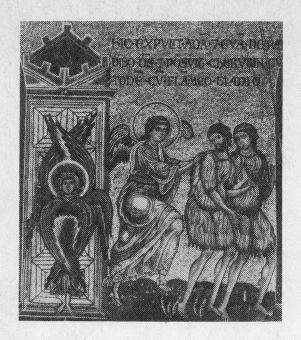

IIa   Expulsion of Adam and Eve, Monreale Mosaic, Alinari
  b   Expulsion and Annunciation, Fra Angelico, Prado

IIIa Christ as Pilgrim greeted by Two Dominicans, Fra
Angelico, Hospice Fresco, San Marco, Alinari
b Christ as Pilgrim, Pistoia, Alinari

IVa   Faus Semblant and Abstinence disguised as Pilgrims,
        Bodleian Library, MS e Mus 65, fol. 95
    b,c Amant as Pilgrim with Rose, Valencia MS

Va   Emmaus Pilgrims, Santo Domingo de Silos Cloister
 b   Emmaus Pilgrims, Christ with Magdalen, Spanish Ivory,
      Metropolitan Museum of Art, New York
 c   Dante and Virgil, Inferno, Vatican MS Lat 4776,
      fol. 39
 d   Belin, Benart, Renart as Emmaus Pilgrims, Roman de
      Renart

VIa   Ulysses' Shipwreck, Vatican MS Lat 4776, fol. 92
  b   <u>Purgatorio</u> as a Pilgrim Ship, formerly Geneva, Bodmer
      MS 247, fol. 95
  c   Neptune and the Argo, British Library, MS 36 Yates
      Thompson, fol. 190

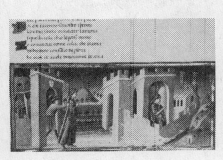

VIIa   <u>Inferno</u>, London, British Library, MS Egerton 943,
       fol.3
   b   <u>Purgatorio</u>, MS Egerton 943
   c   Dante expulsed from Florence, writing <u>Commedia</u>,
       Boethian iconography, British Library, MS 26 Yates
       Thompson, fol. 59

VIIIa Arch of Titus, Morrone
    b Jerusalem Spoils, Morrone
    c Titus in Triumph, Morrone
    d <u>Inferno</u> VIII, Biblioteca Angelica, MS 1102, fol. 7
      Dante and Virgil before Tower and Arch
    e Engraving of Arch of Titus, Virgil's Tower

IXa   Virgil as Aaron, Cato as Moses, <u>Purgatorio</u> I
       British Library, MS Add. 19587, fol. 62
  b   <u>Purgatorio</u> X, fol. 77, Trajan and the Widow
  c   Jerusalem Temple, Sancta Sanctorum with Ark, Moses,
      Aaron, Twelve Tribes, Bibliothèque de l'Arsenal, MS
      5057, fol. 77

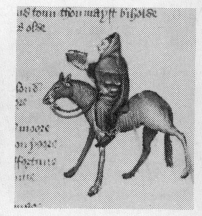

Xa   Pardoner, Bodleian Library, MS Douce 104, fol. 44ᵛ
 b   Sloth, fol. 31
 c   Trajan, "Ye, baw for bokes!" fol. 56
 d   The Ellesmere Clerk, Huntington Library and Museum

XIa The Ellesmere Cook
  b The Ellesmere Physician
  c Boethius and the Physician, Rennes, MS 595, fol. 473
  d Boethius and Philosophy, fol. 473^v

XII   Dante reading the Book of the <u>Commedia</u> to Florence
Fresco, Duomo, Florence, Domenico Michelini, Alinari

XIII   Andrea da Firenze, <u>Via Veritatis</u>, Spanish Chapel,
Santa Maria Novella, Florence. Figure at far right
(stage left) tearing pages from a book is in
scarlet. Alinari

XIV   Autun Tympanum, Angel with Trump of Doom on left,
Compostela and Jerusalem Pilgrims on right, Giraudon